RECRUITING, INTERVIEWING, SELECTING & ORIENTING NEW EMPLOYEES

Fifth Edition

Other Books by Diane Arthur

The First-Time Manager's Guide to Performance Appraisals (New York: AMACOM, 2008; also published in India, Sri Lanka, Nepal, Bangladesh, and Pakistan in 2011)

Recruiting, Interviewing, Selecting & Orienting New Employees, Fourth Edition (New York: AMACOM, 2006; also published in India in 2007)

The Employee Recruitment and Retention Handbook (New York: AMACOM, 2001)

Recruiting, Interviewing, Selecting & Orienting New Employees, Third Edition (New York: AMACOM, 1998; also published in the People's Republic of China in 2000)

The Complete Human Resources Writing Guide (New York: AMACOM, 1997)

Managing Human Resources in Small & Mid-Sized Companies, Second Edition (New York: AMACOM, 1995)

Workplace Testing: An Employer's Guide to Policies and Practices (New York: AMACOM, 1994).

Recruiting, Interviewing, Selecting & Orienting New Employees, Second Edition (New York: AMACOM, 1991)

Managing Human Resources in Small & Mid-Sized Companies (New York: AMACOM, 1987)

Recruiting, Interviewing, Selecting & Orienting New Employees (New York: AMACOM, 1986; also published in Colombia in 1987)

American Management Association Self-Study Publications by Diane Arthur

Performance Appraisals: Strategies for Success (2007)

Fundamentals of Human Resources Management, Fourth Edition (2004)

Successful Interviewing: Techniques for Hiring, Coaching, and Performance Meetings (2000)

Success Through Assertiveness (1980)

RECRUITING, INTERVIEWING, SELECTING & ORIENTING NEW EMPLOYEES

Fifth Edition

DIANE ARTHUR

AMACOM

American Management Association

New York • Atlanta • Brussels • Chicago • Mexico City • San Francisco
Shanghai • Tokyo • Toronto • Washington, D.C.

This publication is designed to provide accurate and authoritative information in regard to the subject matter covered. It is sold with the understanding that the publisher is not engaged in rendering legal, accounting, or other professional service. If legal advice or other expert assistance is required, the services of a competent professional person should be sought.

Library of Congress Cataloging-in-Publication Data

Arthur, Diane.
   Recruiting, interviewing, selecting & orienting new employees / Diane Arthur. — 5th ed.
      p.   cm.
   Includes bibliographical references and index.
   ISBN 978-0-8144-2024-9 (hbk.)
   1. Employees—Recruiting.   2. Employment interviewing.   3. Employee selection.   4. Employee orientation.   I. Title.   II. Title: Recruiting, interviewing, selecting and orienting new employees.
   HF5549.5.R44A75   2012
   658.3'11—dc23
                                                                                              2012005589

About AMA
American Management Association (www.amanet.org) is a world leader in talent development, advancing the skills of individuals to drive business success. Our mission is to support the goals of individuals and organizations through a complete range of products and services, including classroom and virtual seminars, webcasts, webinars, podcasts, conferences, corporate and government solutions, business books, and research. AMA's approach to improving performance combines experiential learning—learning through doing—with opportunities for ongoing professional growth at every step of one's career journey.

Printing number

10   9   8   7   6   5   4   3   2   1

To Warren, Valerie, and Vicki
My Special Network

Contents

Preface

The primary focus of *Recruiting, Interviewing, Selecting & Orienting New Employees,* published first in 1986, then in 1991, again in 1998, and most recently in 2006, remains unaltered: It is still a comprehensive guide through the four stages of the employment process identified in the book's title. The book's wide-based readership is also the same: HR specialists who need in-depth information about the entire employment process; non-HR professionals whose jobs encompass select employment-related responsibilities; and seasoned HR practitioners looking for a refresher in one or more recruiting, interviewing, selecting, or orientation subcategories. The methods and techniques described continue to be applicable to all work environments: corporate and nonprofit, union and nonunion, technical and nontechnical, large and small. They also pertain to both professional and nonprofessional positions. And the book continues to be useful as a reference for training workshops in various aspects of the employment process and as a text for college and other courses dealing with employment issues.

That said, as a reflection of today's evolving workforce, fluctuating economy, and interviewing trends, several topics have been added, expanded upon, or otherwise revised in this fifth edition. For example, an entirely new chapter explores differing applicant and employer workplace perspectives. This includes respective expectations, how personal and professional lives are best balanced, and what questions applicants are likely to ask of prospective employers. Another new chapter relates to the rapidly expanding impact of social networks on the hiring process, including their uses and legal risks, and a comparison of social media with traditional reference checks. A third new chapter examines web-based orientation programs, assessing their advantages and drawbacks, legal concerns, and a contrast of conventional and web-based sessions.

The content of each chapter has been carefully reviewed and updated; for instance, the chapter on references and background checks, Chapter 13, has a new look with expanded content. There are also numerous additions throughout each section, including the impact of a fluctuating economy, establishing and adhering to standards of excellence, expanded recruitment sources for special interest groups, updated electronic recruiting methods, additional electronic recruitment alternatives, electronic record-keeping guidelines, up-to-date legislation, testing, and bias.

Also, the information in Part IV has been completely revised to reflect three distinct types of orientation: organizational, departmental, and web-based.

Appendixes have been modified, most notably the employment application form. There is also the addition of a sample e-mail cover letter.

This newly modified and expanded fifth edition offers the same, easy-to-follow format as the previous version: four distinct sections that replicate the topics identified in the book's title. This compartmentalized approach meets the needs of readers wanting to focus on one or more stages of the employment process at any given time, as well as those who like knowing absolutely when one stage ends and another begins.

As with previous editions, readers are cautioned on two points: First, any reference made to specific publications, websites, services, or institutions is for informational purposes only and is not to be considered an endorsement. Second, this book is not intended to provide legal advice.

Recruiting, interviewing, selecting, and orienting new employees are tangible skills. How well you practice these skills will directly affect many common organizational problem areas, such as employee morale, absenteeism, and turnover. By diligently implementing the methods described in this book, your organization can greatly improve its employment efforts and levels of employee productivity.

D. A.

Recruiting Qualified People

CHAPTER 1

▪ Recruitment Challenges

Employers across the country struggle with similar recruitment challenges, including a tumultuous economic picture that continues to confound labor experts, frustration over the inability to attract and compete for qualified applicants despite long bouts of high unemployment, and efforts to establish and adhere to high standards of excellence. While there may not be any one-size-fits-all solution to these and other recruitment issues, there are limited-risk measures businesses can take that will likely improve employer-employee relations, which in turn will serve to improve productivity and hence profitability.

Weather the Impact of a Fluctuating Economy

No one will dispute that we have been on an economic roller coaster ride for the past several years and will undoubtedly continue to experience unrest, at least in the near future. This unsettling sense of economic instability tends to discourage long-term business planning, which is founded upon a solid core of qualified, motivated employees.

Even after we've settled into a state of calm, experts suggest that business as we once knew it will not resume. An air of uncertainty and concern will hover, challenging human resources (HR) practitioners in all employment-related matters, including hiring. Indeed, many recruiters hesitate to launch aggressive staffing efforts despite knowing that if they do not, jobs will remain unfilled, existing employees will become overworked and unmotivated, and productivity and quality of services or products could ultimately stagnate or decline.

While this scenario is daunting, it need not be prophetic. A three-pronged strategic plan will better enable employers to weather the impact of economic turbulence on recruitment efforts, allowing them to not only survive, but thrive.

1. *Clarify goals by being "S.M.A.R.T."*

    Recruitment—regardless of prevailing or predicted economic conditions—begins with a clear sense of where you're headed as a business. Ask yourself: What is our mission statement? Do we know how each department can contribute to the achievement of short- and long-term organizational goals? Is there an alignment between employee interests and corporate goals? Do we have an accompanying detailed timeline that calls for measurable accomplishments?

While an unstable economy can make goal setting more challenging, it need not deter a business from moving forward. The long-standing "S.M.A.R.T." model for identifying performance standards—establishing goals that are specific, measurable, attainable, realistic, and time-sensitive—is applicable to clarifying business objectives. For example, your company may want to resume increased patterns of production that were averaging 8 percent per year before the onset of the recession. Think S.M.A.R.T.: Instead of saying, "We need to increase production," identify realistic, attainable target figures based on past numbers, competitors' output, and projected staffing requirements. Your mission statement, then, might be, "Our goal is to raise production by 5 percent at the end of this calendar year, and an additional 7 percent by December 31 of next year. This will initially match our competitions' yield and surpass their current production by the end of our second year. In order to succeed we need to expand operations and improve quality control."

Accomplishing specific objectives identified in your mission statement begins with answering the question, "What are the roles most critical to keeping our business strong while we move toward expansion?" Once specific functions and tasks are isolated, you can proceed to update and assess the skills and interests of current staff, focusing on top performers. This process of maximizing core strengths requires matching the scope of each employee's responsibilities with that employee's interests and attributes. This, in turn, lays the groundwork for HR to identify additional hiring needs and map out a productive recruitment initiative.

2. *Practice targeted recruitment.*

Savvy employers understand that regularly identifying key performers and ensuring that they are being fully utilized and motivated is a valuable precursor to recruitment. After experiencing economic setbacks, however, many employers leave openings unfilled, relying instead on their best workers to perform additional duties. This approach may work for the short term, but it is likely to ultimately strain employer-employee relations to the point where top performers move on to other job opportunities when economic conditions allow.

Alleviate the possibility of misusing top talent by viewing economic slowdowns as opportunities, allowing employers to select from among a highly talented pool of candidates who have been downsized or otherwise cut adrift for reasons having nothing to do with their abilities. Recruiting during an economic downturn, then, can actually serve as a tremendous competitive advantage when the economy rights itself, but only if you practice targeted recruitment. If you have established S.M.A.R.T. goals, you're ready to match up business needs with requisite skills and abilities. In this regard, avoid the classic mistake made by many employers when the market is saturated with applicants and assume they will seek you out. This is not the time to practice passive recruitment; instead, be aggressive and target locations and sources where candidates with desirable skill sets are likely to be found. For example, if you want to fill technical support positions, your best bet is to focus on industry-specific, web-based sources (Chapters 3 and 4). This cuts down the amount of time and effort invested in the recruitment process and increases the likelihood of a high return on your investment.

Targeted recruitment also supports efforts to increase workplace diversity by using sources that reach out to underutilized groups, making it more likely that organizations will satisfy their affirmative action goals (Chapter 6).

Simply stated: know what you need and go where your applicants are likely to be.

3. *Clarify your expectations.*

Most applicants come in with a clear understanding of what they expect from a prospective employer. In addition to salary and benefits, the list usually includes a motivating work environment, opportunities for growth and advancement, regular feedback on their work, and a mutually respectful relationship between themselves and their boss. When asked what they want from their employees, however, employers are rarely as specific. Most say that they expect to be able to rely on their employees to perform their jobs in at least a competent manner. But there can and should be more in the way of expectations, regardless of who's driving the economy. As part of your company's targeted recruitment efforts, determine whether prospective employees are likely to help meet its S.M.A.R.T. goals: Are they able to help the organization grow and prosper? What is it about their concrete skill set and intangible qualities, such as interpersonal and organizational skills, that will benefit your business? Be prepared as well to determine whether prospective employees demonstrate a willingness to learn and accept criticism. Now consider traits that are relevant to each particular job. If you're looking for a manager, for example, you'll likely need someone who has demonstrated that she can work well as a team player, has effective conflict resolution abilities, and has the ability to remain calm while dealing with problems. When hiring an administrative assistant, emphasize the ability to maintain cooperative working relationships, flexibility, and effective time-management skills. And a human resources professional should have a keen sense of business, HR, and organizational operations, be a strategic thinker, and be an effective communicator. Of course, there is likely to be an overlap of skills and traits between one job and another, but you can still isolate those attributes that will lead you to the most qualified employee for a specific position.

Well-thought-out and well-written job descriptions will serve as the foundation for effective recruitment (Chapter 5), as will an understanding and application of different questioning techniques (Chapters 7 and 8).

Make Recruitment Efforts Succeed

While every employer deals with similar recruitment challenges, some are more successful than others. The resources successful recruiters use make a difference (Chapters 3 and 4), but there's more involved than that. To achieve the best possible results, proactive employers apply as many of the classic "ABC Guidelines for Successful Recruitment" as possible every time they have a job opening.

ABC Guidelines for Successful Recruitment

As soon as you know there's going to be an opening, either because of a vacancy or due to a newly created position, kick the twenty-six "ABC Guidelines for Successful Recruitment" into high gear.[1] This means being:

- *Attractive.* Promote your organization as the kind of place employees will want to call their place of work. Highlight your most generous and unique benefits, have employees promote your attributes among friends, and publicly pat yourself on the back for accomplishments. In addition, convert failures or shortcomings into strengths, e.g., stating, "Last year you read about our competition; now it's our turn. We've already surpassed Drexel's profits by 12 percent and we're just getting started. Join Hartman, and be part of a winning team!"

- *Believable.* If what you're offering sounds too good to be true, repackage your wares. Skeptical applicants shouldn't have to cross-examine interviewers to determine if your hard-to-believe advertised benefits package is real.

- *Centered.* Identify and focus on anywhere from three to six critical, job-specific competencies; that is, qualities or traits that contribute to a person's ability to effectively perform the duties and responsibilities of a given job. Clearly communicate and adhere to them in your recruitment efforts. For example, here are key competencies that have been identified for a project manager: apply technical expertise to solve business problems, focus on key elements of a project, motivate and work effectively with a wide range of people, and negotiate in order to accomplish goals.

- *Diligent.* Effective recruitment requires hard work. Gather together a team of focused individuals who will invest the effort needed to recruit from a pool of qualified candidates.

- *Empathetic.* Take into consideration an applicant's needs and interests in relation to organizational goals in order to strike a balance and find common denominators between the two. For example, if an applicant expresses an interest in becoming an integral member of the management team within five years, but the job she's applying for is a support position with little likelihood of promotion, it's likely she'll grow disenchanted and leave shortly after being hired.

- *Flexible.* If you've tried one recruitment source and it's not yielding the kind of results you need in a reasonable period of time, move on to others. Do this even if it's a recruitment source you've relied heavily on in the past, with good results.

- *Greedy.* Tell yourself that your company is entitled to be staffed by the best possible workforce and seek out those applicants who maximally meet your needs. Aim high, but be realistic and don't drag out the recruitment process for an unreasonable period of time hoping to find the ideal employee as opposed to the best fit.

- *Hip*. Stay informed and current when it comes to the latest developments in recruitment, as well as what sources and techniques your competitors are using.

- *Informative*. Anticipate what applicants are likely to want to know about a job and your company and be prepared to tell them, either verbally or in some form of written or electronically generated material.

- *Judicious*. Exercise sound judgment when matching applicants with jobs. Avoid decisions dictated by emotion or resulting from pressure to fill an opening.

- *Knowledgeable*. Be thoroughly familiar with the parameters of the job, as well as how it interfaces with other positions, the department, and the company. Also, be aware of how other organizations view this job in terms of responsibility, status, and compensation.

- *Linear*. Think in terms of a series of straight lines connecting the applicant, the job, and the company. This practice helps keep you on track and accomplish your goal of staffing openings as quickly as possible with the most suitable employees.

- *More*. Review your current recruitment efforts and think of what else you could be doing. Take each of the key words in these guidelines and ask yourself if you can be *more* attractive, *more* believable, *more* centered, *more* diligent, and so on.

- *Notorious*. Strive to become the brand-name organization everyone has good things to say about. Your goal is to become the company applicants want to work for and other companies want to imitate.

- *Open-minded.*Whether you're recruiting IT specialists, engineers, or secretaries, view the job from the applicant's perspective. Ask employees in the classifications you're trying to fill to identify key elements of the job as well as what they like best so you can emphasize those aspects to applicants.

- *Persistent*. Continue exploring various recruitment sources until you find the person who will be the best fit. Resist pressure to settle or compromise your standards if you're unable to fill an opening right away. Instead, re-examine the sources you've chosen and adjust as needed.

- *Quick*. The moment you discover you're going to have an opening, act on it. Spread the word among employees, run an ad, post the position online, do whatever you can to spread the word that you have a job to fill.

- *Realistic*. It's one thing to seek out the best possible applicant for a job, yet quite another to hold out for the ideal employee who may only exist on paper or in your mind. Adhering to job-specific competencies will enable you to remain realistic.

- *Sensible*. Carefully determine the best recruitment source based on a number of factors, including the nature of the job and the current job market.

- *Tireless*. If you relax your recruitment efforts, chances are another organization will grab the applicant you failed to pursue.

- *Unified*. Make certain everyone concerned with the recruiting effort is working toward the same goal—that is, that they agree with regard to sought-after qualities and skill sets.

- *Vocal.* Openly and clearly express the qualities and skills you need in an applicant to agencies or others assisting your company with a job search.
- *Watchful.* Look for signs that confirm the recruitment sources you're using are producing the kinds of results you want and that the applicants they're producing possess both the tangible and intangible qualities you need.
- *Xentigious.* I made this word up (the last two syllables rhyme with "litigious") to mean "keep it legal." Regardless of how desperate you are to fill an opening, never, ever, step outside the boundaries of what's legal—it's just not worth it.
- *Youthful.* Be youthful both in thinking and spirit in order to compete for top performers, especially the scarce but vitally important group of younger workers. Specifically, think in terms of what's important to younger workers in relation to working conditions, hours, perks, and a balance between work and personal time.
- *Zealous.* Applicants are more likely to be interested in becoming part of a company if the recruiters are enthusiastic and appear to genuinely enjoy working there. Accordingly, consider briefly sharing some of your experiences with the company, offering vivid images of how great it is to work there.

Let's take a look at how these guidelines may be applied to a typical recruiting scenario. Roger has worked for eighteen months as a customer service representative with Cromwell, Inc., a computer sales/service firm with approximately two thousand employees. He has just informed Anita, the assistant vice president of HR, of his intentions to resign, offering two weeks' notice. She's fairly certain that there's no one else in the company who can do Roger's job, which means she has to find a replacement from the outside and bring that person on board, ideally before Roger leaves. This is going to be a challenge and Anita needs to begin her search immediately (*quick*).

She starts out by listing four essential qualities of a customer service rep: excellent interpersonal skills, empathy, patience, and effective listening skills. She thinks for a moment and then adds, "interested in improving departmental procedures" (*centered*). Now where can she go to find someone fast? She immediately posts the job on Cromwell's website, and then recalls a colleague from the last regional meeting of HR practitioners who commented that he'd had luck using a particular agency that specializes in placing customer service representatives and administrative assistants (*hip*) (*sensible*). Anita has successfully used this agency in the past and decides to get in touch with them now. She e-mails the following message to Jim, her contact there:

> **Please call me right away about an immediate opening we have for a customer service representative. The money is competitive and the benefits are great, including four weeks' vacation, health club membership, transportation vouchers, and prepaid legal services (*attractive*). In fact, I'm pretty sure we offer a better benefits package than anyone else in our business (*believable*). Just give anyone who's interested the link to our benefits page (*informative*). Send the applications to my HR rep, Sandy. She's doing the initial screening, and then I'll conduct the interviews (*knowledgeable*).**

Jim, we need someone who has great interpersonal skills, listens well, can be patient when customers get agitated, and is empathetic; also, someone who's interested in getting involved (*vocal*). Ideally, I'd like to see applicants with experience in our industry (*greedy*), but I'll consider anyone with solid customer service experience (*realistic*). The important thing is that we get someone who requires minimal training and will work well in this environment (*linear*). As always, stress the fact that we pride ourselves on being an equal opportunity employer. And be sure to mention that we won an award last year for our efforts in workplace diversity (*xentigious*).

As soon as she finishes e-mailing Jim, Anita calls her employee relations manager, June. Anita says, "Would you please post Roger's opening? I don't think we've got anyone in house for the job, but let's be sure. I also want to let our staff know so they have a chance to make referrals. Talk with Roger, too. He might know someone who would be interested (*flexible*). Come down to my office this afternoon and I'll give you the particulars."

Anita sticks her head out of her office and calls out to Sandy. "Roger is leaving and we need to fill his job fast. I need you to make filling this job a priority: you know, screening applicants on the phone and lining up interviews. We've got to be organized and focused—he's only giving us two weeks' notice" (*diligent*).

Anita sits back in her chair and reflects on what she has done thus far with regard to the customer service opening. She's satisfied that she has gotten the recruitment search off to a good start and has everyone working toward the same goal (*unified*).

The next morning, Anita receives a call from Jim. "I've got two top-notch people for you to see, both with prior experience. One of them says he's heard good things about Cromwell and has been hoping something would open up so he could apply" (*notorious*). Anita schedules appointments with both applicants for later that day. Meanwhile, she learns from June that one of their employees has referred a friend of his for the job, as has Roger. Anita schedules them for interviews as well.

Before meeting the four applicants, Anita goes over a checklist of things to do: She reminds herself to try and understand the applicants' needs and interests in relation to company goals (*empathetic*), exercise sound judgment based on skills and abilities (*judicious*), and be practical in making a selection (*realistic*). She also knows that potential employees are more likely to be interested in joining the company if she comes across as enthusiastic, so she thinks of a few especially interesting experiences she's had since joining Cromwell two and a half years ago (*zealous*).

Anita interviews the four applicants and comes away unimpressed. She contacts Jim to ensure that he understands the qualities she's seeking (*vocal*). She checks Cromwell's website to see if anyone has expressed an interest in the job online, and then talks to June to make certain employees understand the nature of the job before making referrals (*watchful*) (*persistent*) (*tireless*). Anita leaves her office disappointed but not disheartened. She knows she's applying the ABC Guidelines for Successful

Recruitment, thereby improving her chances of finding a good replacement for Roger. She just has to persevere.

Attract and Compete for Qualified Applicants

Despite the economy's impact on employment—that is, regardless of who's in the "driver's seat" at any given point, applicants or employers—it's critical that recruiters continually work hard to attract and compete for top performers. Applicants have their own personal lists of "must haves," even during times of high unemployment when people are likely to be less selective and more grateful for a job, sometimes any job. If forced to deviate from that list and take a job they really don't want, chances are that when the market shifts (and it will), they'll act on harbored feelings of resentment and leave at their earliest opportunity. A workforce of disgruntled workers is guaranteed to hurt even the most successful business.

Here, then, is my advice with regard to attracting and competing for applicants: Go after applicants with no less vigor during your least productive work cycles than you do during your most productive, profitable times. It will keep your skills sharpened and you'll earn a reputation for being employee-focused, as opposed to self-serving. Being perceived as fair can earn you big points when the economy shifts to work against employers.

That said, let's look at some specific ways of attracting applicants. Keep in mind that this is not about recruitment sources; we'll discuss those in Chapters 3 and 4. This is about determining what you have to offer that would make someone want to be your employee. Remember, while you're interviewing applicants and deciding if they're right for your company, they're also interviewing you and deciding if you're the right fit for them.

All That Glitters . . .

Let's get the issue of "stuff" out of the way right up front. Giveaways are great, but too much in the way of freebies and perks can come across as little more than a desperate attempt to "buy" an applicant. In addition, employees quickly become accustomed to these perks, whether it's bringing pets to work, concierge services, or free catered lunches. If unmotivated by their jobs, employees will probably grow restless and simply require more stuff. To avoid earning the reputation of being long on talk and short on substance, as well as incurring high turnover costs, you need to put as much energy and thought into keeping employees motivated as you devote to your efforts to attract them.

If you're determined to offer tangible goods as a means of attracting applicants, follow these three simple rules:

1. *Find out what your competitors are giving away.* If you can match or top their perks, fine; just be careful not to get caught up in a game of who can "outgift" whom.

2. *Offer perks, regardless of market conditions.* You'll be viewed as generous when the economy favors employers, and consistent when it favors applicants and employees.

3. *Don't make promises you may not be able to keep.* For example, avoid telling prospective employees that they can look forward to a sizable bonus at year's end if that's not certain to happen.

Better yet, get personal. A shotgun approach to perks may find a few targets, but you're likely to be more successful if your giveaways suit the personal tastes of the recipients. Personalization also shows effort and interest on your part and is more likely to accomplish the desired results. While you certainly can't be expected to know what each individual likes, there are a few approaches that will more closely appeal to everyone's tastes. One is to offer would-be employees catalogues from which they can choose gift items. Another is to have generic categories, such as "membership," and allow recipients the option of perhaps joining a health club rather than a country club. You might also have a list of a dozen or so comparably valued perks and allow applicants to chose three that appeal to them.

First Impressions

Many years ago I went on a job interview with a publishing firm in New York City. I sat opposite the desk of my interviewer, with my back to the open doorway. Within minutes, I became uncomfortably aware that my interviewer's attention had been diverted by a conversation between two HR employees outside his door. They were speaking rather loudly, so I couldn't help but hear them discussing an applicant they had seen for "my" position. If that wasn't awkward enough, my interviewer suddenly called out, "Hey! Come and talk to me when I'm done here! I'd like to hear more about her!" The interview continued, but it was over as far as I was concerned. When they called back for a second meeting, I declined.

Negative first impressions can have a lasting effect. Consider these examples of initial encounters between an employer and a prospective employee, and imagine being on the receiving end:

- A recruiter for a top financial services firm schedules a recent graduate from a top school for a series of interviews, keeps her waiting, and then, without explanation or apology, has the receptionist announce that the interviews need to be rescheduled.

- An interviewer for an insurance company eats lunch during his meeting with a prospective employee, stating that he doesn't have time for both lunch and the interview.

- An applicant for a printing/graphics company has to compete with the radio as her interviewer explains that he isn't about to miss an important announcement concerning his favorite team.

- A recruiter excuses herself during an interview to reschedule an appointment with her therapist.

Would you be interested in working for any of these companies? If the economy is working against you, then you might be more inclined to look the other way. I guarantee, though, you will never forget an off-putting first impression. Applicants are not invested at this stage; the company, on the other hand, stands to lose a potentially valuable employee and earn a reputation for being an undesirable place to work. In addition, organizations need to bear in mind that applicants are far more than just potential employees: They are likely to be consumers of your product or services and could well end up working for your competition. Word about an employer's hiring practices spreads fast, and you can count on applicants sharing their job search experiences with others.

It's not difficult for a business to earn a reputation as an attractive place to work by projecting a positive first impression. This can be accomplished in eight effortless ways:

1. Allot a sufficient amount of time for each interview so as not to appear rushed.
2. Be courteous.
3. Be prepared.
4. Devote the interview to focusing fully on the applicant, not texts, e-mails, or phone calls.
5. Display a sense of pride in and involvement with your company.
6. Exhibit enthusiasm and interest.
7. Keep appointments.
8. Remain professional at all times.

Brand Imaging as a Competitive Edge

Brand imaging can give you an edge when competing for qualified applicants. A company's brand is what differentiates its products or services from others. Recruiters from well-known businesses need not describe to applicants what that they make or do. Think about companies like Microsoft, Procter & Gamble, Sara Lee, Disney, and PepsiCo, and you will immediately conjure up an image of their products. Some are so well known that all you have to do is mention initials, like IBM, HP, AOL, KFC, and BMW. Others are quickly recognized simply by their logos, like Nike and McDonald's. With recognition comes a sense of identity, or what the brands stand for. For example, Rolex represents quality, Burger King means fast food, and Starbucks suggests trendy coffee.

Companies such as these understand that consumers buy not only a particular product or service, but also the images associated with that commodity. They tend to stand out in a field of similar commodities, sometimes even when they are not as cost-effective, reliable, or otherwise desirable. It stands to reason, therefore, that applicants will be drawn to brand names and choose them as places of employment over lesser known businesses in the same field.

While it's certainly true that lesser-known and unknown organizations must work harder at cultivating their brand image, even those giants that are household names continually work at brand redevelopment. The bottom line is that every organization needs to hone its brand image.

Brands involve public perception. Exhibit 1-1 is a simple yet revealing questionnaire you can use to start thinking about your organization's overall image and what you can do to enhance it.

Exhibit 1-1. Assessing Your Organization's Overall Image

A workplace should identify the most prominent images with which it wants to be associated and then strive to reinforce these images with customers, clients, and the public. Answer these questions to learn what you can do to enhance your organization's overall image:

1. What does our organization stand for?
2. What have our customers, our clients, and the public come to expect from us?
3. When our company's name is mentioned, what are people likely to envision?
4. When our name is mentioned, what would we like people to envision?
5. What must we do to get people to change how they envision us?
6. Which of these words or terms are people likely to associate with our product or service?

Cleanliness	Innovativeness
Consistency	Integrity
Dependability	Quality
Fun	Quick service
Good service	Reliability
Good value	Safety
	Other _____

7. Which of these words or terms do we *want* people to associate with our product or service?

Cleanliness	Innovativeness
Consistency	Integrity
Dependability	Quality
Fun	Quick service
Good service	Reliability
Good value	Safety
	Other _____

8. What must we do if we want to be perceived as more _____?

Lightening Up

Some time ago, I was asked to conduct a training program for an investment bank. As we began to discuss the contents of the workshop, the HR manager interrupted and said, "I'm less concerned with the 'what' than I am with the 'how.' How are you going to keep the managers interested in the subject matter?" That was a fair question, so I proceeded to describe some of the learning techniques I thought were appropriate. Once again, he interrupted, this time to ask, "What I mean is, do you have any games that they can play?" I was silent for a moment. As a matter of fact, I did, but this was an investment bank—not exactly the type of environment that comes to mind when you think of playing games. The HR manager apparently anticipated my reaction and responded by saying, "I think I know what you're thinking: This is a serious environment where we keep our heads down and work, work, work. That's not far from the truth, and that's why we need a change. I believe fun and humor help boost morale, and hence improve productivity; wouldn't you agree?" In fact, I did agree and was delighted to comply; I went on to talk about some of my favorite "fun" training tools.

Mark Twain said, "Laughter which cannot be suppressed is catching. Sooner or later it washes away our defenses, . . . and we join in it . . . we have to join in, there is no help for it."[2]

Experts say that when we laugh we release endorphins, which are a natural hormone that combats stress. Laughter helps us relax, keeps us positive and focused, and gives us renewed strength. Furthermore, it is contagious—hearing someone else laugh compels others to join in.[3] Everyone, to a lesser or greater extent, likes to laugh and have fun, but typically "play" is reserved for before coming to or after leaving work. Does laughter and fun belong in the workplace? A lot of people think so, although there is some disagreement as to whether the best sort of fun is planned—e.g., staging contests and competitions, holding theme days, providing "joybreaks" during which workers can listen to comedy tapes or read cartoons, arranging entertainment—or encouraged to develop spontaneously.

Proponents of fun work environments see an increase in the ability to attract applicants, and higher levels of employee enthusiasm, group cohesiveness, employee satisfaction, and employee creativity. Conversely, they see a decline in anxiety and stress, boredom, turnover, absenteeism, and interpersonal conflicts. Opponents express concern over possible negative repercussions resulting from fun at work, such as equipment damage, sexual harassment claims, and increased errors.

The list of companies that promote fun in the workplace remains headed by Southwest Airlines. Cofounder and former CEO Herb Kelleher (he stepped down in 2008) promoted this philosophy: "I think people should have fun at work. It should be an enjoyable part of their life. . . . I think most of us enjoy fun, and why not at work as well as at play? And so we've always encouraged people to be themselves, not be robotic, not be automatons."[4] This thinking continues under the leadership of Gary Kelly, and as a manifestation of this prevailing philosophy, Southwest encourages employees to "express their sense of humor on the job, to act spontaneously, and to make their work fun."[5] This concept contributes to the unique and positive culture for which Southwest is known.

Another company that encourages fun at work is Hyland Software, the largest software company in northeast Ohio, with more than nine hundred regional employees. The company's commitment to showing workers that they are appreciated is demonstrated in such activities as paper airplane flying contests and paintball. They are so committed to encouraging their employees to have fun that the "Careers with Hyland Software" page of their website states, "Our company's culture—one that values hard work balanced with fun times and community outreach—hasn't changed its focus a bit since day one."[6]

There are plenty of other organizations that promote fun at work. The three-thousand-plus employees at Under Armour—the Baltimore, Maryland, developer, marketer, and distributor of performance apparel—can enjoy a fully operational basketball court.[7] At Google, the Internet giant based in Mountain View, California, employees have access to a climbing wall.[8] And Zappos.com, the online shoe retailer, voted number six out of the one hundred best companies to work for in 2011, promotes a "happy culture" and an atmosphere of ". . . fun and a little weirdness."[9]

If you're thinking about whether you should promote an employee-friendly and fun work environment, consider this: Businesses that promote fun in the workplace, such as those mentioned above, believe that doing so gives them an edge when it comes to competing for qualified applicants. During the employment interview, let applicants know that you encourage the integration of fun and humor into employees' daily routines as a way to balance the tension that work inevitably produces. Simple practices such as encouraging employees to play with toys at their desks, participating in group games during breaks, and assigning humorous descriptions of stressful projects can all project your company as a great place to work.

Establish and Adhere to High Standards of Excellence

Regardless of the state of the economy, top-notch applicants are more likely to be drawn to quality-driven businesses than to those that are in the news for allegedly lowering standards to maximize profits. Establishing and adhering to high standards of excellence, then, is a major recruitment challenge for every organization, regardless of how well-known your brand name may be.

Companies dedicated to quality know that this commitment impacts every aspect of their business, including strategic planning, project management, and marketing. It is an ongoing process that actually ends with recruitment, at which time employers can proudly highlight evidence of their high standards via their products and services.

High levels of performance permeate corporate and nonprofit work environments alike. An example of the latter includes The Standards for Excellence Institute, an organization dedicated to raising the level of ethics and accountability within the nonprofit community. Their guidelines provide benchmarks as they relate to conflicts of interest, financial and legal matters, fund-raising, and public affairs.

Some especially outstanding organizations can point to awards they have received for establishing and adhering to high standards of excellence. The Malcolm Baldrige National Quality Award is one such coveted prize that acknowledges businesses demonstrating exceptionally high standards of excellence, workforce engagement, and innovation. Organizations that are able to boast receipt of this honor include Honeywell Federal Manufacturing & Technologies (a subsidiary of Honeywell International), a manufacturer of nuclear components with approximately 2,700 employees at locations in Missouri and New Mexico; and AtlantiCare, a health care provider in New Jersey with more than five thousand employees.[10]

Organizations that focus on high standards of excellence establish specific goals and hold employees accountable for achieving them. At the Children's Hospital at Montefiore (CHAM), one of the most technologically advanced hospitals in the world, there are seven key standards all employees strive to regularly demonstrate: respect; effective communication; sensitivity; professionalism; exceeding expectations; courtesy; and teamwork. One by-product of this effort is that CHAM has been recognized as one of the best children's hospitals in the country by *U.S. News & World Report* for four consecutive years as of this writing, most recently in 2011–2012.[11]

Establishing and adhering to standards of excellence is likely attract a higher caliber of applicants; it also could very well result in greater loyalty, lower turnover, elevated levels of performance, and greater profits. It remains, therefore, a laudable recruitment challenge.

Summary

Today's employers are compelled to wrestle with numerous recruitment challenges, including an unstable economic recovery, making recruitment efforts succeed, competing with other organizations to attract qualified applicants, and establishing and adhering to high standards of excellence.

To successfully deal with these challenges, readers are encouraged to apply as many of the twenty-six "ABC Guidelines for Successful Recruitment" as possible every time there is an opening. For example, be *attractive* by promoting your organization as the kind of place employees will want to call their place of work, *flexible* with regard to accessing different recruitment sources, and *notorious* as you strive to become the brand-name organization everyone has good things to say about.

It's also critical to continually work hard to attract and compete for top performers, regardless of the state of the economy and who's in the "driver's seat"—applicants or employers. This will keep your recruitment skills sharpened and earn you a reputation for being employee-focused, as opposed to self-serving. While offering tangible goods as a means of attracting applicants has some merit, giving too much away can come across as little more than an attempt to "buy" an applicant. If you are going to offer perks, find out what your competitors are giving away. Better yet, do all you can to have your giveaways suit the personal tastes of the recipients, thereby showing effort and interest on your part. Avoid conveying negative impressions, especially those that occur during the initial contact with an applicant. As part of your initiative to compete for qualified applicants, work to enhance your overall brand image and strive to promote fun in the workplace.

Finally, make every effort to establish and adhere to high standards of excellence. Regardless of the state of the economy, top performers are more likely to be attracted to quality-driven businesses that demonstrate a commitment to workforce engagement and accountability.

CHAPTER 2

Applicant and Employer Perspectives

The way applicants and employers view a particular job or judge its importance to career and organizational development can have an enormous impact on the relationships they cultivate with one another, with colleagues, and with others in the workplace. Differing views may also taint levels of motivation and commitment on both ends. Diverse perspectives that prevail between applicants and employers during the recruitment stage of the hiring process can produce unfortunate results for everyone concerned: Applicants may decide to walk away from what they perceive to be an incompatible or undesirable work environment, and employers may prematurely decide that an applicant is not be the best fit for their corporate culture.

It's not unreasonable to think that applicants and employers will likely characterize a company's work environment or culture differently, see the need for balancing work with one's personal life from a different perspective, or have varying workplace expectations. What employers believe motivates workers and what employees themselves may describe as a positive work environment may also differ. The goal is to prevent these distinctions from resulting in ineffective employer-employee relations.

Corporate Culture

Every organization—whether corporate, nonprofit, service-driven, or product-driven—has a unique, definable culture, that is, a specific environment characterized by numerous factors, including organizational structure, workspace allocation, policies and procedures, expectations, job titles, acceptable attire, benefits, and perks. While every business shares these features overall, they differ in specificity, making each workplace distinct. Think about some of your past jobs. Were the environments interchangeable? In addition to the inevitable learning curve attached to each position, wasn't there also an adjustment in terms of the setting and surroundings? Recall the way people interacted and the relationships between coworkers, managers and employees, senior management and staff: Was it the same everywhere? What about rules? Were they more stringent in some jobs, less so in others? Could you come in a few minutes late and not be criticized in one place, but chastised for the same deed in another? How about the clothes you wore to work? Was there more traditional business attire in some, while dress down/casual in another? All of these elements are part of uniqueness that sets one workplace apart from others; it's what we refer to as the corporate culture, a term that applies to every workplace, whether corporate or not.

Most of us give little thought to corporate culture while we're working in an environment that's compatible with our personal style, habits, and preferences, but as soon as we're part of a workplace that's different, we react. Consider Richard, a hardworking and skilled manager, dedicated to his job. Downsized in a turbulent economy after eight years of loyal service, he considers himself fortunate to find another position that's similar in duties and responsibilities, albeit it in a very different office environment. He gives little thought to the latter as being problematic, assuming he will quickly adjust. Unfortunately, Richard soon learns that the corporate culture of his new job differs dramatically from what's he's used to in a number of ways. For example, at his old company Richard knew exactly who reported to whom. There was a clear chain of command and delineation of duties. As a manager he followed a clearly written policies manual that left no doubt as to how to handle various employee-related matters. Furthermore, every manager in the company followed the same procedures. Now, in his new workplace, everyone seems to make things up as they go along. There appear to be more exceptions than rules, and Richard finds himself increasingly frustrated to the point of distraction. He begins to question his managerial abilities and wonders if he's made a mistake in taking the job.

Then there's Jacqueline, an associate with a small firm, accustomed to working in a corporate culture that encourages and rewards employee participation in the decision-making process. Despite being largely satisfied with her position and the environment in which she works, Jacqueline is looking for a change that will enable her to shave time off from her three-hour daily commute. She is offered and accepts a similar job closer to home. Unfortunately, Jacqueline quickly learns that the reduced travel time doesn't compensate for what she's given up. Of particular concern is that members of senior management hand down all decisions, and employees are discouraged from expressing their views. While she tries to adapt over a period of several months, Jacqueline has trouble keeping her thoughts to herself, especially those she believes would bring about cost savings and improved services. This soon produces inharmonious employer-employee relations, which in turn results in reduced motivation, poor performance, and ultimately decreased productivity. For the first time in her career, she receives a less-than-satisfactory performance review.

If asked, it's unlikely that Richard or Jacqueline would make a connection between changes in their work performance and a different corporate culture, but that is actually the basis for what's going wrong. They would undoubtedly argue that it shouldn't matter, that they could function effectively regardless of the prevailing office atmosphere. But in truth, the factors cited, as well as many others that can be quite subtle and intangible, can directly impact job performance. To further muddy the waters, there are often subcultures within departments that seem to have their own sets of rules, or lack thereof. If that's not what a person is accustomed to, the results can be problematic.

In recognition of the important role corporate culture plays, some organizations identify specific business ethics, expected employee behaviors, strategies, goals, and desirable means for achieving these goals in their mission statement. More often than not, however, a company's corporate culture is unspoken. New hires absorb it, if you will, through observation and interaction with coworkers over time after coming aboard. Sometimes it works out, and sometimes it doesn't.

Heads Up

Clearly, it would be beneficial to employers and applicants alike if information about the corporate culture were revealed in advance. There's a simple four-step process recruiters can follow to accomplish this:

1. Ask applicants to describe the environments they're accustomed to working in. Then ask them to isolate aspects of that environment that they most enjoy and those that they dislike, elaborating on both responses.

2. Ask applicants to provide a description of the perfect workplace. What makes it idyllic? How far from their ideal is what they're accustomed to? If there were one aspect of their ideal workplace that they would want above all else, what would it be?

3. Relate their answers to the components of your corporate culture, using the checklist in Exhibit 2-1 as a guide. For example, if an applicant says that the most important aspect of a corporate culture is to receive ongoing feedback, and you know that your managers are well-advised on the merits of coaching and counseling, then that's a potentially good match. If, on the other hand, an applicant shares that he prefers to work on his own, seeking advice or assistance on an as-needed basis, then there could be a problem; you know for a fact that the climate of your company is such that managers tend to micromanage and that this practice is not discouraged.

4. Discuss those elements that replicate what the applicant is accustomed to as well as any that reflect his ideal work environment in relation to your organization. Don't shy away from any negatives—it's better to talk about such matters now rather than having them surface after he's come aboard. There may even be ways to convert what's different or undesirable into something that's beneficial for all concerned. For instance, individuals accustomed to gym membership through their jobs could research the benefits of fitness and its impact on work productivity and reduced benefits costs. That kind of data might just be what it takes to convince management to sign everyone up at the local fitness center.

Work and Personal Life Balance

Surveys can be simultaneously misleading and useful. While the specific numbers and percentages reported by different sources can sometimes appear to conflict with

Exhibit 2-1. Corporate Culture Checklist

Here's a checklist of some corporate culture components that you can reference when recruiting prospective employees:

- Acceptable attire
- Aligning career goals with those of the organization
- Employee career planning and goal setting
- Expectations concerning extracurricular events, such as participation in company-sponsored sports and other recreational activities
- Expectations concerning work performance
- Flexible work hours
- Fun in the workplace
- How problems are solved and decisions are made
- How people address one another
- Independent work
- Office space allocation
- Ongoing feedback regarding work performance
- Ongoing educational and training opportunities
- Organizational and departmental goals, and expectations of employees with respect to achieving these goals
- Organizational structure
- Primary means of communication
- Rules concerning the décor of an employee's workspace
- Skills, characteristics, and behaviors the company both disapproves of and values
- Stress reducers, such as gym memberships
- Teamwork

one another, suggesting extraneous information, the overall patterns they reveal can be helpful. This observation applies to varied reports on balance between work and the personal lives of workers. Consider, for example, a survey conducted by Strategy-One in August 2010, which reported that 89 percent of more than a thousand employees said that work and personal life balance is an issue.[1] The survey went on to state that of the 89 percent, 54 percent indicated that it was a "significant" problem. Additional information from the report suggests that 43 percent of those surveyed believe their employers could do a better job of addressing the work/life balance issue. An additional point was made that 44 percent of men between the ages of 34 and 54 felt that they do not have sufficient balance. Interestingly, the economy did not appear to play a significant role on employee feedback.

Another survey, conducted by Glassdoor.com between April 2010 and March 2011, suggests that only 43 percent of American workers are dissatisfied with their work and personal life balance.[2]

While the numbers in these two surveys significantly differ, two common factors emerge: (1) work and personal life balance is an issue deemed worth surveying, and (2) a sufficient enough number of individuals are dissatisfied to make it a legitimate workplace issue.

It's safe to say, then, that employees are concerned with striking a balance between the amounts of time they devote to work and how much time is left over for their personal lives. Whether they want more time to devote to family-related activities, educational pursuits, or recreational endeavors, workers increasingly want more flexibility and control of the allocation of their time. This does not translate into less dedication to the job; it merely means there's more to life than work, no matter how gratifying one's job may be.

Just how concerned are employers with work and personal life balance for their employees? Understandably, businesses are focused on maximizing productivity to increase profitability, but at what cost? A corporate culture that promotes long work hours with little personal life balance can result in increased stress levels, reduced motivation, frustration, resentment, low output, and poor performance.

Some companies are better at acknowledging the need for balance than others. Nestle Purina PetCare, for example, actually references work/life balance on their website and has been rated number one in the aforementioned Glassdoor.com survey.[3] MITRE (a not-for-profit national technology resource), SAS Institute (a major producer of software), FactSet (a financial data and software company), and United Space Alliance (a spaceflight operations company) ranked numbers two through five respectively on the list of successfully meeting employees' need for balance.

Work/life balance has become more of an issue today for a very simple reason: One of the detriments of our ever-advancing electronic age is that we are always, either actually or theoretically, at work. Nearly everyone can be reached via some electronic device anywhere, at any time. If you're at a sporting event for your son, you can easily be summoned back to the office on your phone via a call, e-mail, text, or tweet. If you should be on vacation, someone at work can readily access you for much-needed information to complete a project or report without so much as actually speaking with you. Electronic communication, then, has blurred the lines between work and personal lives, creating a greater challenge for balance than ever before.

Work and personal life balance can readily be used as a recruitment incentive. Promoting flexible work alternatives, leave options, and on- and off-site child and/or elder care provisions are just a few of the offerings that illustrate ways your organization can encourage balance, providing an incentive for applicants to select your workplace over others. Workers with greater job autonomy are likely to feel motivated, demonstrate an increased sense of loyalty, produce quality products, and provide greater customer satisfaction, even during difficult economic times.

Applicant Expectations

One of my favorite interview questions is, "What do you think an employer owes an employee in addition to salary and benefits?" (Naturally, I also ask the converse of this: "What do you think an employee owes an employer?") This is an important topic to probe, since employee and employer expectations do not always mesh. All too often, talented workers quit or are asked to leave due to a conflict over what one expects of the other. These expectations usually have to do with matters other than money or benefits. That's because salary and benefits are known, discussed, and agreed to prior to hiring. Other, often intangible factors such as employer-employee relations are not always adequately explored in advance. These topics are typically viewed as secondary or even irrelevant and are overlooked. In truth, however, what one person expects from another in a work relationship can be the measure of success or failure.

I generally ask the question about expectations near or at the end of an interview after I've compared the applicant's tangible skills, knowledge, and interests with the requirements and tasks of the job. I also like to wait until we've established a rapport and the interview is winding down, suggesting that the "hard" part is over. This way the interviewee is at ease and more likely to be forthcoming with a sincere response. Here's a sampling of some of the most frequent responses I've received over the years:

- "A willingness to communicate."
- "Allowing me to be part of the decision-making process."
- "Applying rules consistently."
- "Appreciation of my work."
- "Availability."
- "Career growth opportunities."
- "Letting me know that what I'm doing is making an impact."
- "Providing a positive work environment."
- "Providing a safe workplace."
- "Respect."
- "Taking my work seriously."
- "Treating everyone fairly and equitably."

I've received these revealing answers during both sound and turbulent economic times, when applicants have had the upper hand and vice versa, and from representatives of every generation.

When I receive one of these or other similar, generic responses, I continue, probing for in-depth information. Even though I dislike and try to avoid stereotypical descriptions, I acknowledge that there are certain traits that characterize each generation, setting them apart from one another in some significant ways, including employer expectations. One valuable resource for identifying employer expectations by varying demographic groups is the Center for Generational Studies, a private research firm in Aurora, Colorado (1-800-227-5510; www.generationaldiversity. com). The center offers valuable insight concerning workplace expectations of four key generations: Matures, Baby Boomers, Generation X, and Millennials. (The names assigned each group and where each generation begins and ends demographically are not absolute.)

Matures

Mature workers, also called Traditionalists or the Silent Generation, are defined by the center as those born prior to 1946. They are said to value hard work and standardized work ethics, take pride in their work, adhere to rules, have a deep sense of responsibility, and do not expect additional recognition or compensation. They believe policies and procedures should be applied uniformly, maintain a methodical approach to business, and adhere to a focused corporate vision. Indeed, they view any training they receive as contributing to organizational goals as opposed to enhancing personal development. Job security is of vital importance to members of this generation, as is loyalty and commitment. Consequently, they are more likely to tolerate mundane and repetitive work, asking only for clear direction and reinforcement. Not surprisingly, they favor face-to-face meetings or phone calls as means for communicating. Indeed, the idea of staying with one employer for their entire careers is not at all unusual, even if the job is less than ideal. They also appreciate predictable outcomes.

Baby Boomers

These workers were born between 1946 and 1964. In contrast with Matures, who came of age during times of economic depression, Baby Boomers grew up in the midst of economic prosperity. Still, like Matures, they believe in working hard and putting in long hours, but unlike members of the generation before them, they expect to be acknowledged publicly for their work and rewarded for their efforts, hence the label "Me Generation." Competitive and independent, they additionally expect a workplace that allows work schedule flexibility, emphasizes teamwork, and encourages individual workers to make an impact. Baby Boomers associate themselves closely with their professions and as such resist retiring even when they can afford to do so, although many are working considerably longer than they'd anticipated because they have exhausted their assets. These Baby Boomers must continue to support not only themselves, but post–college aged children as well as aged parents; hence the label "sandwich generation."

Generation X or Xers

Generation X or Xers were born between 1965 and 1980 and have a different view of work than their predecessors. Having witnessed their Mature and Baby Boomer grandparents and parents laid off despite years of dedication and loyal service, they don't see the necessity of putting in excessively long hours or working extra hard to impress employers they perceive as not likely to be concerned with their well-being. Instead, they believe in "working smarter," which often translates into developing transferable skills and devoting less time on the job. They have a more casual regard for authority than Matures and Baby Boomers, and they place limited value on policies. Loyalty to one's self outweighs loyalty to one's employer. They are also more likely to demand work/personal life balance from their employers. They further value being able to work independently, focusing more on outcomes than tasks. In addition, Xers expect training and development opportunities that will advance their own career goals.

Millennials

Millennials, also referred to as Generation Y or Nexters, are workers born between 1981 and 1999. They are defined first and foremost by technology, as opposed to work ethics, and expect employers to continually provide them with cutting-edge equipment. When it comes to communication, they favor texting, IMing, and tweeting, and they have limited patience for e-mails and even less for phone conversations or face-to-face meetings. They also believe in integrating fun with work, appreciate a diverse workplace, and strive to make a difference. Millennials additionally expect immediate feedback and rapid results. Like Generation X, they are proactive when it comes to career advancement and believe in acquiring as many experiences as possible. As such, they are not wedded to any one employer for long periods of time and regularly seek new opportunities. Whereas Matures and even Baby Boomers might view this as disloyal, Millennials see it as being practical; why stay in a job that's not at once stimulating and rewarding?

Beyond Millennials

Experts are already looking to label and characterize the next generation of workers, those born between 2000 through 2010. They are being called Homelanders, Generation Z, Generation M (for multitasking), the Internet Generation, and Digital Natives. Since members of this generation have not yet entered the workforce, it's premature to try and identify their workplace expectations or to characterize them other than to say that by the time they begin work they will have had lifelong use of technologically generated communications, including many, no doubt, that are yet to be developed. It's also anticipated that they will be the most racially and culturally diverse group.

Not surprisingly, we already have a label for those born after 2010: Generation Alpha or Gen A. Social researcher Mark McCrindle predicts that this may very well be our biggest generation to date. Stay tuned.

Employer Expectations

Beyond a specific set of tangible skills that match those needed to perform a particular job, what do employers expect from their employees? Most identify a standard list of intangibles, including the ability to communicate effectively, analytical thinking, technical literacy, adaptability, interpersonal skills, multicultural awareness, organizational skills, problem-solving abilities, and teamwork. These can all be identified during the employment interview through carefully worded questions that will lead to making an informed decision (Chapters 7 and 8).

It's likely that these skills would strike applicants from every generational category as reasonable, but here's where it gets interesting: Employers also have a list of "values" that they want their employees to demonstrate. They consistently identify ten categories of personality traits and personal characteristics they expect employees to demonstrate: (1) honesty and integrity, (2) a solid work ethic, (3) reliability, (4) responsibility, (5) loyalty, (6) a positive attitude, (7) energy, (8) self-motivation, (9) professionalism, (10) a willingness to take on additional tasks.

In addition to being more difficult to discern because of the interviewing skills required to elicit relevant answers, these traits are not likely to be perceived as being connected with members of every generation. For example, a solid work ethic is something more likely to be identified with Matures and Baby Boomers than with Xers and Millennials. I'm not saying that this is necessarily an accurate portrayal, but it is a likely assumption. So if a recruiter is focused on work ethic as a key factor, the recruiter may be more inclined to look for an older applicant. The same perception may hold true for loyalty. The reverse may be the case, however, when it comes to looking for someone who is energetic and self-motivated; these are traits typically associated with Millennials. Matters become even more complicated when recruiters factor in reporting relationships. Can a Mature successfully work for a Millennial? How about vice versa?

After all is said and done, is there a way to align applicant expectations with those of employers? The answer is a resounding "yes," assuming both sides are willing to do a little work. Applicants may be able to piece together information available online about most companies to determine, to some extent, what employee traits organizations consider important. Then they will need to compare those traits with their own to decide whether they want to proceed with the application process. They can also get some clues as to whether the company is likely to value and meet their expectations by reading staff testimonials and talking with current and former employees. Of course, they can ask specific questions during the interviews as well.

For employers, the task begins with acknowledging typical generational personality traits and personal characteristics while at the same time avoiding across-the-board assumptions. It also means becoming familiar with the generic employee expectations identified earlier and honestly identifying those that are consistent with their particular corporate culture. Once these two steps have been accomplished, it will be left to interviewers to ask questions that will reveal whether there is a match between what a particular applicant is looking for and what the employer expects in return.

One company that exemplifies how the integration of employee and employer expectations can be achieved is Trader Joe's, the multibillion-dollar national specialty grocery chain that has managed to accomplish corporate growth while fostering an environment of interesting work, thereby keeping turnover levels low and employee loyalty levels high. The last observation is especially interesting since many of Trader Joe's workers are young college graduates, representative of the Millennial generation, typically characterized as being disinclined to stay with any one employer for long periods of time. The primary reason young workers stay loyal to Trader Joe's is because the company demonstrates that they value employees' opinions and provide immediate feedback on suggestions, all of which are taken seriously and many of which are acted upon. They also believe that happy employees make for better relations with customers, which stimulates spending. This means that working for Trader Joe's is fun—another important workplace ingredient for Millennials. The environment is informal; employees get to wear cool Hawaiian shirts, are encouraged to joke around with one another as well as with customers, and generally feel good about being at work.

This is not to say that Trader Joe's does not have high expectations of its employees or that it is focused entirely on hiring Millennials. Their starting salary and benefits are considered generous, which attracts workers from every age group. In addition, they offer extensive formal training, something that has cross-generational appeal. The company also promotes many of the generic applicant expectations cited earlier. Specifically, in addition to providing a positive work environment, they have a strong upward and downward chain of communication, strongly provide career growth opportunities, and treat employees with respect.

Trader Joe's has been recognized as one of the world's most ethical companies of 2010[4] and has appeared on Supermarket News' listing of top seventy-five retailers for 2011.[5] It must be doing something right.

Applicants' Questions

While interviewers control the exchange between themselves and prospective employees, they should also anticipate questions applicants may ask of them. Long gone are the days when applicants only asked about benefits and how much money they would be paid. Far more sophisticated and concerned about how a particular job fits in with their lives overall, today's applicants are more likely to pose detailed questions about the company itself and the role they can expect to play. While the prevailing state of the economy and their current work status will impact the nature and depth of applicants' questions, employers are advised to view every job opening at all times from the perspective of a potential employee, and be prepared. Even if all these questions aren't posed—and it's unlikely that they all will be—knowing the answers and thinking like an applicant will better prepare you for the interview.

Here's a sampling of questions employers can anticipate from applicants:

Questions About the Job Description
- Is there a written job description for this position? May I see it?
- Who prepared the job description? Did incumbents have input?
- Is there a job description for every job?
- May I see the job description for the position this one reports to?
- How frequently are job descriptions reviewed?

Questions About the Interviewer

- How long have you worked for this company?
- What made you decide to work here?
- Has the company been supportive with regard to helping you meet personal career goals?
- Looking back to the time of hire, has everything worked out the way you'd hoped?
- What's the best thing about working here? The least desirable?

Questions About the Company

- I've read about the company's growth over the past five years and its projected goals for the next five years. How does this job fit in with regard to helping the company achieve its next set of goals?
- Given the current state of the economy, what assurance can you offer that my position will not be eliminated?
- What has the company done in the past to avoid layoffs?
- What percentage of senior management consists of members of protected groups?
- How does that percentage compare with five years ago?
- What are the greatest challenges this company currently faces?
- Who are your greatest competitors? What makes them a threat?

Questions About the Corporate Culture

- How would you describe the company's corporate culture?
- How highly does the organization value employee input?
- How strictly are policies and procedures followed? Are they consistently applied?
- How important is teamwork?
- Is there a written organizational chart with a formal flow of command? May I see it?
- What does the company expect from its employees? What's the most important trait?
- How diverse is the company's workforce?

Questions About the Person to Whom the Position Reports

- How long has she been in the job?
- How would you describe her management style?
- How many people does she currently have reporting to her? What are their positions?

- What's the turnover rate been like in her department since she's been in charge?
- What are some of the reasons she's rejected applicants in the past?

Questions About Prior Employees

- Can you tell me about the strengths of the incumbent and prior employees?
- Why did they leave?
- How long did they work here?
- Was their work style similar to that of the manager and/or department head?
- What mistakes did they make that I should avoid if I were to be hired?

Questions About the Job

- In addition to what I've read in the job description, what can you tell me about the day-to-day activities of this job?
- Approximately what percentage of time would I be expected to devote to each task?
- What would you describe as the best and least desirable aspects of this job?
- What are the most valuable skills an employee can bring to this job?
- What is the greatest challenge connected with this job?
- Will I be able to strike a balance between work and my personal life?
- Who will make the final hiring decision?
- When can I expect to hear from you?

Questions About the Job in Relation to Other Departments

- How does this job interrelate with jobs in other departments?
- What role does this job play in helping the department and/or other departments achieve their goals?
- How frequently would I interact with representatives from other departments?
- How interrelated are the goals of each department?
- Do different departments ever work together on projects? How frequently? Can you give me an example of the type of project we'd work on together?

Questions About Salary, Growth Opportunities, and Benefits

- Based on my skills and experience, what salary are you offering me?
- How frequently are pay increases implemented?
- Are increases tied to performance reviews?
- Does the company have a formal metrics plan in place for measuring and rewarding performance?
- Does the company have a policy of looking within when there's an opening before recruiting from the outside?

- Is the position I'm applying for part of a job family?
- Assuming I perform satisfactorily, what is the logical next step in terms of advancement?
- Does the company have a formal career-planning program?
- Is there a mentoring program?
- What is the company's policy concerning training opportunities?
- Does the company offer tuition reimbursement?
- I understand that I will be provided with detailed benefits information if I'm hired, but can you tell me what you consider to be the best benefit the company offers its employees?
- What can I get here in the way of benefits that I'm unlikely to be offered elsewhere?

Summary

Applicants view work differently than do employers. While that's not particularly surprising, the ways this distinction manifests itself and the extent to which it can impact employer-employee relations may be. Beginning with a work environment's unique culture, qualified applicants may find themselves ill at ease with their environment once hired, to the point where they become less motivated and productive. Recruiters can prevent this from happening by both clearly communicating information about the corporate culture prior to hire and determining the type of environment in which applicants are most comfortable working.

Another aspect of work that can strain employer-employee relations is the way in which applicants and employers view the importance of work/personal life balance. Businesses are, understandably, focused on maximizing productivity to increase profitability, and most employees are all too willing to help achieve this goal. But employees also require balance between the amount of time and energy they devote to work and to their outside lives. Employers would do well to use work/life balance as a recruitment incentive by promoting flexible work alternatives and other offerings. This lets prospective employees know that employers are aware and respectful of their need for balance, which provides incentive for them to select your workplace over others.

Perhaps the greatest source of friction between employees and employers lies in their respective expectations of one another. Both groups could convincingly argue that their expectations are reasonable and appropriate. Unfortunately, they don't always mesh. The matter becomes more complicated when you factor in certain traits that typically characterize each of four generations: Matures, born prior to 1946; Baby Boomers, born between 1946 and 1964; Generation X, born between 1965 and 1980; and Millennials, born between 1981 and 1999. While drawing conclusions based on generalities is ill-advised, one must acknowledge that these traits set members of each generation apart from one another in some significant ways, including employer expectations. Employers would do well to become familiar with what members of each of these generations wants and identify those that are consistent with their corporate culture. They can then ask questions during the employment interview that will reveal whether there is a sufficient match between what a specific individual requires, what the employer is willing or able to give, and what they expect in return.

Finally, recruiters need to anticipate and be prepared for questions applicants may ask of them. Knowing the answers and thinking like an applicant will better prepare them for the interview.

CHAPTER 3

Recruitment Sources

"I need a customer service rep—fast!" "I'm losing my public relations manager—do you know anyone who can replace her?" "The employment agency I've been using keeps sending me unqualified applicants; they just don't seem to get what I'm looking for!" "We're getting a ton of resumes in response to our ad for a warehouse supervisor, but no one is qualified!" "Our website is outdated; I'm still getting resumes for a job we filled two weeks ago!" "Our top competitor lost their best technical specialist the same time we did and they hired a dynamite replacement a week later; we still can't find anyone. What are we doing wrong?" "The labor pool keeps changing and I can't keep up—are we in an economic upswing or downswing this week? Are we in charge or are the employees? Help!"

Can you relate to any of these phrases? You're not alone if you can; these are common cries heard these days throughout businesses nationwide. Filling a vacancy or a newly created position poses numerous challenges, but it all comes down to this: Where can you find qualified applicants in the least amount of time for the least amount of money?

Some organizations ignore the multitude of options available and use the same source each time. While this may produce a pool of qualified applicants from which to choose, repeatedly using the same recruitment sources can make you susceptible to charges of systemic discrimination: the denial of equal employment opportunity through an established business practice, such as recruitment. Even though the discrimination may be inadvertent, the disparate effect it produces may develop into a prime area of vulnerability for employers. Relying on the same recruitment source each time a particular position becomes available could have an adverse impact on members of certain protected groups lacking the same access as others to that source. This, in turn, could translate into the inadvertent but no less illegal denial of equal employment opportunity.

Electronic recruitment will be reserved for separate discussion in Chapter 4.

Prerecruitment Considerations

Consider four factors before embarking on a recruitment campaign: how much money is available, how quickly the opening must be filled, whether you need to reach a wide audience, and the exemption level of the available position.

Recruitment Budget

The amount of money allocated for recruitment can greatly affect your options. For example, display ads and search firms can cost several thousands of dollars with no guarantee of attracting a substantial number of qualified applicants. On the other hand, some of the most effective recruitment sources, such as employee referrals, cost very little.

Quick Results Recruitment Sources

Openings can occur suddenly and unexpectedly, usually when employees decide to leave with little or no notice. Being prepared is your best defense. Begin by ensuring that your employee data bank is up to date; this way you can turn to existing staff as an immediate resource, even if it's an interim replacement until you've hired some-one permanently. In addition, have an employee referral program in place. Launch it as soon as you know there's an opening, spreading the word to as many employees as possible. Focus, too, on recruitment sources most likely to yield immediate results, such as applicants who were previously interviewed and assessed. You might do well to turn to your preemployment training pool, if you have one, or consider hiring contingency workers as a stopgap measure.

Broad-Based Recruiting

Some positions are highly specialized and more difficult to fill. To improve the chances of a job match, reach out to as many applicants as possible. Employment agencies and search firms may be helpful in this instance, although they tend to recommend nearly everyone when the requirements are broad. Ads in newspapers and journals can be effective also. Consider advertising in out-of-town publications for hard-to-fill openings, and be prepared to accommodate the travel needs of viable applicants.

Exemption Status

The Fair Labor Standards Act defines *exempt* employees as workers who are legally precluded from receiving overtime compensation; that is, employers do not have to pay professionals for overtime. The term *nonexempt* literally means not excused from overtime compensation, or, stated another way, entitled to receive overtime pay. The distinction is significant in that recruitment sources that produce qualified exempt or professional applicants may not work as well for nonexempt applicants. For example, direct mail recruitment, search firms, campus recruiting, job fairs, research firms, and professional associations could produce qualified exempt applicants, whereas high school guidance counselors, government agencies, advertising in the classified section of newspapers, and employment agencies are more likely to yield a choice group of nonexempt applicants.

Of the factors indicated—cost, immediacy, audience, and level—a specific recruitment source may meet some criteria but not others. Employers are advised to explore the ramifications of using each resource in relation to these four factors, deciding which are most important for a given job opening.

Newspaper ads provide a prime example. They are expensive but are more likely to yield immediate results. If they appear in the most likely to be read section of an appropriate paper on the right day of the week at the right time of year and contain the necessary text, newspaper ads will reach a wide audience at the level you're trying to reach.

Proactive and Reactive Recruitment

After examining the four prerecruitment criteria, consider how aggressive you need to be to fill a particular opening. If immediacy is a primary factor, search out proactive recruitment sources that will make a concerted effort to find employees. Proactive recruitment requires direct involvement on the part of the recruiter. It's the reverse of reactive recruitment where you wait for applicants to apply, hoping that the best fit is among them.

Some recruitment sources are inherently reactive, by their very nature prohibiting recruiters from aggressively pursuing applicants. Consider one of the most popular recruitment sources, employee referrals. HR provides employees with the job description and a list of requirements and waits to see who among their friends, family, and acquaintances is interested. The onus for referring applicants is on the employees. This is cost-effective and an employee morale booster since employees making referrals resulting in placement are usually rewarded, and it could work if time is not a factor. For example, perhaps you have an employee who wants to retire but is willing to wait until a replacement is found, or maybe a department head is thinking about creating a new position but doesn't need to fill it immediately. More often than not, however, time is crucial. When an employee resigns, you usually need to move fast, and that means being proactive.

Proactive recruiters start looking for a replacement as soon as they learn of an opening. They expand their recruitment pool to encompass other than traditional recruiting sources and aggressively go after applicants. When you're in control of who's being targeted, you're more likely to find qualified applicants and choose the one who makes the best fit. With direct mail recruiting, for example, employers contact specific applicants known to have certain skills and knowledge. While the response rate is usually low, around 2 percent, at least you know that those responding are viable options.

Another example of proactive recruitment is preemployment training that provides a supplemental workforce of people who have been recruited through conventional means and trained in job- and industry-specific matters. They are then placed in a standby pool. When there's an opening, employers can turn to this supplemental workforce and select a suitable applicant. While there's no guarantee that the person who would make the best fit will remain in the pool waiting to be offered a job, the odds are in your favor during times of high unemployment and if you provide the person with an incentive.

Professional associations and inter-HR networking can also provide employers with an opportunity to proactively recruit. Direct contact with potential employees or communication with others in your field can often put you in touch with qualified applicants.

Special Interest Groups

Taking a shotgun approach to recruitment in terms of who will be drawn in by whatever source you're using may result in a qualified applicant pool, but certain special interest groups may need to be targeted directly in order to minimize inadvertent violations of certain equal employment opportunity laws. This approach is also likely to produce a more diverse pool of applicants, thereby potentially enhancing productivity and profitability and increasing your global appeal.

Begin targeting special interest groups by developing a keener insight into the characteristics of the generations as identified in Chapter 2. Then consider those recruitment sources most likely to appeal to members of the following select employment groups:

Older Workers

Many Mature and Baby Boomer workers who are eligible for retirement are instead opting to stay actively employed. Some seek part-time jobs to supplement Social Security and other sources of income, while others compete for positions with the same verve and energy as applicants who are considerably younger because their identities are so closely connected with their work. Still others need to continue working full-time because they can't afford not to.

Because older workers are statistically shown to be more likely to come aboard with a strong work ethic, are more reliable and loyal, have higher retention rates, and bring with them invaluable experience, employers are wise to seek them out for hire. The only reported possible disadvantage to hiring members of the Mature and Baby Boomer generations is their failure to keep up with technology, but that is becoming less and less of a factor as our lives become increasingly electronically connected.

Employers can take a proactive approach to hiring older workers by using these and other similar recruitment sources:

- Advertise in sections other than the classified, i.e., television or sports sections, to reach older adults who are not actively looking.
- Advertise on radio and television shows that have demographics of Mature- and Baby Boomer–aged listeners and viewers.

- Approach senior citizen community centers.
- Ensure that your marketing materials show older people, both as employees and as recipients of your products or services, and distribute these materials in locations frequented by older workers.
- Participate in open houses and career fairs sponsored by organizations such as American Association of Retired Persons (AARP) and the Veterans Administration (VA).
- Partner with professional organizations that attract older workers.
- Rehire retirees who have industry-specific experience.
- Sponsor open houses and second-career fairs specifically for older adults.
- Try Forty Plus, a nonprofit organization that offers support to executives and professionals seeking jobs.
- Turn to company-sponsored alumni groups.
- Use language in job ads that encourages older workers.

Youth

It's challenging to write about nonelectronic recruiting sources for Millennials since they are so intrinsically linked with web-based recruiting sources. Still, there are other ways to recruit young workers:

- Approach businesses that are known for hiring seasonal help and ask about their top former workers.
- Conduct job fairs that identify benefits and perks likely to appeal to young workers.
- Work with colleges and set up on-campus recruitment drives.
- Contact various branches of the armed services since some young people opt for the military as an alternative to college.
- Find out where Millennials like to hang out, e.g., local coffee shops and bars, and distribute company-related literature there.
- Encourage young employees working for you to refer their friends.
- Ensure that your marketing materials show young people, both as employees and as recipients of your products or services.
- Look to businesses—including your own—that offer internships, and consider recent participants.
- Prepare company brochures that emphasize new technology, training, and promotional opportunities as well as geographic alternatives.

Women

There are a number of recruitment sources that specialize in placing women. Some are generic, several are linked to certain professions, and others reflect women of specific ethnicities:

- Association for Women in Mathematics
- Association for Women in Science
- Black, Indian, Hispanic and Women in Action
- Business and Professional Women, Inc.
- National Association of Professional Asian American Women
- National Coalition of 100 Black Women
- National Institute for Women in Trades, Technology & Science
- National Organization for Women (NOW)
- National Women in Management, Inc.
- Society of Women Engineers
- Women Employed
- Women in Science and Engineering
- Women in Technology International

Recruiters seeking to increase the number of women in their workforce can also share job openings with pediatricians' offices and schools. Many women will also be drawn to employers offering not only the usual benefits but on-site or off-site child care and flexible hours.

Minorities

The term *minority* as used here is intended to encompass a broad spectrum of ethnic groups including, but not limited to, African Americans, Hispanics (e.g., Puerto Ricans, Cuban and Mexican Americans, and people originally from more than twenty additional Central and South American nations and Spain), Asian Americans (e.g., Korean, Japanese, Chinese, and Filipino Americans), and Native Americans. Many will be drawn to employers offering not only the usual growth opportunities and benefits, but also a multicultural or diverse environment. As with women, there are numerous organizations that specialize in placing minorities. Some are broad-based, while others specialize according to occupation and/or ethnicity:

- American Association of Blacks in Energy
- American Coalition of Filipino Veterans
- American Indian Science and Engineering Society (AISES)
- American Society of Engineers of Indian Origin (ASEI)
- Asian American Leadership Empowerment and Development (LEAD)
- Hispanic Alliance for Career Enhancement (HACE)
- National Action Council for Minorities in Engineering (NACME)
- National Association of Asian-American Professionals
- National Black MBA Association

Applicants with Disabilities

People with disabilities are considered the single most underutilized labor resource. One of the primary reasons has to do with how we perceive them. Many of us are locked into an image of someone in a wheelchair. In reality, the term *disabled* encompasses a broad spectrum of impairments. Categories include visual, hearing, and speech impairments; heart disease; developmental disabilities such as cerebral palsy; mental illness; acquired immune deficiency syndrome (AIDS) or human immunodeficiency virus (HIV)–positive status; and limitations resulting from accidents. Experts say that each of us has a 20 percent chance of developing a disability during our working lives.

Another reason commonly cited for failing to actively pursue applicants with disabilities is cost. Laws stipulate that employers must make reasonable accommodations for applicants with disabilities, unless such accommodation results in undue hardship. In determining whether a given accommodation would result in undue financial hardship, the law assesses the overall size of an organization, the nature of its business, and the type of the required accommodation.

Recruiting people with disabilities requires a proactive approach, beginning with establishing relationships with agencies that represent or train people with disabilities before openings occur. Here are some specific resources that may be helpful:

- Disabled American Veterans
- Kennedy Institute—Support Employment Program
- Learning Disabilities Association of America (LDA)
- National Alliance for the Mentally Ill (NAMI)
- National Federation of the Blind
- National Organization on Disability
- Operation Job Match
- President's Committee on Employment of People with Disabilities
- Technical Vocational Institute—Special Services
- U.S. Department of Health and Human Services
- U.S. Department of Labor—Office of Disability Employment Policy

The Unemployed

Being laid off, downsized, or excessed no longer has the stigma attached to it that it once had. The economy is in turmoil as an increased number of businesses buy one another out, merge, dissolve, or consolidate, making all employees vulnerable.

Recruiters are starting to view this group of workers as a viable recruitment source. By partnering with similar businesses that are undergoing major reorganizations, a growing number of employers are creating win-win scenarios: downsized workers find new employment, and recruiters fill their openings with experienced people ready to hit the ground running.

Recruiting unemployed applicants requires proactive thinking. Businesses need to establish ties with companies with similar employee pools well before there are signs of trouble, agreeing on how a shift in employers could take place. Having a formal transition program in place at both locations is ideal, complete with counseling services made available to displaced workers.

Interns

Interns are often viewed as contingency or temporary workers, retained for a limited period of time or for specific assignments instead of as members of a special interest group eventually available for full-time hire. If you're inclined to see interns this way, you could be robbing your organization of valuable future talent. Hiring former interns has many advantages. They know your organization and what's expected of them; you, in turn, are familiar with their style of work, strengths and areas requiring improvement, work ethics, and interpersonal skills. One could say that you've had a chance to try one another out before making a commitment. The primary disadvantage of hiring interns is time. Interns are often students who work for businesses during the summer, performing tasks that relate to their major course of study. If they first come to you as freshmen or sophomores, you'll have to be patient and wait two or more years until they graduate before you can bring them on board as full-time employees. The wait, however, may be worth it.

Former Employees

Employers used to adhere to strict "no rehire" policies, but in an erratic economy former employees are rapidly becoming a viable recruitment source as employers increasingly contact former employees, striving to convert former employees into new hires.

In some instances, rehires are brought in at a higher level or as in-house consultants, earning more salary and benefits than they did the first time around. This can send a negative message to a company's current workforce—that the best way to get ahead in an organization is to leave it and then come back.

If your organization wants to recruit former employees for rehire, carefully review their work history before making contact. Delve deeply into reasons for termination: Was it voluntary or forced? Look at their past performance reviews, identifying any problem areas, and talk with their former supervisors to review their skill sets. Also, explore what they've been doing since leaving your company.

Traditional Recruitment Sources

Traditional recruitment sources are methods for finding employees that are easily recognized, conventional in nature, acceptable to most types of organizations, and appropriate for filling a wide range of positions. Before embarking on a traditional recruitment campaign, remember to consider the four factors discussed earlier in this chapter: how much money is available, how quickly the opening must be filled, whether a wide audience must be reached, and the exemption level of the available position. In addition, carefully weigh the advantages and disadvantages of each source before proceeding.

Here are some of the most commonly used traditional recruitment sources. Exhibit 3-1 provides key advantages and disadvantages for each source.

Advertising

Advertising, whether in newspapers or professional publications, remains one of the most popular and effective nonelectronic means for soliciting applications. Careful planning of content, timing, and location is likely to generate a large targeted response, often resulting in hiring.

To increase your chances of finding top-notch applicants through advertising, apply these ad placement strategies:

- Capture the job hunter's attention through the location of the ad, an appropriate job title, graphics, use of white space, and the placement of a logo.
- Provide just enough information to pique the job hunter's interest so that the job hunter establishes a connection between your needs and her skills.
- Design your ad to be the last one a job hunter wants to read, using language that creates an image of how great employment with your company would be.

Be sure the language in your ads doesn't violate equal employment opportunity (EEO) laws and regulations. Such language would include an age preference using terminology such as *young man* or *mature woman;* using certain other subjective terms, such as *attractive;* or stating a preference for either gender. With regard to the latter, it is important to note that masculine or feminine terms do not automatically constitute an EEO violation. The Equal Employment Opportunity Commission (EEOC) has issued a policy statement regarding sex-referent language in employment advertising, noting that terms such as *patrolman* or *meter maid* have become "colloquial ways of denoting particular jobs rather than the sex of the individuals who perform those jobs." The statement continues with "the use of sex-referent language in employment opportunity advertisements and other recruitment practices is suspect but is not a per se violation of Title VII." (Title VII is part of the Civil Rights Act of 1964.) The EEOC goes on to urge employers to clearly indicate their intent to consider applicants of both genders whenever sex-referent language is used. Including a statement confirming nondiscriminatory intent such as "equal employment opportunity employer, male/female" is recommended.

Campus Recruiting

Students are generally attracted to companies that enjoy a good reputation, are successful, will look impressive on their resumes, have shown a past interest in their school, and keep up with technological change. To gain students' attention, many employers are replacing traditional company recruitment brochures with technologi-

Exhibit 3-1. Key Advantages and Disadvantages for Traditional Recruitment Sources

Traditional Recruitment Source	Advantages	Disadvantages
Advertising	Reaches a wide audience	Costly
Campus Recruiting	Can select top students Opportunity to groom future management	Hard to assess potential
Contingency Workers	Can fill jobs in a hurry	Possible legal ramifications
Direct Mail	Personalized Selective	Time-intensive May not be opened
Employee Referrals	Employee morale booster if referrals are hired Expeditious Inexpensive	Employee demotivator if referrals are not hired Possible systematic discrimination
Employment Services	Access to large labor pool	Cost
Former Applicants	Good public relations	Outdated records
Government Agencies	Cost-effective	Limited scope
Job Fairs	May fill several openings in a short period of time	May not be able to hire anyone
Job Posting	Morale booster	Managers feel lack of control
Military Outplacement	Hands-on experience Strong work ethic Experience in teaming and managing	Lack of general business skills
Networking	Expanded base of possible applicants	Lack of control
Open Houses	Good public relations May fill several openings	Costly Time-consuming
Outplacement Firms	Large numbers of applicants	Incomplete picture of intangibles
Professional Associations	Personal referrals	Someone else's rejected applicants
Radio and Television	Reaches a wide audience Reaches prospects not actively looking for a job	Can be costly
Research Firms	Allows for greater involvement in the interviewing process	Services end upon contacting applicants

cal tools that go beyond providing the standard company history, products, services, customers, work environment, culture, and answers to typical questions. Students today are looking for information telling them what life is like in the company, how people treat one another, and if the company has received any bad publicity recently. This offers students a comprehensive sense of what working for the company would be like.

Some organizations are conducting online, interactive chat sessions, or webinars, with students who are majoring in subjects that are of particular interest to the hiring company. Others are posting videos on the web with content that specifically targets Millennials, including career opportunities. This approach allows businesses to reach out to students without leaving their offices; it also lets students know that they are technologically savvy.

Professor programs are another method of school recruitment. Professors identify students who are high-potential applicants and take information about a company back to their students after meeting with management and observing employees at work. A variation of the professor program is when company executives teach courses at selected schools, giving them direct access to students with demonstrated potential.

Many businesses limit themselves to a handful of target schools, developing relationships with them and identifying future employees as early as a student's sophomore year. These target schools are generally selected based on the quality of their academic programs, the school's reputation, and the diversity of the student population.

Employers unable to compete for top students from prestigious colleges are urged to recruit from lesser-known schools that may be just as strong in academics and programs. For many jobs, even at a managerial level, a person's educational credentials may take a back seat to other skills and job-related knowledge not necessarily acquired through formal education.

Contingency Workers

Contingency workers are those who put in less than a full forty-hour week without comprehensive benefits, carrying portable skills from job to job. Their work is literally contingent, or dependent, on an employer's need for them. Most hold one or two assignments within a six-month period. Contingency assignments are available in virtually every field and profession. Part-timers, temps, freelancers, contract employees, and consultants all fall under the "contingency" umbrella.

People accept contingency jobs for a variety of reasons. Teachers during school vacations, peripheral workers such as retirees who no longer want to work full-time, those having child care or elder care responsibilities, college students, and displaced workers may seek contingency assignments for additional income. Others look to contingency work as a path to long-term employment. Some take temporary assignments to improve skills or gain exposure to a particular work environment. Many enjoy the flexible work schedules that can accompany contingency assignments. Still others accept contingency work as a stopgap between full-time jobs.

Companies generally hire contingency workers when they're pressed to fill an opening in a hurry or to provide a service for a specified period of time.

Increasingly, the courts are examining the relationship between companies and their contingent workers. *Enforcement Guidance: Application of EEO Laws to Contingent Workers Placed by Temporary Employment Agencies and Other Staffing Firms*, prepared by the EEOC, helps employers address the application of federal employment antidiscrimination statutes to individuals placed in job assignments on a contingent basis. The Internal Revenue Service (IRS) is also interested in your relationship with contingency workers. Employers are urged to review the IRS's "twenty-factor test" to determine if individuals are properly classified as contingency workers.

Direct Mail

Companies use direct mail campaigns to target specific individuals. The first step is determining whom to contact. Since the expected response rate is low—between 0.5 and 2 percent—you will need several different mailing lists. List information may be obtained through professional associations, business directories, and trade groups. *Direct Mail List Rates and Data*, published by Standard Rate and Data Service, Inc., can offer additional assistance. You may also opt to hire the services of direct mail specialists or consultants to help plan and implement your mail campaign. Obtain a copy of the *Mailer's Guide* from the local post office for guidance on most efficiently sending your materials.

Your letter should contain a clear, brief, easy-to-read message. The first sentence should inform the reader of your purpose and interest. Include information about the requirements of the job, its duties and responsibilities, and its benefits. Try to anticipate any relevant questions an applicant might ask and provide brief answers. Also, ask for a referral. In the event your initial prospect is not interested in the position, she may know of someone who is.

Employee Referrals

One of the most expeditious, cost-effective, and morale-boosting recruitment sources is a company's own employee referral program. This method entails "spreading the word" as soon as a position becomes available. The manager in charge of the department with the opening tells her employees to tell people they know who might be interested in applying. Employees, especially those proven to be valuable and reliable human resources, can often lead their company to prime applicants.

To maximize the effectiveness of this method, employers offer incentives of varying worth to employees who refer individuals who are ultimately hired and complete a predetermined period of employment with a satisfactory performance evaluation. These are usually cash awards, ranging from one hundred dollars for nonexempt hires to several thousand dollars for top-level executives. In addition to cash bonuses, some employers offer savings bonds, gift certificates, and merchandise. For especially hard-to-fill openings, employers have been known to grant trips and cars.

Employee referral programs generally translate into a win-win for all concerned: Employees respond favorably to the incentives, and employers spend considerably less than they would for other recruitment sources such as advertising or employment services. Just avoid using employee referrals exclusively so as not be accused of systemic discrimination.

Employment Services

Employment services include agencies and search firms. Agencies generally recruit for nonexempt and some exempt jobs, while search firms typically handle professional openings with a minimum salary figure.

There are two primary reasons employment services are so popular with employers. First, these services have access to a large labor pool and can readily scout the market for qualified applicants. This includes seeking out applicants who are seemingly content with their current jobs. Second, they often fill positions more quickly than a company can on its own.

The most significant reason for not retaining an employment service is the cost.

Before agreeing to register an opening with either an employment agency or a search firm, consider these five guidelines:

1. Be certain that the service will evaluate applicants and refer only those who meet the standards you've stipulated. Too often, agencies merely forward resumes to a client without first screening the applicant.

2. Be firm about the job's requirements and refuse to consider anyone who doesn't meet them. Forward a copy of the job description to avoid misunderstandings.

3. Require a written agreement detailing the fee arrangement. Some search firms will refund a percentage of the fee if employees placed because of their efforts are terminated within the first three to six months of work.

4. Be selective in determining which employment services will receive your business. Meet with and interview representatives in advance to make certain that they clearly understand your objectives. Establish their degree of knowledge in the specific field for which they will be recruiting, and make certain you feel comfortable working with them. Ask for information regarding their methodology, experience, and track record. Don't hesitate to ask for references to gauge their reputation in the field. Also be sure that the person you meet is the one handling your account.

5. Be clear in stating, in writing, that you are an equal opportunity employer and share information about your organization's affirmative action and diversity programs. Clearly stipulate that you expect them to comply fully with all employment laws (they are bound by Title VII) and that you will terminate your relationship if they should violate these laws.

Once you have decided to work with a particular employment service, encourage their representatives to learn as much as possible about both your organization and job openings. The more information they have, the better able they will be to meet your needs effectively and expeditiously.

With thousands of placement agencies and firms in the United States, an employer can afford to be selective when choosing the one that best meets its needs.

Former Applicants

Previously rejected applicants could become excellent future employees. There are often several qualified applicants for one opening; choosing one does not necessarily mean all the others are unqualified. If a similar position opens up, checking back with them could lead to hiring with little effort on your part.

A simple database can help you log and keep track of all applications received. Retrieve applicants according to the job for which they originally applied, areas of expertise, relevant education, and areas of interest.

Upon contacting former applicants, be sure to update their records. What have they done since applying to your company? Have they added to their skill set? Do they have additional, applicable educational credentials? Whom can you contact for an update on their work? A new round of interviews will be necessary, even if you were part of the initial interviewing process.

Consider being proactive by keeping in touch with viable former applicants even when you don't have suitable openings. Periodically follow up with them so that when a suitable opening comes along, you don't have to take the time to reestablish contact and update your records.

Government Agencies

Government agencies are valuable recruitment sources for entry-level and other non-exempt openings. Many organizations, like welfare-to-work agencies and local non-profits such as those serving individuals with disabilities, provide basic life skills and job training to their clients. In addition, they may offer English as a second language (ESL) training and help those who have not graduated from high school to acquire their general education development (GED) certification. Some nonprofit agencies also provide short-term mentors to new workers to help them as they settle into their jobs with your company.

There is usually no cost to employers for any of these services. In fact, businesses may be entitled to additional savings. If, for instance, a company hires someone transitioning from welfare to work, they could save in federal income tax per employee. Contact the IRS for qualifying conditions and required forms.

An additional benefit to recruiting via government agencies is that clients are usually unemployed and therefore eligible to begin work immediately.

Job Fairs

Job fairs allow recruiters to interview several applicants in a short period, usually one or two days. Businesses typically hold their own job fairs, either on company premises or at various geographic locations. Some recruiters prefer to attend specialized job fairs, such as those targeting applicants in specialized fields such as engineering, or focusing on placing members of specific groups, like women, minorities, or people with disabilities.

Whether conducting their own job fair or attending someone else's, recruiters typically conduct a series of brief interviews during the fair so they can maximize the number of applicants they see. Once they've established mutual interest, arrangements are made for applicants to come to their place of business for in-depth interviews.

If all goes well, you may hire several people for what it would cost to hire one employee using an employment service.

Job Posting

Job posting is an internal recruitment process whereby existing staff members can apply for openings before recruiters explore outside sources. Employees are provided with a succinct job description identifying the job's department, location, exemption status, salary grade and range, work schedule, requirements, primary duties and responsibilities, and working conditions. A closing date by which time all applications must be submitted is also provided. The standard deadline is generally from one to two weeks. Some employers require interested employees to receive permission from their existing managers before applying; others request notification, and still others respect the confidentiality of the process until a decision has been reached. A sample job posting form appears in Appendix A, and a sample job posting application form is shown in Appendix B.

Employees who apply for jobs via job posting are considered in the same way as any outside applicant. If a qualified applicant is found, arrangements for a starting date in the new position are made between the existing department head, human resources, and the new department head. Two weeks is usually allowed for finding a replacement to fill the position being vacated.

Some organizations have a policy of posting all openings; others post only nonexempt positions. Some steer clear of job posting altogether. Reasons offered for this include the following:

- Managers may want to promote someone they've been grooming, and thus don't want to consider anyone else.
- Managers may resent employees who apply for jobs outside their department, tending to take such a move personally.
- Losing an employee to job posting may mean waiting a long time for a replacement who may not be as qualified.

- Some companies prefer to bring in "new blood" rather than recycling existing employees.

Promoting or transferring employees from within offers several advantages:

- It usually creates an opening at a lower, easier-to-fill level.
- The company saves considerable time and money by transferring someone already familiar with the organizational structure and methodology.
- The process boosts employee morale.
- Hidden talent may be uncovered.

The success of a job-posting system depends largely on how well it is designed and monitored. Consider stipulating the following as conditions: (1) employees must be with a company for at least one year; (2) they must be in their current position for at least six months; (3) the maximum number of jobs for which they may apply within one year is three; (4) they must have received a rating of satisfactory or better on their most recent performance review. These guidelines may mitigate the problem of the "revolving door" employee who opts to apply for virtually every job posted.

Military Outplacement

While lacking in general business skills, former military personnel often come with hands-on experience in a variety of tasks, tend to have a strong work ethic, and understand organizational structure. They also have a background of providing support, both up and down the chain of command, and prior training in teaming as well as managing. In addition, the physical fitness requirements of military service tend to transform veterans into healthy employees. This can mean reduced costs for health care claims and fewer workdays lost to illness.

According to the 1991 Defense Authorization Act, the office of the secretary of defense must provide employment assistance to separating military service personnel. Originally dubbed the Defense Outplacement Referral System (DORS), the program is now known as Job Search and is linked with America's Job Bank. Job Search offers a no-cost referral program for companies registering at http://dod.jobsearch.org/register.

There are several other programs that can facilitate your company's publication of job openings and recruitment from the ranks, including the Retired Officers Association, the Army Career and Alumni Program, the Non-Commissioned Officers' Association, and Transition Assistance Online.

Networking

Consider this scenario: Tess works for a public relations firm and is having trouble finding an entry-level assistant who fits in with her corporate culture. She attends a

PR association meeting and mentions her plight to Tony, a colleague from another firm. Tony comments that he recently received a resume from Rob, a friend of his son's, who is about to graduate from college and wants to work in PR. Tony forwards Rob's resume to Tess, who calls him in for an interview and ultimately hires him.

This cost-effective expanded form of networking is an example of how recruiters would do well to broaden their scope of contact. Talk to people all the time and tell them what you're looking for in the way of skills and traits. Get the message out there, because you just never know.

Open Houses

Organizations hosting an open house generally run ads in numerous geographic locations, as well as post notices on their company websites. These ads announce a recruitment drive for specific dates at varying sites. Unless the company is well-known, a description of the company's product and reputation are included, along with highlights of its benefit package. All available jobs are listed as well. On the advertised date, company recruiters gather to greet and interview interested applicants. As with job fairs, recruiters want to maximize the number of applicants they see during their open house event; therefore, arrangements are made for in-depth interviews with qualified applicants at a later time.

Outplacement Firms

Companies generally retain outplacement firms to help select employees find new jobs following termination because of workforce reductions or other factors unrelated to job performance. In addition to serving as an effective source for those seeking guidance in finding new employment, outplacement firms can also assist employers who, while cutting back on staff in some departments, may need to hire in others. Most of these firms are staffed with generalists who do not specialize in placing people in particular occupations or fields. Therefore, they may know of a number of applicants meeting a variety of job specifications. In addition, the immediate availability of job seekers referred by outplacement firms can be a big plus.

One disadvantage of interviewing outplacement firm referrals is that these applicants may not provide a clear overview of their intangible qualities. The traumatic experience of losing a job and the stress of having to market oneself, added to the pressure of finding new employment, can greatly impact an applicant's self-image. This in turn can affect how prospective employers perceive the applicant.

Professional Associations

Joining a professional association gives you an opportunity to network with colleagues from other organizations. For HR specialists this can mean exchanging information about the market in general and specific job openings in particular. If you have either interviewed or reviewed the resume of some viable applicants, you can share this information with your professional colleagues, assuming you have the applicants' permission to do so. Hopefully, your colleagues will do the same for you. This cost-effective, effortless exchange could result in new hires.

A variation on this technique is to join professional associations in those fields related to your recruitment responsibilities. The associations' membership directory, mailing list, placement service, and publications could provide the names of your company's future employees.

Radio and Television

There are two main advantages to using radio or television advertising to fill an opening. First, you will appeal to a large audience in a short period of time. Second, you can reach and tempt prospects not actually looking for a job. This can be a real plus when you have hard-to-fill positions.

In the past, employers have tended to shy away from radio and television advertising primarily because of the cost. But while still ranked among the more expensive recruitment sources, the media, especially radio, has become more financially accessible. The growth of independent radio stations and cable television has created greater opportunities for employers with limited budgets.

Proponents of radio advertising emphasize that radio often reaches people when "their guard is down," that is, when they are not necessarily thinking about job hunting. For example, they may have the radio on while getting ready for work in the morning or sitting in traffic, commuting to and from their jobs. Companies looking for applicants in particular fields should research what music, talk shows, news, or sports these individuals are likely to prefer and run ads on those stations.

Television advertising receives high marks from supporters because aspects of the job can be demonstrated as well as described. Done well, this can encourage job seekers to respond.

Research Firms

Research firms may be described as abbreviated full-service executive search firms, providing about one-half the services. Their primary function is to provide organizations with information about potential high-level professional employees; the interview and evaluation is then up to the employer.

After determining the specifications of an available position, research firms target those companies likely to have employees meeting the job requirements. They then go on to identify specific potentially qualified employees, relating this information to the client company. Contacting well-established persons within a given industry to request personal recommendations of potential employees is a variation on this procedure.

At this point, most research firms terminate their services, although the client company may ask the firm to make the initial contact with the targeted applicants.

The purpose of this phase is to clarify qualifications and to determine mutual interest.

Research firms are most useful when a company is looking for a cost-effective way to recruit top-level professionals or when they want more hands-on involvement in the interviewing process.

When evaluating the services of a research firm, consider whether the company services a wide range of industries or specializes in one particular field. Also determine its success rate and reputation. Ask for references from satisfied clients to determine the extent to which the research firm provided client companies with applicants whose qualifications reflected the job's specifications. In addition, find out how long it took for a firm to produce the applicants and how many job offers were extended to applicants as a result of the research firm's efforts.

Innovative Recruitment Sources

Innovative recruitment sources are less conventional than traditional sources. Some may be considered quirky or unusual, appealing only to certain work environments during specific market conditions, while others are gradually making their way over to the traditional side of the ledger. Often they're used when traditional recruitment sources don't yield the results needed in terms of quality applicants or timelines. As with traditional sources, it's advisable to review the four prerecruitment factors discussed earlier: how much money is available, how quickly the opening must be filled, whether a wide audience must be reached, and the exemption level of the available position. Following are some of the more popular innovative recruitment sources. Exhibit 3-2 offers key advantages and disadvantages for each source.

Airplane Banners

Imagine a picturesque summer day; you're at the beach, enjoying the sun and surf. The furthest thing from your mind is work, current or future. Then you hear the sound of an engine; you follow the sound upward and see a banner lazily trailing behind a plane, advertising jobs.

The scene could just as easily be a sporting event or a concert, anywhere where tens of thousands of would-be employees might congregate. Contact companies like AdsThatFly.com, Airsign.com, and Heli-Banner (http://www.aerial-media.com/heli-banners) about flying your ads.

While airplane banners certainly are attention-getters, many object to them as being intrusive and unprofessional.

Banners and Signs

Your business can use banners and signs as successful recruitment tools if it occupies a separate building that's located on a main street. Drape a banner across the front

Exhibit 3-2. Key Advantages and Disadvantages for Innovative Recruitment Sources

Innovative Recruitment Source	Advantages	Disadvantages
Airplane Banners	Attention-getters	Intrusive Unprofessional
Banners and Signs	Cost-effective	Requires busy location
Billboard Advertising	High-volume attention-grabber	Limited amount of information
Bumper Stickers	Incentives for employees as part of employee referral program	Not taken seriously
Company-Sponsored Social Events	Cost-effective	Reaches a limited number of people
Competitions	Opportunity to evaluate skills before extending a job offer	Time-consuming
Customers, Clients, and Guests	Employee has in-depth knowledge of what it's like to work for you	Rejection or termination could sever relationship
Fast-Track Training	Provides marketable skills	Fails to support long-term advancement
Kiosks	Easy for a person to apply	Unmonitored applicant flow
Medical Offices	Cost-effective	Low response volume
Movie Ads	Can attract people not necessarily actively looking for a job	Intrusive
On-Site Recruitment	Can reach a wide audience Time-saver Good public relations	Lots of unqualified applicants
Preemployment Training	Creates trained workforce	No guarantee trained workers won't apply skills elsewhere

of your building or post a sign inviting customers, clients, and passers-by to stop in to inquire about employment opportunities. The banner or sign can simply state that there are jobs available, or it can list the openings, which would require you to prepare a new banner or sign each time a different job is added. Unless your business has brand-name recognition, identify your product or service in a few words. Be sure to specify how interested applicants should contact you.

Banners and signs are real "you never know" recruitment sources. The investment is minimal and the payoff could be substantial. On the other hand, they can look carnival-like, leaving would-be employees to wonder if they should take such come-ons seriously.

Billboard Advertising

Since most people view billboards while driving, they're limited in the amount of time they have to take in details. As such, an effective billboard ad needs to catch one's eye immediately, offering a minimal amount of information. This usually limits a company to a sparsely worded statement about employment opportunities, an enlarged logo, company name, and contact information in an easy-to-recall format.

Billboard ads seem to work most effectively for lodging, restaurants, and airlines, and they generally target nonexempt-level workers.

Bumper Stickers

Bumper sticker ads offer little space for your message and there isn't much one can do to make the stickers visually outstanding. Also, unless someone is stuck in traffic directly behind a car sporting a bumper sticker, there's very little time to read what's written. For these reasons, companies that advertise on bumper stickers usually include little more than a generic statement about employment opportunities and note, in large letters, their easy-to-remember contact information.

If company employees are willing to place this inexpensive form of advertisement on their cars' bumpers, employers may get some viable nonexempt applicants. Consider this a variation on employee referrals and offer bonuses to any employee whose bumper sticker results in a new hire.

Bumper sticker ads may be viewed as an act of desperation by job seekers and therefore not taken seriously.

Company-Sponsored Social Events

If your organization goes in for huge social events to celebrate special occasions, such as picnics on Independence Day, encourage employees to bring family and friends. Then set up a "job opportunities" table with a list of openings and brochures. This form of recruitment requires an investment of only some additional food and one or two employees willing to answer questions from interested applicants.

Competitions

Competitions ask a selected number of interested applicants to spend the equivalent of anywhere from a couple of days to a week or more competing for a job. Sometimes the job is an executive position, but it could also be a low-end professional opening.

During the competition, applicants learn new skills and then apply them to simulated job-related tasks under the scrutiny of selected company human resources and departmental representatives. In addition to their ability to learn and perform specific tasks, contenders are evaluated on relevant intangible skills, such as problem solving, ability to interact with others, decision making, and communication. Anyone may drop out or be eliminated at any time. At the end, one person is awarded the coveted prize: a job.

While competitions per se are new, they bear a close resemblance to job tryouts, a process used by some businesses before extending a job offer to see whether a person will fit into a corporate culture. Even though applicants enter into job tryouts or competitions voluntarily, companies need to be careful about the matter of money. Can you have people working for you for a week without paying them? As long as the participants are learning new skills, employers are not likely to be required to pay them, as it is considered education. Compensation may be required, however, when it comes to actual work performed. Talk with an attorney before proceeding.

Customers, Clients, and Guests

One increasingly popular innovative recruitment source is encouraging customers, clients, and guests to become employees. This is especially helpful for small businesses that, over time, develop relationships with their clientele and get to know a great deal about them. These regulars, through interaction with company employees, learn the product, understand the culture, have an understanding of what it's like to work there, and are thus able to make informed decisions about being an employee.

The one real negative to hiring customers, clients, or guests could be that if the customer-turned-employee applies for a job and is either rejected or doesn't do well once hired, that person is unlikely to continue to frequent your business.

Fast-Track Training

Fast-track training, often offered by community colleges and completed in one to six months, enables individuals to acquire specific skills and make themselves more marketable. Attendees include students, those who are unemployed seeking training for new jobs, employees wanting to improve existing skills, and those with minimal work experience seeking specialized abilities.

Proponents say that these practical, accelerated programs meet the needs of both businesses and job seekers. Critics argue that these crash courses offer little to support long-term advancement and can't provide skills like critical thinking.

Kiosks

You see them at airports, shopping malls, or in large stores: kiosks where customers can interrupt shopping to apply for a job. These businesses view all customers as potential employees and want to make it as easy as possible for them to fill out applications. Most of these are web-enabled, making the process quick and easy.

A variation on the web-based kiosk theme is to have company representatives stationed throughout or in front of their stores, clipboard and applications in hand, ready to approach would-be employees. Sometimes sales associates actually include a job application in your bag along with your purchase and receipt. Their attitude is, "it couldn't hurt."

This approach may generate many applications, but companies have no way of monitoring their quality.

Medical Offices

Some employers focus on attracting members of specific groups into their workplace by posting job openings in medical offices. These include offices of gynecologists, obstetricians, and pediatricians to attract women, doctors specializing in geriatrics to draw older workers, and physical therapists to entice those with physical disabilities. Fliers are usually left with the receptionist so that anyone interested can contact the employer.

This is a cost-effective, easy way to reach out to targeted populations, but the approach hasn't been shown to generate a high volume of applications.

Movie Ads

You get to the movies in plenty of time to grab a tub of popcorn and a drink. You find a seat and settle in, ready for the show to begin. Imagine, now, in addition to clips of upcoming shows, you see your company's name on the screen advertising job opportunities! Recruitment ads at movie theaters are a proactive way to target captive, unsuspecting audiences. The amount of information is kept to a minimum, usually just the company name, easy-to-remember contact information, and either a list of openings or a statement about job opportunities. Some employers try to link their promotions to specific movies and anticipated types of viewers; others go for the shotgun approach and just run their ads, regardless of what's showing.

On-Site Recruitment

On-site recruitment is limited to the types of businesses that attract large numbers of people to their locations each day and can be quite effective, especially for nonexempt-level positions. For example, railroad companies may place pamphlets that describe employment opportunities on car seats; airlines might do the same with seats on planes; department stores might attach fliers to packages at cashier stations; and fast food chains or family restaurants might describe job openings on tray liners and table tents.

The brief message, which usually describes the benefits of working for the company, is often framed in bright, eye-catching colors and graphics. Pictured, too, may be people reflecting diverse traits and characteristics. Interested applicants are invited to visit, call, or go online for an application.

Preemployment Training

Preemployment training ensures the hiring of those applicants "guaranteed" to possess the basic knowledge and skills needed to perform a given job. This is typically accomplished through a program that offers, free of cost to participants, various skills training. These individuals are not necessarily being trained for specific jobs, nor are they being offered employment. The emphasis is on preparation, so that if and when jobs do become available, the trained individuals will be considered first. Employers benefit by having an available workforce of skilled individuals from which to choose, without wasting time screening untested applicants. In addition, once hired, program graduates need not devote the first several days, or in some cases weeks, to learning their jobs. Participants benefit by acquiring marketable skills and being first in line for employment opportunities. Of course, there's no guarantee the trained workers won't take what they've learned and apply it elsewhere.

Summary

Before embarking on a recruitment campaign, consider four factors: how much money is available; how quickly the opening must be filled; whether you need to reach a wide audience; and the exemption level of the available position.

Next, consider how aggressive you need to be to fill a particular opening. If immediacy is a primary factor, search out proactive recruitment sources that will make a concerted effort to find employees. Proactive recruitment requires direct involvement on the part of the recruiter. It's the reverse of reactive recruitment, where the recruiter waits for applicants to apply, hoping that the best fit is among them.

Taking a shotgun approach to recruitment in terms of who will be drawn in by whatever source you're using may result in a qualified applicant pool. Certain special interest groups, however, may need to be targeted directly in order to minimize inadvertent violations of certain equal employment opportunity laws. This approach is also likely to produce a more diverse pool of applicants, potentially enhancing productivity and profitability and increasing your global appeal. Begin targeting special interest groups by developing a keener insight into the characteristics of the generations as identified in Chapter 2. Then consider those recruitment sources most likely to appeal to members of select employment groups, such as youth, applicants with disabilities, and former employees.

Numerous recruitment sources will yield excellent applicants. Decide from among dozens of traditional and innovative sources. Traditional sources are easily recognized, acceptable to most types of organizations, and appropriate for filling a wide range of positions. Innovative sources are less conventional, generally appealing to certain work environments during specific market conditions, and used when traditional recruitment sources don't yield the results needed.

CHAPTER 4

Electronic Recruiting

Long-time HR specialists undoubtedly recall receiving stacks of resumes sent either by employment services in response to newspaper ads, or via one of the other more traditional recruitment resources described in Chapter 3. Too busy to do them justice during a typical workday, you probably loaded these resumes into your briefcase and dutifully reviewed them during the commute home or after dinner in front of the TV (muted, of course). When you came across a resume longer than two pages (one page, as the evening grew later), you groaned, fighting the temptation to "file" it for violating the unwritten law against submitting a resume that's too long for a tired HR professional to review at the end of a busy day.

The process of receiving and reviewing resumes has changed dramatically over the past decade. Increasingly, employers are using the Internet to recruit, either by developing web pages of their own or by linking up with web-based job search services. Applicants, too, are preparing and transmitting many more resumes electronically, thereby relieving recruiters from being inundated by thousands of paper resumes. The Internet, then, is rapidly moving up in the ranks of recruitment, as greater numbers of applicants and employers communicate with one another, computer to computer.

Definition of an Internet Applicant

To comply with record-keeping requirements and to preclude charges of discrimination, the Office of Federal Contract Compliance Programs (OFCCP) of the U.S. Department of Labor has provided organizations with this definition of an "Internet Applicant."[1]

1. An individual submits an expression of interest in employment through the Internet or related electronic data technologies;

2. The contractor considers the individual for employment in a particular position;

3. The individual's expression of interest indicates the individual possesses the basic qualifications for the position; and

4. The individual at no point in the contractor's selection process prior to receiving an offer of employment from the contractor, removes himself or herself from further consideration or otherwise indicates that he or she is no longer interested in the position.

Applicant status is not impacted by level of qualification according to this definition. That is, even if someone does not meet the minimum requirements of a job, that person is still considered an applicant if he meets the applicant criteria. In this regard, the "basic qualifications" could be, but are not required to be, identified in a job description. These qualifications do need to be advertised to potential applicants or, if not advertised, established in advance by making and maintaining a record of such qualifications. Preemployment tests are not considered basic qualifications under the Internet Applicant rule. Basic qualifications must be established prior to the beginning of the selection process.

Here are some examples of when individuals would be considered applicants according to the OFCCP's definition:

- If someone completes a profile and forwards a resume in response to an ad posted by an organization.
- If a person posts a resume on an Internet resume bank without expressing an interest in a specific job with a particular employer, that person would become an applicant if the employer contacts him or her about a specific job and the person expresses interest.

Here are some instances whereby individuals would not be considered applicants:

- Transmitting a resume to the "jobs" e-mail address on a company's website without indicating interest in a specific job
- Posting a resume on any major job board
- Being passed along by a company that has an applicant's resume to another company without first determining the person's interest in a particular job
- Casually browsing the web

The OFCCP's definition applies exclusively to the Internet and related technologies, including resume banks, job boards, organizational websites, resume databases, and online job listings. The 1978 Uniform Guidelines on Employee Selection Procedures and their subsequent rulings issued in 1979 and 1980 continue to apply to those who submit paper resumes.

Electronic Resumes

Some employers still encourage applicants to submit paper resumes via snail mail or fax, while increasing numbers prefer resumes that are delivered electronically.

Proponents of the electronic format offer the following as reasons for discouraging paper resumes:

- Paper costs considerably more than the average electronic file of six kilobytes.
- Processing paper into an electronic format takes longer than processing an originally electronic file into a paper format.
- Mail delivery is slow: The average U.S.-based letter takes three days to deliver; the average electronic transmission takes three seconds.
- Electronic files can be formatted, extracted, and otherwise manipulated countless ways. They can also be incorporated with other data or stored in various applications or systems.

Paper resume supporters argue that electronic resumes are often difficult to read and lack a professional look. In addition, they argue, some applicants express concerns about confidentiality and privacy, as well as fear that one's resume will get lost in a mile-high cyber pile, so they continue to favor a mailed paper resume. Accordingly, if businesses don't offer a paper resume option, these applicants may bypass them entirely and ultimately become someone else's employees.

Whatever your personal preference, everyone agrees on one thing: Reading electronic resumes is unlike reading paper resumes. While the focus remains the same—searching for information that reflect a person's ability to perform a job—the presentation and format of that information is dramatically different. As one recruiter put it, "What pleases a computer is likely to bore a person."

Electronic Cover Letters

Resume-writing guides recommend including cover letters regardless of whether the resume is submitted in paper or electronic form. Indeed, few employers seriously consider a resume without an accompanying letter that identifies the specific job or type of job sought as well as highlights of the submitter's qualifications. Cover letters can grab a recruiter's attention by suggesting a preliminary fit between job and applicant, so savvy applicants word theirs carefully.

These are critical components of an electronic cover letter:

- *Including the cover letter in the body of the e-mail rather than as an additional attachment,* as some systems either block multiple attachments or can't handle them.
- *Using the subject line wisely.* That means including the job number as well as a succinct statement about the applicant's qualifications. Generally, this means extracting key words that are likely to grab the recipient's attention, such as "5 yrs.' mgr. exper. in finance." The key words here—5 yrs.; managerial; finance—match the job requirements and are therefore likely to catch the reader's eye.
- *Presenting a professional look.* E-mail cover letters are no different from traditional paper letters in terms of salutations, spacing, punctuation, grammar, spelling,

and closings. Typos can make the difference between a resume that's considered and one that's not. Also, the content of the first paragraph should both hook and sell the reader.

• *Highlighting key job-related words.* Since electronic cover letters and resumes will likely be filed in a database, recipients are looking for job-specific words.

• *Using a simple format,* as in black font, normal size (12-point), and standard typeface, e.g., Times Roman, on a white background.

• *Following company requirements* and not sending more or less than what's requested.

• *Making it easy on the reader.* State, in clear and concise terms, the job you're applying for and why you're the best fit, including brief examples demonstrating relevant accomplishments and how they can benefit a potential employer. In other words: here's the job, here's the person. If it's an exploratory letter, identify possible suitable job titles.

• *Demonstrating knowledge of the employer.* This is a nice touch if not overdone. For example, an applicant might write, "Now that Bixby Industries has expanded its product base as a result of its acquisition of Triad Inc., I would like to offer my extensive expertise in marketing and become a part of your exciting new work environment." This shows that the applicant has taken the time to do some research and, further, has bothered to incorporate that research into a personalized letter.

• *Keeping it brief.* If it takes more than fifteen or twenty seconds to read, it's too long.

A sample electronic e-mail cover letter reflecting these components appears in Appendix C.

Electronic Resume Formatting

Employers expect all resumes—paper or electronic—to be organized either by function (whereby skills are grouped into categories) or chronologically (jobs and education are listed in reverse chronological order). In addition to education and experience, resumes should reflect honors or awards, publications, and other accomplishments.

Successful electronic resumes, however, reflect a different format and wording than traditional paper resumes. A major distinction has to do with the emphasis on nouns instead of verbs. Since searches are done by key words that describe required skills and tasks to be performed, computers are programmed to zero in on terms such as "team leader" as opposed to "lead a team." Buzzwords or descriptors that refer to the essential traits required to perform a job are also relevant. The more buzzwords the computer picks up, the more qualified an applicant appears. Savvy applicants know to place the most relevant buzzwords at the beginning of their resumes since many programs are limited in the number of items they will scan for and so usually start at the beginning of the document.

Computers like things to be kept simple:

- No more than seventy characters per line to preclude problems with different e-mail programs
- Lots of white space to show where one topic has ended and another has begun
- Design elements that preclude the use of underlining or italics and rely instead on strategically placed asterisks or dashes
- Minimal use of abbreviations and special characters, such as the copyright symbol (©) and the ampersand (&).
- The use of all upper case letters for headings

Computers also favor typical words that everyone is likely to know, although they also seek maximum usage of industry jargon. These resumes are usually in an ASCII format, that is, plainly formatted and unadorned.

Company Career Websites

Companies that put up their own career websites or that advertise on a job opportunity section on their corporate site are recruiting proactively and increasing their chances of finding suitable employees.

Company Career Website Objectives

Before spending a lot of money and effort loading up your website with attractive graphics and inviting verbiage, be clear about your primary objective. Think twice if you're tempted to answer, "to lure applicants." Any recruiter who has ever used a recruitment source that did not carefully target applicants with the required credentials or skills knows that this answer is not totally accurate. As awful as it is to run an ad and only get a handful of responses, it's far worse to get inundated with responses from unqualified applicants. This can happen if your job posting fails to clearly identify the parameters of the position.

Rather than taking a hit-or-miss approach targeting no one in particular, plan your postings with a specific objective in mind: attracting qualified applicants whose backgrounds and interests are compatible with the culture and offerings of your organization. This statement identifies your company as unique and immediately sets it apart.

What Applicants Are Looking For

Many job hunters report that they can learn a great deal about a potential employer from its website. Based on photos, terminology, design, and areas of emphasis, applicants can determine if a company is likely to be a good fit for them.

To succeed at attracting applicants to their career websites or career opportunity sections, businesses need to focus on four areas: content, navigation, branding, and functionality. In this regard, here are some factors to consider:

- Make job listings easily accessible.
- Keep postings current.
- Avoid slow-to-load images.
- Don't get carried away with the latest bells and whistles unless they serve a purpose and are consistent with your corporate image.
- Keep screening questions simple and to a minimum.
- Allow submission options, e.g., online applications or e-mail.
- Offer a resume builder tool.
- Offer cut-and-paste capability so applicants can edit an existing resume.
- Provide information about the history of your organization, its products or services, the culture, and benefits of working there.
- Provide information about the geographic area, including housing, taxes, schools, and recreational and cultural activities.
- Enable applicants to register to receive updates about new jobs.
- Ensure that the contents are in full compliance with employment laws.
- Provide a calendar of career-related events.
- Review visits to your website to identify patterns.
- Test out your website numerous times before launching it.

In addition, talk with colleagues and competitors to determine who uses their web pages and the kind of feedback they're receiving. Consult with your technical staff, other employees, and even external applicants about what they expect to find on a web page and what turns them off. Information from these sources can supplement advice from outside web experts.

Getting Started

New websites are generally organized according to job function, geographic location, or business unit. A statement of the organization's mission is offered, as is generic information about the work environment and benefits of working there. A table of contents allows job seekers to browse topics of interest, including specific job offerings. Experiment and ask for feedback from staff, consultants, and applicants as to which format is likely to draw the greatest number of qualified job hunters.

The overall appearance and visual design of a website creates an important first impression on applicants and affects their interest in continuing. For example, too much text can cause readers' eyes to glaze over, and huge graphics that slow loading down to a crawl are likely to make viewers impatient. Strike a balance between smaller graphics that load quickly and meaningful text to capture and retain the interest of job hunters.

Companies generally start with a web presence. This is a bare-bones home page that provides the company name, geographic locations, contact information, basic information about the company's history and primary product areas, and whom to contact. The site's text, tone, and look should reflect the company's corporate culture. These pages are later upgraded, depending on requests received for more information, as well as the company's own observations and advice from consultants. On average, start-up pages are redesigned two to three times in the first twelve to eighteen months.

Solicit Professional Help

Many organizations solicit professional help in setting up their websites. Before making a commitment to outside consultants, however, verify their effectiveness by talking with businesses, preferably ones similar to yours, that have used them. Here are some questions to ask previous clients of potential consultants:

- Do they have both technical expertise and design experience?
- How helpful were they in a setup situation?
- How patient were they in explaining terms and processes to nontechnical HR people?
- Did they bother to find out what your company was all about in terms of products, market, and direction?
- Did they acknowledge that you know your business best and therefore should either write the text for your site or at least contribute to it?
- Did they make suggestions as to the best format and design of your website?
- Did they advise you as to appropriate equipment for high-speed access?
- Did they try to start you off with more than you needed?
- Did they continue to offer support services after building your website?
- Did they recommend upgrades to your site after a probationary test run?

Website Upkeep

Once established, maintaining a website is crucial. Job listings should be current; few things prove more irritating for applicants than sorting through old listings and dated information. Also, keep up to date with regard to new capabilities, colors, backgrounds, and effects, such as flash demos. And to keep from appearing complacent, give the site a facelift every six months or so.

The issue of exposure is also essential. Even the most expensive website is ineffective if not seen or accessed. Employers often purchase hypertext links or hotlinks, buttons that lead directly into its server from popular employment service sites. This allows web surfers to jump from one site to another, ensuring easier access and greater exposure.

It's also a good idea to track how often the site is being accessed and what pages are the most popular. Tracking the number of hits on each page can offer insight into how the website should be redesigned and what features should be revised, included, or eliminated down the road.

Company Career Website Guidelines

Here are some additional guidelines to help make your career website a success:

1. *Make searching for job openings easy.* A user-friendly website means making available an employment button in a prominent place on your homepage and offering a resume-building service or forms that route the data into your e-mail or database.

2. *Make the site navigable.* Broad appeal is an important ingredient to website success. For people who know exactly what they want, speed and easy access are crucial. People who like to browse, on the other hand, will want to explore, interacting with stimulating graphics and interesting text.

3. *Be prepared to respond to applicants quickly.* In describing the recruitment capabilities of the Internet, a frequent user accurately notes that it "offers incredible new opportunities to disappoint." After applying for a position within only minutes, applicants expect a quick response. If they don't get it, chances are they'll lose interest and move on.

4. *Maintain an up-to-date employment opportunity database.* The importance of keeping a website current cannot be overemphasized. If you cannot manage this internally, hire the services of a company that can.

5. *Balance content with design.* Maybe appearances shouldn't matter to job seekers, but they do. As with display newspaper ads, visual appeal will draw applicants to your page and the content will pique their interest.

6. *Keep it organized.* Serious job seekers want to focus on the relevant data right away. While some may want to browse the entire site, taking it all in, others will zero in on what you have to offer, decide if they're interested, and apply. If this can't be done with ease, chances are they'll move on to another site.

7. *Take advantage of all the information you can learn about your web visitors.* You will not hire every applicant expressing an interest in your company, but you can collect data about them that may prove useful to recruitment strategies later on. One of the pluses of electronic recruiting is that everything is measurable. Decide what you want to know and there's bound to be an Internet service that can provide it. For example, it may be helpful to determine which schools or organizations visitors of your website have attended and belong to, respectively. Or perhaps you're interested in what other pages visitors look at. This kind of information can be valuable to the ongoing re-evaluation of your career website.

8. *Don't say too much.* Many companies believe that applicants can make more informed decisions if they have access to a maximum amount of information. In fact, it's more effective to provide just enough information to create a level of interest on the part of job hunters, encouraging them to apply. Think in terms of supplying answers to these questions: What are the primary duties and responsibilities of the job? What are the qualifications required to perform the job? Why would someone want to work for you? How can they apply?

Internet Job Boards

In addition to advertising on your company's career website, you can post job openings on a variety of Internet job boards. Here are some of the most popular types of job boards (Note: The author does not, by referencing specific job boards, necessarily endorse these sites or ensure their continuation beyond the date of this writing):

• *General Job Boards.* These are the most commonly used means of online recruiting. Companies post jobs and applicants respond, either to the system, which sends the application on to the company, or directly to an e-mail address.

Resume banks are extensions of general job boards, providing employers with the option of previewing resumes and paying for the contact information. Some of the most popular, enduring job boards include Monster.com and CareerBuilder.com.

• *Industry-Specific Boards.* Industry-specific boards target applicants with experience or interest in your particular type of business. It's not uncommon for these boards to offer free trials and rock bottom sign-on prices. Some examples include computerwork.com (owned by JobServe.com) for computer jobs; healthcareers.com (owned by TargetJobs.com) for positions in the health care industry; higheredjobs .com for education; engcen.com for engineering; jobsinthemoney.com (owned by Dice.com) for the field of finance; ultimateinsurancejobs.com for insurance jobs; and pharmadiversityjobboard.com for work in the pharmaceutical industry.

• *Professional Associations.* As with industry-specific boards, professional associations target applicants with experience or interest in your field. Most professional associations offer either free posting as a benefit to their members or they post and review resumes for a nominal fee. An example of a professional association for human resources is jobs.shrm.org.

• *Resume Blasters.* Resume blasters, such as resumeviper.com, are free for employers; applicants pay to "blast" a resume to recruiters who have identified desirable skills and competencies.

• *Government Sites.* Government sites are often thought of as a wasteland, difficult to navigate and difficult to find anyone whose skills match your needs. You can narrow your focus, however, by posting jobs on state sites and clearly identifying the skills you're seeking. Government sites include usajobs.gov, federalgovernmentjobs .us, and federaljobsearch.com.

- *Diversity Sites.* Targeting diversity sites for various ethnicities, people with disabilities, and the like can not only produce qualified applicants but help you meet affirmative action goals as well. A word of caution: Some diversity sites claim to focus on placing specific groups, e.g., minorities, when in reality they're little more than links to larger, generic job boards. Here are some diversity sites: womenforhire .com for women; nul.org/employment-network for African Americans; nativejobs .com for indigenous peoples; latpro.com for Latinos; aaede.org for Asian Americans; and eop.com for people with disabilities.

- *Targeted Applicants.* If there's a way to personalize a largely impersonal recruitment source, this is it. A project manager works one-on-one with you to prepare a virtual profile of your business and then helps you with specific job postings. These postings are then e-mailed to a specific group of registered applicants who have been targeted based on their skills. After reviewing your profile, these applicants can contact your company to discuss job opportunities.

- *Streamline Services.* These services automate your recruitment efforts and applicant tracking, saving you time. They usually link a job-posting page onto your home website and allow you to post your openings on several job boards. One of the benefits to these streamline services is that they are flexible and customize according to your needs. Most charge a monthly fee.

- *School Job Boards.* Most colleges and universities, as well as high schools, offer job boards. These sites are similar to traditional job boards, generally targeting seniors and graduates. Look, too, for national sites that link schools.

- *Outplacement Services.* Outplacement firms will often post your jobs for free on their job boards. You can also keep in touch with companies issuing layoffs or experiencing mergers; they will usually allow you to post your job openings on their job boards.

Some employers prefer using their company websites over job boards, viewing the latter as largely ineffective because of the amount of competition on them, as well as the number of resumes the employers have to peruse before finding a viable candidate. According to one study, companies review more than two hundred resumes per job on job boards before finding the right match, while only going through about thirty per job on their own career site.[2] Many believe applicants applying for jobs at a certain company's website are more likely to have relevant experience. Still, even though job boards may attract a range of qualified applicants, it is said that about 25 percent of hires come through job boards.[3]

Additional Electronic Recruitment Alternatives

Some employers prefer electronic recruitment tools that fall somewhere in between full-out company websites and job boards, such as LinkedIn, a business/social site used primarily for professional networking. The site allows individuals to connect with prospective employees as well as colleagues and business prospects. For organizations with job openings, this means a greater scope of contact with prospective employees. LinkedIn members can create professional profiles detailing their professional skills and employment experiences; companies can add the "Apply with LinkedIn" button to their job postings. Then, with one click of the mouse, interested applicants can apply using their LinkedIn profile. As part of the submission process, employers can request a cover letter as well as other pertinent information.

Still others are following the lead of Marriott International Inc., which screens applicants according to how well they perform on a unique social media game.[4] Patterned after the Facebook games FarmVille and CityVille, the game at Marriott—entitled My Marriott Hotel—lets applicants manage various aspects of a hotel, beginning with the restaurant's kitchen. Players score points for good customer service and turning a profit. The game also allows applicants to create and manage their own restaurant.

My Marriott Hotel is used primarily to interest applicants up to the age of 35 (a possible EEO red flag), acknowledging that social media in general appeals to younger workers. Once a viable interest is established, applicants are directed to Marriott's career site.

Because Marriott is an international operation, the game can be played in multiple languages, including English, Spanish, French, Arabic, and Mandarin.

Marriott International is a credible member of the hospitality field. It has appeared on the Fortune 100 Best Companies to Work For list since the list's inception in 1998, and was named one of the Hottest Employers of 2010 by *Bloomberg Businessweek*.

Marrriott's use of a Facebook game to attract applicants is an example of how popular social media is now. The public relations and communications firm of Burson-Marsteller tells us just how popular social media has become.[5] It reports that in 2011, 77 percent of Fortune Global 100 companies relied on Twitter, 61 percent had a presence on Facebook, 57 percent had YouTube channels, and 36 percent had corporate blogs. At the time of this writing, one out of every ten of these companies used social media for career information or jobs. Chapter 14 explores the use of social media as a selection tool.

International Electronic Recruitment

Websites offer a global presence as an increasing number of companies are posting their job openings online in more than a hundred countries. Not surprisingly, most of these sites are produced in English. Since English is the most widely spoken language in the world, this may seem advantageous. For many people, though, English is a second language. They may be familiar with the basic structure of the language and be able to converse in it or read it, but they may not be aware of the nuances we so often use without regard to whether they constitute "proper English."

It's impractical, costly, and excessively time-consuming to prepare variations of each web page in several different languages. You can, however, develop one site in one language that most people will be able to understand. This requires a focus on how you speak and read the English language. Here are some guidelines:

1. *Avoid jargon.* These are made-up words that can interfere with a clear, precise message. The meaning may confuse readers and slow them down. Clearly, industry-unique buzzwords or acronyms are appropriate, but only if you're fairly certain that the vast majority of your readers will understand their precise meaning.

With terms that are ambiguous, provide a definition the first time the word or term appears in the text. It's also a good idea to review the document from the perspective of someone outside the culture of an American organization. If you have the slightest suspicion that readers will not share the intended meaning, either spell it out or make a clearer choice.

2. *Select proper word usage.* The English language is full of words that are confused with one another. For example, do you know the difference between *assure, ensure,* and *insure; affect* and *effect; adapt* and *adopt; advise* and *inform;* or *accept* and *except?* We all probably learned the meanings of these words at some point in our education, but when it comes time to use these words in a sentence, we often play a guessing game as to which one is correct. To people for whom English is a second language, correct word usage is very important. They probably know the difference between *continual* and *continuous* and would find disturbing text that confuses the two.

3. *Use proper grammar, punctuation, and spelling.* Web writing is unique in that spaces between many words are eliminated and periods often appear in the middle of sentences. Despite this, the actual text of your job offerings should consist of proper grammar, punctuation, and spelling. Again, people for whom English is a second language are more likely to be aware of rules of grammar and pick out errors. These errors could be viewed as a carelessness that is representative of your organization, which could influence an applicant's decision to submit an application.

4. *Do not avoid clichés.* For business writing, I would say the opposite, but in writing Internet text for a population consisting largely of people for whom English is a second language, clichés can actually be helpful. Certain overused, stock phrases are probably familiar and more likely to accurately convey your meaning.

5. *Be careful about how you use numbers.* Something as simple as noting a resume filing date can be incorrectly interpreted by someone from another country. For example, in Europe, the numbers are reversed; a filing date of 12/11/13 would be interpreted as meaning November 12, 2013, instead of December 11, 2013.

6. *Consider the colors you select for graphics.* In many countries, colors have distinct, important, and sometimes religious meanings. Misusing a color on your website can result in lost applicants. For example, in some cultures, purple is the color of royalty, while in others it is associated with mourning and death.

You may choose to have your current website translated, graphics included, into another language. Many translation companies will do this for a nominal per-page fee, priced according to the content, number, and complexity of graphics involved. While doing this may appear to solve any potential problems associated with presenting your web page in English, there is a wrinkle that comes with translation. The alphabet of other languages may have characters not found in English; therefore, you may need a separate product that can create websites in multiple languages. Likewise, if you decide to browse foreign-language websites, enlist the services of companies that will translate pages into English.

Electronic Recruiting Risks

Joseph Beachboard, a partner in the law firm of Ogletree, Deakins, Nask, Smoak & Stewart, alerts employers to some of the risks associated with electronic recruiting.[6] His first concern has to do with resume-screening software. While screening software is intended to, and often does, help recruiters select the best applicants by searching for key words or phrases, Beachboard suggests that there is significant legal risk if one selects software that categorically excludes members of certain protected groups. For example, if the software isolates words and terms that people in various protected categories do not typically use, then they could not possibly be selected for consideration. Stated another way, if the software identifies words that are most commonly used by Caucasians and not by members of other ethnic groups, then only Caucasian applicants would be contacted, considered, and ultimately hired. This practice creates a disparate impact and could result in charges of systemic discrimination, the denial of equal employment opportunity through an established business practice—in this instance, recruitment.

Another risk associated with electronic recruiting has to do with Internet access. For instance, as a population, older workers are reportedly less comfortable with searching for jobs online than are younger workers. Therefore, if employers rely heavily on electronic recruitment, they are potentially excluding many qualified older applicants, again potentially supporting claims of disparate impact and systemic discrimination.

Applicant tracking is another electronic recruiting risk. With employers receiving thousands of resumes electronically, it can be an overwhelming task to maintain applicant flow data; that is, maintaining information about who's applying.

Because it's so easy for individuals to submit resumes electronically, many do so without much thought as to where the jobs are; they just send their resumes to as many sites as possible. Someone in Texas could apply for an opening in California and not even realize it. This creates a potential electronic recruiting risk for employers: which states' laws govern the collection of data? Texas laws are more liberal than those in California when it comes to the amount of information employers can collect. Hence, if you're collecting information from someone in California and the job is in Texas, you have to carefully determine whose laws govern. Matters such as these are best reviewed and determined by legal counsel.

Beachboard also cautions recruiters against saying too much on a website. His concern is that with an unlimited amount of space on a website, employers have a tendency to volunteer more than they should about who would make the best applicant. Depending on just what's said, this could result in charges of discrimination. This concern extends to e-mail communications between employers and applicants. By their very nature, e-mails are informal; accordingly, inappropriate statements or non-job-related questions could be posed, resulting in charges of discrimination.

Many of these risks can be reduced if employers vary the recruitment sources they use. Despite the many advantages of electronic recruiting, employers must remember that there are many other effective means for finding qualified applicants, as identified in Chapter 3. Constantly ask yourself, "Am I reaching a wide range of people and sidestepping legitimate charges of disparate impact and systemic discrimination?"

Summary

The Internet is moving up in the ranks of recruitment as greater numbers of applicants and employers communicate with one another computer to computer.

To comply with record-keeping requirements and to preclude charges of discrimination, employers are urged to become familiar with and comply with the OFCCP's definition of an "Internet Applicant." It applies exclusively to the Internet and related technologies, including job boards and organizational websites.

While electronic resumes currently dominate the marketplace, paper resumes still have their supporters. The focus remains the same—searching for information that reflect a person's ability to perform a job—but the presentation and format of that information is dramatically different. As one recruiter put it, "What pleases a computer is likely to bore a person." Differences between electronic and paper resumes begin with the cover letter and go on to include resume formatting.

Many organizations favor establishing a company career website as their primary recruitment tool. Before proceeding, employers are advised to consider what applicants are looking for and seek professional help for advice on efficient setup and upkeep.

Other businesses prefer to post job openings on a variety of Internet job boards. These include general sites, industry-specific boards, professional associations, resume blasters, government sites, diversity boards, and school job sites. Still others favor electronic recruitment tools such as LinkedIn that fall somewhere between full-out company websites and job boards.

Electronic postings for international recruitment produced in English require an understanding of factors that will determine how clear your message is likely to be. This includes avoiding jargon, selecting proper word usage, and using numbers and graphics carefully.

Increased Internet exposure brings with it a host of electronic recruiting risks. For example, employers need to be concerned about the legal risks of selecting resume-screening software that may categorically exclude members of certain protected groups. Applicant tracking is another electronic recruiting risk. Many of these risks can be reduced if employers vary the recruitment sources they use.

PART II

Interviewing Applicants

CHAPTER 5

Interview Preparation

A commonly held but erroneous belief is that interviewing does not require any real preparation. The perception is that an interview is little more than two people sitting down together having a conversation. As they talk, one person—the interviewer—asks questions, while the other—the applicant—answers the questions. Whether or not a job offer is extended depends on just how well the applicant answers the questions.

Such an impression is largely based on observations of interviews being conducted by seasoned interviewers who certainly can make employment interviews seem like effortless conversation. It is, however, an inaccurate impression; these interviewers have actually put a great deal of work into this casual front and have completed a number of preparatory steps before meeting their applicants.

Do a Job Analysis

The process of interview preparation begins with a thorough job analysis. This includes a review of the position's responsibilities, requirements, reporting relationships, environmental factors, exemption and union status, salary, benefits, and growth opportunities. This important task provides necessary answers to four key questions:

1. Am I thoroughly familiar with the qualities being sought in an applicant?
2. Are these qualities both job-related and realistic?
3. Can I clearly communicate the duties and responsibilities of this position to applicants?
4. Am I prepared to provide additional relevant information about the job and the company to applicants?

Duties and Responsibilities

Job analysts (typically HR specialists) should make it a point to spend time in the department where openings exist, observing and conversing with incumbents as they perform various aspects of the job, as well as talking with managers in charge about their perspective of the scope of work involved. If possible, they should also seek out people who previously held the position to shed light on how the job may have evolved. Visiting on more than one occasion will enable the job analyst to observe a typical day. If personal visits aren't feasible, lengthy conversations with several departmental representatives will suffice.

In reviewing the duties and responsibilities of an opening, job analysts will want to determine if the duties and responsibilities are realistic in relation to other factors, such as previous experience and education. Equally important is determining if they're relevant to the overall job function and if they overlap with the responsibilities of other jobs.

Job analysts should review the duties and responsibilities of a job each time a position becomes available. Even if an opening was filled six months ago and is now vacant again, assessing its current status will ensure that no major changes have occurred in the interim. This, in turn, will guarantee up-to-date job information and accuracy when discussing the position with potential employees.

Education and Prior Experience

The process of job analysis continues with identifying appropriate educational and prior experience prerequisites. This can best be accomplished when managers and HR representatives join together to ask these key questions:

- What skills and knowledge are needed to successfully perform the primary duties and responsibilities of this job?
- What makes these skills and knowledge necessary?
- Why couldn't someone without these skills and knowledge perform the primary functions of this job?
- Are the requirements consistent with the job duties and responsibilities?
- Are we influenced by the background of the present or last incumbent?
- Are we subjectively considering our own personal expectations of the job?
- Are we compromising because we're in a hurry to fill the job?
- Are we unrealistically searching for the ideal applicant?
- Are we succumbing to pressure from others, e.g., senior management, as to what are appropriate job requirements?
- Are the requirements in accordance with all applicable equal employment opportunity laws?

Arbitrarily setting high minimum standards in the hope of filling a position with the most qualified person can backfire. For example, suppose you're trying to fill a first-line supervisor's spot and you decide on someone who not only has a great deal of hands-on experience, but is also well-rounded. To you, this translates into someone with at least five years of supervisory experience and a four-year college degree.

If asked some of the questions just suggested, you would probably conclude that these requirements are too stringent for a first-line supervisory position. You would also want to modify them for reasons of possible discrimination. But even if there were no applicable employment laws, there is a good reason for setting more flexible standards: If you came across an applicant who fell short of this experience and educational profile but who met other intangible requirements and came highly recommended, you would not be able to hire him. It would be difficult to justify hiring someone not meeting the minimum requirements of the job, especially if you also rejected applicants who exceeded them.

In addition to asking yourself these basic questions regarding experience and education, there is a way of setting requirements that doesn't paint you into a corner and still allows you to be highly selective. By using carefully worded terminology you can choose the applicant who best combines relevant concrete and intangible requirements. Suggested phrases include:

- Demonstrated ability to _____ required.
- In-depth knowledge of _____ required.
- Extensive experience in _____ required.
- Knowledge of _____ would be an advantage.
- Proven ability to _____ required.
- We are looking for an effective _____.
- Proven track record of _____ needed.
- Substantial experience in _____ essential.
- Familiarity with _____ would be ideal.
- Degree relevant to _____ preferred.
- Degree in _____ preferred.
- Advanced degree a plus.
- College degree in _____ highly desirable.
- An equivalent combination of education and experience.

These sample phrases all provide employers with latitude to select someone who may be lacking in one area, such as formal education, but compensates with additional experience. The use of such terms does not mean compromising hiring standards; rather, it means taking care to avoid setting requirements that cannot be justified by the specific duties of the job, while at the same time offering the widest range of choice among applicants.

Intangible Requirements

To lend balance to a lack of specific educational or experiential requirements, or to round out the concrete requirements of a position, job-related intangible criteria can be helpful. Depending on the job, these intangibles may be relevant:

- Cooperative working relationships
- Decision-making ability
- Effective time-management skills
- Even disposition
- Flexibility
- Organizational skills
- Problem-solving ability
- Self-confidence
- Successful delegation skills

These intangible factors can be significant, but only when examined in relation to the requirements of the opening. That is, in addition to determining any relevant education and experience prerequisites and examining the scope and degree of responsibilities, you should explore the question of what type of individual would be most compatible with the position. This may best be determined by learning as much as possible about such factors as the amount of stress involved, the extent of independent work permitted, and the overall management style of the department. The combined information should translate into a profile of the person who will make the best fit.

Keeping this profile in mind as job seekers are considered can be helpful, particularly if two or more applicants meet the concrete requirements of the job. You can then compare intangible job-related criteria to help make the final decision. Intangibles can also be helpful in evaluating applicants for entry-level jobs for which there are few, if any, concrete educational and experience prerequisites.

Be careful when making comparisons based on intangibles, since the meaning of certain terms can be highly subjective. For example, some of the more popular applicant evaluation phrases—the person has a bad attitude, a winning personality, or a nice appearance—may not translate the same way for everyone. Furthermore, such descriptions really do not tell anything substantive about what the person can contribute to a job. So be careful not to weigh intangible elements too heavily or select someone solely on the basis of any of these factors. If considered at all, such factors must be job-related, not based on personal bias.

Reporting Relationships

Another facet of job analysis has to do with reporting relationships. In this regard, ask yourself the following questions:

- What positions will this job report to, both directly and indirectly?
- Where does this job appear on the department's organizational chart?
- What positions, if any, report directly and/or indirectly to this job?
- What is the relationship between this job and other jobs in the department in terms of level and scope of responsibility?
- What is the relationship between this job and other jobs in the organization?

These questions all pertain to positions, as opposed to specific individuals. Once you've determined the nature and level of a reporting relationship, you can factor in any relevant personality traits of the person to whom the opening reports. For example, if the department head with an opening for an assistant is known to have a short fuse, you would be wise to seek out someone who has demonstrated in past jobs the ability to effectively deal with such outbursts.

Work Environment

A job's work environment consists of four distinct areas: physical working conditions, geographic location, travel, and work schedule. A work environment checklist appears in Appendix D.

Physical Working Conditions

Physical working conditions encompass such factors as working in areas that may not be well-ventilated, exposure to chemicals or toxic fumes, working in cramped quarters, working in a noisy location, and sitting or standing for long periods. If working conditions are ideal, few interviewers will hesitate to inform prospective employees. After all, this helps sell the company and the job and perhaps even compensates for areas that fall short, such as the starting salary or benefits package. If the working conditions leave something to be desired, however, the tendency is to omit reference to them when discussing the job in the hope that once employees begin work and discover flaws in the work environment, they'll opt to adjust rather than leave. Unfortunately, what frequently happens is that new employees resent the deception and either quit, develop poor work habits, or harbor feelings of resentment over being had.

Problems of poor morale or high turnover as they relate to unsatisfactory working conditions can easily be prevented. Ask applicants to describe past and current physical working conditions, then accurately describe the working conditions of the available job. If an unpleasant condition is temporary, by all means say so, but don't make anything up. Again, ask applicants to compare experiences with similar conditions. As they talk, watch as well as listen to their answers. There may be a contradiction between an applicant's verbal and nonverbal responses. Skilled interviewers are able to separate and evaluate both. Issues of actively listening and nonverbal communication will be developed in subsequent chapters, but for now, suffice it to say that if an applicant verbally states that she doesn't mind standing seven hours a day, but you sense hesitancy through her body language, pursue the subject until you're more certain of the truth.

Another way of assessing potential employees' reactions to less-than-ideal working conditions is to show them where they would be working if hired. Unless it's logistically impractical, a quick trip to the job site should be part of the interview. This way there will be no surprises and a new employee knows exactly what to expect.

Geographic Location

As stated, when possible, show potential employees where they would be working if hired. If recruiting from a central office for positions in satellite branches, be specific in the description of the job site and offer visual depictions, realistically illustrating the location where an opening exists.

Sometimes a position calls for rotation from one site to another. As with physical working conditions, ask the applicant about any prior experiences they've had with job rotations before describing the working conditions of each location and how long each assignment is likely to last. Through your questioning, determine if they would prefer to settle into a work routine where they're familiar with the environment, the commute, and the other workers, or if they would prefer the variety offered by a rotational position. It's important that you know so you can determine the best fit for the job.

Travel

Talk with applicants about whether they travel for their current employer or did so in former jobs. Then discuss the geographic span and expected frequency of job-related travel. Tell applicants, too, how much advance notice they can generally expect before having to leave. In the case of local travel, applicants will want to know whether they will be expected to provide their own transportation. They will also want to know how reimbursement for job-related travel expenses are handled.

Work Schedule

Employees, especially at the nonexempt level, need to know what days of the week they're expected to work, how many hours they're being paid for, when to report to work each day, and when they may leave. If alternative work arrangements are available, applicants need to know their options. They will also want to know how much time is allotted for meals, as well as other scheduled breaks throughout the day.

Exemption Status

The Fair Labor Standards Act (FLSA) defines the term "exempt" to mean precluded from overtime compensation; that is, an employer is not required to pay exempt employees for time worked beyond their regularly scheduled workweek. This generally pertains to executives, managers, and some supervisors. The term "nonexempt" means not precluded from overtime compensation. Full-time nonexempt employees, such as clerical workers, must be paid for any time worked beyond their regularly scheduled workweek.

To assist with exemption classification, the Department of Labor offers a series of requirements that must be met before someone can be classified as exempt. These requirements were revised in 2004, replacing the long-standing dual Salary and Duty Tests with the singular Standard Test. Revisions include an increase in the minimum salary for determining exemption status to $455 per week and revising stipulations for the executive, administrative, and professional duties tests.

The Standard Test helps employers determine the exemption status of their workforce. The actual work or duties performed by employees, not their job titles, determines exemption status. With most positions there is no question as to whether they are exempt or nonexempt: employees earning less than $455 per week, regardless of duties performed, are considered nonexempt. Some jobs, however, fall into a gray area and are not as easily categorized. Fact sheets are available at www .dol.gov.

Union Status

The National Labor Relations Act (Wagner Act) clearly states, "Employees shall have the right to self-organization, to form, join, or assist labor organizations, to bargain collectively, through representatives of their own choosing, and to engage in other concerted activities, for the purpose of collective bargaining or other mutual aid or protection."

If you're interviewing applicants for union positions, be prepared to tell them if they're required to join, information relative to initiation fees or required dues, and, essentially, what being a union member entails. Do not express your personal opinions regarding unions or try to influence them, either for or against. Also avoid inquiries about their present views toward unions or questions about past union involvement. Your job is to be informative and descriptive only.

Salary Ranges

Whether this information is disclosed to an applicant at the initial interview is a matter of company policy, but interviewers should certainly know what a job pays so they can determine if an applicant warrants further consideration. If, for example, there is an opening for a benefits specialist offering an annual salary of between $55,500 and $63,750, and an applicant is currently earning $57,900 a year, there's no problem. On the other hand, if there's an opening for a purchasing manager with a salary range of between $83,500 and $97,500, and an applicant is currently earning an annual salary of $96,500, there's cause for concern. What's your company's policy when it comes to starting a new employee so close to the maximum of the salary range? If you offer the maximum, will this person accept an increase of up to $1,000? What about subsequent salary increases? Does your company "red circle" employees who are at the ceiling of their ranges so that they remain frozen until either the salary structure is re-evaluated or the position is reclassified?

Other salary-related issues may arise. An applicant may currently be earning considerably less than the minimum salary you're offering for what may be considered comparable work. It could be that the applicant is currently underpaid or not being altogether forthright about his actual duties and responsibilities. This calls for a more thorough line of questioning during the interview regarding the level and scope of tasks he is presently capable of performing.

Applicants sometimes indicate that they are currently earning considerably more than the maximum for an available position, but are receptive to taking a pay cut. This doesn't automatically translate into being overqualified or that, if hired, they'll get restless and leave the job. There are a number of explanations as to why someone would be willing to take a reduction in pay, such as the opportunity to work for a specific company, the desire to learn new skills or enter a new field, or an inability to find suitable work in one's own profession.

Related to the issue of salary is the sign-on or hiring bonus. Previously reserved for executive-level, highly specialized, or hard-to-fill positions, the bonus is now becoming a means for attracting talent at all levels. It is generally calculated at 5 to 20 percent of the base salary, depending on the scope and difficulty of the job. Some companies tie the bonus to an agreement with the employee not to leave the company for a specified period.

Benefits

Describing your company's benefits package can be an excellent selling point, especially for hard-to-fill positions. Recruiters are advised to prepare a forty-five- to sixty-second summary of company benefits, such as medical and disability insurance, dental coverage, life insurance, profit-sharing plans, stock bonus programs, vacation days, personal days, leaves of absence, holidays, and tuition reimbursement.

Be careful not to give the impression that a discussion of your company's benefits means the applicant is being seriously considered for a job. Make it clear that providing this information is part of the interview process and that the selected applicant will receive more comprehensive benefits information if a job offer is extended.

Growth Opportunities

Most applicants are interested in whether they will be able to move up in an organization. It is therefore helpful to know about the frequency of performance appraisals, salary reviews, and increases; policies regarding promotions; relationship of a position's level and scope of responsibilities to that of others within a job family; policies governing internal job posting; likelihood of advancement; tuition reimbursement plans; and training.

It's important to provide an accurate account of growth opportunities to preclude the possibility of morale problems developing later on. For example, if an applicant is applying for a position that is one step removed from the top position in a given job family, and that position has been occupied by the same person for the past ten years, the opportunity for growth by way of promotion is unlikely. There are, however, other ways to grow, such as an expansion of responsibilities that could, in turn, lead to the creation of a new job classification.

Prepare a Job Description

The primary purpose of a job description is to identify the essential function of a job, that is, those tasks that are fundamental to the position. It clarifies the role of the job and what the incumbent is expected to accomplish. Essentially, a job description forms the groundwork for an agreement between an employer and the incumbent as to expected job performance results. Accordingly, the language should be concise, straightforward, uncomplicated, and easily interpreted.

Every position in an organization should have a job description, whether it's generic or specific. Generic job descriptions are written in broad, general terms and may be used for several similar positions in different departments of the same company. For example, there may be one generic job description for "administrative assistant," rather than a separate administrative assistant job description for each department. Specific job descriptions define the duties and tasks of one particular position, such as "vice president of human resources." They are written when a position has unique responsibilities that distinguish it from other, similarly titled jobs.

Job descriptions are multipurpose tools that can be used in virtually every aspect of the employment process:

Clarifying relationships between jobs	Grievance proceedings	Recruitment
Interviewing	Salary structuring	Demotions
Job posting	Selection	Disciplinary actions
Outplacement	Training	Employee orientations
Performance appraisals	Transfers	Exit interviews
Promotions	Work flow analyses	

Since job descriptions can be used for many different purposes, employers should take care to write them as comprehensively as possible. Initially, this will require a fair amount of time, but it will prove well worth the effort.

Here are fifteen guidelines for writing job descriptions:

1. *Arrange duties and responsibilities in a logical, sequential order.* Begin with the task requiring the greatest amount of time or carrying the greatest responsibility.

2. *State separate duties clearly and concisely.* This way anyone can glance at the description and easily identify each duty. Identify each task as essential or nonessential—a requirement of the Americans with Disabilities Act of 1990 (ADA).

3. *Avoid generalizations or ambiguous words.* Use specific language and be exact in your meaning. To illustrate: "Handles mail" might be better expressed as "sorts mail" or "distributes mail."

4. *Don't try to list every task.* Use the phrase "primary duties and responsibilities include" at the beginning of the job description, and close with the phrase "performs other related duties and responsibilities, as required."

5. *Include specific examples of duties wherever possible.* This will enable the reader to more fully understand the scope of responsibility involved.

6. *Use nontechnical language.* A good job description explains the responsibilities of a job in commonly known terms.

7. *Indicate the frequency of occurrence of each duty.* One popular way of doing this is to have a column on the left side of the list of tasks with corresponding percentage representing the estimated amount of time devoted to each primary duty.

8. *List duties individually and concisely rather than using narrative paragraph form.* A job description is not a novel.

9. *Don't refer to specific people.* Instead, reference titles and positions. Incumbents are likely to change positions long before the positions themselves are revamped or eliminated.

10. *Use the present tense.* It reads more smoothly.

11. *Be objective and accurate.* Describe the job as it should be performed, not as you would like to see it performed.

12. *Stress what the incumbent does instead of explaining a procedure that is used.* For instance, use "records appointments" rather than "a record of appointments must be kept."

13. *Be certain that all requirements are job-related and are in accordance with equal employment opportunity (EEO) laws and regulations.* This will preclude the likelihood of legal problems developing later on.

14. *Eliminate excessive verbiage.* Most job descriptions can be completed in a page or two. The length of a job description does not increase the importance of the job.

15. *Use action words.* These words describe a specific function, such as *organize*. One word should stand out within a sentence as most descriptive, a word that could readily stand alone. Action words will also convey to the reader a degree of responsibility. For example, compare "directs" with "under the direction of." Try to begin each sentence with an action word; the first word used should introduce the function being described. Here's a list of sample action words that employers can refer to when writing job descriptions:

accepts	acts	administers	advises	allocates
analyzes	anticipates	approves	arranges	ascertains
assigns	assists	audits	authorizes	balances
batches	calculates	circulates	classifies	codes
collects	compiles	conducts	consolidates	constructs
consults	coordinates	corrects	correlates	counsels
creates	delegates	deletes	designs	determines
develops	devises	directs	disseminates	documents
drafts	edits	ensures	establishes	evaluates
examines	facilitates	figures	files	fills in
fines	follows up	formulates	furnishes	generates
guides	identifies	implements	informs	initiates
inputs	inspects	instructs	interprets	interviews
investigates	issues	itemizes	lists	locates

maintains	manages	measures	modifies	monitors
negotiates	notifies	observes	obtains	operates
organizes	originates	outlines	oversees	participates
performs	plans	prepares	processes	proposes
provides	pursues	rates	receives	recommends
records	refers	renders	reports	represents
requests	researches	reviews	revises	routes
schedules	screens	selects	signs	specifies
studies	submits	summarizes	supervises	tabulates
trains	transcribes	transposes	troubleshoots	types
utilizes	verifies	writes		

After writing a job description, ask yourself a series of questions to confirm its contents:

- What is the purpose of the job?
- Will the jobholder supervise the work of others? If so, can I provide job titles and a brief description of the responsibilities of those supervised?
- What duties will the jobholder perform regularly, periodically, and infrequently? Can I list these in order of importance?
- What degree of supervision will be exercised over the jobholder?
- To what extent will instructions be necessary when assigning work to the jobholder?
- How much decision-making authority or judgment is to be allowed the jobholder in the performance of required duties?
- What are the working conditions?
- What skills are necessary for the successful performance of the essential functions of the job?
- What authority will the jobholder have in directing the work of others?
- At what stage of its completion will the manager in charge review the jobholder's work?
- What equipment will the jobholder be responsible for operating? Am I able to adequately describe the equipment's complexity?
- What would be the cost to management of serious errors that the jobholder might make in the regular performance of required duties?
- What employees within the organization, and customers or clients outside the organization, will the jobholder interact with on a regular basis?

The exact contents of a job description will be dictated by the specific environment and needs of an organization. What follows provides the basic categories of job information required for most positions:

Date

Job analyst

Job title

Department

Reporting relationship

Location of the job

Exemption status

Salary grade and range

Work schedule

Job summary

Job requirements, including education, prior work experience, and specialized skills and knowledge

Duties and responsibilities, distinguishing between those that are essential and nonessential

Physical environment and working conditions

Equipment and machinery to be used

Other relevant factors, such as degree of contact with the public or customers and access to confidential information

A job description form reflecting these categories appears in Appendix E.

A database of well-written job descriptions provides any organization with an understanding of how the job contributes to the achievement of company-wide goals, as well as offering a solid legal base with respect to employment-related decisions made relative to that job. Once a job description is written, review it each time that position becomes available or on a semiannual or annual basis to make certain the content or requirements of the job have not changed.

Find the Best Fit

Jack had just interviewed three applicants for a customer service representative opening at the large retail store for which he worked. All three met the basic requirements of the job and appeared capable of performing the essential functions of the job as identified in the job description. But something bothered Jack about each of them:

- The first applicant had a great deal of relevant experience and demonstrated a thorough understanding of the job duties. There was no doubt in Jack's mind that she could do the job. What bothered him was a nagging sensation that she would resist adjusting to a new environment and would fail to work in concert with the other representatives.

- Applicant number two was the least experienced but indicated a great willingness to learn and work hard. He was pleasant enough, but Jack had a troublesome image of him reporting to Eliza, the manager in charge of the department. During the interview, the applicant had indicated that at his former job, there had been a slight verbal altercation between himself and another employee—a woman; his boss, also a woman, had "taken sides" against him. He felt there may have been some gender bias involved.

• The final applicant had a sufficient degree of experience. Jack had no trouble picturing her working alongside the other representatives and taking direction from Eliza. What troubled him was that she didn't seem interested in doing anything beyond what was expected. There was no willingness to help the other representatives, as was often needed during the company's peak holiday season.

What should Jack do? He knows there is no ideal employee, but each of these applicants fell short in areas critical to the successful performance of the job. Should he keep looking?

The answer is "yes." Jack should keep looking, but not before he clarifies what he's looking for. The requirements and areas of responsibility identified in a job description are excellent indicators of the skills connected to a job. However, they cannot unveil what a person is willing to do once on the job or how well his bank of intangible skills will enable him to fit within a new organizational culture. It's these elements together that produce the best possible employee: that is, the best fit.

The best fit begins with identifying what someone has accomplished, either at past jobs or through the performance of relevant non-job-specific tasks. By asking questions that will yield specific, measurable, and verifiable responses (Chapters 7 and 8), and comparing the answers with the particulars identified in the job description, recruiters can largely determine what a person is capable of doing. In other words, they can isolate someone's tangible skills and abilities.

The next stage of determining the best fit has to do with what a person is willing to do with these tangible skills and abilities. Recruiters can relate past performance to the future by asking competency-based questions (Chapter 7). When doing this, always bear in the mind an important question: What is the likelihood that a person will approach a task in a new work environment the same way as in a former job? Since we are essentially creatures of habit, it's likely that an applicant will approach a problem, make a decision, or communicate in essentially the same way. Therefore it is important to ask for specific examples of how past performance relates to the performance of specific job-related tasks for the available position.

The final stage of identifying whether a person will be the best fit concerns a host of intangible qualities. Depending on the job and the work environment, these could include:

• Ability to adjust to sudden changes in direction
• Ability to work as an integral member of a diverse team
• Capability of functioning effectively in a different work environment
• Degree of flexibility
• Disposition toward working with others whose approach to problem solving may differ from their own

- Interest in learning from those whose work style differs from their own
- Knack for multitasking
- Outlook on accepting direction from someone whose communication style differs from what they're accustomed to
- Tolerance for working with individuals of varying degrees of effectiveness
- Willingness to accept criticism

This combination of what a person can do, is willing to do, and relevant intangible factors will result in the best fit.

Review the Application and Resume

Always review the applicant's completed application and/or resume prior to the interview. There are two main reasons for doing this. First, you will begin to become familiar with the person's credentials, background, and qualifications as they relate to the requirements and responsibilities of the job. Second, you can identify areas for discussion during the interview.

Whether paper or electronic, the application should reflect each organization's own environment. For example, the application form for a highly technical company will differ from one used by a nonprofit organization. Some companies have more than one form: one for professional or exempt positions, another for nonexempt positions.

When designing an application form, it's important to remember that all categories must be relevant and job-related. This is critical from the standpoint of compliance with EEO laws. In this regard, familiarity with federal laws is not sufficient since many state laws are more stringent, and where there is a difference, the stricter law prevails. Oversight or ignorance of the law does not provide immunity. Appendix F contains a generic sample job application form with categories that are applicable to many positions in most work environments.

While resumes differ from applications in terms of format and appearance, the same basic information should appear. This includes work history and educational accomplishments. Career objectives are also typically cited.

Following are ten key areas to consider when reviewing a completed application or resume. Each of these categories should be considered if relevant to the responsibilities of a particular position:

1. *Scan the overall appearance of the application or resume.* Is it easy to read and navigate? The handwriting on applications should be legible, paper resumes should be printed and generally no longer than two pages, and electronically generated resumes should comply with stipulated requirements. The contents of applications and resumes should be grammatically correct and the language easy to understand. Cover letters should demonstrate added interest on the part of the applicant.

2. *Look for any blanks or omissions.* This is easy with an application form; with a resume, check to see that basic information relating to work and education has not been excluded. Make note of anything that's missing so you can ask the applicant about it during the face-to-face interview. Some employment application forms are poorly designed, as are some electronic resume formats. This can cause applicants to inadvertently overlook certain questions or categories. Or it may be that an applicant purposely omitted certain information. If this is the case, it's up to you to find out why and to determine during the interview the importance of what's missing.

3. *Review the applicant's work history and make a note of any time gaps between jobs.* If an applicant indicates that he took some time off between jobs to travel throughout Europe, make a note of it, but avoid passing judgment. Fill in the gaps and worry about drawing conclusions after the interview process is completed.

4. *Consider any overlaps in time.* For example, the dates on an application may show that the applicant was attending school and working at the same time. Of course, this is possible if the person was taking online classes, but you still need to verify the accuracy of all dates, especially if the places of employment and school were separated by hundreds of miles.

5. *Make a note of any other inconsistencies.* To illustrate, say there is an applicant with an extensive educational background who has been employed in a series of nonexempt jobs. This may be because she has degrees in a highly specialized field and cannot find suitable work, or it may be that her educational credentials are misrepresented. It's up to you to find out.

6. *Consider the frequency of job changes.* People voluntarily leave jobs for many reasons, including an inaccurate description of the work at the time of hire, an improper job match, personality conflicts on the job, inadequate salary increases, limited growth opportunities, and unkept promises. Some employees, knowing that they're doing poorly, voluntarily terminate their employment just prior to a scheduled performance evaluation. Then there are instances when employees are let go for reasons unrelated to performance: a company shuts down for economic reasons, major organizational changes result in the deletion of positions, or a contingency assignment is completed and there is no additional work to be done. Of course, employees are also terminated for poor performance.

When reviewing an applicant's employment record, avoid drawing premature, negative conclusions regarding the frequency of job changes. Determining what constitutes a frequent change is highly subjective and often driven by the economy. Too often interviewers set arbitrary guidelines, sometimes patterned after their own work history. You may decide that changing jobs more often than once every two years is too frequent and that this translates into unreliability. At this stage of the interview process, though, you simply do not have enough information to make such a decision. After all, you haven't even met the applicant yet. Make a note that you want to discuss his pattern of job changes and move on to the next category.

7. *Be objective when evaluating a person's salary requirements.* In our society it's assumed that everyone wants to make more money. While money is one of the most

commonly cited reasons for changing jobs, you will undoubtedly come across applicants who are willing to take a job at a lower salary than they were previously or are currently earning. The reasons for this, as cited earlier, vary. The message here is not to draw premature conclusions.

It is significant to note that factoring in information relevant to salaries earned in past positions may be a violation of the Equal Pay Act of 1963, which prohibits paying women less than men for performing substantially equal work. This could occur where an employer learns that a woman has been earning considerably less in previous jobs than has a man with comparable skills. If both are hired for the same type of job to perform substantially equal work and are offered starting salaries that are, say, $2,000 above their previous salaries, and they both perform at comparable levels of effectiveness during their respective terms of employment, the pay differential between the two will widen that much more with each performance review. Consider, for example, a man who is hired as a database administrator at a starting salary of $70,000 and a woman who is hired to perform comparable work at a salary of $63,500. Both receive an "excellent" evaluation at the time of their first performance evaluation, resulting in a 5 percent increase. The original $6,500 gap between their respective salaries has just increased to $6,825, as the male employee's annual earnings rise to $73,500 and the woman employee's salary increases to only $66,675. If their performance levels remain comparable at the time of their next review, warranting another 5 percent raise, the gap will increase to $7,166, since the man will now be earning $77,175 and the woman will only be making $70,009 (essentially what the man was offered at the time of hire). Over time, presuming continued comparable performance, this pay gap will continue to widen. Such a pay difference based on past earnings could be a violation of the Equal Pay Act if it is perceived to be a differential based on sex.

Remember, too, not to hire anyone below the minimum range for a job.

8. *Carefully review the applicant's reasons for leaving previous jobs.* Look for a pattern. For example, if the reason given for leaving several jobs in a row is "no room for growth," it may be that this person's job expectations are unrealistic. While this explanation could be perfectly legitimate, it could also be a cover-up for other, less acceptable reasons. This is a key area to explore in the face-to-face interview.

9. *Make a note to ask for elaboration of duties that are not clearly described on the application or resume.* Job titles may also require explanation. Some titles are not functional or descriptive and therefore fail to reveal their scope of responsibility. Examples of such titles include "administrative assistant" and "vice president." Sometimes titles sound quite grand, but upon probing, you discover that they carry few substantive responsibilities.

10. *Review the application or resume for "red-flag" areas.* This is any information that doesn't seem to make sense or leaves you with an uneasy feeling. Here's a classic example: The application asks for the "Reason for Leaving Previous Jobs." The popular answer "personal" should alert you to a possible problem. Many interviewers assume that they have no right to pursue this further, that to do so would be an

invasion of the person's privacy. This is not true. You have an obligation to ask the applicant to be more specific. If people begin to volunteer information about their home life and personal relationships, then you must interrupt and ask them to focus on job-related incidents that may have contributed to their decision to leave. Also note that "personal" is frequently a cover-up for "fired."

Set the Stage

Allowing sufficient time for meeting with an applicant and conducting that meeting in an appropriate environment are two critical components to successful interviewing.

Allow Sufficient Time for the Interview

When determining how much time to allot for each interview, think about the entire process, not just the portion devoted to the face-to-face meeting. Time is needed before the interview to review the application and/or resume; during the interview for both you and the applicant to ask questions and for you to provide information about the job and company; and after the interview to write up your notes, reflect on what took place, set up additional appointments, and check references. Additional time may also be required before or after the interview for testing.

Considering all that must be done, just how much time should be set aside for each interview? Much depends on the nature of the job, that is, whether it is nonexempt or exempt. Generally speaking, more time is needed for interviewing professionals, usually a total of 90 to 120 minutes, with 60 to 90 minutes for the face-to-face meeting. This amount of time should be sufficient for you to gather the necessary information about an applicant's qualifications and to get a good idea of job suitability and applicant interest. If the actual face-to-face interview runs much beyond 90 minutes, it's likely to become tiresome for both the applicant and the interviewer. A 60- to 90-minute interview leaves approximately 30 minutes to be divided between the pre- and post-interview activities, including reviewing the application and resume, rereading the job description, preparing key questions, conducting tests, and arranging subsequent interviews.

In the case of interviews for nonexempt positions, approximately 45 to 75 minutes should be allotted, with 30 to 45 minutes for the face-to-face meeting. More concrete areas are usually probed at this level, such as specific job duties, attendance records, and the like. These take less time to explore than do the numerous intangible areas examined at the exempt level, such as management style, level of creativity, and initiative.

These time frames should be used as guidelines only. Be flexible in the amount of time allotted, but also be aware of these general parameters because they can help you acquire sufficient information and avoid discussing irrelevant factors. For example, if you find that your interviews are over within fifteen minutes, you may not be phrasing your questions properly; that is, you could be asking closed-ended questions as opposed to competency or open-ended questions (Chapters 7 and 8). It may also be that you're not adequately probing suspicious areas, or perhaps simply don't know what questions to ask. If, on the other hand, your interviews last much beyond forty-five minutes for a nonexempt position or ninety minutes for an exempt position, it's likely you're either talking too much or that the applicant has taken control of the interview. It's not unusual for applicants lacking sufficient job-related experience to steer interviewers away from questions regarding their job suitability. By diverting the interviewer's attention and talking a blue streak about irrelevant matters, applicants hope to cloud the real issue of whether they're qualified for the job. Of course, some people simply like to talk a lot and don't intend to be devious. Regardless of the motive, however, interviewers are cautioned against allowing applicants to take control of the interview. This is less likely to happen if you're aware of the recommended time frame for an interview.

To help maximize the time set aside for meeting with applicants, consider these scheduling guidelines:

1. *Interview during the time of day when you're at your peak.* If you tend to slow down around midmorning, but then pick up again around 1 p.m., it would be best to schedule interviews during the afternoon hours. Likewise, if you're at your best first thing in the morning, late-afternoon appointments would be unwise.

2. *Take a five-minute break between interviews.* The time can be used for just about anything, including taking a short walk, getting a cup of coffee, stretching, responding to a few e-mails, or doing other work. The break will help you feel more in control of your interview schedule and allow you to focus fully on your next applicant.

3. *Avoid conducting more than four or five interviews in one workday.* While this may not always be possible, you can space your interviews with other work in between. In so doing, you'll find that your attention level during the interviews, as well as during the other work, is likely to improve.

Plan an Appropriate Environment

If applicants are expected to talk freely they must be assured that others can't overhear what they're saying. This is particularly important when discussing sensitive matters, such as why they're leaving their present jobs. Hence, interviewers are obliged to ensure privacy. While not everyone has his own office, everyone has access to privacy. This may mean borrowing someone else's office when it's not being used, using the company cafeteria or dining room during off-hours, or sitting in a portion of the lobby that is set apart from those areas receiving the most traffic. Such options may be preferable if your own office has partitions instead of full floor-to-ceiling walls. Sounds can easily carry over and around partitions, and people can peer over the top if the walls are short.

Interviewers should ensure that there are a minimum number of distractions. Obvious distractions include your phone ringing, people walking into your office during the interview, or papers requiring attention left exposed on top of your desk. Some interviewers claim that such distractions are actually beneficial in that they allow for an assessment of how the applicant handles interruptions. This is unlikely. Distractions and interruptions waste valuable time for both the applicant and the interviewer. Moreover, the applicant may be left with an unfavorable impression of the interviewer in particular, and possibly the organization overall.

A more subtle distraction, but one that can interfere as much as a phone ringing or a person barging in, is the interviewer's own thoughts. Thinking about all the work that needs to be done may not only prevent you from focusing fully on the applicant but may even result in resentment toward this person for keeping you from it. To guard against this tendency, remind yourself just prior to meeting an applicant that the sooner you fill the opening the sooner you can move on to other tasks. It might also help if you cleared off your desk and turned off your computer before the job applicant sits down for the interview.

Interviewers should also ensure that the applicant is comfortable. It's a simple fact that if the applicant feels comfortable, you'll be assured of a more productive meeting. Comfort level is not determined by how much furniture there is in your office, whether you have rugs on the floor, or if your office overlooks a scenic view. It's your behavior and general approach to the interview that will largely determine the comfort level of the applicant. If you come across as friendly, appear genuinely interested in what the applicant has to say, and have made an effort to ensure privacy and prevent interruptions, then the interview surroundings are not going to matter a great deal. Ideally, offer the applicant a choice of seats. If space is limited, however, and there's only one chair in addition to yours, that's all right too. What matters is that the applicant feels welcome.

The most common office seating arrangements between an interviewer and an applicant include:

- The applicant and interviewer seated on either side of a desk
- The applicant's chair on the side of the desk
- The applicant and the interviewer sitting on chairs across from one another, away from the desk
- The applicant and the interviewer seated at a table, either next to or across from each other

There is no one proper relationship between your seat and the applicant's seat. Some interviewers feel that desks create barriers between themselves and the applicant. If this is how you feel, then desks do indeed become barriers. Also, some interviewers want to see as much of the applicant as possible so they can better assess nonverbal communication. If you're comfortable seated behind your desk, though, then by all means sit there.

Plan Basic Questions

Plan a handful of questions that will serve as the foundation for your interview. The job description is an excellent source for this. By reviewing the job description, you can easily identify what skills are required, and then proceed to formulate the questions you'll need to ask to determine whether applicants possess these skills and are likely to be the best fit. Hypothetical situations can also be developed and presented to applicants to enable them to demonstrate their potential.

Be careful not to prepare too many questions or become too specific during this stage of preparation. If you have an extensive list of detailed questions, the tendency will be to read from that list during the interview. This will result in an overly structured session, which could make the applicant feel ill at ease. In addition, with a lengthy list of questions, interviewers are likely to feel compelled to cover the entire list and will often end up being redundant. Again, this can result in the applicant feeling uncomfortable and wondering whether you are really listening to her responses.

Limit yourself to preparing about a half-dozen general questions. Once you get into the interview, the other questions that need to be asked will follow as offshoots of the applicant's answers. In fact, if your first question is broad enough, the applicant's response should provide you with numerous additional questions. An example of an effective first question might be, "Would you please describe your activities during a typical day at your current (or most recent) job?" As you listen to the applicant's response, note any areas that you want to pursue further.

This one question alone could yield enough information to fill an entire interview if you listen closely to the applicant's answer and use portions of it as the basis for additional questions. Consider, for example, the applicant who is currently working as a customer service representative. Suppose you asked him the question, "Would you please describe your activities during a typical day at your present job?" and he provided a scant response: "Well, let's see. Each day is really kind of different since I deal with customers and you never know what they're going to call about; but basically, my job is to handle the customer hotline, research any questions, and process complaints."

If you were to leave this answer and go on to another question, you would be overlooking a wealth of information. The applicant has handed you four valuable pieces of information worthy of exploration:

1. His job requires dealing with a variety of people and situations.
2. He "handles" a customer hotline.
3. He "researches" questions.
4. He "processes" complaints.

Here are some additional questions you can ask, based on the applicant's own comments:

"What is the nature of some of the situations with which you are asked to deal?"
"Who are the people who call you?"
"What is the process that someone with a complaint is supposed to follow?"
"What is your role in this process?"

"Exactly what is the customer hotline?"

"When you say that you 'handle' the hotline, exactly what do you mean?"

"What do you say to a customer who calls on the hotline?"

"What do you say to a customer who calls with a specific question?"

"Has there ever been a time when you did not have the answer being sought by a customer? What did you do?"

"What do you do when a customer isn't satisfied with the answer you've given him? Give me a specific example of when this has happened."

"Tell me about a time when a customer was extremely angry. What happened?"

"Tell me about a time when a customer demanded to speak to someone else."

"Describe a time when you had to handle several demanding customers at the same time."

"Describe a situation in which a customer repeatedly called, claiming his problem had still not been resolved. How did you handle it?"

"How much of your time is devoted to researching answers?"

"Describe the research process, including the resources you use."

"How do you prepare for each day, knowing that you will probably have to listen to several people complaining about a variety of problems?"

These are just some of the questions triggered by the applicant's vague response to one broad, open-ended question. The answers to each of these questions are also likely to result in further inquiries that will ultimately provide you with a clear picture of the level and scope of this individual's current bank of responsibilities.

This single open-ended question is so comprehensive that it alone could suffice as the only prepared question you have before beginning the interview. Most interviewers, however, feel better prepared if they have additional questions planned; furthermore, applicants lacking prior work experience cannot provide information about a typical workday. Here, then, are some additional questions that may be prepared before the interview. Note that all are broad enough so that the answers will result in additional questions.

For Applicants with Prior Work Experience

- "What (do/did) you like most and least about your (current/most recent) job?"

- "Describe a situation in your (current/most recent) job involving _____. How did you handle it?"

- "What (are/were) some of the duties in your (current/most recent) job that you (find/found) to be difficult and easy? Why?"

- "Why (do/did) you want to leave your (current/most recent) job?"

- "How do you generally approach tasks you dislike? Please give me a specific example relative to your (current/most recent) job."

For Applicants with Formal Education but No Prior Work Experience

- "What were your favorite and least favorite subjects in (high school/college/ other)? Why?"
- "Describe your study habits."
- "Why did you major in _____?"
- "How do you feel your studies in _____ prepared you for this job?"

For Applicants without Formal Education or Work Experience

- "Here are a series of hypothetical situations that are likely to occur on the job. How would you handle them?"
- "What has prepared you for this job?"

Summary

Even the most seasoned interviewer prepares prior to meeting with an applicant. The process begins with a thorough job analysis, including a review of the position's responsibilities, requirements, reporting relationships, environmental factors, exemption and union status, salary, benefits, and growth opportunities. Job descriptions aid in this process by identifying the essential functions of a job, that is, those tasks that are fundamental to the position. A database of well-written job descriptions provides organizations with an understanding of how the job contributes to the achievement of company-wide goals, as well as offering a solid legal base with respect to decisions made relative to that job.

In addition to reviewing the particulars of a job, employers seeking a match between a job and an applicant need to determine the best fit, that is, what a person has demonstrated he can do in terms of tangible skills, whether he's willing to apply those skills and knowledge to your organization, and what intangible skills and attributes he has that will benefit the job.

Interviewers should always review the applicant's completed application and/or resume prior to meeting with him. This will ensure familiarity with the person's credentials, background, and qualifications as they relate to the job, so that interviewers can identify areas for discussion during the interview.

Interviewers are advised to allow sixty to ninety minutes for the actual face-to-face meeting with exempt applicants, and thirty to forty-five minutes for interviewing nonexempt applicants. Additional time should be allocated for reviewing the application and/or resume, testing, writing up notes, reflecting on what took place, setting up additional appointments, and checking references. Employers should provide a private and comfortable environment for interviews. They should also prepare a half-dozen or so questions in advance to serve as the foundation for the interview.

CHAPTER 6

Interviewing and Legal Considerations

Pick up a newspaper on any given day and you're likely to read about the most recent in an ongoing series of employment discrimination settlements. These cases involve all forms of discrimination, including race, religion, sex, and age. For example, in June 2011 the Supreme Court blocked a sex discrimination class action suit against Wal-Mart. The case was considered the largest employment discrimination case in the nation's history, but the Court ruled unanimously that a class action lawsuit involving more than 1.5 million women could not proceed, reversing a decision by the Ninth Circuit Court of Appeals in San Francisco. While plaintiffs could still pursue individual suits, there would be much less money at stake than the projected billions of dollars.

What does any of this have to do with you personally if you make a concerted effort not to discriminate? The answer is easy, albeit disconcerting: If you're in HR and anyone in the organization is charged with discrimination, you are certain to be involved in what is often a lengthy legal process. If you're personally accused of employment discrimination, justly or not, you will find yourself embroiled in each step of the lawsuit. You may even be called upon to provide input if you're not in HR or personally involved with a particular charge of employment discrimination. That's because anyone having anything to do with any aspect of the employment process is expected to have a basic knowledge of EEO laws. Unintentional violations due to a lack of knowledge are not excusable.

The information contained in this chapter is current as of this writing and is not intended to represent legal advice. Readers are urged to consult with legal counsel in all equal employment matters.

Employment Legislation

Federal employment laws exist to ensure individuals the right to compete for all work opportunities without bias because of their race, color, religion, sex, national origin, age, or disability. Many state laws extend beyond this coverage to matters such as sexual orientation. Certain aspects of key employment legislation may not appear on the surface to relate directly to interviewing, but a closer examination reveals a correlation with the interviewing process. For example, the Equal Pay Act of 1963 requires equal pay for men and women performing substantially equal work. While this does not relate specifically to determining job suitability, interviewers need to understand the parameters and ramifications of the law to ensure that they are not in violation. This could occur if women are offered lower starting salaries than men based on their respective current rates of pay instead of on the scope of work to be performed or on qualifications.

These laws also protect employees being interviewed for internal promotions or transfers.

The following employment laws and categories of discrimination represent major federal statutes, rules, and regulations. The list is not all-inclusive. Employers are urged to obtain a copy of each of these and other laws relevant to their places of business. Unless otherwise noted, copies of the laws may be obtained from:

Equal Employment Opportunity Commission (EEOC)
Department of Labor
1801 L Street, NW
Washington, D.C. 20507
202/663-4900
http://www.eeoc.gov/

State and local laws may differ and should also be considered. Failure to comply with any of these laws could result in costly litigation.

Civil Rights Act of 1866

Many people are surprised to learn that employment-related laws have been around for nearly 150 years. One of the earliest pieces of legislation was the Civil Rights Act of 1866. The portion most relevant for today's employers is Section 1981, Title 42, which ensures all people the same "equal rights under the law . . . as is enjoyed by white citizens . . . to . . . make and enforce" contracts.

Essentially, this has been interpreted to mean that discrimination against non-whites in the making of written or implied contracts relevant to hiring and promotions is illegal. This law was originally intended to support charges of race discrimination and was expanded in 1982 to include national origin discrimination. It applies to all employers regardless of the number of employees.

Over the years, this early civil rights act has been a significant weapon against employers in that it permits the plaintiff to seek punitive damages in addition to compensatory damages such as back pay. Moreover, it provides for a jury trial.

While the awards for violation of this act can be substantial, the claimant must establish *intent* to discriminate on the part of the employer. That is to say, it is necessary to prove that the employer deliberately denied an individual an opportunity for employment or promotion on the basis of his race or national origin. This is to be distinguished from establishing *effect*, which means that while one or more representatives of an organization did not intend to deny someone equal employment opportunity on the basis of his race or national origin, the effect of a certain employment practice, such as exclusively using employee referrals as a recruitment source, was discriminatory. It is usually more difficult to establish intent to discriminate than it is to show effect.

Civil Rights Act of 1964

This is probably the best-known piece of civil rights legislation and the most widely used, in that it protects several classes of people and pertains to so many employment situations, including interviewing. Title VII of this act prohibits discrimination on the basis of race, color, religion, sex, or national origin in all matters of employment, from recruitment through discharge. Criteria for coverage under Title VII include any company doing business in the United States that has fifteen or more employees. Title VII does not regulate the employment practices of U.S. companies employing American citizens outside the United States. Violations are monitored by the EEOC.

Violators of Title VII are generally required to "make whole," which includes providing reinstatement, if relevant, and back pay. Jury trials are not allowed.

Plaintiffs in Title VII suits generally need not prove intent; rather, they may challenge apparently neutral employment policies having a discriminatory effect.

Many claimants sue for violations of both Section 1981, Title 42, of the Civil Rights Act of 1866 and Title VII of the Civil Rights Act of 1964.

Equal Pay Act of 1963

The Equal Pay Act of 1963 (EPA) requires equal pay for men and women performing substantially equal work. The work must be of comparable skill, effort, and responsibility, performed under similar working conditions. Coverage applies to all money-related aspects of the employment process including starting salaries, annual increases, and promotions. This law protects women only; men who feel they are being discriminated against in matters of pay may claim violation of Title VII. Criteria for coverage is at least two employees.

Unequal pay for equal work is permitted in certain instances, such as when wage differences are based on superior educational credentials or extensive prior experience. This pay difference, however, should diminish and ultimately disappear after a number of years on the job, assuming job performance supports equivalent pay increases.

Comparable Worth

An important issue related to equal pay is comparable worth. Several states have implemented programs for comparable worth pay whereby employers are required to compare completely different job categories. Those held predominantly by women, such as nurses and secretaries, must be compared with those occupied predominantly by men, such as truck drivers and warehouse workers. Point systems determine the level of skill involved in the job, as well as the economic value of each position. If the classifications dominated by women are deemed comparable to those dominated by men, adjustments are made to reduce the difference in pay.

The important distinction between comparable worth and equal pay is that in order to claim violation of the EPA, identical job classifications must be compared. Therefore, if a woman accountant believes that she is not being offered a rate of pay equal to that of her male counterpart who is performing substantially equal work, she may have sufficient cause to claim violation of the EPA. On the other hand, comparable worth compares different job categories. For example, if a clerk-typist believes that the value of her work is comparable to that of a male custodian hired to work for the same employer, she might sue on the basis of sex discrimination. Since there is currently no federal law that deals specifically with comparable worth, she would sue for violation of Title VII.

Businesses are urged to voluntarily assess their employment practices and work toward minimizing gender-dominated categories.

Age Discrimination in Employment Act of 1967

The federal Age Discrimination in Employment Act of 1967 (ADEA), as originally written, protected individuals from ages 40 to 65, and then to age 70. A 1978 amendment permitted jury trials, which gave claimants more power. Effective January 1, 1987, Congress unanimously approved, and President Reagan signed into law, H.R. 4154, amending ADEA by extending its protection to those beyond the age of 70. Now, most private sector and federal, state, and local government employees cannot be discriminated against in matters of pay, benefits, or continued employment regardless of how old they may be. The act also pertains to employees of employment agencies and labor organizations, as well as to U.S. citizens working outside the United States.

ADEA contains an exemption for bona fide executives or high-level policy makers who may be retired as early as age 65 if they have been employed at that level for the preceding two years and meet certain criteria, including exercising discretionary powers on a regular basis; having the authority to hire, promote, and terminate employees; and having a primary duty to manage an entire organization, department, or subdivision. Contact the EEOC for detailed guidelines.

The general criterion for coverage under ADEA is employment of at least twenty employees. Part-time employees are included when calculating coverage.

Rehabilitation Act of 1973

Section 501 of this federal law prohibits discrimination against persons with disabilities by contractors doing business with the federal government totaling $2,500 or more per year. Those employers who are government contractors, do business totaling $50,000 or more per year, and have fifty or more employees must prepare an affirmative action plan to comply with the act, although hiring and promotion goals and timetables are not required under this plan. Section 504 requires employers receiving federal financial assistance to take affirmative action in hiring and promoting qualified workers with disabilities.

The act protects "any person who (1) has a physical or mental impairment that substantially limits one or more of the person's major life activities, (2) has a record of such an impairment, or (3) is regarded as having such an impairment." Included in this definition are former drug addicts and recovering alcoholics. Current drug or alcohol users are not protected. Individuals with of acquired immune deficiency syndrome (AIDS) and AIDS-related conditions are also covered by this act.

An employer's obligation extends to making a reasonable effort to accommodate the person's disability, as long as such accommodation does not create an undue hardship. Undue hardships are determined by considering such factors as the size of the organization, the type of work involved, and the nature and cost of such accommodation. For example, job restructuring might be required if the person with the disability can perform the essential functions of the job, but requires assistance with one remaining aspect of the work, such as heavy lifting. Other aspects of job restructuring may include revised procedures, providing readers or interpreters, or modification of equipment. Any adjustment, including alternations to facilities that do not create an undue hardship, may be required.

Resources that assist in modifying facilities and equipment to accommodate workers with disabilities include the Job Accommodation Network (http://janweb .icdi.wvu.edu/).

Americans with Disabilities Act of 1990

In July 1990, President George H. W. Bush signed landmark legislation prohibiting all employers, including privately owned businesses and local governments, from discriminating against employees or job applicants with disabilities. Exempt are the federal government, government-owned corporations, Native American tribes, and bona fide tax-exempt private membership clubs. Religious organizations are permitted to give preference to the employment of their own members. The law requires every kind of establishment to be accessible to and usable by persons with disabilities. This legislation, titled the Americans with Disabilities Act of 1990 (ADA), pertains to employers with fifteen or more employees and is monitored by the EEOC.

Under the ADA, the term *disability* is defined the same as in the Rehabilitation Act of 1973, that is, as a physical or mental impairment that substantially limits an individual's major life activities. The definition also encompasses the history of an impairment and the perception of having an impairment. Examples of disabilities that are covered include impaired sight and hearing; muscular conditions such as cerebral palsy and muscular dystrophy; diseases like cancer, AIDS, diabetes, and epilepsy; cosmetic disfigurements; emotional disturbances; stuttering; smoke sensitivity; tension; and depression. In fact, there are more than one thousand different impairments that are covered by this act. Current users of illegal drugs or alcohol are not protected by the ADA. Also, people with contagious diseases or those posing a direct threat to the health or safety or others are not covered by this act.

Recently, the EEOC has focused on the issue of discrimination against individuals with intellectual disabilities. This includes people with an IQ below 70 and those with significant limitations in adaptive skills. The EEOC has issued a guide with examples of situations in which such intellectual disabilities are protected by the ADA.

Under the ADA, employers are required to make a "reasonable accommodation" for those applicants or employees able to perform the "essential" functions of the job with reasonable proficiency. Reasonable accommodation includes job restructuring, allowing part-time or modified work schedules, reassignments, hiring additional workers to aid employees with disabilities in the performance of their jobs, and installing new equipment or modifying existing equipment. An accommodation is considered unreasonable only in those instances where undue physical or financial hardship is placed on the employer. Such hardship is determined according to the overall size of an organization in relation to the size of its workforce, its budget, and the nature and cost of the required accommodation.

Essential functions are loosely defined as tasks that are "fundamental and not marginal," according to the Senate report on the ADA. Employers are encouraged to conduct a detailed review of each job to determine which functions are essential. This should include an assessment of the amount of time devoted to each task.

The ADA also refers to what an employer may require in the way of preemployment physical examinations. According to the act, employers cannot single out individuals with disabilities for medical exams. If they are shown to be job-related and consistent with the requirements of the job, medical exams are permitted after an offer of employment has been made, prior to the start of work. In this instance, an employer may condition an offer of employment on the results of the exam.

Pregnancy Discrimination Act of 1978

The Pregnancy Discrimination Act of 1978 (PDA) recognizes pregnancy as a temporary disability and prohibits sex discrimination based on pregnancy, childbirth, or related conditions. Pregnant applicants may not be denied equal employment opportunities if they are able to perform the essential functions of the available job. Likewise, women must be permitted to work as long as they are capable of performing the essential functions of their current job or any job to which they may be promoted or transferred.

If an employer insists on establishing special rules for pregnancy, such rules must be dictated by business necessity or related to issues of health or safety.

Fetal Protection

An important concern related to pregnancy discrimination has to do with fetal protection. Whether an employer may bar women of childbearing age from jobs that involve toxic substances, X-rays, lead exposure, or the like is an issue that has been addressed by the EEOC in a series of fetal protection guidelines. The guidelines require employers to first determine if there is substantial risk of harm to an employee's potential offspring from exposure to a workplace hazard. To accomplish this, employers should rely on scientific evidence of the risk of fetal or reproductive harm from exposure and the minimum period of time required for exposure to cause harm. Then the employer should assess its policy and determine whether there is a reasonable alternative that would be less discriminatory than exclusion, such as a temporary assignment to another nontoxic job or wearing a personal protection device.

Religious Discrimination Guidelines

The EEOC guidelines define religion and religious practices as "moral or ethical beliefs as to what is right and wrong, which are sincerely held with the strength of traditional religious views." In 1972, Congress amended that portion of Title VII pertaining to religion in the workplace by expanding the definition to include an individual's right to "all aspect of religious observance and practice, as well as belief, unless an employer demonstrates that he is unable to reasonably accommodate an employee's or prospective employee's religious observance or practice without undue hardship on the conduct of the employer's business." This amendment placed the burden on employers to prove their inability to reasonably accommodate an individual's religious practices.

As with accommodating persons with disabilities, what constitutes an undue hardship depends on a number of factors, including prohibitive cost. Undue hardship must be provable.

Certain work assignments might also require some adjustment if an individual raises religious objections. For example, a foreign work assignment to a country whose prevailing religious practices conflict with the beliefs of an individual might be the basis for that individual's request to work at a different location. Every effort should be made to accommodate such a request.

Balancing an individual's religious beliefs with an organization's dress and grooming practices may also become an issue. Unless safety is a factor, the employer should make a reasonable effort to accommodate religious-based attire and grooming.

Religion and work should be kept separate, meaning that employers have the right to require "quiet and unobtrusive" observance.

National Origin Discrimination Guidelines

The EEOC's "Guidelines on Discrimination Because of National Origin" preclude denial of employment opportunity because of an individual's ancestry, place of origin, or physical, cultural, or linguistic characteristics. There are four main areas pertaining to employment:

1. Citizenship requirements may not be valid if they have the purpose or effect of discrimination on the basis of national origin.

2. Selection criteria that appear to be neutral on first glance may have an adverse impact on certain national groups.

3. Speak-English-only rules may be considered discriminatory when applied at all times.

4. Ethnic slurs maybe considered national origin discrimination and must not be tolerated.

Immigration Reform and Control Act of 1986

The Immigration Reform and Control Act (IRCA) makes the employment of illegal aliens unlawful and establishes requirements for employers to determine an individual's authorization to work in the United States. The act applies to employers with four or more workers.

The Immigration and Naturalization Service (INS) determines what constitutes an acceptable document proving work eligibility and identity. Some documents establish both identity and employment eligibility; in instances where these are not produced, documents establishing identity in addition to documents establishing employment eligibility are required.

Employers must examine documents that establish an individual's identity and eligibility to work in the United States before completing the required I-9 form. This examination should be made subsequent to the final hiring decision to avoid violation of IRCA's antidiscrimination provisions. Employers face penalties for hiring unauthorized employees and for failure to properly complete and maintain I-9 forms.

Immigration and Customs Enforcement (ICE) has recently begun to increase the number of audits aimed at uncovering illegal hirings. Businesses are typically given three days to present their I-9 forms. If found guilty of knowingly violating verifications laws, employers have ten additional business days in which to rectify matters. If they do not, ICE may issue fines of up to $1,100 for each illegal employee, impose criminal charges, and recover assets.

Antidiscrimination provisions of the Immigration and Nationality Act regulate unfair practices during employment eligibility verification.

Drug-Free Workplace Act of 1988

Employers holding contracts with, or receiving grants from, the federal government of $25,000 or more must meet certain posting and record-keeping requirements and must develop policies prohibiting the unlawful manufacture, distribution, possession, or use of controlled substances in the workplace. The act does not make a definitive statement about requiring drug testing.

Civil Rights Act of 1991

The primary intent of the Civil Rights Act of 1991 is to provide appropriate remedies for intentional discrimination and unlawful harassment in the workplace. It extends beyond the Civil Rights Act of 1964's Title VII, "make-whole" remedies of back pay, reinstatement, and some attorneys' fees in several ways:

- Coverage is extended to U.S. citizens employed at a U.S. company's foreign site.
- The burden of proof is placed on employers to show lack of discrimination.
- Jury trials are permitted.
- Awards of compensatory and punitive damages are permitted in cases of intentional discrimination.
- Victims of intentional sex discrimination are permitted to seek compensatory and punitive damages up to $300,000, depending on the number of employees an organization has.
- Victims of race discrimination are permitted to seek unlimited damages.
- A "glass ceiling" commission has been established to develop policies for the removal of barriers to women and minorities seeking advancement.
- "Race norming," or the practice of adjusting test scores by race, is banned.

Family and Medical Leave Act of 1993

Administered by the Wage and Hour Division, the Family and Medical Leave Act (FMLA) requires employers of fifty or more employees to grant up to twelve weeks of unpaid, job-protected leave in any twelve-month period to eligible employees for the birth or adoption of a child or for the serious illness of the employee or a spouse, child, or parent.

The FMLA has undergone several changes since its inception. Amended by the 2008 National Defense Authorization Act, the revised FMLA allowed up to six months of leave for family members caring for military veterans injured while on active duty and up to twelve weeks of leave due to any "qualifying exigency" to family members of service men and women called to active duty. In 2009 the final FMLA regulations made additional changes to the law, including new notice forms to be used and new medical certification requirements. The 2010 National Defense Authorization Act further amended the FMLA by expanding military benefits to the National Guard, military reserves, or regular armed forces when called to active duty in a foreign country. Furthermore, eligible employees may take up to twenty-six weeks of leave in a single twelve-month period to care for family members with a serious injury or illness that occurred or was aggravated while on active duty. These may be individuals currently serving in the military or a veteran up to five years after leaving military service, even if the injury did not become apparent until after the person became a veteran.

Uniformed Services Employment and Reemployment Rights Act of 1994 (USERRA)

USERRA prohibits discrimination of employment based on military membership or service. Generally, a person re-employed by an employer is entitled to the seniority, status, pay, and other rights and benefits the employee would have received if the employee had remained continuously employed. Employers are expected to train or retrain returning service members so that their skills are upgraded. The law also provides for alternative re-employment positions if the returning service member cannot perform the duties of her original position. When employment is reactivated the employee is generally protected from discharge for one year except for cause.

Genetic Information Nondiscrimination Act of 2008 (GINA)

GINA prohibits discrimination against individuals in all matters of employment on the basis of genetic information of the individual or the individual's family members. It further prohibits an insured or self-insured health care plan from denying eligibility for health care coverage or from adjusting premium or contribution rates under a plan based on an individual's or family member's genetic information.

Lilly Ledbetter Fair Pay Act of 2009

This act stipulates that an unlawful discriminatory act occurs each time an employee receives her paycheck, benefits, or other compensation that reflects a discriminatory practice. This resets the 180-day statute of limitations for filing an equal pay lawsuit with each new discriminatory paycheck.

Employment Non-Discrimination Act (ENDA)

As of this writing, ENDA is a bill proposed in Congress. Civilian, nonreligious employers with fifteen or more employees would effectively be prohibited from discriminating against individuals on the basis of their sexual orientation, including heterosexuality and gender identity. The act has been introduced in every Congress, with the exception of the 109th, since 1994.

Currently, fifteen states and the District of Columbia have policies that protect against sexual orientation and gender identity discrimination in employment in the public and private sectors: California, Colorado, Connecticut, Hawaii, Illinois, Iowa, Maine, Minnesota, Nevada, New Jersey, New Mexico, Oregon, Rhode Island, Vermont, and Washington. Six additional states have laws that protect against discrimination based on sexual orientation alone: Delaware, Maryland, Massachusetts, New Hampshire, New York, and Wisconsin. Many companies voluntarily provide equal rights and benefits to their lesbian, gay, bisexual, and transgender employees.

President Obama reportedly supports the current bill.

Employment- and Termination-at-Will

Employment laws and categories of discrimination do not preclude the employment- and termination-at-will doctrines, which grant employers the right to terminate, at any time for any reason, with or without cause, the employment of an individual who does not have a written contract defining the terms of employment, provided such termination does not violate state or federal laws. In exercising this right, employers are unlikely to incur legal liability.

Employees have additional rights protecting them from arbitrary acts of termination-at-will. The broadest form of protection, implied covenants of good faith and fair dealing, requires employers to prove "just cause" before terminating an employee. Public policy rights may also protect employees from being fired for exercising rights such as "whistle-blowing"—public disclosure of illegal actions taken by one's company—or for refusing to perform illegal acts on behalf of an employer. Moreover, the issue of implied contract rights may arise when the protection provided by statements on the employment application form, in employee handbooks, or in other company documents is interpreted as a binding contract. In this regard, employers are advised to develop at-will policies for inclusion in these documents. A sample employment-at-will statement appears in Appendix F. It conforms to the following preemployment at-will guidelines:

- *State the at-will principle.* It is important to declare that your offer of employment is neither an employment contract nor a guarantee of employment.
- *Avoid making statements regarding job security.* Steer clear of phrases such as "We treat employees of (company name) like members of our family."
- *Avoid stating a prospective employee's salary in yearly numbers.* A statement of annual salary may imply a one-year employment contract. Instead, use weekly, biweekly, or monthly numbers.
- *Avoid using the term "probationary period."* It implies that, once a given period of time is over, an individual is there to stay. Likewise, avoid the term *permanent employee;* instead, substitute *regular employee.*

In addition to including at-will statements on their application form, employers can minimize the possibility of wrongful discharge allegations and put the company in a better position to successfully defend against such action by implementing additional safeguards and ensuring that:

- Application forms are in full compliance with applicable EEO laws.
- Everyone involved with the employment process is skilled in effective and legal interviewing skills.
- Applicants clearly understand the content and scope of responsibility of the position they're being considered for before a job offer is extended.
- Job descriptions are accurate and job standards are consistent with what is required.

Because the legal issues involving employment- and termination-at-will are still evolving, employers are advised to have all written materials pertaining to the employment process reviewed by legal counsel.

Noncompete Agreements

Also known as nonsolicitation agreements or restrictive covenants, noncompete agreements are designed to protect an employer's trade secrets, customer and marketing lists, and confidential knowledge about the employer acquired by an employee while on the job. Noncompete agreements—most commonly used in the computer industry, some professional partnerships, high-tech industries, and engineering environments—are usually presented for signature as a condition of employment or when a worker is promoted to a sensitive position. These agreements are intended to take effect upon termination, at which time employees may be restricted from working for a competitor for a specified period of time, often one to two years; working at the same or a comparable job in the same industry during a certain time frame; or working in a defined geographical area for a competitor.

The current trend is toward protecting employees by placing limitations on the extent to which an employer can restrict a former employee's right to work. There are no federal laws dealing directly with noncompete agreements, but there are some state laws.

Negligent Hiring and Retention

Negligent hiring and retention may occur when employers fail to exercise reasonable care in hiring or retaining employees. Increasingly, employers are being held liable for harmful acts committed by their employees both in the workplace and away from it. Named in such lawsuits are usually the employer, the employee who caused the injury, and the person directly responsible for hiring. Findings of personal liability are not uncommon. Negligent hiring actions have been brought by employees as well as by innocent third parties, such as customers, visitors, and clients injured by the criminal, violent, or negligent acts of an employee.

Plaintiffs must prove that the employee causing the injury was unfit for hiring or retention, that the employer's hiring or retention of that employee was the cause of the plaintiff's injuries, and that the employer knew or should have known of the employee's unfit condition. Generally, the deciding factor is whether an employer can establish that it exercised reasonable care in ensuring the safety of others. Reasonable care may include conducting relevant preemployment testing, checking references, investigating gaps in an applicant's employment history, verifying academic achievements, conducting a criminal investigation, checking an applicant's credit history, or verifying the individual's driving record. The type of position an employee is hired for typically plays a role in how extensive the investigation should be. For example, unsupervised positions in which the employee has a great deal of contact with customers, clients, visitors, or other employees may require more in-depth pre-employment investigation than would jobs that are highly supervised.

Juries may not be sympathetic to the difficulties an employer encounters in obtaining relevant background information on which to base a hiring decision. Employers in court because of negligent hiring or retention charges report that juries often find for the plaintiff. The trial of such actions may involve the examination of a number of issues, including what the employer actually knew about the individual, as opposed to what it tried to ascertain; whether the potential risk to others could have been reasonably discovered through interviews or reference and background checks; and whether the risk to others was greater because of the nature of the job. Consideration of these questions may implicate the employer in an act of negligent hiring or retention. Employers should note that such lawsuits might prove more costly than typical employee litigation because of potentially higher awards of punitive damages.

It's apparent from all this that preventive measures are an employer's best defense against charges of negligent hiring or retention. In this regard, employers are advised to do the following:

- Conduct comprehensive employment interviews.
- Investigate all gaps in employment.
- Conduct job-related preemployment tests.
- Conduct thorough reference and background checks.
- Keep written notes of information received when checking references.
- Decide whether a criminal investigation is warranted, based on information received.
- Immediately investigate any allegations of employee misconduct.
- Consult with legal counsel when in doubt as to what course of action to take.

Record-Keeping Requirements

Employers are obliged to retain documents according to certain federal and state stipulations, and longer if a claim or government investigation is conducted or threatened. This requirement appears in the record-retention provisions of most federal and state EEO laws, as well as the Sarbanes-Oxley Act of 2002 (SOX). Enacted as a reaction to several major corporate and accounting scandals, SOX requires greater accountability of all U.S. public corporate boards, management, and public accounting firms. Individuals who tamper with records or documents can be fined and imprisoned for up to twenty years.

As with certain aspects of key employment legislation that may not appear on the surface to relate directly to interviewing, a closer examination of record-keeping requirements reveals an important correlation with the interviewing process for new hires as well as for promotions and internal transfers.

Federal Retention Requirements

Some of the specific record-keeping requirements for relevant laws are summarized as follows:

- *Age Discrimination in Employment Act.* Employers with twenty or more employees must keep payroll or any other records containing the name, address, birth date, occupation, rate of pay, and weekly compensation of each employee for three years.

- *Americans with Disabilities Act.* Employers with fifteen or more employees must retain all HR records involving a person with a disability, whether they have hired that person or not. With specific regard to interviewing, keep requests for reasonable accommodation with job applications. All records must be kept for one year from the date the record was made or an employment action was taken, whichever is later.

- *Civil Rights Act of 1964, Title VII.* Employers with fifteen or more employees must retain all HR records, including resumes, applications, interview notes, and test results for one year. EEO-1 reports must be retained for one year by employers with one hundred or more employees, and federal contractors with fifty or more employees.

- *Consolidated Omnibus Budget Reconciliation Act.* While employers that offer group health insurance benefits are not required to maintain records for any specific period of time, experts recommend three years.

- *Employee Retirement Income Security Act.* All employers with employee benefit plans must retain records for six years.

- *Equal Pay Act.* All employers must retain FLSA-required records, as well as wage rates and descriptions of wage differentials for individuals of both genders for three years.

- *Executive Order 11246.* All employers with federal contracts or subcontractors should retain HR records relating to their affirmative action programs for a recommended period of three years. Affirmative action plans must be updated annually and retained for two years.

- *Family and Medical Leave Act.* Employers with fifty or more employees must keep detailed payroll and leave-related records for three years.

- *Immigration Reform and Control Act.* I-9 forms must be kept by all employers for three years or one year after termination, whichever is later.

- *Occupational Safety and Health Act.* Employers with ten or more employees must maintain certain forms as they relate to injuries and illnesses for five years: Specifically, these are forms 300, 300A, and 301. Records of medical exams required by this act or records relating to employee exposure to toxic or hazardous materials must be kept for thirty years after termination.

- *Older Workers Benefit Protection Act.* Employers with twenty or more employees are required to maintain pay-related information for three years.

- *Rehabilitation Act of 1973.* Public employers and federal contractors or sub-contractors must keep HR-related records for applicants and employees with disabilities for two years (one year for employers with fewer than 150 employees and $150,000 in government contracts). Employers should also keep a record of complaints and actions taken under the act.

State Retention Requirements

Most states' nondiscrimination laws have document-retention requirements that must be met in addition to federal stipulations. Thus, employers in some states will have to retain files for longer than the federally mandated period. For employers with locations in multiple states, this means reviewing the file-retention requirements in each state.

Employers may have to retain files for their defense in several types of legal actions, including charges of state common law fraud, tort claims, and contract claims. For example, an applicant could accuse an employer of fraud by claiming the employer misled him about the particulars or availability of a job. Tort claims could result from inferences of defamation and invasion of privacy. Contract laws may be brought into play when employees take issue with their employment contracts, both written or oral.

This last point—employment contracts—becomes especially complex when you consider that the retention periods for written and oral contracts can vary in the same state. Florida, for example, has a four-year statute for oral contracts, but a five-year statute for written contracts; in Illinois, there is a five-year statute for oral contracts, but a ten-year statute for written contracts. To further complicate matters, some states interpret written contracts broadly to include e-mail correspondence.

In many states there is something called a "catch-all statute of limitations" that covers all claims not covered under a specific statute of limitations. This is usually six years. Rather than trying to follow the myriad rules concerning retention, many employers opt to adopt the six-year rule across the board, hoping it will cover most fraud, tort, and contract claims.

State record-keeping requirements cover multiple topics, including apprenticeships, child labor, health and safety, employee access to HR records, unemployment, and workers compensation.

With regard to applicants who are not hired, federal nondiscrimination laws require a one-year record-retention period. Some states, however, have longer requirements, such as California, where applicant records must be retained for two years.

Employers are advised to weigh the risks of failing to retain files for the entire length of a statute of limitations against the potential costs, e.g., administrative expenses. If at all possible, retain all records for the longest statute of limitations period and then some.

Electronic Record-Keeping Guidelines

The Uniform Electronic Transaction Act (UETA) stipulates that electronic records have the same status and protection as paper records and that electronic signatures have the same status as those in ink. Employers are permitted to substitute electronic documents for paper documents if the following conditions are met:

- Electronic documents are easily printed out;
- Electronic copies accurately replicate the original paper documents;
- Backup procedures and security systems are in place to safeguard against damage to electronic documents; and
- Electronic documents can be easily accessed by the Office of Federal Contract Compliance Programs (OFCCP).

Experts recommend a multitiered security system in order to maintain confidentiality and limited access.

Once documents have been transferred to an electronic format, employers may destroy the originals. Most employers opt for shredding, although many are hesitant and keep certain original records pertaining to employment contracts, settlement documents, and anything that has been notarized. In general, then, documents that are difficult to authenticate are retained in their original form.

As with paper records, electronic records containing I-9 information and medical, employment, and EEO records must be kept in separate files.

While not required of all records, there is a general four-year retention rule recommended by many attorneys, even if federal or state requirements suggest shorter periods of time. This applies to employee name, gender, and address; social security number; date of birth if a minor; work schedule; total wages paid each pay period, dates of payment, overtime, tips, and other forms of compensation other than an employee's regular rate of pay; contracts and collective bargaining agreements; terms and conditions of employment; and forms W-4 (federal tax withholding) and W-2 (report of annual wages and the amount of taxes withheld).

Most experts recommend keeping HR files of all applicants, including those not hired, for two years from the date of an employment action. HR files include job ads and responses; applications and resumes; tests, including physicals; records of rejecting applicants for hire; and accounts of reasonable accommodation. I-9 forms should be kept for three years after the date of hire or one year after the date of an employee's termination, whichever is later.

Records need to be dated and accessible, and ready to be produced in twenty-four to forty-eight hours. Records relating to employment and medical matters must be kept in separate files.

Affirmative Action

Because Title VII did not immediately have the desired effect on discrimination, a series of executive orders was issued by the federal government, first by President

Kennedy in 1961 and later strengthened by President Johnson in 1965. The best known, Executive Order 11246, contained an EEO clause that required companies doing business with the federal government to make a series of commitments. Three of the most significant commitments are to:

1. *Practice nondiscrimination in employment.* When a company does business with the federal government, it is on the basis of a contract; should the company discriminate in its interviewing and hiring practices, it would effectively be violating its contract. The ramifications of this could be severe, including contract cancellation and debarment, meaning that the government would no longer do business with that company.

2. *Attain affirmative action goals.* This commits a company to hiring, training, and promoting a certain percentage of qualified women and minorities. The actual percentage is based on the number of women and minorities in a specific geographic location, referred to as a Standard Metropolitan Statistical Area (SMSA). Employers should contact the Office of Federal Contract Compliance Programs (OFCCP) to determine the most recent requirements for separate affirmative action plans pertaining to different establishments.

3. *Obey the rules and regulations of the Department of Labor.* This agreement extends to allowing periodic checking of its premises by labor representatives to ensure compliance with the other two commitments identified here.

Affirmative Action Plans (AAPs)

Increasingly, employers are adopting formal, written AAPs even where these are not required, in an effort to correct racial and gender imbalances in the workplace. These plans include internal auditing and reporting systems that measure progress toward achieving a bias-free work environment.

Written AAPs should encompass a minimum of seven key elements:

1. A policy statement
2. Internal dissemination of the policy
3. External dissemination of the policy
4. Positive utilization efforts
5. A review of internal procedures
6. Implementation, development, and execution
7. The establishment of a complaint procedure

Affirmative action guidelines may be obtained by contacting the Department of Labor at www.dol.gov/index.htm.

Currently, the OFCCP requires federal contractors and subcontractors to develop written AAPs where fifty or more workers are employed and the employer engages in $50,000 worth of business annually with the federal government. Other stipulations pertain to employers with contracts of varying amounts ranging from $10,000 to $5 million or more, as well as employers in certain industries, such as construction. Contractors are expected to maintain proper documentation and make records of compliance available to the OFCCP.

In the absence of a written AAP, it is more difficult to provide credible evidence that the employer is making a bona fide effort to correct real or perceived discrimination.

Diversity

Any AAP should be temporary, to be abandoned and replaced by a diversity-driven work environment once workplace equity has been achieved. Diversity-driven work environments go beyond affirmative action by nurturing individuality and making changes to suit the needs of employees without sacrificing business goals. Diversity reflects all the factors that identify us. The term extends beyond race, religion, sex, or national origin. It includes the multitude of ways in which we are unique and at the same time similar, such as customs, language, lifestyle, mental abilities, personality, physical characteristics, sexual orientation, socioeconomic status, talents, values, and work styles.

The ultimate goal of a diverse workplace is for everyone to work together toward achieving common organizational objectives while prospering individually. Achieving organizational goals requires flexibility and cooperation; the onus for adaptation cannot be placed solely on those employees outside the dominant culture, i.e., the culture to which the people in power belong. In order for a business to grow and profit, everyone must make a commitment to diversity. This commitment begins with open-mindedness during the interviewing process.

Advantages of Diversity-Driven Work Environments

There are many advantages to seeking a diverse workforce. Employers are able to select from a larger labor pool, enhancing the chances of finding qualified applicants. Such applicants reflect a variety of backgrounds and experiences, increasing the degree of talent and extent of contributions they bring to the organization. Employees will appreciate the multicultural environment provided and are thus likely to be more motivated and have a better attitude, resulting in higher productivity. A diversity-driven work environment can also result in fewer discrimination charges and lawsuits.

Having a diverse workforce is especially critical in companies that reach out to a diverse customer or consumer base. With changing demographics in the United States, and many businesses operating on an international level, it makes good business sense to have a workforce that reflects the needs of an organization's diverse customers.

Companies that invest in diversity as a long-term commitment may also enjoy significantly better financial results than those that do not.

Discrimination Charges

Individuals who believe their employment rights have been violated may file a charge of discrimination with the EEOC.

The following information is required to file a charge of discrimination:

- The name, address, and telephone number of the person or party bringing charges
- The name, address, and telephone number of the organization alleged to have committed the act of discrimination, as well as the total number of employees, if known
- A description of the alleged violation
- The date of the alleged violation
- Why the person believes she was discriminated against: race, color, religion, sex (including pregnancy), national origin, age, or disability
- Signature

The EEOC has strict requirements with regard to filing dates for charges of discrimination. A charge must be filed with the EEOC within 180 days from the date of the alleged violation. This 180-day filing deadline may be extended to 300 days if a state or local antidiscrimination law covers the charge.

If an organization is deemed guilty of discrimination, whether intentional or by practices that have a discriminatory effect, it may be required to comply with a host of remedies, including:

- Back pay
- Hiring or reinstatement
- Promotion
- Reasonable accommodation
- Other actions that will make a person "whole," that is, restore her to the status she would have had were it not for the discrimination
- Attorneys' fees
- Expert witness fees
- Court costs

Compensatory and punitive damages may also be imposed in matters of intentional discrimination. Damages may compensate for actual monetary losses, future monetary losses, and for mental anguish and inconvenience. Punitive damages may be imposed if it is found that an organization acted with malice or reckless indifference (the federal, state, and local governments are exempt from punitive damages).

Employers may also be required to take corrective action to cure the source of the discrimination and minimize the chances of its recurrence. This often translates into government-imposed affirmative action goals and training.

Avoid Discrimination Charges

While there is no absolute way of preventing applicants or employees from charging your organization with discrimination, there are guidelines you can follow to minimize the chances.

• *Make certain your hiring criteria are objective, uniformly applied, and consistent in effect.* By applying job criteria across the board that do not have a greater negative impact on any one group, you are demonstrating fair employment practices.

• *Show job-relatedness.* Every criteria you set, each question you ask, and every decision you make should be job-related.

• *Focus on making sound hiring decisions that properly match an applicant's skills, knowledge, and interests with a job's duties and responsibilities.* This should lead to fewer terminations, which is significant, since firing is the act that triggers many lawsuits.

• *Pay attention to questionable "red-flag" areas on an applicant's application or resume.* Do not proceed with the interviewing process until you're satisfied that these areas have been thoroughly explored.

• *Conduct reference checks and, if relevant, background checks.* While this is not always easy or even possible to do, making the effort may reveal important information that can influence your decision to extend a job offer, as well as provide protection against charges of negligent hiring and retention should you make the wrong hiring decision.

• *Think like a juror.* To avoid actions that generate lawsuits, think about how a juror might interpret your actions. For example: Did the employee understand, as a result of the interviewing process, what the employer would expect of him once hired? Did the employer follow policies and procedures known to the employee?

• *Treat all employees equally.* Most lawsuits alleging any form of discrimination are based on failure to treat employees consistently, reasonably, and fairly. This includes overt discrimination as well as more subtle forms of discrimination, such as stereotyping, patronizing, and favoritism. Note that "equal treatment" does not mean "identical treatment." It means ensuring that each employee has the same opportunity for consideration as every other employee.

• *Respect an employee's legal rights.* In addition to civil rights, these include the right to:
  —A safe workplace
  —Refuse to perform illegal acts without fear of retaliation
  —Not be defamed
  —Be free from harassing treatment
  —Participate in certain union activities
  —Compensation according to the Fair Labor Standards Act
  —Certain benefits under the Employee Retirement and Income Security Act (ERISA)

Some employees may have additional rights as a result of written or implied contracts (e.g., based on the language on employment applications or in employee handbooks).

• *Honestly appraise employees.* Negative performance appraisals are challenging to write, but they can save you a lot of trouble later on. It's hard to justify termination on the basis of poor performance with a file filled with glowing reviews. If an employee exhibits performance problems, identify them and together set goals for improvement. If, ultimately, you end up terminating the employee, an unjust termination lawsuit will be more difficult to sustain.

• *Take allegations seriously and act promptly.* Whether allegations are of sexual harassment or other forms of misconduct or illegal acts, responding quickly and appropriately will often defuse a situation and preclude a lawsuit.

Questions to Avoid Asking

Stated in the simplest of terms, if it's not job-related, don't ask. What's job-related? Education and training and previous work or military experience as they relate to the requirements and duties and responsibilities of the job. Just about everything else is off limits.

The number of topics to avoid may be great in comparison with those about which you can legally inquire, but the latter can generate hundreds of legitimate, job-specific questions and answers that will help you determine job suitability. The others will provide limited responses about personal qualities that may be interesting but have no bearing on ability.

In general, the categories to steer clear of during the employment interview, whether on the application form or during the face-to-face meeting, relate to race, color, religion, sex, national origin, age, and non-job-related disabilities and genetic information.

It is significant to note that even if applicants volunteer the non-job-related information, you are still liable if the information is used illegally. Suppose you inform an applicant that the available position requires travel. You then ask if she foresees any problem in leaving for a business trip with very little advance notice. She responds, "Oh, that will be no problem at all. My mother has been babysitting for my three kids ever since my divorce last year." The applicant has just volunteered information regarding two categories that are not job-related: children and marital status. If she is rejected, she might claim discrimination on the basis of this information, even though you did not solicit it.

Should an applicant provide information you should not have, do not write it down or pursue the subject. Tell the applicant that the information is not job-related and that you want to return to discussing her qualifications in relation to the job opening.

Exhibit 6-1 identifies the most common categories and questions to avoid during the employment interview, both verbally and via the application form. Related rec-

Exhibit 6-1. Preemployment Questions Asked Verbally and/or Appearing on Applications Forms

Subject	Questions Not Recommended	Recommended Questions
Name	What is your maiden name? Have you ever used any other name? Have you ever worked under another name? Have you ever changed your name?	Have you ever worked for this company under a different name? Is additional information relative to a change in name, use of an assumed name, or nickname necessary for us to check your work record? If yes, please explain.
Address	Do you own or rent your home? How long have you lived at this address?	What is your address? Where do you live?
Age	How old are you? What is your date of birth? Are you between 18 and 24, 25 and 34, etc.?	Are you above the minimum working age of _____?
Physical Appearance	How tall are you? How much do you weigh? What is the color of your eyes and hair?	None
Citizenship and National Origin	Of what country are you a citizen? Where were you born? Where were your parents born? Are you a naturalized or a native-born citizen? What is your nationality? What kind of name is _____?	Are you a citizen of the United States? If you are not a U.S. citizen, do you have the legal right to remain permanently in the United States?
Marital Status	What is your current marital status? Have you ever been married? Divorced? Do you wish to be addressed as Mrs., Miss, or Ms.?	None
Children	Do you have any children? How many children do you have? What child-care arrangements have you made? Do you intend to have children? When do you plan to have children? If you have children while employed, will you return to work?	None

Police Records	Have you ever been arrested?	Have you ever been convicted of a (crime? felony? crime greater than a misdemeanor?). Please explain. (NOTE: Applicants may not be denied employment because of a conviction record unless there is a direct correlation between the offense and the job, or unless hiring would constitute an unreasonable risk [Correction Law Article 22-A Sec. 754]).
Religion	What is your religious background? What religious holidays do you observe? Is there anything in your religious beliefs that would prevent you from working the required schedule?	None
Disabilities	Do you have any disabilities? Have you ever been treated for any of the following (list of diseases and illnesses)? Do you now have, or have you ever had, a drug or alcohol addiction? Do you have physical, mental, or medical impediments that would interfere with your ability to perform the job for which you are applying? Are there any positions or duties for which you should not be considered because of existing physical, mental, or medical disabilities?	Can you perform the tasks required to carry out the job for which you have applied with or without accommodation?
Photographs	Any question requiring that a photo be supplied before hire.	None
Languages	What is your native language? How did you learn to speak _____?	What is the degree of fluency with which you speak/write any language, including English? (Ask only if job-related.)

(continues)

Exhibit 6-1. Continued.

Subject	Questions Not Recommended	Recommended Questions
Military Experience	Have you ever served in the armed forces of any country? What kind of discharge did you receive?	What is your military experience in the armed forces of the United States?
Organizations	What clubs, organizations, or associations do you belong to?	What clubs, organizations, or associations, relative to the position for which you are applying, do you belong to?
References	A requirement that a reference be supplied by a particular kind of person, such as a religious leader.	Please provide the names, titles, addresses, and phone numbers of business references who are not related to you other than your present or former employers.
Finances	Do you have any overdue bills?	None
Education	Are you a high school or college graduate? When did you attend high school or college?	Questions about the applicant's academic, vocational, or professional education, including the names and locations of the schools, the number of years completed, honors, diplomas and degrees received, and the major courses of study.
Experience	Any question regarding experience unrelated to the job.	Any questions regarding relevant work experience.

ommended questions are also shown. Many of the recommended inquiries appear on the application form in Appendix F.

Bona Fide Occupational Qualifications

Sometimes the requirements of a position seem to be discriminatory in nature. For instance, jobs that specifically request a male or a female appear on the surface to be discriminatory. Upon closer investigation, however, it could become evident that the EEO concept of bona fide occupational qualification (BFOQ) would prevail. By definition, a BFOQ is a criterion that appears to be discriminatory but can be justified by business necessity. For example, an employer may have an opening for a model to show a new line of designer dresses. In this instance being female would be a

BFOQ. An example of an unacceptable BFOQ would be a position requiring heavy lifting where only male applicants are considered. The requirement of lifting can be tested; all applicants—male and female—could be asked to lift the weight normally required on the job. Those unable to perform this task would not be considered. This would include all men as well as all women who could not meet the lifting requirement. Likewise, women able to lift the weight must be given an equal opportunity for the job.

BFOQs may apply to religion, gender, age, and national origin, but never to race. Furthermore, general company preference does not constitute a legitimate BFOQ. The most valid BFOQ or business-necessity defense is safety.

When there is doubt, the following business-necessity guidelines should be applied:

- Document the business necessity.
- Explore alternative practices.
- Ensure across-the-board administration of the practice.
- Ensure that the business necessity is not based on stereotypical thinking, arbitrary standards, or tradition.

There are very few instances in which BFOQ applies. For example, certain categories, such as security-sensitive jobs, may make BFOQs of some of the inquiries that are not generally recommended.

If you believe that your requirements qualify as BFOQs, check with the EEOC before proceeding.

Applicant Tracking

The EEOC and the OFCCP require private employers of one hundred or more employees and federal government contractors or subcontractors with fifty or more employees and contracts in excess of $50,000 to identify their workforce by job category as well as by race, ethnicity, and gender in the EEO-1 report to be filed annually on September 30 with the EEOC. The preferred method of filing is via the web-based filing system. Companies should expect to receive their EEO-1 filing materials no later than mid-August. Instructions on how to file are available on the EEOC's website at http://www.eeoc.gov/employers/eeo1survey/howtofile.cfm.

Recent revisions to the EEO-1 form include those pertaining to ethnic and racial categories as well as job categories.

Ethnic and racial changes include:

- The addition of a category, "Two or More Races."
- The division of the category "Asian or Pacific Islander" into two separate classifications: "Asian" and "Native Hawaiian or other Pacific Islander."

- "Blacks" are renamed "Blacks or African American."
- "Hispanics" are renamed "Hispanic or Latino."
- Self-identification replaces visual employer identification.

Job classification changes include:

- The category of "Officials and Managers" is divided into two levels based on responsibility and influence: Executive/Senior Level Officials and Managers, and First/Mid-Level Officials and Managers.
- Business and financial occupations have been moved from the Officials and Managers category to the Professional category.

The OFCCP uses EEO-1 information primarily to determine which business to select for compliance evaluations.

Summary

Federal employment laws exist to ensure that all individuals have the right to compete for all work opportunities without bias because of their race, color, religion, sex, national origin, age, or disability. State statutes often extend beyond protection provided by federal legislation. Employers are urged to familiarize themselves with all relevant employment laws and categories of discrimination.

These laws do not preclude the employment- and termination-at-will doctrines, which grant employers the right to terminate the employment of an individual without a written contract defining the terms of employment. But employees have rights protecting them from arbitrary acts of termination-at-will. The broadest form of protection, implied covenants of good faith and fair dealing, requires employers to prove "just cause" before terminating an employee.

Negligent hiring and retention may occur when employers fail to exercise reasonable care in hiring or retaining employees. Increasingly, employers are being held liable for the acts of their employees both in the workplace and away from it. Plaintiffs must prove that the employee causing the injury was unfit for hiring or retention.

Employers are obliged to retain documents according to certain federal and state stipulations. This requirement appears in the record-retention provisions of most federal and state EEO laws. In some states, employers are required to retain employee files for longer than the federally mandated period. The Uniform Electronic Transaction Act (UETA) stipulates that electronic records have the same status and protection as paper records. Employers are permitted to substitute electronic documents for paper documents if certain conditions have been met.

Affirmative action is the result of a series of executive orders issued by the federal government to ensure equal employment opportunity. Many federal contractors and subcontractors are required to have written plans.

Diversity-driven work environments go beyond affirmative action by acknowledging the distinctiveness of each employee and by making changes to suit the needs of all. The ultimate goal of a diverse workplace is for everyone involved to work together toward achieving common organizational objectives, while prospering individually.

Those who believe their employment rights have been violated may file a charge of discrimination with the EEOC.

To avoid discrimination charges, ask only job-related questions during employment interviews, that is, questions about experience and education as they relate to the requirements, duties, and responsibilities of the job. Make certain, too, that your application forms contain only job-related questions.

The EEOC requires most employers to break down their workforce by job category as well as by race, ethnicity, and gender. This is accomplished by filing an annual EEO-1 report.

CHAPTER 7

Competency-Based Questions

I've conducted hundreds of interviewing workshops, with some being more memorable than others. A particular session stands out because one of the participants, a manager named Dan, proved the merits of competency-based questions to himself. Toward the end of the first day Dan firmly stated, "It really doesn't matter what people have done in the past—all that matters is what they're willing to do."

He was taken aback when I told him that I agreed. He said, "You just stated that competency-based questions make the most effective types of questions since they assess an applicant's demonstrated abilities as they relate to the requirements and responsibilities of a particular job. How can you say you agree with me when I say all that matters is what a person is willing to do?"

"That's simple," I replied. "But before I answer, let me ask you a question. How can you determine what a person is willing to do?"

Dan thought briefly and then replied, "This is probably a trick question because the answer is so obvious, but here goes: you ask them!"

I smiled. That was exactly what I thought he would say. "Dan," I continued, "suppose you have an opening for a project manager. One of the key qualities is teamwork. What are you going to ask your applicants?"

Dan responded, "Well, I could ask them to describe how they work with other members of a team."

"And what do you think they'll say?" I asked.

"I guess they'll say they work well with other members of a team," Dan replied.

"Right," I said. "What have you learned about how they work with other members of a team?"

"Not much," Dan confessed. "All right, then I would ask a specific question, like 'suppose you're working as a member of a team and you hit a snag because one of your coworkers isn't doing her share of the work; what are you going to do?'"

"Much better," I said. "But don't you think she's likely to tell you what you want to hear?"

Dan was becoming frustrated, so I decided to return to his original question. "Dan, the reason I can agree that all that matters is what a person is willing to do and also maintain that competency-based questions should form the foundation of any interview is that competency-based questions allow you to project, with a high degree of certainty, just what a person is willing or likely to do. Let me illustrate with teamwork. The last question you posed is excellent, but it's incomplete; you still don't know if what the applicant says is what she really will do or if she's just saying what she anticipates is the 'correct' answer. Imagine, however, continuing with, 'tell me about a time at your last job when that happened?' Her response is going to entail a specific, job-related experience involving teamwork. Since we're all creatures of habit, it's likely she'll approach a similar teamwork challenge the same way in the future as she did in the past."

Dan was chagrined, but he was receptive to hearing more about the merits of competency-based questions.

Key Competency Categories

For our purposes, a competency is defined as a skill, trait, quality, or characteristic that contributes to a person's ability to effectively perform the duties and responsibilities of a job. Competencies are the gauges for job success. Identifying job-specific competencies enables you to assess how effective a person has been in the past, and therefore how effectively he is likely to perform in future jobs. While every position requires different competencies, there are four primary categories:

1. Tangible or measurable skills
2. Knowledge
3. Behavior
4. Interpersonal skills

Most jobs emphasize the need for one category over the others, but every employee should be able to demonstrate all four competencies to a greater or lesser extent.

Tangible Competencies

For many jobs today tangible, concrete, or technical skill is critical to success. Tangible competencies demonstrate what applicants have accomplished in past jobs. For example, a sampling of competencies for a technical job includes having overall technical know-how; tailoring technical information to different audiences; applying technical expertise to solve business problems; staying technologically current; understanding the technologies of the organization; optimizing technology; balancing multiple projects; and communicating project status.

Although these concrete competencies are indisputably necessary and should certainly be thoroughly explored during an interview for a technical job, the other three categories should be examined as well. The reason for this is simple: a person brings much more than measurable skills to a job. Complex beings that we all are, we also bring an array of knowledge, behaviors, and interpersonal skills, all of which contribute to our success or failure on the job. This is true regardless of the job or grade level.

Consider this situation: There are two openings for the same type of job and two people are hired, both of them technically competent. One of them, Paul, has slightly more experience than the other, Justine, but both possess outstanding technical know-how. After one year Justine's performance review reveals that she is doing above average work, while Paul's indicates borderline, barely adequate performance. Why? Paul has trouble focusing on the key elements of a project and does not interact well with customers. In addition, while Justine responds well to feedback, Paul views suggestions as criticism. His poor performance evaluation is a result of several nontechnical issues. What went wrong?

Looking back, the interviewer in this scenario focused all of his questions on the applicants' technical capabilities, erroneously assuming that inquiries relating to the other competencies were irrelevant for a technical job. Had he asked Paul questions about how he interacted with customers in past jobs, or asked for examples of how Paul handled past projects, he might not have extended a job offer despite Paul's technical expertise.

Knowledge-Based Competencies

The second competency—knowledge—concerns what applicants know and how they think. Included in this category are project-management skills, problem-solving abilities, decision-making skills, the ability to focus on key elements of a task, time management, and the ability to use resources effectively. Many of these are considered intangible qualities, more difficult to measure and quantify than concrete skills, but no less important. Every job, regardless of level, requires a certain degree of knowledge. Even an entry-level position demands some degree of decision making or problem solving. Interviewers should ask knowledge-related questions appropriate to the level and nature of a job to determine not only what applicants know, but also how they think. This is especially important when jobs don't require previous measurable experience, which would preclude you from drawing conclusions based on past job-related experiences.

Behavior

The third competency concerns how an applicant behaves or acts under certain conditions. Suppose the position calls for a high level of client satisfaction. In past client-oriented jobs, was this applicant committed to developing lasting partnerships with clients? Did she keep clients informed of key developments? Did she follow up to ensure client satisfaction? If she worked as part of a team, or led a team, did she help team members focus on client requirements? Did she incorporate client views in decision making? There are numerous questions you can ask applicants with regard to job-specific behaviors that will reveal whether they'll behave effectively in your company's environment.

Interpersonal Skills

The fourth and final competency category involves interpersonal skills, that is, how applicants interact with others. Do they actively listen? Can they exercise self-control when upset? Are they self-motivated and able to work effectively with a wide range of people? Do they respect the views and ideas of others? Are they receptive to feedback? Can they manage conflict effectively?

Every job requires some degree of interaction with others. Regardless of how competent they may be at what they do, what they know, and how they behave, if job applicants are unable to interact effectively with their managers, coworkers, employees, customers, or clients, then their work and the work of others will suffer. Interviewers must ask questions, therefore, that focus on how the applicants interacted in past situations similar to those that are likely to occur in your organization.

Impact of Competencies

Whether you're in HR or a manager, it's not hard to understand how focusing on one set of competencies at the expense of the other three can negatively impact your role as a representative for your organization. If the people you hire exhibit problems, it reflects on your judgment and abilities. It also makes your day-to-day job more difficult, resulting in possible morale, motivational, and productivity concerns. Hiring the wrong people can also be costly.

On the positive side of the ledger, by hiring all-around qualified applicants you get more out of a person. These employees are also more likely to enjoy their work and remain with your company, resulting in a positive impact on turnover rates and recruitment expenses. Productively is also likely to improve, as will levels of customer and client satisfaction.

Job-Specific Competencies

Each job thus requires competencies from all four categories of tangible skills, knowledge, behavior, and interpersonal skills. It also necessitates a different set of *job-specific* competencies, based on the particular responsibilities involved.

Several sources will determine which competencies are relevant for each opening. Information about the job is generated primarily by the job description (Chapter 5). You can also gather additional information from job requisitions and postings. Also, talk with department heads, managers, and supervisors having an in-depth understanding of the opening. They will be especially helpful with the tangible and knowledge competencies. Incumbents often prove helpful, too, since they can probably provide information regarding the behaviors and interpersonal skills needed for the job.

Once you've acquired information about the job, isolate job-specific competencies. This is a two-step procedure: (1) make a list of all the required competencies, and (2) identify each competency according to its category. By example, consider an account representative. Here's a partial list of competencies needed to successfully perform this job, as determined by examining an HR department–generated job description and posting and conversations with a director of sales and two incumbents. Note that the list consists of both requirements and responsibilities:

Requirements

- Experience in managing and executing product sales
- Ability to examine, question, evaluate, and report sales
- Ability to match timelines and meet deadlines

Responsibilities

- Sells business's products
- Assists in the development and implementation of sales plans
- Documents quote and sales contract review
- Reports sales performance to director of sales
- Interprets technical documents as they relate to sales and contracts for company products
- Interfaces and communicates effectively with technical and nontechnical staff

Now you're ready to identify each competency according to its category. Review what each of the competencies represents: "Tangible" skills reflect what applicants can do, "knowledge" refers to what they know and how they think, "behaviors" reveal how they act, and "interpersonal skills" indicate how they interact. Return to your list and mark each one with a "T" for tangible, "K" for knowledge, "B" for behavior, or "I" for interpersonal skills. Note that a competency can reflect more than one category:

Requirements

T/K/B	Experience in managing and executing product sales
T/K/B/I	Ability to examine, question, evaluate, and report sales
B	Ability to match timelines and meet deadlines

Responsibilities

T/K	Sells business's products
T/K	Assists in the development and implementation of sales plans
T/K	Documents quote and sales contract review
T/K	Reports sales performance to director of sales
T/K	Interprets technical documents as they relate to sales and contracts for company products
B/I	Interfaces and communicates effectively with technical and nontechnical staff

Now go back over your list to ensure that all four categories are represented. You will no doubt see a greater emphasis of some competencies over others (in the case of the account representative, the emphasis is on tangible skills). Also, where competencies are paired, tangible and knowledge generally fall together, as do behaviors and interpersonal skills. Sometimes, a competency reflects all four categories. Go back and seek out additional information if all four categories are not represented. Perform this critical step before meeting an applicant to ensure that you'll probe all relevant areas during the interview.

Having isolated job-specific competencies, you're ready to correlate what the job requires with what the applicant has to offer. Information about the applicant can come from several sources. Two of the most comprehensive sources are the completed employment application and a resume. Since information appearing on applications and resumes is unlikely to be the same, it's a good idea to require an application from everyone submitting a resume. Applicants should be instructed to answer all the questions and not to respond to any questions with "see resume."

Referrals can also yield valuable applicant-related information. If applicants come to you as a result of staff word-of-mouth recruiting, the referring employee can provide helpful job-related information. Perhaps the two worked together as account representatives in the past; that could yield information about an applicant's technical, knowledge, and behavior competencies. Maybe your employee supervised the referral in a past job; important information about interpersonal skills may emerge from that relationship. When considering data from referrals, try not to be influenced by irrelevant factors. For example, if the referral comes from a colleague for whom you have little regard, you could be biased against the applicant before even meeting him. Avoid this trap by adhering to job-related competencies, derived from the four primary competency categories.

References (Chapter 13) can also provide valuable information about an applicant. Try to contact at least three former employers to establish a pattern. If one former manager indicates that the applicant was a problem from the outset and was glad when he resigned, but two others suggest that he was outstanding, it's likely that there were other issues impacting the first reference. You'll need to probe further to ensure a clear picture.

Characteristics of Competency-Based Questions

Competency-based questions focus on relating past job performance to probable future on-the-job behavior. The questions are based on information relevant to specific job-related skills, abilities, and traits; the answers reveal the likelihood of similar future performance. The process works because past behavior is shown to be an indicator of future behavior. Be careful not to translate this last statement as reading, "Past behavior predicts future behavior" or "Future behavior is the same as past behavior." Proponents of the competency-based approach to employment interviewing plainly point out that past behavior is an indicator only. No one can predict with absolute certainty how someone will behave in a job. There are too many variables that can affect a person's performance, among them:

- A significant change in the work environment
- The approach, attitude, or personality of a manager
- Difficulties in an employee's personal life
- A long-term or degenerative illness or disability
- A department's dramatic departure from established procedures
- Mergers, acquisitions, or economic downturns
- The introduction of a new organizational philosophy
- What is perceived as being an unfair performance review or salary increase
- Being bypassed for a promotion

Any of these factors alone can alter how an employee approaches work, and even the most compatible, conscientious, dedicated workers can be affected. Since interviewers cannot anticipate these influences when they first meet an applicant, they need to develop a line of questioning that will project, as accurately as possible, how an employee is likely to behave. This is best accomplished by asking the applicant to draw from the past.

For example, suppose you have an opening that is known for its emergency projects and tight deadlines. You can find out if a person is up to the challenge by asking about similar experiences in the past. Here's how you might phrase the question: "Tell me about a time in your last job when you were given an emergency project with what you believed to be an unrealistic deadline. What did you do?" Suppose the applicant's response indicates a firm grasp of how to handle this type of situation. You still need to know if the applicant was required to interrupt her normal workload frequently to tend to emergencies, or only once in a while. In addition, you will want to know if the rest of her work suffered while she tended to the emergency project. Some revealing, follow-up competency-based questions would be:

"How many times, in a typical month, did this sort of emergency occur?"

"Describe the system you had for effectively dealing with these emergencies and the impact it had on the rest of your work."

"Who else was involved in meeting these deadlines?"

"What was your role vis-à-vis theirs?"

"Was there ever a time when you felt the deadline could not be met? What did you do?"

Competency-based questions seek specific examples. These examples will allow you to project how an applicant is likely to perform in your organization. If the environment, conditions, and circumstances are essentially the same in the person's current or previous company as in yours, then your task has been made simple. Of course, this is rarely the case. That's why you need to extract information about all four competency categories. You need to know not only if the applicant knew what to do and how to think, but also how to act and interact. Answers to the above follow-up questions will reveal how competent the applicant is in all four categories when confronted with demanding emergency projects.

Competency-based interviews, then, allow you to make hiring decisions based on facts. They are structured, job-specific, and focused on relevant concrete and intangible qualities. In addition, they are legally defensible.

Interviewers should note that competency-based interviews do not consist entirely of competency-based questions: Chapter 8 will explore additional employment interview questioning techniques. Nevertheless, competency-based questions should represent about 70 percent of any interview, supplemented by other types of questions. They will improve the interview by:

- Identifying the skills and characteristics needed to succeed in a specific work environment
- Isolating the competencies required for a given job
- Earmarking relevant experiences necessary to have acquired these competencies
- Clarifying what applicants have learned from their experiences
- Determining whether applicants can apply what they have learned to a given job and work environment

Competency-Based Lead-Ins

When preparing competency-based questions, remember two things: They require specific examples concerning what the applicant has done in the past, and they should tie in directly with job-specific competencies.

That said, competency-based questions are among the easiest questions to formulate. If the job requires the ability to oversee a project, you could ask the applicant:

"Tell me about a time when you had to oversee a project: what was the extent of your responsibilities?"

"Tell me about a specific project you worked on; I'm interested in learning about the roles of everyone involved."

"What did you do in your last job to successfully complete a particularly difficult project?"

Or perhaps the job involves working extensively as a member of a team. The questions might include:

"Describe the circumstances under which you most recently worked as a member of a team."

"Tell me about a specific time when you worked as a member of a disparate team. How did you resolve any differences that arose?"

"Tell me about a specific instance in which you made suggestions that were not acted upon."

"Describe a time when you thought you should have led a team because of your knowledge or expertise, but someone else was selected. How did you feel and what did you do?"

Each of these competency-based questions is introduced by a lead-in phrase that alerts the applicant to an important fact: that you want specific examples. Here's a sampling of competency-based lead-ins:

"Describe a time when you . . ."

"Give an example of a situation in which you . . ."

"Tell me about an instance when you . . ."

"Tell me about a specific job experience in which you . . ."

"Give me an example of a specific occasion when you . . ."

"Describe a situation in which you were called upon to . . ."

"Describe the most significant . . ."

"What did you do in your last job in order to . . .?"

"Tell me about a time when you didn't want to _____; what happened?"

"Describe a situation in which you felt _____; what was the result?"

By the time you've asked the third or fourth competency-based question, applicants will realize that you expect a specific response whenever you begin with a lead-in phrase.

When to Ask Competency-Based Questions

Effective competency-based employment interviews are structured to ensure control by the interviewer and coverage of the four key competencies. They are also, as previously stated, legally defensible. For maximum effectiveness, competency-based interviews should consist of five stages: rapport building, introductory, core, confirmation, and closing. Each has a specific purpose and should take up a designated approximate percentage of the interview. Competency-based questions are highly effective in some stages, minimally effective in others, and relatively useless in others. A summary of the five interview stages, their approximate percentages of time, and the level of effectiveness in asking competency-based questions appears in Exhibit 7-1.

1. *Rapport building.* This is the stage during which applicants are encouraged to relax and feel at ease with the interviewer. Non-job-related topics are discussed, such as the weather or the applicant's commute. The rapport-building stage should

Exhibit 7-1. The Five Interview Stages

Stage	Purpose	Percentage of Time	Level of Effectiveness in Asking Competency-Based Questions
Rapport Building	Put applicant at ease	2 percent	None
Introductory	Beginning of applicant assessment	3 percent	Minimal
Core	Gather information about job-specific skills, knowledge, behavior, and interpersonal skills	85 percent	High
Confirmation	Verify information acquired thus far	5 percent	Minimal
Closing	Last chance for interviewer to cover relevant competencies	5 percent	High

represent approximately 2 percent of the interview. Competency-based questions are ineffective during this stage.

2. *Introductory.* The initial questions an interviewer poses are intended to help still-nervous applicants feel at ease. These questions should encourage the applicant to talk about a familiar topic, such as his current or most recent job. In addition, the first few questions should be broad enough to generate additional questions, as well as allowing the interviewer to begin assessing relevant verbal and organizational skills. This stage should represent about 3 percent of the interview. Competency-based questions during the introductory stage are minimally effective.

3. *Core.* During this segment interviewers gather information about job-specific skills, knowledge, behavior, and interpersonal skills. It allows for an examination of the applicant's past job performance and projects future performance based on explicit job-related examples. Interviewers can ultimately make hiring decisions based on facts as opposed to intuitive feelings. The core stage should represent approximately 85 percent of the interview, with as much as 65 percent of it devoted to competency-based questions. The effectiveness of asking competency-based questions in the core stage is high.

4. *Confirmation.* During this stage interviewers can verify what they learned about job-specific competencies during the core stage. Topics of discussion should be limited to those aspects of work experience and education already discussed during the core segment. The confirmation stage should represent approximately 5 per-

cent of the interview. The effectiveness of asking competency-based questions in the confirmation stage is minimal.

5. *Closing*. This final stage is the interviewer's opportunity to ensure that she has covered all relevant competencies needed to make an effective hiring decision. It is also the applicant's last chance to sell himself—to say how and why he would be an asset to the organization. The closing stage should represent approximately 5 percent of the interview, with most to all of it taken up with competency-based questions. The effectiveness of asking competency-based questions in this stage is high.

Developing Competency-Based Questions

The information you've gathered through job descriptions and other sources, combined with the applicant's background, will yield a great deal of information about a possible job match—if you know how to phrase your questions properly. Since nearly three-quarters of an interview involves asking for specific examples related to past job performance, interviewers need to convert topics about which they seek information into competency-based questions. Note that it's not always necessary to ask questions in the interrogative form; statements can often be just as effective.

Developing competency-based questions or statements is best accomplished by first listing the primary duties and responsibilities of the job. Let's assume there's an opening for an assistant to the director of human resources. A partial list of tasks reads as follows:

- Recruits and interviews applicants for nonexempt positions; refers qualified applicants to appropriate department managers.
- Performs reference checks on potential employees.
- Helps director of human resources plan and conduct each month's organizational orientation program.
- Assists in the implementation of policies and procedures; may be required to explain or interpret certain policies.
- Assists in the development and maintenance of up-to-date job descriptions for nonexempt positions throughout the company.
- Assists in the maintenance and administration of the organization's compensation program; monitors salary increase recommendations as they are received to ensure compliance with merit increase guidelines.

Now isolate the first task: *"Recruits and interviews applicants for nonexempt positions; refers qualified applicants to appropriate department managers."*

Refer to the list of competency-based lead-ins listed (previously in this chapter) and attach them to components of this task. Here's what you'll get with very little effort:

"Describe a time when you had a nonexempt position open for an unusually long period of time; how did you eventually fill it?"

"Give an example of a time during which you referred an applicant to a department manager whom you believed should have been hired, but your referral was rejected. How did you resolve your differences with that manager?"

"Tell me about a time when you had more applicants than you could handle."

"Tell me about a specific job experience in which you hired someone who later didn't work out."

♪ "Give me an example of a specific occasion when you and a department head didn't agree on the requirements for a nonexempt opening. What happened?"

♪ "Describe a situation in which you were called upon to fill several openings in one department simultaneously."

"Describe the most significant recruiting experience you've had to date."

"What did you do in your last job to convince a department head to hire someone?"

"How often in the last year were you called upon to recruit for especially hard-to-fill openings? Tell me about those openings and what ultimately happened."

"Tell me about a time when you didn't want to continue using a long-time recruiting source; what happened?"

"Describe a situation in which you felt uneasy with the answers given by a particular applicant; what was the end result?"

Of course, you don't have to use all the lead-ins and you can substitute some with your own. This is exemplified with the remaining tasks, beginning with the second task, *"Performs reference checks on potential employees."*

"Describe your process of conducting references. How do you follow up with former employers who fail to respond to your inquiries?"

"Describe a time when you received negative references on an applicant that the department manager wanted to hire anyway; what happened?"

"Tell me about a time when you went back to an applicant with a negative reference and asked if he could explain why he felt the former employer had given the poor reference."

"Tell me about a reference that sounded too good to be true and later turned out to be just that."

"Tell me how you go about obtaining references with former employers who will only verify dates of employment?"

"Tell me some of the questions you ask former employers to determine job suitability."

"Describe a situation in which you received conflicting references from two of an applicant's former employers; what did you do?"

"Tell me about a time when you called the former manager of an applicant your company was interested in hiring and she referred you to the HR department."

"How do you handle the verification of school records? Please give me an example of a specific time when you applied this method; what happened?"

"Tell me about a time when an applicant apparently falsified educational credentials; what did you do?"

"Describe an instance in which you received negative references on an applicant after she had already started work; what happened?"

The next task is *"Helps director of human resources plan and conduct each month's organizational orientation program."* Here are some questions using competency-based lead-ins:

"What did you do in your last job to ensure that the orientation program ran smoothly and effectively?"

"Tell me about a time when you were asked questions during orientation to which you did not have answers."

"Describe an instance when speakers you had lined up as part of orientation didn't show up, printed materials weren't ready, or something went wrong with the equipment. What did you do?"

"Tell me some of the things you did in preparation for your first orientation that you no longer do; why have you stopped?"

"Describe the relationship between you and the other orientation developers and participants."

"Tell me about a time when you didn't follow up with orientation attendees who were required to provide feedback; what happened?"

"Tell me about some ideas you might have had for making the orientation experience more meaningful and more helpful to new hires that were adopted; how about some ideas that were not considered."

The next area to probe is *"Assists in the implementation of policies and procedures; may be required to explain or interpret certain policies."* Some useful competency-based questions include:

"Tell me about your role in implementing and interpreting HR policies and procedures for employees."

"What is the nature of some of the calls you receive from employees with regard to policies and procedures?"

"Describe a situation in which an employee required additional information about an HR policy and became upset with the explanation. What did you do?"

"Has there ever been a time when an employee challenged the accuracy of a policy or procedure? Tell me about it."

"Give me an example of a specific occasion when a longtime policy was revised. What was your role?"

"Describe a company policy or procedure that generates the most questions or concerns. Why do you think that is?"

For *"Assists in the development and maintenance of up-to-date job descriptions for nonexempt positions throughout the company,"* the following competency-based questions will be helpful:

"Describe your responsibilities when it comes to developing job descriptions."

"Tell me about some of the job categories for which you are responsible."

"Describe how you gather information for job descriptions."

"Tell me about a time when you had difficulty developing a job description. Why do you think that was?"

"Have you ever been in a situation where the incumbents and their managers described a job differently? What was the outcome?"

"How do you ensure that job descriptions remain up to date?"

"Give me an example of a specific occasion when a job's responsibilities, its corresponding grade, and salary range did not seem to coincide. What happened?"

"What do you do to improve your proficiency in developing and maintaining accurate job descriptions?"

The final area is *"Assists in the maintenance and administration of the organization's compensation program; monitors salary increase recommendations as they are received to ensure compliance with merit increase guidelines."* Consider asking:

"Describe your responsibilities in relation to your organization's compensation program."

"Tell me how performance appraisals relate to salary increases."

"Tell me about a time when you received a salary increase recommendation from a department head for an employee whose documented job performance was below average."

"Describe the most challenging aspect of your compensation responsibilities."

"Give me a specific example of a time when an employee objected to the amount of his recommended increase. What was your role in resolving the dispute?"

"Describe a time when an employee was already at the top of her range, but whose performance warranted a raise. What happened?"

These six tasks alone resulted in dozens of questions that will yield a great deal of job-related information, reflecting all four competency categories. Additionally, by practicing active listening skills (Chapter 9), the applicant's answers to these questions are likely to result in even more job-specific questions.

With the half-dozen or so preplanned questions described in Chapter 5, and information contained in the job description, applicant's application, and resume, competency-based questions should flow freely during the interview.

Formulating these questions is painless and the process is highly productive, enabling you to make an effective hiring decision.

Generic Competency-Based Questions

Among the most effective competency-based questions are those that are generated by job descriptions and resumes/applications. These provide a direct correlation between the position and the applicant. Sometimes, though, interviewers need to explore other aspects of an applicant's eligibility to provide a complete picture of how well an applicant will fit within the corporate culture, contribute to a team, or function under the direction of a certain management style. Job-specific competency-based questions may not be sufficient to determine whether this fit exists.

Isolating some key, job-related categories and posing a series of generic competency-based questions can help provide the balance needed to ultimately identify the best overall fit for a job.

Exempt Categories and Competency-Based Questions

Here is a list of generic categories that apply to many exempt positions and a series of related competency-based questions:

Decision Making

● "Tell me about a time when you had to make an unpopular decision; what was the outcome?"

● "Describe a time when you were angry about an unfair decision; how did you react?

"Give me an example of a time when you made a decision that didn't turn out the way you'd planned; what happened? What, if anything, would you do differently?"

"Tell me about a decision you had to make to meet an unrealistic deadline; what happened?"

"Tell me about the most productive decision you've ever made. Now tell me about the most unproductive decision you've ever made."

Problem Solving

● "Tell me about a recent problem at work; how did you resolve it?"

● "What did you do in your last job to encourage your staff to resolve their own problems?"

"Describe the most challenging problem you've had to resolve at your current job; what made it challenging and how did you resolve it?"

● "Give me an example of what you initially perceived as a problem but later turned out not to be."

"Describe a situation in which you felt overwhelmed by a problem; what was the outcome?"

Communication

"Describe a time when you had to made a presentation to senior management; how did you prepare?"

"Give me an example of a time when you made a presentation and were asked questions to which you didn't have the answers. What did you do?"

"Tell me about a time when you were compelled to communicate bad news to an employee. What were the circumstances? What happened?"

"Describe how you keep staff apprised of goings-on in the department and company-wide. Tell me about one time when this form of communication broke down; what was the outcome of the breakdown?"

"Describe a situation in which you were called upon to write a report and the contents were misinterpreted; what happened next?"

Delegation

"Tell me about a time when you delegated tasks to a staff member who failed to follow through. What happened?

"Describe an instance in which you opted to perform a task outside the scope of your job description rather than delegate it."

"Give me an example of a time when you delegated a long-term project. How did you determine and communicate who would perform certain tasks?

"Give me an example of a time when an employee complained about a task you delegated; what happened?"

Time Management

"Describe a time when the amount of time you'd set aside for a task proved insufficient; how did you compensate?"

"Tell me about an instance when you had to meet several crucial deadlines simultaneously."

"Give me an example of a specific occasion when you were unable to meet a deadline. What, if anything, would you do differently?"

"How do you ensure that you always have enough time to accomplish your work? Describe a time when you applied this approach and it worked; now tell me about a time when it didn't work; what happened?"

"Tell me how you prioritize your assignments and budget your time."

"Think of a time when you had a number of people working on different aspects of a project; now describe the timeline you developed for completion and how you ensured that each stage was being met."

Nonexempt Categories and Competency-Based Questions

Here's a list of generic categories that apply to many nonexempt positions and a series of related competency-based questions:

Ability to Follow Instructions

"Tell me about a time when you were given instructions but had difficulty following them."

"Describe a time when you were given incomplete instructions; what did you do?"

"Tell me about a specific instance in which you were given instructions that didn't make sense, but you hesitated to ask for clarification; what happened?"

"Describe a situation in which you disagreed with instructions for completing a task."

"Give me an example of the type of instructions that you find easiest to follow; most difficult."

Telephone Skills

"Tell me about a specific job experience in which an irate customer kept calling your boss, who told you to 'handle it'; what did you do?"

"Describe a time when your supervisor said the information you recorded on a call slip was incomplete or incorrect."

"Give me an example of a time when you had trouble understanding someone on the phone."

"Tell me about an instance when you had a great deal of work to do but the phones kept ringing; what did you do?"

"Tell me about a time when a particular member of management called your supervisor to complain about how you spoke with her; what happened?"

Juggling Multiple Tasks

"Tell me about a time when you were given assignments by several supervisors, all due at the same time; how did you prioritize the work?"

"Describe an instance when you thought you'd been given too much work to do."

"Tell me about a situation whereby you didn't want to work overtime, but you knew it would be the only way you were going to get all your work done. What did you do?"

"Give me an example of a time when you felt you were being asked to juggle more tasks than everyone else in the department."

"Describe an occasion when your supervisor expressed appreciation for how well you juggled multiple tasks."

Exempt and Nonexempt Categories and Competency-Based Questions

Here is a list of generic categories that may apply to both exempt and nonexempt positions and a series of related competency-based questions:

Ideal Work Environment

"Tell me about the best work environment in which you've ever worked; how did it compare with your concept of the ideal work environment? Now tell me about the worst work environment in which you've ever worked; how did it compare with your concept of the ideal work environment?"

"Tell me about three aspects of your current work environment that you would change if you could."

"Describe a task you've been asked to perform in a less-than-ideal environment. How did you cope?"

"Give me an example of a job that on the surface appeared to be ideal, but later turned out to be far less than ideal."

"Tell me about a time when you didn't want to take a job because of the work environment, but you were later glad you did."

Employer/Employee or Coworker Relations

"Give me an example of a time when you had to deal with a difficult coworker. How did you handle the situation?"

"Tell me about the most productive employer-employee relationship you've ever had. What made it so productive? How about the least productive employer-employee relationship?"

"Tell me about a time in your current job when you made a suggestion about a better way to perform a process. What was your employer's reaction? How did it affect your relationship?"

"Tell me about a specific instance in which you felt a coworker took credit for your work; what did you do?"

"Describe a meeting during which your coworker blamed you, in front of your boss, for an error that you hadn't made."

Strengths and Areas Requiring Improvement

"Tell me about a time when you were able to convert an area requiring improvement into a strength."

"What did you do in your last job to improve one particular area requiring improvement?"

"Identify three of your greatest strengths and tell me about three separate occasions in which you were able to apply them."

"Describe a situation in which an area requiring improvement adversely impacted your coworkers. What would you do differently if given the opportunity?"

"Which of your strengths do you apply when faced with a crisis?"

Working Under Pressure

"What do you do at work to relieve stress?"

"Tell me about a time when you made mistakes because you were working under too much pressure. What was the outcome?"

"Describe an instance in which you thrived working under pressure. Please be specific."

"Please provide your personal definition of what working under pressure means; give me an example of when those circumstances prevailed at your last job; how did you handle the pressure?"

"Tell me about a specific job experience in which you were working under pressure because of ineffective leadership. What did you do?"

Motivation

"Tell me about a job that provided a motivating environment; please describe that environment in detail."

"Describe an aspect of your current job that you find especially motivating."

"Tell me how you motivate yourself to perform tasks you dislike."

"Describe a situation in which you felt unmotivated. What happened? What, if anything, did you do to feel more motivated?"

Summary

A competency is a skill, trait, quality, or characteristic that contributes to a person's ability to effectively perform the duties and responsibilities of a job. Identifying job-specific competencies enables you to assess how effective a person has been in the past and therefore how effectively she is likely to perform in your organization. There are four primary competency categories: tangible or measurable skills, knowledge, behavior, and interpersonal skills. Most jobs emphasize the need for one category over the others, but every employee should be able to demonstrate competencies to some extent in all four categories. Every job also requires a set of specific competencies, based on its individual requirements and responsibilities.

Competency-based questions focus on relating past job performance to probable future on-the-job behavior. The questions are based on information relevant to specific job-related skills, abilities, and traits; the answers reveal the likelihood of similar future performance. The process works because past behavior is an indicator of future behavior.

Competency-based questions seek specific examples and are introduced by lead-in phrases that alert applicants to this end. They are also structured, job-specific, and legally defensible. Hence, you are able to make hiring decisions based on facts.

Competency-based questions should constitute about 70 percent of any interview, supplemented by other types of questions.

For maximum effectiveness, competency-based interviews should consist of five stages: rapport building, introductory, core, confirmation, and closing. Each has a specific purpose and should take up a designated approximate percentage of the interview.

Although the most effective competency-based questions are generated by job descriptions and resumes/applications, interviewers may need to explore other aspects of an applicant's eligibility to provide a complete picture of how well an applicant will fit within an organization's culture. Isolating some key job-related categories and posing a series of generic competency-based questions can help provide the balance needed to ultimately identify the best overall fit for a job.

CHAPTER 8

Additional Types of Questions

A former student of mine who had completed one of my courses on interviewing skills sent me an e-mail about three months later, reporting that he's been able to apply much of what he'd learned. He commented that at the time, he'd thought I was making too big a deal about the importance of asking different types of questions, that initially he'd seen nothing wrong with simply asking, "Tell me about yourself." I wrote back that I was delighted he'd found the class useful and queried, "What's the most important thing you learned about asking questions during an employment interview?" His response came back immediately: "I learned that any thought can be expressed in a number of different ways. The wording you choose will determine how much information you receive and how useful that information is in making a hiring decision."

I knew he was copying that statement from his notes, but I didn't care. His response demonstrated an understanding of the power of words during an interview and how extensively the wording of a question impacted the end result. I was also thrilled that he no longer used the "Tell me about yourself" question, which I consider to be among the worst ever asked. It lacks direction and structure and invites applicants to volunteer illegal information.

I wrote back, "Good for you, your organization, and all the applicants you interview! Can you impress me further by telling me the types of questions you ask?" I received his answer within minutes: "In addition to posing competency-based questions during most of the interview, I present open-ended, hypothetical, probing, and some closed-ended questions. And even though you didn't ask, I'll tell you what questioning techniques I avoid: trait, multiple choice, and forced choice, because these types of questions usually result in meaningless or misleading information."

Once again, I recognized my own words, and as before, it didn't matter. He'd walked into my class believing that the wording of questions was irrelevant and left appreciating the role well-worded questions play in the selection process. Mission accomplished.

Open-Ended Questions

By definition, open-ended questions require full, multiple-word responses. The answers generally lend themselves to discussion and result in information upon which the interviewer can build additional questions. Open-ended questions encourage applicants to talk, allowing the interviewer an opportunity to actively listen to responses, assess verbal communication skills, and observe the applicant's pattern of nonverbal communication. It also allows the interviewer time to plan subsequent questions. Open-ended questions are especially helpful in encouraging shy or withdrawn applicants to talk without the pressure that can accompany a competency-based question requiring the recollection of specific examples.

The partial interview with a customer representative applicant in Chapter 5 illustrates these points. His answer to the open-ended question, "Would you please describe your activities during a typical day at your present job?" was vague: "Well, let's see. Each day is really kind of different since I deal with customers and you never know what they're going to call about; but basically, my job is to handle the customer hotline, research any questions, and process complaints." However, it yielded four categories for additional questions:

1. His job requires dealing with a variety of people and situations.
2. He "handles" a customer hotline.
3. He "researches" questions.
4. He "processes" complaints.

Many of the follow-up questions were open-ended:

"What is the nature of some of the situations with which you are asked to deal?"
"Who are the people who call you?"
"What is the process that someone with a complaint is supposed to follow?"
"What is your role in this process?"
"Exactly what is the customer hotline?"
"When you say that you 'handle' the hotline, exactly what do you mean?"
"What do you say to a customer who calls on the hotline?"
"What do you say to a customer who calls with a specific question?"

"What do you do when a customer is not satisfied with the answer you have given him?

"How do you prepare for each day, knowing that you will probably have to listen to several people complaining about a variety of problems?"

Bear in mind that asking open-ended questions such as these allows applicants to control the answers. Such inquiries are most helpful, then, when used to form a foundation for competency-based questions that direct an applicant to provide specific responses supplemented by examples. Take one of the open-ended questions just listed: "What do you do when a customer is not satisfied with the answer you've given him?" That's a perfectly legitimate question relative to the responsibilities of a customer service representative. The applicant may reply, "I tell them I'm sorry they're dissatisfied with my answer and that I wish I could be more helpful." That generic answer tells you little about how this applicant interacts with customers—the essence of his job. Now is the time to follow up with a competency-based question: "Give me a specific example of when this happened." The applicant must now draw from a real situation involving her interaction with a customer. The information her answer yields will help you evaluate a critical job-related skill.

Open-ended questions, then, can result in descriptive monologues, lacking substance or verifiable information. Without further probing, such responses are not useful in painting an accurate picture of an applicant's job suitability.

Any open-ended question can be made more substantive by converting it into or supporting it with a competency-based question. For example, "How would you describe your ability to deal with difficult customers?" is open-ended. The competency-based version reads, "Describe a situation in which an irate customer held you responsible for something that was not your fault; what did you do?"

There are two additional possible problems with open-ended questions. The applicant's response may include information that is irrelevant or that violates EEO laws. As soon as this occurs, the interviewer must bring the applicant back to the focus of the question. One way to do this is to say, "We seem to have strayed from the original question of why you left your last job. I'd like to get back to that." Another effective response might be, "That information is not job-related. Let's get back to your description of a typical day at the office." This is especially appropriate if information being volunteered has the potential for illegal use.

Another concern is that open-ended questions may be too broad in scope. The classic request "Tell me about yourself" illustrates this point. Questions that require applicants to summarize many years in a single response are also not effective. An example of this would be "Describe your work history" when you are addressing an applicant who has worked for more than thirty years. Instead, say, "Please describe your work experience over the past five years." This is still open-ended, but it establishes useful boundaries.

Here are further examples of generic, work-related, open-ended questions. Note that in those instances where several questions appear as one, they are intended to be asked separately. Also, the effectiveness of many of these queries would be enhanced if they were followed up with competency-based questions. For example, consider the first open-ended question: "What is your description of the ideal manager?" For maximum effectiveness, the interviewer could then ask, "Tell me about a time when you worked for someone you initially perceived as being the ideal manager, but ultimately was not. What changed?" "Describe someone who was far removed from being your idea of an ideal manager; what were some of the traits he exhibited?" "Tell me about the effect an ideal manager had on your work, as opposed to a manager who was less than ideal; please be specific." You get the idea.

Generic Open-Ended Questions Relating to Work Experience

"What is your description of the ideal manager? Employee? Coworker? Work environment? Work schedule?"

"How would you describe yourself as an employee? Coworker? Manager?"

"What kind of people do you find it difficult/easy to work with? Why?"

"What do you feel an employer owes an employee? How about what an employee owes an employer?"

"What were some of the duties of your last job that you found to be difficult? What made them difficult? What about duties that you found to be easy? What made them easy?"

"How do you feel about the progress that you've made in your career to date? Where are you career-wise in terms of where you thought you'd be five years ago? What happened?"

"How did your last job differ from the one you had before it? Which one was preferable? Why?"

"Of all the jobs you've had, which did you find the most/least rewarding? Why? What makes a job rewarding?"

"In what ways do you feel your present job has prepared you to assume additional responsibilities?"

"What does the prospect of this job offer you that your last job did not?"

"Why do you want to leave your current job?"

"What are you looking for in a company?"

"How does your experience in the military relate to your chosen field?"

"What immediate and long-term goals have you set for yourself?"

"What would you like to avoid in future jobs? Why?"

"What do you consider to be your greatest strength? What are the areas in which you require improvement? How would you go about making these improvements? What have you done thus far to make improvements?"

"What aspects of your work give you the greatest satisfaction?"

"How do you approach tasks you dislike? How does this approach differ from how you approach tasks you like?"

"How do you manage your time?"

"How do you go about making a decision?"

"What have past employers complimented/criticized you for?"

"What types of work-related situations make you feel most comfortable? Uneasy?"

"What is the most difficult/rewarding aspect of being a _____?"

"If you were asked to perform a task that was not in your job description, how would you respond?"

"How do you go about discussing job dissatisfaction with your boss?"

"What, if anything, could your previous employers have done to convince you not to leave?"

Generic Open-Ended Questions Relating to Education

Here are some additional open-ended questions, this time dealing with education:

"What were your favorite and least favorite subjects in high school/college? Why?"

"What subjects did you do best in? Poorest in?"

"Why did you decide to major in _____?"

"Why did you decide to attend _____?"

"What career plans did you have at the beginning of college? How did they change?"

"How did high school/college prepare you for the 'real world'? How did it fail to prepare you?"

"What did you gain by attending high school/college?"

"If you had the opportunity to attend school all over again, what, if anything, would you do differently?"

"How do you feel your studies in _____ have prepared you for this job?"

"Describe your study habits."

"Describe any part-time jobs you had while attending high school/college. Which of your part-time jobs did you find most/least interesting?"

"What advice would you give to someone who wanted to work and attend school at the same time?"

"What did you find to be most difficult about working and attending school at the same time?"

"What could the department head of the course you majored in have done to make the curriculum more interesting?"

"How did you approach required courses that were not of particular interest to you?"

"Describe what you consider to be characteristics of the ideal teacher."

Hypothetical Questions

Hypothetical questions are based on anticipated or known job-related tasks for the available opening. The questions are phrased in the form of problems and presented to the applicant for solutions. The questions are generally introduced with words and phrases like the following:

"What would you do if . . . ?"

"How would you handle . . . ?"

"How would you solve . . . ?"

"In the event that . . ."

"If . . ."
"Assuming . . ."
"How would you avoid . . . ?"
"Consider this scenario . . ."
"What would you say . . . ?"
"Suppose . . . ?"
"How would you go about . . . ?"

Hypothetical questions allow for the evaluation of reasoning abilities, thought processes, values, attitudes, creativity, work style, and one's approach to different tasks.

Although the answers to hypothetical questions can produce important information, interviewers are cautioned against expecting correct answers. Without familiarity with the organization, applicants can offer responses based only on their previous experiences. Such answers, then, are based on how they think rather than what they know.

An important distinction between hypothetical and competency-based questions is that hypotheticals ask applicants to project what they might do in a fictitious, albeit realistic, scenario, whereas competency-based questions draw from the actual experiences of the applicant. The former is based on conjecture, the latter on fact.

Consider the distinction between two differently worded questions on the subject of unreasonable work demands. The first example is worded as a hypothetical question:

> **"If you were a manager and your team complained about having to meet some unreasonable demands presented by one of the company's top clients, how would you go about satisfying both the client and your staff?"**

Now let's reword the question to be competency-based:

> **"Tell me about a time when, as a manager, your team complained about having to meet some unreasonable demands presented by one of the company's top clients; how did you go about satisfying both the client and your staff?"**

The wording of the first question directs the applicant toward the realm of possibilities. She is likely to answer using words like "I would" or "I could." There is no way of knowing if she's providing you with what she believes is a good answer and the one you want to hear, or if this is actually what she would do. In the second question, however, she must draw from a real situation and describe what happened. Could she make something up? Sure, it's possible, but applicants can't be certain as to what you already know or what can be confirmed. It's more difficult to lie about something that can be checked out than it is to speculate about something that has not yet happened.

Naturally, the competency-based version requires a similar experience to draw from. If, after reviewing the applicant's resume, you're unclear as to whether the applicant has experienced a similar situation in the past, word the question this way:

> **"As a manager, have you ever been in a situation where your team complained about having to meet some rather unreasonable demands presented by one of the company's top clients? If so, how did you go about satisfying both the client and your staff? If not, draw from your expertise as a manager and imagine such a scenario; what would you do to satisfy both the client and your staff?"**

Here are additional samples of hypothetical questions:

- "How would you handle an employee who was consistently tardy?"

"How would you go about discussing job dissatisfaction with your boss?"

- "How would you handle a long-term employee whose performance has always been outstanding, but who recently has started to make a number of mistakes in his work?"

"What would you say to an employee who challenged your authority?"

"What would you do if an employee went over your head?"

"Consider this scenario: You've just given a presentation and are asked a series of answers to which you do not know the answers. What would you do?"

"Suppose you are a member of a team and disagree with the way the others want to approach a project; how would you go about trying to change their minds?"

"How would you address an employee whose personal problems are interfering with her work performance?"

"If you were given a task that created an undue amount of pressure, what would you do?"

"How would you avoid conflict with coworkers? Your employees? Your manager? Clients?"

Hypothetical questions are also appropriate for applicants with limited or no work experience, such as graduating students. They are also helpful in interviews for jobs with little or no tangible requirements.

Probing Questions

These are questions that enable interviewers to delve more deeply for additional information. Best thought of as follow-up questions, they are usually short and simply worded. There are three types of probing questions:

1. *Rational probes* request reasons, using short questions such as "Why?" "How?" "When?" "How often?" and "Who?"

2. *Clarifier probes* are used to qualify or expand upon information provided in a previous response, using questions such as "What caused that to happen?" "Who else was involved in that decision?" "What happened next?" and "What were the circumstances that resulted in that happening?"

3. *Verifier probes* check out the honesty of a statement. For example, "You state on your resume that you currently work closely with the officers from your customers' firms; please tell me exactly what you have done for them."

Applicants who have trouble providing full answers usually appreciate the extra help that comes from a probing question. These also show the applicant you're interested in what she's saying and want to learn more.

Interviewers are cautioned against asking too many probing questions consecutively, as they tend to make applicants feel defensive. In addition, try to show interest with your accompanying body language. Do this by maintaining eye contact, nodding, and smiling. Avoid staring or raising your eyebrows, as these gestures can suggest disapproval.

Here are additional examples of *rational probing questions:*

"What kind of people do you find it difficult/easy to work with? *Why?*"

"Do you take over for your manager when she is away? *How often?*"

"What motivates you? *Why?*"

"What is the greatest accomplishment of your career to date? *Why?*"

These further illustrate *clarifier probing questions:*

"Who or what has influenced you with regard to your career goals? *In what way?*"

"You said earlier that your team failed to meet the last deadline; *what do you believe caused that to happen?*"

"Before you said that you were part of the decision to revamp your company's compensation structure; *who else was involved in that decision?*"

"You've described part of what took place when your company downsized; *what happened next?*"

"What are some of the problems you encountered in your last job? *How did you resolve them?*"

"Please give me an example of a project that did not turn out the way you planned. *What happened?*"

"What is your definition of company loyalty? *How far does it extend?*"

Additional examples of *verifier probing questions* include:

"What would your former manager say about how you handled the Grisham deal?"

"How would your former employees describe your management style?"

"What would your coworkers say about your contributions to the last team project you participated in?"

"Earlier you stated that you led a team from your company that had linked up with a team from World Energies, Inc. to work on developing a new communications device. Tell me about the roles and responsibilities of three specific members from World Energies."

Closed-Ended Questions

These are questions that may be answered with a single word—generally yes or no. Closed-ended questions can be helpful in a number of ways: They give the interviewer greater control; put certain applicants at ease; are useful when seeking clarification; are helpful when you need to verify information; and usually result in concise responses. Also, if there is a single issue that could terminate the interview, such as the absence of an important job requirement, then asking about it up front in a direct, closed-ended way can disclose what you need to know quickly and succinctly.

Interviewers should avoid relying on closed-ended questions for the bulk of their information about an applicant's job suitability. Except under certain circumstances, answers to closed-ended questions provide limited information, resulting in an incomplete picture of the person's abilities and experiences. Also, you will be unable to assess the applicant's verbal communication skills if they are relevant.

Ask closed-ended questions to serve the functions described above, but not as a substitute for open-ended or competency-based questions. Any question that can be answered by a single word can be converted into an open-ended question. For example, "Did you find your last job to be rewarding?" can easily be changed to "What aspects of your last job did you find to be especially rewarding?" In most instances, the information yielded by the open-ended version will be more valuable.

Closed-ended questions can also be converted into competency-based questions. Asking, "Have you done a good amount of public speaking?" will result in a single-word answer and tell you little about the applicant's experience with public speaking. The open-ended version of this question, while better, still doesn't tell you much: "What is your experience with public speaking?" Making this a competency-based question, however, will provide you with a job-related, detailed response: "Tell me about a time when you had to address a large audience. How did you prepare for it?"

Here are examples of functional, closed-ended questions relating to work:

"How often do you travel in your current job?"

"Are you aware that the starting salary for this job is $1,200 per week?"

"Based on what you have told me so far, am I correct in understanding that you prefer working independently rather than as part of a team?"

"How many times did you step in for your manager in the last three months?"

"Earlier you said that the most challenging part of your job is conducting new hire orientations; just before you indicated you favor conducting interviews. Am I to understand that you consider the two areas to be equally rewarding?"

Here are examples of functional, closed-ended questions relating to education:

"What subject did you do best in? Poorest in?"

"What did you major in? Minor in?"

"How many hours a weeks did you work while carrying a full credit load in college?"

"What was your grade-point average in your favorite subject? Least favorite subject?"

Questioning Techniques for Different Stages of the Interview

Chapter 7 identified the five stages of a competency-based interview: rapport-building, introductory, core, confirmation, and closing. Competency-based questions make up as much as 65 percent of the core stage and the entire 5 percent of the closing. The remaining 30 percent of the interview is divided between open-ended, hypothetical, probing, and closed-ended questions.

Rapport-Building Stage

This stage, representing a scant but important 2 percent of the interview, sets the tone for the rest of the meeting. The purpose is to put applicants at ease, thereby encouraging them to communicate openly and allowing you to determine job suitability. Closed-ended questions that are casual in nature and focus on non-job-related topics will accomplish this goal.

Here are some examples of neutral, rapport-building, closed-ended questions:

"Did you have any trouble getting here?"

"Were you able to find parking nearby?"

"How was the traffic getting here?"

"Were the directions we gave you helpful?"

"Isn't it a beautiful day?"

"When you think it will stop raining?"

"What do you think about this string of 80 degree days we're having in late October?"

As you can see, all these questions are about the same two topics: commuting and the weather. Boring? Perhaps. But they are clearly the safest areas to inquire about without running the risk of saying something controversial or job-related. Don't worry about being repetitious in asking the same set of rapport-building, closed-ended questions of every applicant; they're not likely to compare notes with one another after their interviews. Chapter 9 will further discuss establishing rapport.

Introductory Stage

As stated in Chapter 7, the introductory stage represents just 3 percent of the interview and is intended to accomplish two key objectives: to help still-nervous applicants feel at ease and to allow the interviewer to start assessing their job suitability. These objectives are best accomplished by posing two or three open-ended questions. This is the most effective type of question to ask at this stage because the applicant will begin talking and relax more, while you actively listen to their responses and start making some preliminary job-suitability decisions.

Introductory questions should be about topics familiar to the applicant, so as not to create undue pressure, and broad enough to generate additional questions by you. One question that satisfies both of these criteria is "Would you please describe your activities during a typical day at your current job?" This question can accomplish a great deal:

- It helps to relax a still-nervous applicant by allowing him to discuss a familiar subject.
- The open-ended nature of the question encourages the applicant to talk, giving you an opportunity to assess verbal and organizational skills.
- It allows you time to begin observing the applicant's pattern of body language.
- It provides information upon which you can build additional questions.

The question is not foolproof, however. An applicant could respond with, "Well, that's kind of hard to do. No day is really typical." If this happens, be a little more specific in your wording to help the applicant get started. Try adding, "I can appreciate that. Why don't you just pick a day—say yesterday—and describe what you did."

Once the applicant begins to outline specific tasks, you can interject, "Do you do that every day?" By breaking the question down and encouraging the applicant to talk, you should be able to get the required information and move on to the next question.

Additional effective open-ended questions to start off with include:

"Can you give me an overview of your past experiences with benefits administration?"

"Why don't we begin with your current job; would you describe your involvement in the day-to-day operation of your department?"

"In your job as a public relations manager, how do you go about preparing press releases?"

"Working as a legal assistant sounds very challenging; what are your primary responsibilities?"

"If you were asked to write a summary of your primary duties and responsibilities, what would you include?"

"I'm interested in learning more about what being an internal consultant entails; please tell me what you do in that capacity."

Core Stage

As the term implies, this is the most substantive segment of the interview. Here the interviewer gathers all relevant information about the applicant based on the four categories of tangible skills, knowledge, behavior, and interpersonal skills, examining them in relation to the requirements and responsibilities of the job. As stated in Chapter 7, this stage represents 85 percent of the interview, with as much as 65 percent of it devoted to competency-based questions. That leaves about 20 percent of the time to be divided between four other types of questions: closed-ended, open-ended, probing, and hypothetical. The last two should receive shared emphasis, say about 5 percent each, with open-ended questions receiving about 8 percent and closed-ended carrying the balance.

Closed-ended questions allow you to zero in on specific issues, usually for purposes of verification or clarification. They are useful when you need a tightly worded response in order to proceed with the interview.

Open-ended questions generally focus on how an applicant approaches tasks. They serve as effective setups for subsequent competency-based questions, testing out the validity of preceding answers.

Probing questions asked during the core of the interview will allow you to gather additional information from answers to competency-based, open-ended, and hypothetical questions. Their main function, whether rational, clarifier, or verifier in nature, is to allow you to delve deeper. Asking too many consecutive probing questions can come across as an interrogation. It also means you're not asking a sufficient number of substantive questions.

Hypotheticals lend balance to competency-based questions. While the latter focus on specific examples from past job experiences, hypotheticals present realistic job-related problems for solution. Where one is founded on facts, the other is based on supposition. Interviewers can compare what a person has done with what she might do, looking for similarities and further examining situations that stand out. Hypotheticals are also valuable for applicants with limited or no prior work history. Remember, hypotheticals evaluate how the applicant thinks as opposed to what she knows.

Consider this Chapter 7 reference to an opening for the assistant to the director of human resources. The partial list of tasks reads as follows:

- Recruits and interviews applicants for nonexempt positions; refers qualified applicants to appropriate department managers.

- Performs reference checks on potential employees.

- Helps director of human resources plan and conduct each month's organizational orientation program.

- Assists in the implementation of policies and procedures; may be required to explain or interpret certain policies.

- Assists in the development and maintenance of up-to-date job descriptions for nonexempt positions throughout the company.

- Assists in the maintenance and administration of the organization's compensation program; monitors salary increase recommendations as they are received to ensure compliance with merit increase guidelines.

We have already developed dozens of competency-based questions based on these six tasks. Now let's simulate a segment of the core stage, integrating open-ended, hypothetical, probing, and closed-ended questions to support the competency-based questions. Each question is identified by "CB" for competency-based, "OE" for open-ended, "H" for hypothetical, "P" for probing," and "CE" for closed-ended:

Interviewer: How would you describe your ability to handle a disagreement with a department head over the requirements for an opening? (OE)

Applicant: I'd like to think I'm pretty diplomatic.

Interviewer: Why don't you pick a situation that occurred recently; tell me about it. (CB)

Applicant: Well, we had an opening for a security guard at one of our branches two weeks ago. The branch manager wanted me to hire someone who was at least six feet tall and weighed more than two hundred pounds.

Interviewer: Why? (P)

Applicant: We'd had a string of attempted robberies at that branch; the manager thought someone who looked big and imposing would threaten would-be thieves.

Interviewer: What happened? (P)

Applicant: I explained that height and weight requirements had a greater negative impact on women and men of certain ethnic groups and therefore could not be justified.

Interviewer: How did the manager respond? (P)

Applicant: Not very well, actually. He insisted that height and weight requirements were job-related.

Interviewer: What did you say to that? (P)

Applicant: I said that if he could show me that, statistically, security guards who were at least six feet tall and weighed two hundred pounds were more successful in thwarting robbery attempts, then I would be able to use these as job requirements. Otherwise, I felt we were opening the company up to possible charges of discrimination.

Interviewer: And . . . ? (P)

Applicant: He backed off and realized what he was asking for was unrealistic. The job is still open, by the way.

Interviewer: Would you say that your rapport with the manager has been adversely affected by this exchange? (CE)

Applicant: No.

Here's another example:

Interviewer: How would you describe your skills in checking references on applicants under serious hiring consideration? (OE)

Applicant: Good.

Interviewer: Tell me about a time when you checked a reference on an applicant the department wanted to hire, only to find that the person's former employer had several less-than-favorable things to say about him? (CB)

Applicant: That's never happened.

Interviewer: Imagine that happening, if you will. How would you handle the situation? (H)

Applicant: Well, I'm not sure.

Interviewer: Okay. Let me ask you this: Have you ever received information from an applicant that conflicted with what was on the resume? (CE)

Applicant: Yes.

Interviewer: Think about one of the times that occurred and tell me what did you did. (CB)

Applicant: Oh, sure. Okay, I see what you're going for. I did a lot of probing and comparing of information till I uncovered the truth. In the situation you described, I guess I would ask a series of questions to determine if the former employer was being factual or had a bias.

Interviewer: What are some of the questions you would ask? (P)

Applicant: I'd ask for specific examples to back up his statements. Then I'd compare what he said with what I learned during the interview. I'd also try to contact more than one former employer to see if there was a pattern.

The combination of open-ended, hypothetical, probing, and closed-ended questions in support of competency-based questions in these two examples will allow the interviewer to better evaluate the applicant's job suitability.

Confirmation Stage

The confirmation stage offers the interviewer an opportunity to verify what she's learned thus far about an applicant's job-specific competencies; no new topics should be introduced. It represents about 5 percent of the entire interview and should be divided between open- and closed-ended questions, with a slightly heavier emphasis on open-ended. A competency-based question may occasionally be appropriate.

Consider these three closed-ended examples based on the interview for the assistant to the director of human resources interview described in the core stage:

1. "Based on what you have told me thus far, am I to understand that you view yourself as being diplomatic when it comes to handling disagreements with department heads?"

2. "Am I correct in understanding that you have not experienced checking a reference on an applicant the department wanted to hire, only to find that the person's former employer had several less-than-favorable things to say about him?"

3. "When we talked earlier about job descriptions, you stated that you assist in their development and maintenance. Is that for exempt and nonexempt job descriptions?"

The single-word answers to these questions will verify whether you have drawn accurate conclusions. The applicant will also have an opportunity to clarify any misunderstood points, if need be.

Sample open-ended questions during the confirmation stage for this same position include the following:

"I'm interested in learning more about your role in your company's monthly organizational orientation program. Would you please clarify for me the extent and nature of your responsibilities?"

"Earlier you stated that you currently assist in the implementation of policies and procedures; what exactly does that mean?"

"I need a clearer picture of when and to whom you explain or interpret these policies and procedures; would you give me some additional information about this?"

"Tell me more about your responsibilities vis-à-vis your organization's compensation program; specifically, tell me about monitoring salary increase recommendations in relation to compliance with merit increase guidelines."

Not only will these open-ended questions help clarify and confirm preceding information, they let the applicant know that you've been paying attention.

Closing Stage

This the "last chance" stage of the interview: the interviewer can ensure coverage of all relevant competencies needed to make a screening or hiring decision, and the applicant has one last opportunity to sell himself. It represents 5 percent of the interview and should be devoted to competency-based questions such as:

"What additional examples of your work with difficult customers would help me make a hiring decision?"

"Provide me with a specific example of your dealings with the GHK model that will help me understand your level of expertise in this area."

"What more can you tell me about your work with employee assistance programs that will illustrate your experience in this area?"

"What additional examples of your knowledge and/or expertise can you offer in support of your candidacy for this position?"

If applicants leave your office believing they've had every opportunity to present a complete and comprehensive picture of their job suitability, then it probably means you've acquired the information needed to determine a job match.

Questioning Techniques to Avoid

I once received a resume that I later dubbed my "ay! yai! yai!" resume. Three pages were devoted to a string of no less than fifty "I" statements: "I am analytical. . . ." "I have excellent interpersonal skills. . . ." "I am good at solving problems. . . ." and so on. At the end of the third page I still didn't know anything about the applicant's skills, abilities, or knowledge. That's because I had just finished reading a classic "trait" resume, that is, one that is big on meaningless rhetoric but short on substance.

Questions That Yield Trait Responses

Applicants may also provide trait responses during the interview as a substitute for specific examples. This is likely to happen in response to an open-ended question when an applicant lacks sufficient expertise and is hoping to impress you with fancy words and phrases. For example, if you were to ask, "What is your greatest strength?" the applicant could reply, "I excel at problem solving." Good question, good answer, right? Not really. What have your learned about the applicant? Absolutely nothing. If you want to know about a person's strengths, try the two-pronged approach. Ask the open-ended trait question first: "Describe your greatest strength," and then follow up with the competency-based question, "Give me an example of how you've used your greatest strength at your current job." Now if the applicant says, "I excel at problem solving" in response to the first question, she must back it up with a specific example. If she cannot back it up or if she rambles on with more rhetoric, you know she's giving you just so much verbiage.

Trait responses are also more likely to take you away from exploring a person's "darker side." Applicants naturally stress strengths and attributes, and interviewers have a tendency to focus on the positive, hoping for the perfect match. Consequently, relevant negative characteristics are overlooked, only to surface after the person has been hired. Interviewers are urged to explore negative information by asking competency-based questions that will provide evidence about past mistakes and problems. Additional open-ended, hypothetical, probing, and closed-ended questions in these areas will also give you a balanced picture of the applicant's strengths and areas requiring improvement.

When an applicant is bombarding you with self-praise it's hard to remember that the person probably can't do everything equally well. So as you ask about a person's strengths, examine the flip side and ask, "Tell me, what is about yourself that you would like to improve on? Specifically, tell me about a time when that characteristic surfaced and hindered your ability to achieve desired results."

Loaded or Multiple-Choice Questions

Another type of question to avoid is the loaded or multiple-choice question. Applicants should never feel forced to choose between two or more alternatives. That kind of setup implies that the correct answer is among the options you've offered, negating other possibilities. The applicant is likely to feel inhibited, and you're apt to miss out on valuable information.

Sometimes interviewers resort to loaded questions because they've lost control of the interview. If you want to regain control, ask a series of closed-ended questions, then return to more meaningful competency-based questions or one of the other types of questions described earlier in this chapter.

Consider the following examples of loaded questions—ones *not* to ask. Each one is paired with a rewording of the question that is more meaningful.

Don't Ask: "How do you go about delegating tasks: according to what a person has proven he can do, demonstrated interest, or random selection?"

Do Ask: "Describe how you go about delegating assignments. Give me an example of when you've done this."

Don't Ask: "Would you describe your management style as being proactive, reactive, controlling, or involved?"

Do Ask: "How would you describe your management style? Give me an example of how and when you've recently applied this style."

Don't Ask: "Would you say the greatest motivator for working is money or the pleasure one derives from doing a good job?"

Do Ask: "What would you say is the greatest motivator for working? Why do you think this is so?"

Don't Ask: "Would you describe your previous manager as easygoing or was she a stern taskmaster?"

Do Ask: "How would you describe your previous manager in terms of her work style and interaction with employees?"

Don't Ask: "Would you like to stay in this field for the rest of your career or do you think you would like to do something else?"

Do Ask: "What are your short- and long-term career goals?"

Leading Questions

Another type of question to avoid is the *leading question,* one that implies that there is a single correct answer. The interviewer sets up the question so that the applicant provides the desired response. Here are some examples of what *not* to ask:

"You do intend to finish college, don't you?"

"Don't you agree that most workers need to be watched very closely?"

"When you were in school, how much time did you waste taking art and music classes?"

It's obvious from the wording of these questions that the interviewer is seeking a particular reply. When leading questions are asked, the interviewer can't hope to learn anything substantive about the applicant.

Summary

Competency-based questions should be supplemented throughout the interview by a combination of open-ended, hypothetical, probing, and closed-ended questions. Open-ended questions, requiring full, multiple-word inquiries, are most meaningful when asked during the introductory, core, and confirmation stages. Most open-ended questions can be made more substantive when followed by competency-based questions. Hypothetical questions are based on anticipated or known job-related tasks, phrased in the form of problems and presented to the applicant for solutions. They evaluate a person's reasoning abilities and thought processes. Hypotheticals are suitable during the core stage of the interview. Probing questions are short and simply worded, allowing interviewers to delve more deeply for additional information. Like hypotheticals, they are reserved for the core stage. Closed-ended questions may be answered with a single word—usually yes or no. They should never be substituted for open-ended or competency-based questions. Closed-ended questions should constitute the rapport-building stage and contribute to the core and confirmation stages.

There are three types of questions interviewers should avoid asking: those that yield trait responses, loaded questions, and leading questions. Trait-generating questions result in answers that are filled with rhetoric but little substance. They also prohibit you from exploring negative information, that is, examining both an applicant's strengths and areas requiring improvement to provide a balanced picture. Loaded or multiple-choice questions offer limited options from which the applicant is forced to choose. And leading questions imply that there is a single correct answer.

CHAPTER 9

Interview Components

Many new as well as experienced interviewers prepare sufficiently for their meetings with applicants, but don't know how to proceed when they're face-to-face. What should they do first? Jump right in with the first question? If so, what should that first question be? Should they let the applicant start out by asking a few questions? Or perhaps the interviewer should begin by providing information about the job and the company; but won't that give too much away? Is there a correct order in which information should be provided and received? Maybe no one should say anything at the outset—should interviewers allow silence so the applicant can settle in and feel at ease? But isn't silence awkward? Won't that make the applicant feel even less comfortable? And once the process is underway, how can interviewers encourage applicants to continue talking but still keep them on track? Then there's the matter of ending the interview: Is there a point when interviewers know definitely that it's time to close?

These are all excellent questions concerning the components of an interview. Let's identify and explore these components and make some sense out of how to proceed with the face-to-face meeting.

Establish an Interview Format

Every interview requires a structured format. The format is beneficial to both interviewers and applicants. It provides interviewers with a checklist of sorts, ensuring coverage of all the necessary information and assuring applicants of a comprehensive exchange of information. The format of an interview should incorporate five critical phases:

1. *Making introductory remarks* concerning what is to take place during the interview.
2. *Asking questions* about an applicant's education and prior work history as they relate to the requirements of the job, as well as about relevant intangible categories.
3. *Providing information* about the job opening and its salary and benefits and about the organization.

4. *Answering questions* about the job and the organization.

5. *Informing the applicant as to what happens next* before ending the interview on a positive note.

The order in which interviewers cover these five phases is largely a matter of preference, with the exception of the first and last phases; telling the applicant what's about to take place obviously must occur at the outset, and informing the applicant as to what will happen following the interview needs to take place at the end.

Phase One: Making Introductory Remarks

Telling the applicant what's about to take place may seem unnecessary: both parties know it's a job interview. But the way this is conveyed sets the tone for the meeting and alerts the applicant as to what to expect over the next hour or so. Here's one example of how you might start out:

> "Good morning, Mr. Turner, my name is Dan King. I'm going to be interviewing you for the position of marketing representative with Walsh Enterprises. I'll begin by giving you an overview of the company and then ask you some questions about your background and qualifications. Then I'll describe the responsibilities of the job. At that point, I'll answer any questions you may have about the opening and the company. Before we end, I'll let you know what happens next and when you can expect to hear from me."

This is a highly structured approach that can come across as overly formal unless accompanied by the appropriate body language and tone of voice. Certainly, with this format there will be no doubt as to the content of the interview. New interviewers tend to favor this approach since it clearly conveys that the interviewer is in control.

Here's another example of how you might start things off:

> "Hi, Bob, I'm Dan King. I see you're applying for a marketing rep opening here at Walsh. Excellent! Why don't I talk a little bit about our company while you tell me some things about yourself. If you think of any questions as we're talking, just jump right in and ask me—no need to wait until the end."

This opening reflects a casual, unstructured approach, placing a greater onus on the applicant to be a partner in the interview process. Seasoned interviewers unconcerned about losing control of the meeting often opt for this approach.

Here's a third sampling of how to begin:

> "Hello, Mr. Turner; nice to meet you. I'm Dan King, vice president of human resources. As you know, we're here today to discuss your application for the marketing representative opening with

Walsh Enterprises. We'll do that by talking about your experience
and qualifications, the job itself, and our organization. I encourage you to ask any questions you might have; it's important that
we're both on the same page in terms of what the job entails and
what we're looking for in our next marketing rep. Before you leave
I'll let you know the next step."

This is a softer approach, but no less thorough. The specific components are
blended together so that the order in which areas are going to be covered is unclear.
The applicant understands that the interview will be comprehensive, that the interviewer is in the driver's seat, and that he needs to pay attention to ensure getting
the most out of the session. As with the previous example, this approach is best
used by interviewers with a fairly high level of confidence in their ability to maintain
control of the meeting.

Some interviewers have a preferred opening that they use consistently. Others
are flexible, quickly assessing an applicant's general composure and comfort level
prior to beginning and adjusting their approach accordingly. Practice and develop a
style that works best for you. It's as important that you're comfortable with the
format as it is for the applicant to feel at ease.

Phase Five: Informing the Applicant as to What Happens Next

Before looking at phases two, three, and four, let's turn to the final stage—telling an
applicant what happens after the interview is over. This is the other aspect of the
format that has a fixed place. Do this when you're sure you have all the information
needed to make an informed decision. Just as some interviewers have trouble knowing how to begin interviews, others are uncertain how to end them. To help you
decide if it's time to close an interview, ask yourself the following questions:

- Have I asked the applicant enough questions about his education and previous experience to determine job suitability?
- Have I adequately described the available position and provided sufficient
  information about this organization?
- Have I discussed salary, benefits, growth opportunities, and other related
  topics to the extent the policy of this company permits?
- Have I allowed the applicant to ask questions?

As with the first stage, what you say at the conclusion of an interview may seem
obvious: "We still have several applicants to consider; we'll be in touch when we've
completed the interviews," or some variation thereof, seems sufficient. But there's
more that can be said or implied, depending on your level of interest in the applicant.
Consider these possibilities:

High Level of Interest

"Thank you for coming in today, Mr. Turner. I've enjoyed talking with you and
learning about your qualifications. I'd like to confirm your continued interest in this

job before continuing (pause while, presumably, the applicant replies affirmatively). As the next step in the interview process, I'd like to arrange for you to meet with our vice president of marketing. I'll call you by the end of the week with a date and time. Meanwhile, please feel free to call me with any questions you may have. Once again, thank you for your time."

Moderate Level of Interest

"Thank you for coming in today, Mr. Turner. I found our meeting to be quite informative. We're in the process of interviewing a number of qualified applicants and hope to reach a decision within the next several weeks. Please feel free to call me with any questions in the interim. You'll be hearing from me, regardless of our decision."

Low Level of Interest

"Thank you for coming in today, Mr. Turner, and for allowing me to review your qualifications for the position of marketing representative. It's been most informative. We're nearing the end of our interviewing process and expect to be reaching a decision by the beginning of next week. I'll contact you at that time. Please feel free to call me if you have any questions."

Each of these closings, even the one reflecting a low level of interest, has a positive tone. That's important from a public relations standpoint; you never know if you'll be considering a rejected applicant for another position or if he might refer a friend. However, notice the distinction in the wording between the three closings. The closing for the applicant for whom there is a high level of interest is the only one that commits to a subsequent interview, revealing continued interest. The closing for the applicant for whom there is a moderate level of interest leaves the door open by allowing an indeterminate period of time before reaching a decision. The closing for the applicant for whom there is a low level of interest identifies a short period of time by which he will be notified.

Phases Two, Three, and Four: Asking Questions, Answering Questions, and Providing Information

Interviewers have flexibility with regard to the order of phases two, three, and four. Here are some popular options:

Option #1

- Make introductory remarks
- Ask questions
- Answer questions
- Provide information
- Inform the applicant as to what happens next

Asking questions immediately following your opening remarks gives you an advantage in that the applicant can't parrot anything he's heard you say about the job as part of his answers. This approach also reveals the applicant's knowledge of the company. It can, however, be unnerving for applicants feeling uneasy and in need of more time to settle in.

Option #2

- Make introductory remarks
- Provide information
- Answer questions
- Ask questions
- Inform the applicant as to what happens next

With the interviewer doing most of the talking at the beginning of the interview, applicants are likely to feel more at ease. Providing too much information before applicants can describe their capabilities, however, may give away the job and feed applicants key information. For example, interviewers may inadvertently describe the kind of person they're looking for to such an extent that an applicant simply repeats this information later on in the interview when describing his skills. If the interviewer is unaware of what he's done, he may erroneously assume that he's just found the ideal applicant.

Option #3

- Make introductory remarks
- Answer questions
- Ask questions
- Provide information
- Inform the applicant as to what happens next

Some interviewers like to invite applicants to ask questions before proceeding. This provides some insight as to the person's current level of knowledge about the job and the company. In all fairness, however, your statements may generate many of the applicant's questions. Asking questions before providing information gives some interviewers a greater sense of control.

Any order you select for phases two, three, and four will work as long as it reflects your own personality and style. If you feel comfortable, the applicant is likely to respond well to whatever format you select.

Put Applicants at Ease

Regardless of the format you select, devote a few moments at the beginning of the interview to putting the applicant at ease. As discussed in Chapter 8, this is accomplished during the rapport-building stage with icebreakers: comments and questions that have no bearing on the job. Their sole purpose is to put the applicant at ease before the actual interview begins. Some popular icebreakers were identified in that segment. Here are some additional neutral questions and remarks:

"Did you have a smooth commute?"

"When we spoke last week you indicated that you were going to take the train in; how did that work for you?"

"That was some blizzard we had last week! How much snow did you get where you live?"

"It's nice to see the sun shining for a change; five consecutive rainy days is enough for me!"

As with the icebreakers listed in Chapter 8, these are all about commuting and the weather, two uncontroversial, non-job-related subjects. Icebreakers about sensitive subjects such as sports, politics, and religion should be avoided. Here are some examples:

"So, do you think the Yankees are going to win another World Series? I sure hope so!

"Which team are you putting your money on for the Super Bowl?"

"Say, did you happen to catch the president's speech last night? What did you think of it?"

"Did you have any trouble at the train station on your way over here? I understand there's a group of protesters tying up traffic. What are those people thinking?"

"Did you read the headlines in this morning's paper?"

"Tonight's debate look like it's shaping up to be a real doozy!"

"I see you stopped off at church on your way over here—I forgot it's Ash Wednesday."

"I take it today isn't one of those less popular religious holidays that you celebrate; me neither. I guess that's why we're both here!"

Just how much time should be spent on icebreakers depends on how comfortable the applicant appears to be. In most instances, fifteen to thirty seconds is sufficient, although sometimes additional time will be needed. Under no circumstances should this stage of the interview continue for more than a couple of minutes. Applicants who are still uneasy after this amount of time will probably not respond to additional small talk. The best thing to do in this instance is to get started.

Get Started

Regardless of whether you opt to start the core of the interview by asking questions, providing information, or answering questions, getting started can be challenging. Some interviewers get caught up in small talk and seem unable to move on. Others want to get started but don't know how to make the transition from the icebreaker stage. Those wanting to begin by asking questions simply don't know what to ask first.

Regardless of which format you favor, consider integrating the topic of your ice-breaker into a transitional statement. For example:

"I'm glad you didn't have any trouble getting here. I'm eager to begin talking with you about your interest in our opening for a marketing representative."

"I'm sorry you had trouble finding parking. I know that those meters where you finally found a space allow only ninety minutes. Why don't we get started, so that you can be sure to get back to your car before the meter expires?"

"With the weather so beautiful, I'm sure that you'd like to get back outside, so why don't we begin?"

"Why don't we get started with the interview; perhaps it will help take your mind off the fact that you got soaked coming over here!"

Each of these statements creates a bridge between one stage of the interview and another, eliminating the awkward silence or stammering that can easily occur.

Balance Listening with Talking

Interviewers need to balance the amount of talking they do with listening. Many interviewers talk too much, erroneously believing that they're more in control of the interview as long as they're talking. In reality, no more than approximately 25 percent of your time should be devoted to talking. Spend this time asking questions about the applicant's qualifications, clarifying points, providing information about the job and the organization, and answering job- and organization-related questions. The remaining 75 percent of the interview should be devoted to listening.

Listening to what the applicant says in response to the icebreaker questions at the beginning of the interview is very different from actively listening during the rest of the interview. Icebreaker listening is very casual; active listening requires greater concentration. Following are some guidelines to active listening:

• *Listen for connecting themes and ideas.* By not focusing on every word, interviewers are better able to concentrate on key job-related information.

• *Summarize periodically.* Applicants don't always provide complete answers to questions at one time. Frequently you need to fit the pieces together. To make certain that you're doing this accurately, periodically stop and summarize. To illustrate: "Let me make certain that I understand exactly what you've accomplished in this area. You weren't directly responsible for running the department, but your boss was away about 20 percent of the time, and during that time you ran the department. Is this correct?" The applicant may then say, "Well, I didn't exactly run the department; if there were any problems, it was up to me to get in touch with her to find out what we should do." This clarifies the scope and extent of the applicant's responsibility.

• *Filter out distractions.* Distractions can include people coming into your office, the phone ringing, and focusing your thoughts elsewhere. The latter can easily occur when applicants aren't interesting to listen to. Maybe the work they do strikes you as being dull, or perhaps they speak in a monotone. When this happens, you may find yourself thinking about that last vacation in Mexico and how you'd prefer being there right now. If you find this happening, consider that not all positions require effective verbal communication skills. The fact that an applicant is not a skilled speaker may be irrelevant to the job. It's unfair to judge people on the basis of how well they're able to hold your interest, unless verbal communication skills are job-related. By not listening actively, you're likely to miss important information that could influence the final hiring decision.

• *Use free information.* Every time an applicant opens his mouth, you get free information. If you don't listen actively, you're going to miss valuable insights. Free information should be the foundation for many of your interview questions.

• *Screen out personal biases.* Don't allow personal views or opinions to interfere with active listening.

• *Acknowledge any emotional states.* Maybe you had a fender-bender en route to work this morning and now you're in a foul mood, or perhaps you're depressed because you just learned you didn't get the promotion you'd hoped for. Emotional states can overshadow your ability to be attentive during an interview. Acknowledge any overriding emotions and exercise self-discipline until after the interview is over.

Thought Speed

This is a wonderful tool that enables interviewers to hone their active listening skills. Here's how it works: Researchers have determined that most people think at a rate of approximately 400 words per minute; we speak at a rate of approximately 125 words per minute. This means that we think faster than we speak. While the applicant is talking, you can use thought speed to accomplish a great deal, including the following:

- Prepare your next question.
- Analyze what the applicant is saying.
- Piece together what the applicant is saying now in relation to something said earlier in the interview.
- Glance down at the application and/or resume to verify information.
- Observe the applicant's body language.
- Mentally check your own body language to ensure that you're conveying interest and understanding.
- Consider how this applicant's background relates to the job requirements.
- Take notes.

Thought speed can also work to your detriment if you anticipate how applicants are likely to complete their responses before they finish; jump to conclusions too soon; compare an applicant's responses with those of a previous applicant; or get too involved in note taking. When applicants ramble or speak in a monotone, your mind can also wander, causing you to tune out. Guard against this by periodically recapping what the applicant has said.

Interpret Nonverbal Communication

Nonverbal communication is vital to the interview process. Often interviewers can learn as much about applicants through their nonverbal messages as from verbal ones. In fact, experts assert that as much as 55 percent of communication is nonverbal, followed by 38 percent that is attributable to tone of voice, and a mere 7 percent that is verbal. One reason for this is that verbal communication is easier to control than nonverbal. Consider the applicant who answers your question about why she's leaving her current job. Her response sounds plausible: "As much as I've enjoyed my job over the past two years, there's just no room for growth. Regrettably, I feel compelled to explore opportunities elsewhere." As she speaks, you notice that she is twisting the ring on her right hand and biting her lower lip. You may not know exactly what's going on at this point, but on some level you understand that her verbal and nonverbal messages are incongruous. Ignoring this inconsistency could result in overlooking significant job-related information and/or poor selection or rejection decisions.

This, then, is an instance during which you should follow up with additional questions to clarify matters: "Can you explain what your expectations were at the time of hire and how your actual experiences differed?" "Will you please help me understand the natural progression in your company for someone in your job classification?" "How long is the average employee in your job classification before advancing?" "Have you clearly conveyed your growth aspirations with your manager? HR? If so, what were their respective responses?" "Tell me about your performance evaluations since joining the company." While asking these additional questions and listening to the applicant's responses, observe her nonverbal messages. Is she still twisting her ring and/or biting her lip? Are there additional nonverbal movements that fail to convey consistency with her verbal answers? If so, it's likely that she is being less than forthright as to her reasons for leaving her current employer.

Since verbal messages are considered less influential, when there is a discrepancy, the nonverbal is likely to be more persuasive. Simply stated, we react to what we see more than to what we hear.

Universal Translations

Reacting to what we see can be useful only to the extent that we are accurately interpreting another person's nonverbal messages. Are there universal translations to nonverbal messages? The answer is both "yes" and "no." Experts tell us that there are seven universal emotions: anger, contempt, disgust, fear, happiness, sadness, and surprise. These emotions are expressed through facial expressions, gestures, and body movements. But each of us expresses these universal emotions in a unique way. True, there are some gestures and expressions that are more commonly interpreted in a particular way: raising one's eyebrows is generally taken to signify disbelief or surprise; sitting on the edge of one's seat suggests anxiety, nervousness, or apprehension; and flaring one's nostrils commonly indicates anger or frustration. But problems arise when we presume to assign universal translations to specific gestures and movements at the exclusion of the role of culture. For example, we tend to think of direct eye contact as respectful, smiling as a sign of interest, nodding up and down as agreement, a firm handshake as confident, and closed eyes as an indication of being tired or bored. But such interpretations may not be accurate cross-culturally. Direct eye contact is considered disrespectful in Korea; in Thailand, smiling masks embarrassment; nodding one's head up and down in Bulgaria means "no"; a firm handshake to Middle Easterners and many Asians suggests aggressiveness; and someone who closes her eyes in Japan is thought to be concentrating.

This difference in interpretation doesn't just occur across diverse cultures. As a result of our individual socialization processes, each of us develops our own pattern of nonverbal messages, and we tend to react to a situation in the same nonverbal way each time it occurs. For example, the applicant who nervously clasps his hands while waiting to be interviewed is likely to do the same thing each time he's nervous.

Hence, although there are no universal interpretations, each of us has our own nonverbal patterns that may be consistently translated if observed over a period of time. During the course of an employment interview, you have an opportunity to observe these patterns if you are perceptive. For instance, the applicant who leans forward while describing her past two positions, but then suddenly sits back as she talks about her current job, is sending you a clear nonverbal message, regardless of what she's saying verbally. Changes such as these can provide you with valuable cues.

First Impressions

I have several colleagues who firmly believe they can tell whether an applicant is qualified for a job within minutes of the applicant's walking into a room. They draw their conclusions based on such external factors as the person's clothes, grooming, and colors worn. All these factors may or may not be relevant, depending on the job—but are they telling to the extent that a person can be excluded from further consideration?

The question must be asked then: Just how accurate are first impressions? Furthermore, how much should they influence our judgment? Should we form an opinion and then proceed to ask questions designed to confirm that opinion? In other words, should we work at making an applicant fit our first impression?

Here's what invariably happens, albeit often on a subconscious level, when we meet someone for the first time: We mentally match the shape and features of his face, hair, and style of dress with those of someone we know. If we conjure up the image of someone that we like, then we're likely to respond favorably, and vice versa. We then move on to focusing on specific external factors, such as glasses, makeup, tattoos, jewelry, and piercings. Once again, we react positively or otherwise. Then, often in a matter of seconds, we draw a conclusion: Qualified or unqualified; suitable or unsuitable.

Whether this ends up being valid is not the point. What is significant is that we all react to nonverbal messages to a greater or lesser extent, consciously or otherwise. Interviewers "size up" applicants, and vice versa. That last part is often overlooked; we tend to forget that applicants are deciding whether they want to work for us. Although there are no universal translations, there are certain gestures and movements that are likely to convey a certain impression. For example, if you want to convey interest, nod your head up and down periodically, keep your arms unfolded, and sit erect in your chair.

Microexpressions

Dr. Paul Ekman, the noted psychologist, researcher in nonverbal communication, and pioneer in the study of emotions, believes that facial expressions are fairly reliable indicators of a person's emotions. Even though we can consciously fake "macro" facial expressions, which can last from one to three seconds, there are also flashes of true emotions that leak through. He refers to these as microexpressions: brief, involuntary facial expressions that are evident even when a person is trying to conceal or repress the seven universal emotions. According to Dr. Ekman, our brains cannot process enough information to fake these mini-bursts of emotional expressions, which can occur in as little as 1/125th of a second (faster than the blink of an eye). When these emotional sparks are briefly revealed, we cannot always tell exactly what emotion is being expressed, only that something is not right . . . that there is a conflict between the verbal and the nonverbal. Since nonverbal communication is harder to control than verbal, we are alerted to an imbalance worthy of further exploration.

Here are some examples of microexpressions that may signify that something is amiss: increased blinking; an exaggerated, broad smile; unusually high or low levels of eye contact; and longer than ordinary pauses before speaking. Exhibit 9-1 exemplifies some of the microexpressions Dr. Ekman believes can reveal the seven universal emotions.

Once you've conditioned yourself to be aware of the seven universal emotions and possible accompanying microexpressions, you can decide how to respond to information you obtain from "reading" these nonverbal clues. Keep in mind that facial expressions—whether macro or micro—do not reveal what is generating an emotion, only that an emotion is occurring. Even when we're unaware on a conscious level of detecting a microexpression, our brain responds by altering our perception of what we see. Say, for example, you observe an applicant with what you would describe as a happy expression on his face. Without any microexpressions

Exhibit 9-1. Microexpressions and the Seven Universal Emotions

Everyone has her own nonverbal patterns, so these examples may not be relevant in every instance. Remember, too, that these are mini-bursts of emotional expressions, thereby often escaping detection.

Anger
• Upper eyelids slightly raised
• Thinning of lips
• Wrinkled forehead

Contempt
• Mouth slightly raised on one side
• Tightening of the mouth

Disgust
• Scrunched up nose
• Narrowing of eyes

Fear
• Eyebrows drawn together
• Open mouth
• Flared nostrils

Happiness
• Corner of lips slightly raised
• Raised cheeks
• "Crows feet" around eyes

Sadness
• Turned down mouth
• Pulled up chin

Surprise
• Dropped jaw
• Widened eyes
• Slightly raised eyebrows

preceding it, you'd be confident in identifying it as happy. But if that same happy expression were preceded or interrupted by a sneering microexpression that you are not conscious of detecting, you'll be more likely to describe that same "happy" face as cunning or untrustworthy. Even if you can't put a label on the expression, you will probably have an uneasy feeling that might lead you to say, "I don't know what it is, but there's something about the applicant that's making me uneasy." As with verbal "red flags," these nonverbal warnings are best addressed by asking additional questions to help clarify matters.

Lying

Can I tell you with absolute certainty when an applicant is telling the truth or lying? I'd like nothing better than to say "yes," but that would be, well, a lie. I can tell you this, however: there are certain gestures and expressions that will help you detect a lie.

Journalist and author Po Brosnon tells us that a typical four-year-old tells a lie, albeit a small one, once every two hours; six-year-olds lessen the time between lies to every ninety minutes; and so it goes as we get older.

You might think, then, that deception becomes fairly easy once we're adults. In fact, it takes a high-functioning brain to take a truth and create an alternate reality. Lying also produces stress, which triggers chemical changes in the brain. These changes have visible effects that can expose someone as a liar if you know what to look for.

While there is no single telltale sign of lying, microexpressions, such as a millisecond-long change in the middle of a smile, can "leak" out, telling the person who sees it that something is not right. In an interview situation, we sometimes refer to this as having a "gut" feeling that the applicant is being less than forthright. But as we just learned, accurately interpreting microexpressions can be tricky. So is there another way? Fortunately, there is. Under normal circumstances, speech and body language happen naturally together. However, when we lie, we have to consciously coordinate our body language with our words. That is, we have to make a concerted effort to select a specific gesture or movement to best match the lie. In addition, when we lie we often feel defensive, which can result in a change in our body language. We may cross our arms, fidget, blink excessively, scratch our nose, or put our hand to our mouth. Sometimes, too, these nonverbal signs are accompanied by verbal clues as applicants try to buy time: asking you to repeat a question, clearing of the throat, coughing, or even avoiding the use of contractions can give the applicant a few extra seconds.

Here are some guidelines that may help you separate liars from truth tellers:

- Establish a baseline; that is, observe the applicant from the very beginning of the interview and look for the applicant's nonverbal patterns.
- Be aware of "red flags" or deviations from the pattern.
- Look for consistency between verbal and nonverbal responses.
- Confirm any suspicions by returning to topics covered earlier in the interview and observe additional changes in body language.
- Be attuned to microexpressions.
- Change the subject. This can take someone who is lying off guard and allow you to further observe microexpressions.

Here's an illustration of how lies can manifest themselves during the course of an interview. Dr. Ekman watched a 2007 interview of New York Yankee Alex Rodriguez by Katie Couric in which Rodriguez denied using performance-enhancing drugs. He subsequently admitted to drug use. Here's some of what Dr. Ekman observed:

• The Gestural Slip: Several times during the interview Rodriguez raised his left shoulder momentarily as he spoke. It was a slight gesture, but enough to suggest something was out of sync.

• Unilateral Contempt: Rodriguez displayed repeated microexpressions of unilateral contempt: a tightening and raising of the corner of the lip that can indicate arrogance or a feeling of moral superiority. Ekman added that this may not mean anything if it's an expression that Rodriguez displays regularly. To find out, he would have to spend time interviewing him about other topics that were not stressful in order to establish a baseline.

• Microfear: When Couric asked Rodriguez if he had ever been tempted to use illegal drugs, he simply said, "No." This verbal response was accompanied by a horizontal stretching of the lips that is often interpreted as an effort to conceal fearfulness. Again, in and of itself, the expression is meaningless; but in combination with repeated half-shrugs and numerous movements at the corner of the lip, Dr. Ekman's suspicions intensified.

• Dr. Ekman also noticed that when Rodriguez denied taking drugs he nodded his head slightly in the affirmative, suggesting a higher probability of lying.

Encourage Applicants to Talk

One of the greatest challenges for an interviewer is encouraging applicants to talk. Some applicant are well-prepared, self-confident, and more than willing to answer your questions. Indeed, it's difficult to prevent some of them from talking too much and for too long. With others, however, talking to an interviewer can be intimidating and unnerving; regardless of how much they may want the job, selling themselves may be very difficult. These applicants need a little help. Here are six ways to encourage applicants to speak freely:

1. *Use repetition.* This encourages applicants to continue talking and helps to clarify certain points. Repeating the last few words of an applicant's statement and letting your voice trail off as a question mark will encourage the person to elaborate. For example, suppose that the last point an applicant made was "The most difficult part of being a manager was that I was in charge of twenty-five people." You could follow up by saying, "You supervised twenty-five people . . . ?" The applicant might then reply, "Well, not directly. I was in charge of three supervisors, each of whom monitored the work of about seven workers." To further clarify, you might then say, "So, you were directly responsible for supervising three people. Is this correct?" The applicant would then state, "Yes, that's correct, although my supervisors always came to me when they were having trouble with their workers."

This dialogue presents a far more accurate picture of the applicant's supervisory responsibilities than did the original statement. Using repetition encouraged the applicant to provide valuable additional information.

2. *Summarize.* Like repetition, summarization allows the applicant to clarify points made up to that point in the interview and to elaborate as necessary. It further ensures an accurate understanding on your part. Summarization may be used at specific time intervals in the interview, say every ten minutes or after a certain topic has been fully discussed. For instance, you and the applicant may have just devoted ten minutes to reviewing his prior work experience as it relates to the available position. At that point, you might say, "Let me make certain that I understand what you've said thus far. All of your employment since high school has been as a mechanic. This includes the time you spent in the Marine Corps. You enjoy this line of work and want to continue doing it. However, you feel that you were underpaid at your last job and that's why you left. Is all of this correct?"

The applicant can now confirm all or part of what you've just summarized. Be careful not to include more than four or five statements in your summary. This way, if part of it is inaccurate or requires clarification, it won't be difficult to isolate. Also, in order to ensure accuracy, make certain to employ the active listening guidelines outlined earlier.

3. *Ask closed-ended questions.* Asking competency-based questions will yield the most information, but some applicants have difficulty talking and may initially respond better to a series of direct, closed-ended questions. These are effective when used for the limited purpose of allowing the applicant to achieve a certain comfort level before moving on to more information-producing forms of inquiry.

4. *Employ certain phrases to encourage applicants to continue talking.* These phrases include "I see," "How interesting," "Is that right?" "Really?" and "I didn't know that." It's important to ensure that none of these phrases expresses an opinion or shows agreement or disagreement; they should merely show interest and under-standing.

5. *Use encouraging body language.* For these phrases of understanding to be effec-tive, they must be accompanied by what is typically interpreted as *encouraging body language.* Examples include nodding, smiling, direct eye contact, and leaning forward. Conveying positive body language consistently throughout the interview will estab-lish your interest in what the applicant is saying and encourage the person to provide additional information.

6. *Silence.* Most people find silence to be awkward and uncomfortable. Conse-quently, interviewers often feel compelled to talk whenever the applicant stops. Unless you are prepared to ask another question, though, talking when you need additional information from the applicant will not help you reach a hiring decision. When the applicant stops talking and you want him to continue, try silently and slowly counting to five before speaking. This pause often compels an applicant to go on. Of course, you must be careful not to carry silence too far. The interview can easily become a stressful situation if you simply continue to stare at an applicant who has nothing more to say or needs your encouragement to continue. However, if you combine silence with positive body language, the applicant should continue talk-ing within a few seconds. Silence clearly conveys the message that more information is wanted.

Keep Applicants on Track

During most interviews, applicants are responsive to the questions asked and format laid out by their interviewers. Sometimes, however, applicants try to take over or distract the interviewer by going off on a tangent. This may be a deliberate attempt to cover up a lack of job-specific knowledge or experience, or it may inadvertently result from an inability to provide detailed responses to challenging competency-based questions. Whatever the reason, interviewers need to be able to keep applicants on track.

The preparation steps identified in Chapter 5 will prove helpful in this regard. In addition, there are other measures interviewers can take to keep the face-to-face meeting moving steadily forward. Following are ten situations during which applicants may try to divert your attention from a discussion of their qualifications, and suggestions for keeping applicants on track:

1. When an applicant asks you to elaborate on your history with the company, say, "Perhaps we could talk about my history with the company at another time; this is your opportunity to convince me that you're the best person for this job; let's return to our discussion of your qualifications."

2. When an applicant tries to change the subject from a discussion of her qualifications to the pictures on your desk, ask, "Since we only have a limited amount of time for this interview, don't you think it would be a better use of our time if we focused on your qualifications?"

3. When an applicant goes off on a tangent while answering a question, interject by saying, "I'm not sure I see how what you're saying relates to the question I asked; allow me to restate it."

4. When an applicant answers your questions with questions of her own, say, "If you could just answer my question before asking one of your own, I'll be certain not to miss any part of your answer."

5. When an applicant insists on discussing positions other than the one she's applying for, pull out the job description and ask that she review it; then say, "I need to know before proceeding any further if you are, in fact, interested in being considered for this position. If you are, we should focus our attention on how you qualify for this job—not others."

6. When an applicant presses for an answer as to whether you're going to hire him, say, "I'm sure you can appreciate that I need to weigh each applicant's responses to key questions before I can make a decision. That said, I'd like to return to those key questions so I can give you equal consideration."

7. When an applicant avoids answering questions directly, say, "I'm having difficulty relating your answers to my questions. That's going to cause problems for me later when I'm evaluating all the applicants' responses. Is there any way you can help me out here, perhaps by answering my questions more directly?"

8. When an applicant starts touching an item on your desk, playing with it, and commenting about it, say, "Why don't I just move that; I know it can be distracting."

9. When an applicant starts talking about personal matters in lieu of her job experience, interrupt and say, "In order for me to determine whether you're the best fit for this job we need to stay focused and discuss job-related matters."

10. When an applicant says or does anything that compels you to stray from the interview format, say, "Let's get back to why you're here and how you're the best fit for this job."

Keep your body language neutral throughout and remain calm. Remember that you're in charge of the interview and it won't take more than a statement or two by you to get an applicant back on track. Try also to get through the interview without forming overly negative opinions. As an interviewer, you're obliged to remain objective and evaluate a host of tangible and intangible factors. Wait until after the interview is over before making a final determination.

Provide Information

Gathering information about the applicant is only part of the interview; providing information is also important. Just as interviewers must decide if applicants are appropriate for a job, applicants must decide whether the job and company are right for them. This is particularly true when unemployment is low and applicants can afford to be selective about job opportunities.

Many applicants come to the interview armed with information about both the company and the job opening. But regardless of how much some applicants presumably or actually do know, interviewers are responsible for informing all applicants about certain aspects of the company and the available position. In this way, applicants will be certain to understand key elements of their prospective employment.

As previously stated, information about the job and company may be provided at the beginning of the interview or may be offered between asking and answering questions. Care must be given, however, not to give away too much regarding the characteristics of an ideal applicant in the early stages of the interview.

Generally, interviewers should inform applicants about the organization in terms of what it does and how long it's been in business, as well as providing brief statements about its origins, current standing among competitors, and the prevailing corporate culture. They should also provide a brief summary of company benefits. Specific information concerning the department that has the opening, including its function, the different tasks performed, how it interrelates with other departments, a description of who's in charge, and the chain of command, is also useful.

This naturally leads to a description of the specific job opening, details of which may be offered by providing the applicant with a copy of the job description. Allow him a few moments to read it and then encourage questions based on its contents. If the job description is comprehensive and well-written, this process will ensure a clear understanding of what the job entails. Be certain to cover growth opportunities available through job posting, career planning, training programs, or other in-house or outside means for career development. Also review any negative features as they pertain to, say, working conditions or the work schedule. Let the applicant react now, during the interview, rather than later as a disgruntled employee.

Whether salary is discussed depends on your company's policy. It's advisable for interviewers to provide at least general information about the range for a given job. Tell the applicant, too, if the salary is fixed and nonnegotiable.

Also, offer a brief description of the neighborhood surrounding the workplace. This might include transportation options, restaurants, stores, and, since we have become increasingly health-conscious, any health/exercise facilities in the area.

Finally, be certain to tell the applicant what will happen after the interview is over. Depending on your level of interest, state approximately when she may expect to hear from you, whether additional interviews are likely, and what to do if she has additional questions. Be certain you have current contact information so there will be no problem with future communication.

Consider the Role of Perception

Before meeting an applicant, interviewers should briefly review the four primary ways in which we form our perceptions and ideas about people. These four aspects of perception—first impressions, information from others, single statements, and ethnocentrism—together form a valuable interview component. Briefly reviewing them when meeting with an applicant can help you avoid hasty rejection or hiring decisions based on nonfactual, subjective factors.

First Impressions

This is the most prevalent and often most damaging way of establishing ideas about people, since we often form first impressions without even realizing it. Interviewers unaware of the importance of perception frequently boast, "The minute he walked in the door, I could tell he was right for the job."

Can you determine job suitability by sizing people up in a split second based on their appearance? It's unlikely. This is not to say that appearance—clothing, colors, and grooming—does not play a role in the selection process. After all, employees represent an organization, and the image they project is a direct reflection on that company. Problems arise, however, when interviewers form preconceived notions of how employees in certain job classifications should look or dress. An accountant, for example, conjures up a different image than does a custodian. If a person applying for a custodial opening came to an interview wearing a suit, you would probably be surprised, but not turned off. But if an accountant showed up wearing jeans and a T-shirt, it's far more likely that you'd form a negative first impression.

First impressions should play a role in your decision-making process, but not at the exclusion of all the other factors to be examined. Don't allow them to act as a substitute for judgment, and try not to form a complete impression until after you've conducted the interview. You may find that the applicant's attire or grooming is the only problem. The person's job skills may be superior to those of all other applicants. At this point you can talk to the applicant about the image your organization wants its employees to project. Then schedule a brief follow-up interview to see if she got the message.

Information from Others

An applicant who comes highly recommended by someone for whom you have high regard can elicit a positive response from you before the actual face-to-face meeting. On the other hand, as stated earlier, if someone you dislike makes a referral to you, it might create a negative bias against the person being recommended. In both instances you're allowing yourself to be influenced by information from others. Instead of assessing the applicant on her own merits, you're assessing the person making the recommendation, transferring your opinion from the referral source to the applicant. As with first impressions, information from others does play a role in the decision-making process. In fact, anything that might supplement what's on an application or resume can be helpful, but it's premature to make an evaluation based on this highly subjective aspect of perception at this stage of the employment process.

Single Statements

Suppose an applicant's response to one of your questions rubs you the wrong way. If you're unaware of the impact that a single statement can have, it could bother you to the extent that you eliminate the person from further consideration. This might occur even though the comment doesn't constitute a valid reason for rejection. Be particularly careful if this should happen during the initial stage of the interview, when you're trying to put the applicant at ease and establish rapport. If you err and mention something relating to, say, politics, the applicant might express a view contrary to yours. If you're not careful, this difference could influence your objectivity in assessing the applicant's job suitability. You will then have taken a single statement—one that is totally irrelevant to the selection process—and allowed it to affect your judgment.

Even single statements that are job-related must be weighed in relation to other qualifying factors. Treat them as red flags and explore them thoroughly, but keep in mind that it's usually a combination of factors that results in the rejection of an applicant.

Ethnocentrism

Ethnocentrism refers to applying our values, standards, and beliefs to judge or evaluate others. Overall, this is a perfectly natural result of the cultural conditioning process to which we are all exposed. In our early years, well-intentioned parents, teachers, and religious leaders teach us to think and act according to certain guidelines. At the age of five or six, few of us question the validity of these guidelines. Unfortunately, many people grow up believing that what they were exposed to as children is the only way to think. This can result in stereotypical misperceptions whereby we assign specific attributes and roles to others based on surface characteristics such as sex, age, or ethnic origin.

Other factors also come into play. For example, you see from a resume that the applicant graduated from Harvard. Your general assumptions about Harvard graduates could lead you to hastily conclude that the person would be an asset to the organization. Negative reactions may also occur. For instance, an applicant may currently be working for an organization from which your brother was recently fired. This negative association could influence your assessment of the applicant's job suitability.

When perceptions are based on ethnocentric thinking, objectivity falls by the wayside. The chances for open, effective communication are blocked when an applicant's responses or nonverbal messages deviate from the interviewer's preconceived notions. Keep in mind that ethnocentrism does not pertain to work-related standards established by the company; rather, it comes into play through the intangible qualities of an individual's style and approach to doing work. It conflicts with objectivity, which is an interviewer's number one obligation.

Summary

This chapter summarizes the following interview component guidelines:

1. Establish a format that encompasses all the important ingredients of an interview. Be sure it reflects your own style and personality.
2. Establish rapport by taking a few moments at the beginning of an interview to put the applicant at ease.
3. Carefully select your first question so that the answer will yield additional categories to explore.
4. Practice active listening skills, concentrating closely on what the applicant says, and talk no more than approximately 25 percent of the time.
5. Look for consistency between an applicant's verbal and nonverbal messages. When there is a discrepancy between the two, the nonverbal is likely to be more persuasive.
6. Encourage applicants to talk via repetition, summarization, direct closed-ended questions, encouraging phrases, positive body language, and silence.
7. Provide information, making certain that the applicant has a clear and complete understanding of both the available job and the organization.
8. Consider the role of perception, and try not be unduly influenced by first impressions, information from others, single statements, and ethnocentric thoughts.

CHAPTER 10

Types of Employment Interviews

Nick Dawkins is the HR manager for Clarisse Inc., a communications company with about nine hundred employees, located outside of Boston, Massachusetts. He currently has several openings to fill, including one for a business office supervisor. Nick has cast a wide recruitment net, using a variety of sources. As a result, he has identified several possibilities, all of whom look impressive on paper. Nick is ready to begin the interview process. He knows he must first carefully screen the applicants before bringing them in for interviews. To do this, he plans on conducting either face-to-face exploratory, telephone, or video screening interviews. Assuming there is continued interest, Nick intends to schedule each applicant for a series of comprehensive interviews: first, there will be the HR interview with himself; next, there will be either a departmental interview with the business office manager or a panel interview with the business office manager and other selected managers; finally, there might be a peer interview with business office colleagues and other supervisors.

By selecting a combination of different types of interviews, Nick is confident he will find the most suitable business office supervisor for Clarisse.

Exploratory Interviews

The purpose of a face-to-face exploratory interview is to establish continued interest on both sides and to determine preliminary job suitability. Assuming these two conditions are satisfied, the next step is to set up a job-specific interview. Exploratory interviews should not serve as substitutes for the in-depth job-specific interview; that is, interviewers should not make decisions to hire based on the exploratory meeting. On the other hand, exploratory interviews can screen out applicants in whom you definitely have no further interest.

What distinguishes an exploratory interview is the amount of time allotted to asking questions. Interviewers must focus on key job-related issues—usually in a period of fifteen to twenty minutes for nonexempt applicants and twenty to thirty minutes for professional applicants—and decide if a full follow-up interview is warranted.

Under these conditions, interviewers often feel pressured into making a decision based on what they perceive to be limited information. Consequently, it can be tempting to dismiss a person for giving an inappropriate answer, or even because of the way he dresses or shakes your hand. Using such non-job-related reasons as the basis for rejection, even at this early stage in the interview process, can be counterproductive for a number of reasons. You may be passing up a viable applicant, the applicant will leave with negative feelings about your organization (which he may well share with others), and it could lead to claims of discrimination based on "intent" (e.g., she contends that the minute you saw that the applicant was a woman, she was excluded from further consideration).

Even though time is limited in an exploratory interview, you can still make decisions based on solid, job-related information. The process of deciding who "passes" an exploratory interview begins with the all-important job description. First, segregate those tasks that are essential; then, from that list, try to identify tasks that require 20 percent or more of the incumbent's time. Companies are required by the ADA to write job descriptions so that each duty is coded as being essential or nonessential. Many employers also note an approximate percentage of time devoted to each task. If there are just a few tasks that require 20 percent or more of the incumbent's time, adjust the percentage downward so that you have somewhere between four and eight essential tasks isolated. If necessary, isolate all essential tasks, even those requiring 5 percent or less of the employee's time, in order to come up with a half-dozen or so duties.

To illustrate, here's a sample job description for a business office supervisor. Preceding each task is an "E" signifying an essential task or an "NE" for nonessential. Following each task is the approximate percentage of time devoted to each task:

(E)   1. Plans, organizes, and controls the billing, receiving, and paying functions for the office. (25 percent)

(E)   2. Reviews financial resources and collects delinquent accounts by direct contact or referral to collection agency. (20 percent)

(E)   3. Prepares and distributes the payroll; establishes and maintains payroll records. (15 percent)

(E)   4. Maintains flow of financial information with other departments. (10 percent)

(NE) 5. Keeps current on new systems, methods, and equipment. (5 percent)

(NE) 6. Performs HR functions in absence of manager; specifically, hiring, training, evaluating performance, and recommending salary increases. (5 percent)

(E)   7. Ensures compliance with government regulations and participates in audits, as required. (5 percent)

(E)   8. Informs management of current financial position and effect of operations by preparing and analyzing various reports. (10 percent)

(NE) 9. Revises policies and procedures relevant to the business office function. (5 percent)

By segregating the essential functions, we end up with this list:

1. Plans, organizes, and controls the billing, receiving, and paying functions for the office. (25 percent)
2. Reviews financial resources and collects delinquent accounts by direct contact or referral to collection agency. (20 percent)
3. Prepares and distributes the payroll; establishes and maintains payroll records. (15 percent)
4. Maintains flow of financial information with other departments. (10 percent)
5. Ensures compliance with government regulations and participates in audits, as required. (5 percent)
6. Informs management of current financial position and effect of operations by preparing and analyzing various reports. (10 percent)

Now we can isolate those tasks that encompass 20 percent or more of the incumbent's time:

1. Plans, organizes, and controls the billing, receiving, and paying functions for the office. (25 percent)
2. Reviews financial resources and collects delinquent accounts by direct contact or referral to collection agency. (20 percent)
   Since only two duties take up 20 percent or more of the employee's time, other tasks need to be isolated:
3. Prepares and distributes the payroll; establishes and maintains payroll records. (15 percent)
4. Maintains flow of financial information with other departments. (10 percent)
5. Informs management of current financial position and effect of operations by preparing and analyzing various reports. (10 percent)

Now we have five of the nine primary responsibilities that represent 80 percent of the job. This condensed job description will enable you to focus on the salient aspects of an applicant's experience and qualifications to determine preliminary job suitability.

Look, too, at the category of "education, prior work experience, and specialized skills and knowledge." Eliminate excess verbiage and separate key requirements. For the business officer supervisor's job, you might extract the following:

1. Extensive experience—billing, receiving, payroll, and collection
2. Ability to prepare/analyze/present financial reports
3. Accounting degree desirable

Now, when interviewing applicants in a limited amount of time, you can focus on just five key tasks and three requirements.

The final step in preparing for an exploratory interview is to plan your format and the types of questions you'll ask. Begin by explaining the purpose of the meeting, verify the available position and, if your company policy permits, the starting salary or salary range. Ask what the applicant currently does (open-ended) and what his current salary is (closed-ended). Then, based on the isolated tasks and educational requirements, ask a series of about six competency-based questions to determine the level and nature of her expertise. Wind down with one or two open-ended and/ or closed-ended questions to confirm what she's told you. Your final question should be, "What else should I know about you in relation to your application for this job?" Probing questions are rarely introduced in exploratory interviews, unless the applicant's responses to competency-based questions are incomplete. Hypotheticals are omitted as well, except where the applicant has no prior work experience to draw from.

Here's a sampling of questions from an exploratory interview with an applicant for the business office supervisor's position:

"Good morning, Jesse. Thank you for stopping by today. I understand you're interested in our opening for a business office supervisor. Is that correct?" (answer) "Very good—let's get started."

"Jesse, this is an exploratory interview. That means we spend a few minutes discussing your interest and qualifications. Then, if it appears that there's a sufficient match between your skills and the position requirements and you're still interested in continuing, we can arrange a more in-depth interview for another time. How does that sound to you?" (answer)

"Let me also confirm that you understand the salary range for this job is $55,500 to $63,000. Do you want to proceed?" (answer) "How does that range fit in with what you're currently earning?" (answer)

"Okay, fine. Let me ask you a few questions."

"First, why don't you begin by telling me about your activities in a typical day at your current job as an office supervisor." (answer)

"I'm interested in learning more about your billing, receiving, and paying responsibilities. Give me one example to illustrate each of these areas." (answer)

"Tell me about a particularly difficult collection you had to make by direct contact." (answer)

"Describe a time when the payroll was delayed; what did you do?" (answer)

"Tell me about another department with which you maintain a steady flow of financial information and the nature of that information." (answer)

"Describe the contents of the most recent financial report you prepared." (answer)

"May I safely assume from what you have told me that the bulk of your work is in billing and receiving?" (answer)

"Am I also to understand that you have not had any experience in direct contact collections?" (answer)

"What else should I know about you in relation to your application for this job?" (answer)

"All right, Jesse; that's all I have for you right now. Is there anything you'd like to ask me at this point?" (answer)

"Thank you for your time and interest. I need to review your answers and will get back to you no later than Friday. Enjoy the rest of the day."

This sample exploratory interview would probably last about twenty-five minutes. Regardless of the outcome, the applicant should leave feeling that he had an opportunity to present his qualifications and will be judged on his abilities in relation to the job requirements. The interviewer, too, can leave the interview knowing he's asked enough relevant questions to make a preliminary decision to either reject the applicant or continue with a more comprehensive job-specific interview.

Telephone Screening Interviews

Telephone screening is intended to accomplish one of two objectives: (1) to establish continued interest in a job applicant that results in an appointment for an in-depth interview, or (2) to determine that an applicant's qualifications do not sufficiently meet the job's specifications. Under no circumstances should telephone screening be viewed as a substitute for the face-to-face interview.

Successful telephone screening depends on establishing and following a certain format. Contact the applicant, confirm his interest in a specific job, and agree on a time to talk. Suggest that an applicant for a nonexempt job allot approximately twenty minutes for the call; an applicant for an exempt job should set aside about thirty minutes.

When the specified time arrives, describe the available position, being careful not to identify the qualities that would make the best fit. Encourage the applicant to ask questions related to the specific opening and the company. Have ready a series of questions to assist you in determining whether continued interest is warranted. Some questions to ask nonexempt-level applicants are:

- "Why are you leaving your present (or last) employer?"
- "What do (or did) you do in a typical day?"
- "What do you like (or did you like) most and least about your present (or last) job?"
- "Why are you applying for this particular position?"

In addition, ask questions relative to any significant aspects of the job. For example, if it requires standing for long periods of time, ask applicants to describe jobs where they've had to do this. Also, describe a typical situation that is likely to occur with this job and ask the applicants to describe how they've handled similar situations in the past.

Appropriate questions to ask exempt-level applicants include:

- "Why are you leaving your present (or last) employer?"
- "Why are you applying for this particular position?"
- "What do you know about this organization?"
- "What have you contributed in past positions?"
- "What contributions do you anticipate being able to make in this position?"
- "What do you expect to receive from this company?"
- "How does this position fit in with your long-term goals?

Then, based on the particulars of the job, ask a series of questions regarding how they have handled certain situations in past positions.

As applicants respond, remind yourself of the purpose of the call: you're deciding whether a face-to-face interview is in order, not whether they should be hired. Take notes as they talk; if the conversation itself is not determinative, reviewing their responses after the call can help you decide whether to schedule an interview. If you do decide to bring them in, these notes can be used as a point of reference and comparison as you repeat some of the questions asked on the phone, seeking more in-depth information.

Be careful not to judge the quality of an applicant's telephone presentation if effective verbal communication skills are not a job-related criterion. On the other hand, some people, especially those in sales or marketing, do very well communicating on the phone; consequently, you must be able to separate style from substance.

Before concluding the conversation, go over a brief checklist:

- Does the applicant understand the job?
- Did you ask questions that will enable you to determine whether further interest is warranted?
- Did the applicant ask pertinent questions?
- Has the applicant expressed interest in the job?
- Does the applicant meet the basic qualifications for the job?
- Is there consistency between the information on the resume or application and what the applicant has told you?

If there's no doubt in your mind that the person should be invited in for an interview, make the invitation before the conversation is completed. If you are not certain and want to review your notes before making a decision, thank the applicant for his time, describe the next step, and estimate when he may expect to hear from you. If you are absolutely certain that the applicant is not suitable for the job, you have two choices: be honest and say that his qualifications are not suitable or that there is a lack of specific expertise or knowledge necessary for the job, or say that you will be reviewing the results of your conversations with all the applicants before taking any further action. If you do reject the applicant outright, be certain to explain your policy on keeping applications and resumes on file and encourage him to apply again in the future for other openings. If you have handled the situation tactfully, the person can hang up feeling good, even though no job interview is forthcoming.

Telephone screening offers numerous benefits. The process enables you to weed out applicants who are not qualified, allowing more time to devote to viable potential employees. It's also an impartial process; that is, neither party can be influenced or distracted by such visual factors as appearance, clothing, or grooming. While these can be important job-related intangibles, they are irrelevant at this screening stage.

Video Screening Interviews

Video screening is growing in popularity as a replacement for telephone screening as businesses expand their applicant searches both nationally and internationally. That's because video screening allows interviewers to observe long-distance applicants while simultaneously talking with them. It also results in cost savings achieved by eliminating travel and administrative costs. Additionally, it allows employers to screen several applicants in the time it would take to interview one person by phone.

Businesses that are interested in video screening often hire the services of an outside source. These sources generally either (1) facilitate a live videoconference between applicants and an employer; (2) provide the company with an unedited recording of a screening session conducted by a professional interviewer; or (3) submit an employer's questions to applicants, who use a webcam to answer. With regard to the latter, applicants are generally first provided with a tutorial as to the technical aspects of the video interview. They are then given approximately thirty seconds to read a question and an additional two minutes or so to answer it. Responses are then e-mailed back to the employer, who compares records of the sessions to see how each applicant answered the questions.

Applicants who find themselves in front of a video camera are usually coached to maximize how they come across. Here are some of the tips they're typically offered:

- Watch how newscasters dress and dress similarly.
- Practice with a webcam in advance.
- Speak clearly and succinctly.
- Don't fidget.
- Pretend that the camera is a real person and maintain "eye contact."
- Avoid sudden movements.
- Use the "picture in picture" feature to see how you appear to your interviewer.

HR Interviews

Employment interviews conducted by HR specialists are both broad-based and job-specific: They are broad-based in that the HR interviewer covers a great deal of general territory, including goals and interests, and they are job-specific because the interviewer delves into the applicant's education and experiences to determine if the applicant has skills and knowledge needed for the job sufficient enough to pass on to the department for further consideration. HR practitioners also need to consider whether a person is the best fit for the organization. Typically, then, the HR interview is the longest and most comprehensive of all interview types.

Let's look at some of the questions Nick, the HR manager at Clarisse, Inc., would ask of Kira, an applicant for the position of business office supervisor. Kira is currently a business office supervisor but doesn't feel she's receiving adequate compensation. She's also frustrated because she wants to learn new skills but there are no training opportunities at her current job.

For purposes of this example, we'll skip over establishing the format, putting the applicant at ease, providing information, and answering questions. Our focus is solely on asking a series of competency-based, open-ended, hypothetical, probing, and closed-ended questions. Note that what follows is not intended to be an all-inclusive list of suitable questions. The applicant's answers would likely trigger numerous additional job-related questions.

Once again, here's the job description:

Primary duties and responsibilities include:

(E)   1. Plans, organizes, and controls the billing, receiving, and paying functions for the office. (25 percent)

(E)   2. Reviews financial resources and collects delinquent accounts by direct contact or referral to collection agency. (20 percent)

(E)   3. Prepares and distributes the payroll; establishes and maintains payroll records. (15 percent)

(E)   4. Maintains flow of financial information with other departments. (10 percent)

(NE) 5. Keeps current on new systems, methods, and equipment. (5 percent)

(NE) 6. Performs HR functions in absence of manager; specifically, hiring, training, evaluating performance, and recommending salary increases. (5 percent)

(E)   7. Ensures compliance with government regulations and participates in audits, as required. (5 percent)

(E)   8. Informs management of current financial position and effect of operations by preparing and analyzing various reports. (10 percent)

(NE) 9. Revises policies and procedures relevant to the business office function. (5 percent)

Education, prior work experience, and specialized skills and knowledge include:

1. Extensive experience—billing, receiving, payroll, and collection
2. Ability to prepare/analyze/present financial reports
3. Accounting degree desirable

Job-Specific Experience and Education Questions

"Kira, please describe your activities in a typical day."

"Are there any other activities you might be asked to perform? What are they?"

● "Of these activities, which would you identify as your primary responsibility?"

"Approximately what percentage of your time would you say you devote to this responsibility?"

● "You've indicated that organizing the billing for your office is your primary responsibility; do you also plan and control the billing?"

"What are your responsibilities with regard to the receiving and paying functions?"

"Tell me about a time when you ran into a problem with regard to organizing the billing for your office; what happened?"

"What would you identify as your second most important responsibility?"

"With regard to this responsibility of preparing payroll, can you tell me about an instance when you couldn't get the payroll out in time?"

"What were the repercussions of not getting the payroll out in time?"

"What procedures are in place as a result of that incident?"

"What was your role in putting those procedures in place?"

"Do you review financial resources and collect delinquent accounts?"

"Who in your department is responsible for doing that?"

"Describe how you keep current with regard to new systems, methods, and equipment."

"How do you ensure compliance with government regulations?"

● "Have you ever participated in an audit? Tell me about it."

● "Tell me about your responsibilities as they pertain to the flow of financial information between departments."

"Describe an instance when one of the other departments didn't receive important financial information in a timely manner and held you responsible—what happened?"

"What HR responsibilities do you perform, if any, in the absence of your manager?"

"Let me make certain I understand what you just said: You don't perform any HR responsibilities but that's one of the tasks you're interested in taking on. Is that correct?"

"Tell me more about your interest in HR—and please be specific."

"Am I to understand that you'd like to eventually move from what you're currently doing into HR? If so, do you have a timeline in mind for doing this?"

"I have a few more questions about your current responsibilities. Are you at all involved with management in terms of preparing or analyzing financial reports? Who is?"

"Tell me about a time when you disagreed with something your manager wanted you to do; what was the end result?"

"Can you describe an instance in which you were asked to perform a task that wasn't in your job description?"

"Of all the tasks you've identified, which do you enjoy the most? The least?"

"Which of these tasks do you find especially easy? Difficult?"

"Prior to working at your current company, did you perform any billing, receiving, payroll, or collection tasks?"

"Am I correct in understanding that all of your experience with accounting is in your current capacity as a business office supervisor?"

"Kira, I have a few questions I'd like to ask you about your education as it pertains to this job. You've indicated that you graduated with a degree in accounting—tell me about some of the accounting courses that you took."

"Which of these did you do well in?"

"Were there any that were especially challenging? Why?"

"Why did you decide to major in accounting?"

Generic Questions to Determine the Best Fit

"Kira, can you give me your definition of the ideal manager?"

"How about the ideal work environment?"

"What would you like to avoid in future jobs?"

"From what I've said combined with what you've read in the job description for this position, what does this job offer that your current job does not provide?"

"Is there anything your current boss could say that would make you want to stay there?"

"What do you consider to be your greatest strength? Give me an example of a time in your current job when you applied this strength."

"Tell me about an area in which you'd like to improve. How do you plan on making these improvements?"

"How would you describe yourself as an employee?"

"How do you approach tasks that you dislike?"

"If you had two tasks due by the end of the day—one that you excel in and enjoy, the other more challenging and less interesting—which would you do first?"

"How would you go about discussing job dissatisfaction with your boss?"

"In what way do you feel your work experiences to date have prepared you to assume additional responsibilities?"

"Tell me about your short- and long-term goals. I'm especially interested in learning more about your interest in HR."

"How can you link your current set of skills with your interest in HR?"

"What educational or training opportunities are of interest to you?"

"What kind of people do you find it difficult to work with? Easy to work with?"

"What do you feel an employer owes an employee? What about what an employee owes an employer?"

⸎ "If you could design the dream job, what would it be? What would you be doing?"

⸎ "What else would you like me to know about you before we conclude?"

Departmental Interviews

Unlike the HR interview, interviews with managers and department heads are less likely to probe general areas of interest or education. Their main focus is "Can this person do the job?" The departmental interview, then, emphasizes job specifics. For this reason, the departmental interview should consist of open-ended, competency-based, and hypothetical questions based on specific job-related duties and responsibilities.

Following Nick's interview with Kira, Nick sits down with the job description for the business office supervisor, Kira's resume, and his interview notes. Based on her experience and responses in relation to the requirements of the job, Nick is hesitant to refer her on. She lacks expertise in a number of essential areas and seems more interested in pursuing a career in HR than in continuing with business. Still, Nadia, the department head, wants to meet with her, so Nick sets up an interview.

Here are some of the job-specific questions Nadia could ask Kira:

"Tell me how you go about organizing the billing for your office—please be specific."

"How do you handle receipt errors?"

"What about payment overages?"

"Describe your logging system."

"What's your approach to collecting delinquent accounts?"

"I have some questions about your responsibilities with regard to your company's payroll system: How do you prepare the payroll? When do you you distribute it? How do you maintain payroll records?"

"What's your take on the Schematic 5500?"

"Describe your system of financial record keeping."

"What do you think of the new Jackal record-keeping system?"

"Tell me about a time when you were blamed for a financial error that wasn't your fault."

"What would you do if I wasn't around and one of the company's VPs started screaming about not having received important financial documents?"

"I need someone to revise policies and procedures relevant to the business office function; have you ever done that?"

"How would you go about doing it? Who would you talk to? How would you gather the information you'd need?"

"What's the most important ingredient in preparing a financial report?"

"What would you do during a government audit if you were held responsible for an error?"

After Kira leaves Nadia's office, she reflects on the interview. Nick was right; Kira is lacking experience with some critical job-specific areas. She will not consider her further.

Panel Interviews

Most interviews involve two people: the interviewer and the applicant. Occasionally, however, the team or panel approach is used. Ideally, this method involves up to three interviewers—usually an HR representative, department manager, and department head. This is commonly done for one of two reasons: (1) to save the time it would take to schedule three separate interviews, and (2) to compare impressions of applicants as they answer questions.

For maximum effectiveness, the role of each participant should be agreed upon ahead of time. Perhaps the HR representative will begin by introducing everyone, making small talk to establish rapport and asking some open-ended and competency-based questions to determine overall job suitability. Then the manager will ask more detailed, job-specific questions, and the department head may also ask job-specific questions as well as assess the applicant's fit within the department. The HR representative might continue with an exploration of the applicant's overall fit with the corporate culture, as well as looking at relevant intangible factors. While each member of the panel need not have a list of specific questions he plans on asking, everyone should agree in advance on their general areas of coverage. It's awkward and unprofessional to have members of a panel bickering over who's going to ask which question or having more than one person asking the same question.

Applicants should always be advised in advance that the panel approach will be used. Otherwise, it can be unnerving for them to find more than one interviewer in the room.

Seating should be carefully arranged. Unlike a one-on-one interview, where the proximity of the interviewer's chair to the applicant's is inconsequential, improper seating in a panel interview situation can create an uncomfortable environment. Do not, for example, surround the applicant's chair. As Exhibit 10-1 illustrates, this places one seat on either side and one directly in front, resulting in a "tennis match" sort of interview, with the applicant continually turning his head from one side to the other, trying to address all members of the team. Instead, either sit at a round table or offer the applicant a seat and form a soft arc in front of the applicant. As Exhibit 10-2 illustrates, this setting is less structured and more conducive to a productive exchange.

If carefully planned, panel interviews can be highly effective. They tend to be more objective because there's less singular interaction with the applicant. In addi-

Exhibit 10-1. Surrounding the Job Applicant

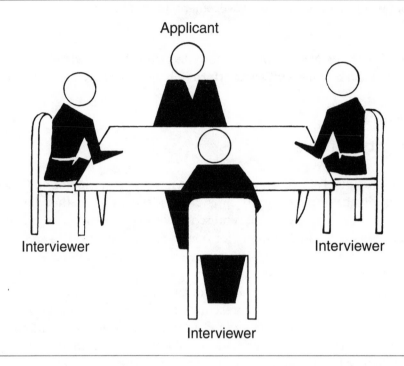

Exhibit 10-2. Suggested Seating Arrangement for Team or Panel Interview

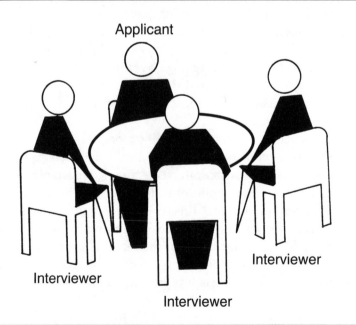

tion, while one of the panelists is talking, the other two can more carefully observe the applicant's body language and take additional time to assess responses to specific questions. Also, if there are three different personality types on the panel, you'll be able to see how the applicant responds to and interacts with these different types. Most importantly, assessments tend to be more accurate and consistent, since everyone is basing their decisions on the same information.

Peer Interviews

Peer interviews involve the potential colleagues of an applicant. The approach has grown in popularity, especially in work environments where teamwork is vital. Most peer interviews are in the form of panels. They should take place at the end of the interviewing process, that is, following any screening interviews, the applicant's interview with HR, and the individual or panel departmental interview.

Participants in a peer interview should be:

- Experienced in the details of the available job
- Aware of job-related intangible factors
- Clear about the relationship of the available job with other jobs in the department and other departments
- Aware of specific problems associated with the job
- Well-versed in how the department functions
- Familiar with the culture of the department in particular, and the organization in general
- Aware of departmental and company goals
- Familiar with the history of the organization
- Sensitive to the issue of diversity
- Free of bias

Structure is critical for peer interviews to succeed. Since most participants of peer interviews are not skilled interviewers, an HR representative usually coaches them in advance. At its most basic level, preparation includes a review of critical factors, a discussion of questions to avoid from a legal standpoint, and a list of recommended general questions to ask. Beyond that, some peer interviews are broken down into specific components, with each participant responsible for probing a particular area. For example, one person could conduct a skills assessment, another could examine how well the applicant is likely to fit in with the culture of the department, and a third could examine the relevance of experiences to the tasks at hand.

Some companies hold mock peer interviews to ensure preparedness. Others invest in extensive training, complete with a detailed checklist of dos and don'ts. Free-form questioning is generally discouraged.

As with panel interviews, three participants are considered ideal for peer interviewing. An HR representative should be present during the process, functioning as the "moderator" of the interview, introducing the applicant to the participants and explaining the process. Beyond that, the HR representative is usually silent, unless one of the interviewers poses an illegal or inappropriate question.

Following a peer interview, participants should compare their observations, using a prepared checklist of relevant topics and corresponding ratings. These ratings should be kept simple, such as "highly qualified," "qualified," "not qualified." At the end, participants can summarize their individual evaluations, again using simple terms like "highly recommend for hire," "recommend for hire," "do not recommend for hire."

The HR representative should be present during these discussions to ensure adherence to relevant topics and objective evaluations. Observations by the peer interview participants should then be compared with those of all preceding interviews. The HR representative, departmental representatives, and members of the peer interview sometimes meet to discuss a particular applicant. This generally occurs when there is a lack of uniformity between everyone's evaluations. If there is disagreement over who would make the best fit, the hiring manager, hopefully backed by HR, should have the final say.

Interviews with Less-Than-Ideal Applicants

Most applicants are eager to make a good impression on their interviewer. They try to answer all questions as fully as possible, project positive body language, and ask appropriate questions. Occasionally, however, you'll find yourself face-to-face with a less-than-ideal applicant, someone who is excessively shy or nervous, overly talkative, overly aggressive or domineering, or highly emotional or distraught.

At the first indication that you're dealing with a less-than-ideal applicant, make certain adjustments in how you proceed with the interview.

Excessively Shy or Nervous Applicants

Within the first few seconds of the rapport-building portion of the interview, it will become apparent if an applicant is especially shy or nervous. Avoid drawing attention to the person's state by saying something like, "I can see that you're really nervous; just try to relax!" Or, "Don't be shy—I'll try to go easy on you!" Statements such as these are only going to make matters worse. Believe it or not, shy or nervous people don't think others notice; calling attention to their behavior could drive them to a point of near implosion.

This type of person needs to be drawn out slowly; a broad, open-ended question might be too intimidating if asked right off the bat. Instead, try a few closed-ended queries to put the applicant at ease. Make them simple, relating to areas likely to make the applicant feel comfortable. Also make certain that your first competency-based or open-ended question pertains to a topic within the individual's realm of experience, which will ensure a certain degree of ease. In addition, try using a softer tone of voice, exaggerated positive body language, and words of encouragement. Let the applicant know that you're interested in what she has to say.

Overly Talkative Applicants

Some applicants seem capable of talking nonstop. They not only answer your questions, but volunteer a great deal more information, much of which is irrelevant, unnecessary, and sometimes illegal. Applicants who are overly talkative may just be extreme verbalizers; on the other hand, they could be engaging in excessive verbiage to distract you from their lack of job-related skills.

Such people are often very personable and really quite delightful to talk with. However, you must remind yourself that you're not there to engage in a social conversation. Your goal is to acquire sufficient information upon which to base a hiring decision.

The key to effectively dealing with applicants who talk too much is control. You must remember that you're in charge of the interview and control the amount of time devoted to their questions and answers. When you've gathered enough information, say to the applicant, "Everything you've told me is very interesting. I now have enough information upon which to base my decision. Thank you very much for your time. You'll be hearing from us by the end of this week."

Sometimes applicants don't respond to this cue that the interview is over. They remain seated and resume talking. If this happens, escalate your efforts. Tell the applicant, "I'm afraid that's all the time we have. I have other applicants waiting. I'm sure you understand." At this point, stand up and extend your hand. As you shake hands, gently guide the applicant to the door.

Overly Aggressive Applicants

Some applicants present themselves in an overly aggressive or hostile manner. Perhaps they've been out of work for a long time, or maybe they've applied for a job with your company before and been rejected. Whatever their motivation, the resulting behavior makes interviewing difficult.

When confronted with an angry applicant, stay calm and maintain your objectivity. Try to find out why the applicant is so upset. Explain that you cannot continue the interview as long as he remains agitated. Your goal should be to complete the interview and judge the applicant as fairly as possible, taking into account any extenuating circumstances. If the applicant's behavior escalates, or he remains hostile, ask the applicant if he's still interested in the position. If so, tell him you need to reschedule the interview.

Domineering Applicants

Sometimes an applicant will try to gain control of the interview, usually to cover up for a lack of sufficient job experience. The attempted takeover may manifest itself in a variety of ways, for instance, by steering the conversation to a discussion of the interviewer's career or hobbies, or discussing books or plants in the office. All is not lost if this happens. Remind yourself that you're in charge and assertively say to the applicant, "Excuse, me, but we seem to have strayed. Let's get back to. . ." If he continues to try to dominate the interview, wait for an opening and state, "We only have a limited amount of time remaining and I still have a number of questions to ask you. Shall we get back on track?"

Highly Emotional or Distraught Applicants

Have you ever had an applicant become highly agitated during an interview? Needless to say, it can be quite unnerving. If this ever happens, extend empathy rather than sympathy; this will enable you to remain objective, in charge, and better able to help the individual regain composure. Resist patting her on the back or asking her to elaborate on whatever it was that set her off. In all likelihood, you'll get an earful of personal information you should not have. Offering the person a few moments of privacy usually enables most applicants to continue with the interview. In some instances, however, it may be preferable to reschedule the interview.

Occasionally, applicants become emotional or distraught when you challenge an answer to a particular question. If this happens, change direction and return to the question later in the interview, perhaps after a better rapport has been established. Emphasize to the applicant that the information is important for continued consideration. This message is usually sufficient encouragement for even the most reluctant applicant. Sometimes it's helpful to pose a series of very specific, closed-ended questions. Another way to encourage applicants to answer is to indicate that you'll be verifying the information she provides during a reference check.

Stress Interviews (How and Why to Avoid Them)

In a stress interview the applicant is deliberately put on guard, made to feel ill at ease, or "tested" for some purpose known only to the interviewer. *This technique is not recommended under any circumstances.* Proponents of stress interviewing claim that they're able to ferret out significant job-related traits, such as how applicants will handle uncomfortable situations that cannot be discovered through effective questioning techniques, assessing nonverbal communication skills, or weighing relevant intangible factors. In truth, stress interviews are often nothing more than a subterfuge for ineffective interviewing skills.

The examples of stress interviews that follow are provided so readers can avoid duplicating them. *Readers are urged to view these as illustrations of what to avoid.*

Stress Interviews in the Office

Stress interviews in the office usually involve various "props," such as chairs, exaggerated body language on the part of the interviewer, or unnecessary, sometimes inappropriate, comments. Here are some examples:

- The interviewer slowly eyes the applicant from head to toe, staring for some time at the applicant's feet. Finally he says, "I never would have worn those socks with those shoes."
- The interviewer makes certain that his chair is elevated considerably higher than that of the applicant.
- The interviewer invites the applicant to sit in an oversized chair, making it difficult for the applicant to rise up and out of it.
- The interviewer invites the applicant to sit in a chair with one leg slightly shorter than the others, causing it to wobble anytime the applicant shifts in her seat.
- The applicant is offered a chair better suited for a toddler.
- The applicant is offered a chair that faces the window. On a sunny day, with the drapes open, the interviewer repositions the chair according to the time of day so that the sun will shine directly in the applicant's eyes.
- The interviewer positions herself in front of a window on a sunny day with the drapes open, thereby causing a "halo" effect around her head.
- The interviewer begins firing questions at the applicant as soon as he enters the room.
- The interviewer doesn't ask the applicant any questions; rather, he simply stares at the applicant, waiting to see what the person will say or do.
- The interviewer asks questions while looking down at her desk or doing other work.
- The interviewer answers the phone during the interview, puts the person on hold, turns to the applicant, and says, "Go ahead; he can wait for a minute."
- The interviewer makes a series of phone calls during the interview.
- The interviewer leaves the room for several minutes.
- The interviewer begins by saying, "Go ahead, impress me."
- The interviewer begins by saying, "Is there anything you'd like to tell me?"
- The interviewer asks the applicant, "Do you always wear your hair that way?"
- The interviewer takes her watch off, places it on the desk, and says, "We have exactly forty-five minutes."
- The interviewer stares at the applicant's watch and says, "You must be rich. Why would you want to work here?"
- After responding to a question, the interviewer asks, "Are you sure that's the answer you want to give me?"
- The interviewer stares at the applicant for some time and finally says, "You're rather young, aren't you?"

Mealtime Stress Interviews

Mealtime interviews are generally reserved for professional-level applicants. They can be appropriate and quite comfortable for both the interviewer and the applicant if the same guidelines that govern office interviews are adhered to. Unfortunately, meals also provide an ideal arena for proponents of stress interviews, based on their perceived justification that eating and drinking habits may be a valid reflection of the applicant's decision-making skills on the job. Consider these examples:

•   The interviewer waits until the applicant has a mouthful of soup before asking a question.

•   The applicant is rejected because he orders a cheeseburger or some other food that requires direct handling with one's hands. The premise here is that an applicant should assume that he'll be asked to review papers during the course of a mealtime interview; this cannot be done with greasy fingers.

•   The applicant is rejected because she orders shrimp scampi when the interviewer orders a chef's salad. The premise here is that the scampi takes fewer than a dozen bites to complete while the salad requires more time to consume; therefore, the applicant will be finished eating long before the interviewer, leaving the interviewer feeling rushed.

•   The applicant accepts an offer of an alcoholic beverage and is rejected because he might have a tendency to drink too much.

•   The applicant refuses an offer of an alcoholic beverage and is rejected because she might be a recovering alcoholic.

•   The applicant is rejected for refusing to check his coat upon entering the restaurant, the assumption being that he's insecure about parting with possessions.

•   The applicant is evaluated on her knowledge of the correct utensils to use during various courses of the meal.

•   The applicant is found acceptable because he orders something from the menu that costs the same or less than what the interviewer orders.

•   The interviewer fires a steady stream of open-ended questions at the applicant as soon as her food arrives, to see whether or not she can eat and talk at the same time.

•   The interviewer tries to slip in some non-job-related, illegal questions during the meal.

•   The interviewer assesses the applicant's level of assertiveness based on how she deals with a disagreeable waiter.

•   The interviewer identifies several other diners who work at the same organization; later in the meal, she asks the applicant about them to determine how closely he was paying attention.

Interviewing Pitfalls

Regardless of the type of interview you're conducting, there are some pitfalls that all interviewers should be mindful of:

- Avoid interrupting the applicant, as long as he is saying something relevant.
- Avoid agreement or disagreement; instead, express interest and understanding.
- Avoid using terminology with which the applicant is unlikely to be familiar.
- Avoid reading the application or resume back to the applicant.
- Avoid comparisons with the incumbent, previous employees, yourself, or other applicants.
- Avoid asking unrelated questions.
- Avoid talking down to an applicant.
- Avoid talking about yourself.
- Avoid hiring an unqualified applicant simply because you are desperate to fill an opening.
- Avoid trying to duplicate someone else's interviewing style.
- Avoid allowing applicants to interview you or to control the interview.
- Avoid hasty decisions based solely upon first impressions, information from others, a single response, body language, or your biases.
- Avoid asking questions, even in a roundabout way, that might be considered violations of EEO laws.
- Avoid judging applicants on the basis of cultural or educational differences.
- Avoid conducting stress interviews of any sort.

Summary

There are many different types of interviews, each serving a specific function in the hiring process. Three of these are screening interviews:

1. *Face-to-face exploratory interviews* establish continued interest on the part of both the interviewer and the applicant, and determine preliminary job suitability.

2. *Telephone interviews* are intended to accomplish one of two objectives: to establish continued interest in a job applicant that results in an in-depth interview, or to determine that an applicant's qualifications do not sufficiently meet the job's specifications.

3. *Video interviews* allow employers to observe long-distance applicants in addition to simultaneously talking with them.

Under no circumstances should face-to-face exploratory, telephone, or video screening interviews substitute for the face-to-face interview.

Other types of interviews constitute comprehensive meetings between the applicant and one or more representatives of the hiring organization. These include:

- *Employment interviews* conducted by HR specialists are both broad-based and job-specific. They are broad-based in that the HR interviewer covers a great deal of general territory, including goals and interests, and they are job-specific because the interviewer delves into the applicant's education and experiences as they relate specifically to the available job opening.

•   *Departmental interviews,* which are conducted by department heads or managers, focus on whether the person can do the job; that is, they emphasize job specifics.

•   *Panel interviews* generally involve three interviewers—usually an HR representative, the department manager, and a department head. Panel interviews save time and allow interviewers to compare impressions of applicants as they answer questions.

•   *Peer interviews* involve potential colleagues of an applicant. Most peer interviews are in the form of panels. An HR representative should be present.

Most applicants are eager to make a good impression on their interviewer. They try to answer all questions as fully as possible, project positive body language, and ask appropriate questions. Occasionally, however, you'll find yourself face-to-face with a less-than-ideal applicant, someone who is excessively shy or nervous, overly talkative, overly aggressive or domineering, or highly emotional or distraught. At the first indication that you're dealing with a less-than-ideal applicant, make certain adjustments in how you proceed with the interview.

Proponents of stress interviews claim that the process allows them to ferret out significant job-related traits by deliberately putting the applicant on guard or at a disadvantage. Stress interviews are not recommended under any circumstances.

Regardless of the type of interview you're conducting, there are certain pitfalls that all interviewers should try to avoid.

Selecting the Best Fit

CHAPTER 11

Documenting the Interview

One benefit of active listening is that interviewers can take notes while the applicant is talking without losing track of what's being said. Thanks to thought speed, you can write down key words and ideas during the interview, then, immediately after, develop your notes more fully. Doing this right away will ensure that you retain important facts.

Remember the Role of Documentation in the Selection Process

Some interviewers believe that note taking will offend applicants or make them uneasy. If you feel this way, tell the applicant at the beginning of the interview that you'll be taking some notes to make certain you have sufficient information upon which to base an effective evaluation. Most applicants actually prefer that you take notes. After all, there are usually a number of applicants competing for one job; how can the interviewer differentiate among all the applicants without notes? In fact, not taking notes could convey a lack of interest on the part of the interviewer.

Interview notes are a permanent record and should be written with care. Most interviewers favor a separate interview evaluation form over a blank piece of paper. There are numerous variations as to the categories that should appear on an evaluation form and the terminology used to evaluate competencies and the applicant overall. Appendix G represents a basic format that distinguishes between essential tangible requirements, job-related intangible requirements, and additional desirable qualities. Significantly, the form calls for comments about the applicant's qualifications in relation to each requirement. In addition, interviewers are asked to support their overall evaluation of "strong," "average," or "weak" with specific examples drawn from the interview. The form also excludes numerical ratings for each qualification, as well as preset tangible and intangible competencies, recognizing that each job calls for a specific skill set. The form also steers clear of highly subjective terms such as "personality" and "appearance." If these traits can be shown to be job-related, the interviewer can add them under the heading "Job-Related Intangible Requirements."

Interviewers are cautioned against writing directly on the employment application. This is considered a legal document and should bear the handwriting of the applicant only, so if there are any corrections to be made or blanks to be filled in, have the applicant do it.

In addition to serving as a permanent record of an interview, documentation enables interviewers to measure each applicant's job suitability against the requirements of the job. Following the interview, place your notes next to the job description. Then simply compare your notes about the applicant's relevant experience, skills, and accomplishments with the requirements, duties, and responsibilities of the available opening. This should make it easy to identify areas in which the applicant shines as well as any skills or experience he lacks.

Documentation may also be used to compare applicants in the final running with one another. Place your postinterview notes on each finalist next to one another, with the job description at the end. Compare the background and qualifications of one person with the other applicants and with the job requirements.

Postinterview notes will additionally prove useful to the original and future interviewers when considering rejected applicants for jobs down the road. Finally, postinterview documentation is frequently scrutinized as potential evidence in employment discrimination suits.

Avoid Subjective Language

Avoiding subjective language, even if complimentary, is an important requirement for effective postinterview documentation. Stated another way, all language that is written down should be objective. For example, saying that an applicant is attractive is a subjective statement. On the other hand, writing that "the applicant's appearance is consistent with the employee image sought by the company" would be objective.

As you can see from this example, objective language generally takes longer to write and requires greater effort. It's easier to say that someone is attractive than it is to write the objective version of the same thought. However, the term *attractive* may not mean the same to everyone as it does to you, hence it would not be useful to future interviewers reviewing your notes, or even to you if your opinion as to what constitutes attractiveness changes over time. In addition, it could create an issue in an EEO investigation.

Following are some additional examples of subjective language that should be avoided:

Abrasive	Acted high	Acted like a real know-it-all
Appears to be rich	A real sales job	A real workaholic
Arrogant	Bad dresser	Boring
Calculating	Careless	Chip on his shoulder
Cocky	Cultured	Curt
Diligent	Easily distracted	Eccentric
Energetic	Erratic	Fake smile

Fidgety	Full of hot air	Good sense of humor
Greedy	Has a bad attitude	Ideal applicant
Ingenious	Interesting	Jovial
Lackluster	Looks like a model	Looks too old
Makes lots of mistakes	Manipulative	Money-hungry
Narrow-minded	Needs polish	No roots
No sense of humor	Not serious about working	Perfect
Personable	Polished	Pompous
Pontificates	Pretentious	Refined
Reserved	Restless	Rude
Sarcastic	Sharp	Shrewd
Sloppy	Sluggish	Smart
Snappy dresser	Somber	Tactful
Too hyper	Too much makeup	Too nervous
Too pushy	Tried too hard	Uptight
Vain		

In contrast, here are some examples of objective language:

- This job requires prior customer service experience; applicant has two years' experience as a customer service representative.

- This job calls for excellent verbal skills; applicant exhibited clear and concise verbal skills during our sixty-minute interview.

- This job includes working with highly confidential matters; applicant has never worked with confidential matters before.

- This job requires employees to be on-call; applicant said one of the reasons he was leaving his current job was because he was on-call and found it "disruptive" to his personal life.

As you can see, these objective versions actually reference relevant portions of the job description, leaving no room for doubt with regard to the applicant's qualifications.

Avoid Recording Unsubstantiated Opinions

Interviewers are cautioned against recording their opinions without sufficient job-related backup. Opinions that stand alone without concrete support imply that the interviewer has drawn some conclusions but has not identified what information these conclusions were based on. These statements generally begin with such telling phrases as:

"I feel . . ."
"In my opinion . . ."
"I believe . . ."
"It is apparent to me that . . ."

"In my judgment . . ."

"I am of the opinion that . . ."

"I think . . ."

"It is my view that . . ."

"To my way of thinking . . ."

"It is obvious to me that . . ."

"To me it is clear that . . ."

"Without a doubt, this applicant . . ."

These broad, summarizing statements do not refer to specific requirements and matching qualifications. Interview notes containing statements such as these would not be useful in determining the applicant's job suitability.

Following are some expressions that illustrate the ineffectiveness of recording opinions. None of the original statements tells us anything about the applicant's qualifications for a given job and all such statements should therefore be avoided. These statements become effective, however, when they are followed by job-related information:

Don't Say: "I feel Ms. Jenkins would make an excellent manager of product planning."

Say: "I feel Ms. Jenkins would make an excellent manager of product planning based on her experience in her present capacity as manager of product planning at Avedon Industries."

Don't Say: "In my opinion, Mr. Martin doesn't have what it takes to be a sales representative."

Say: "In my opinion, based on his lack of sales experience and failure to answer key questions, Mr. Martin does not have what it takes to be a sales representative."

Don't Say: "I believe Ms. Salamander is just what we're looking for!"

Say: "Based on her test scores and accounting expertise, I believe Ms. Salamander is just what we're looking for!"

Don't Say: "It's apparent to me that Mr. Brock can't do this job."

Say: "It's apparent to me that Mr. Brock can't do this job due to his lack of experience in a high-volume working environment."

Don't Say: "In my judgment, Ms. Princeton will make an excellent project manager."

Say: "In my judgment, after assessing her two years' experience as a project coordinator, Ms. Princeton will make an excellent project manager."

Don't Say: "I am of the opinion that Mr. Valentine will make a good addition to our staff."

Say: "I am of the opinion that Mr. Valentine will make a good addition to our staff based on his experience in dealing with crises and working under pressure."

Don't Say: "I think Mr. Turner will make a good mechanic."

Say: "I think Mr. Turner will make a good mechanic based on his three years' previous mechanic's experience."

Don't Say: "It is my view that we would be making a mistake if we hired this applicant."

Say: "It is my view that we would be making a mistake if we hired this applicant due to her lack of public relations experience."

Don't Say: "To my way of thinking, Ms. Davis appears to be just right for the office assistant position."

Say: "To my way of thinking, because of her demonstrated interpersonal skills, Ms. Davis appears to be just right for the office assistant position."

Don't Say: "I consider Ms. Hastings to be excellent secretarial material."

Say: "I consider Ms. Hastings to be excellent secretarial material based on three outstanding references and high test scores."

Don't Say: "It is my view that Ms. Heller will do quite well as a data processing operator."

Say: "It is my view that Ms. Heller will do quite well as a data processing operator after having worked in this capacity for the past two years."

Don't Say: "As I see it, Mr. Green is just right for this job."

Say: "As I see it, Mr. Green is just right for this job due to his accounts receivable background."

Don't Say: "To my way of thinking, Ms. Mendosa will make a great programmer/ analyst."

Say: "To my way of thinking, Ms. Mendosa will make a great programmer/ analyst because of her experience with multiprocessing systems."

Don't Say: "If you ask me, we've found our next assistant vice president of marketing."

Say: "If you ask me, after assessing his background in marketing for the past five years, we've found our next assistant vice president of marketing."

Don't Say: "I believe, with a little training, this applicant will work out fine."

Say: "I believe, with a little training to supplement her limited sales experience, this applicant will work out fine."

You can abbreviate the preferred versions of each of these statements by eliminating their opinion lead-in portions. For example, instead of writing, "It is my view that Ms. Heller will do quite well as a data processing operator after having worked in this capacity for the past two years," drop the lead-in and state, "Ms. Heller will do quite well as a data processing operator after having worked in this capacity for the past two years." Likewise, instead of stating, "As I see it, Mr. Green is just right for this job due to his accounts receivable background," write, "Mr. Green is just right for this job due to his accounts receivable background." And in the case of Ms. Mendosa, instead of recording, "To my way of thinking, Ms. Mendosa will make a great programmer/analyst because of her experience with multiprocessing systems," write instead, "Ms. Mendosa will make a great programmer/analyst because of her experience with multiprocessing systems."

Not only are these versions less wordy and therefore easier to write, they convey a stronger message and appear less tentative.

Refer to Job-Related Facts

There are two documentation techniques that best enable interviewers to assess job suitability, compare the qualifications of several applicants, measure the applicant for future job matches, and preclude the possibility of referencing any information that might violate EEO laws.

The more effective of these two techniques requires referring only to job-related facts. This is a simple process, especially if the job descriptions are well-written and if you practiced active listening techniques throughout the interview. As soon after the interview as possible, refer directly to each duty and requirement of the position and then indicate whether or not the applicant has the necessary skills and experience. In addition, you may want to record direct quotes made by the applicant.

Record Direct Quotes

Directly quoting the applicant is of particular significance when an applicant possesses all the concrete requirements of the job but is lacking some intangible, nonrecordable quality. For example, you're about three-quarters of the way through an interview, and even though the applicant can clearly handle the duties of the job, you have an uneasy feeling about her attitude concerning a number of tasks. Since recording that the applicant has a "bad attitude" would be subjective, you continue to probe until you either resolve or confirm your sense of unease by discovering some job-related reason for rejecting her. For example, among other things, you explore with her that this job requires extensive overtime with little advance notice. Your question to her in this regard might be, "Describe a time in your last job when you were asked to work overtime at the last minute; how did you react?" She replies, "I told my boss I didn't like the idea of being asked at the last minute! I mean, obviously I stayed, but I didn't like it." You might then say, "Are you saying that you have a problem with working overtime, especially on short notice?" She might then reply, "Don't get me wrong; I'll do it, but I would appreciate receiving sufficient advanced notice. After all, there is life after work!"

When it's time to write up this interview, you might state, "This job requires extensive overtime with little advance notice. When asked how she felt about this, applicant replied, 'I'll do it, but I would appreciate receiving sufficient advanced notice. After all, there is life after work!'"

By writing up your notes in this manner, you've clearly indicated that the applicant has effectively eliminated herself because she finds objectionable one of the requirements of the job—working overtime with little advance notice. It also suggests a "bad attitude," without saying as much.

Recording direct quotes can also be helpful when comparing several applicants with similar backgrounds and qualifications.

Let's consider another, more comprehensive illustration of the usefulness of referring directly to the position's duties and requirements and recording direct quotes made by the applicant. Jody is trying to fill the position of administrative assistant to the president of your company. Here's a partial list of essential duties and responsibilities, encompassing approximately 85 percent of the job:

- Schedules all appointments and meetings for the president.
- Arranges the president's travel itinerary, including commutation, reservations, and accommodations.
- Screens all calls and visitors to the president's office.
- Opens, reroutes, and disposes of all electronic and paper correspondence directed to the president.
- Replies to routine inquiries.
- Supervises maintenance of all correspondence and reports sent in and out of the president's office, including confidential information.
- Supervises the work of the president's clerical staff.
- Prepares formal minutes of all board of directors meetings, as well as shareholders and executive committee meetings.
- Prepares various reports required for meetings of the board of directors, shareholders, and executive committee.

As Jody interviews each applicant applying for this position, she refers to the specific job requirements. A partial interview with an applicant named Josh, who is currently working as a senior secretary for the vice president of public relations, might go something like this:

Jody: What are your responsibilities with regard to scheduling appointments and meetings?
Josh: Oh, I do all of that.
Jody: Please be more specific.
Josh: It's my job to see to it that the vice president's calendar is in order; that is, I schedule her appointments and meetings and then every morning, first thing, I go over her calendar with her. If she needs me to make any changes, I get on it right away.
Jody: What about with regard to arranging the vice president's travel itinerary?
Josh: That's my job, too. I even arrange international trips, because my boss trav-

els to Europe about a half-dozen times a year. It's up to me to book her hotel reservations, travel plans, and everything like that.

Jody: Tell me about a time when you thought her travel plans were all set, but then something went wrong.

Josh: Well, one time she flew to Rome, but when she arrived at her hotel they didn't have her reservation. It took them over an hour to straighten out the mess and find her a room in another hotel; by then, it was too late for her to change before making a big presentation. She was pretty mad at me, but it wasn't my fault.

Jody: Why do you think she was mad at you?

Josh: Because I was supposed to make the reservation—which I did. But I can't be held responsible for what some hotel clerk in Rome does!

Jody: What do you do when someone calls or stops by your office and wants to speak with or see your boss?

Josh: By now, I pretty much know whom she wants to see and whom I should turn away. I use my judgment and may tell someone she's in a meeting and can't be disturbed. I also offer my help. Sometimes the person has a question that I can answer.

Jody: Tell me about a time when someone insisted, saying it was urgent that he see her.

Josh: That actually happened last Friday morning. I remember because she really was in a meeting—her weekly staff meeting. The VP of human resources said it was an important matter concerning one of her employees. I buzzed her and she came right out.

Jody: What are your responsibilities with regard to the vice president's mail, including e-mail?

Josh: I open all the mail, including anything marked "confidential." Then I sort and prioritize everything so she can review it. Even though I know what can be discarded and what's important, she likes to go through everything herself. She's kind of a control freak.

Jody: What do you mean when you say she's a control freak?

Josh: Well, she likes to add her personal touch to most things.

Jody: Like what?

Josh: In addition to sorting through her own mail, she likes to place her own phone calls. She also likes to greet people rather than having me take them in to her. I guess that's about it.

Jody: How do you feel about that?

Josh: I don't mind. It's that much less for me to do!

Jody: Let's turn our attention to another aspect of this job. What is the extent of any supervisory responsibility you may have?

Josh: I don't have any.

Jody: Am I correct in understanding, then, that you do not delegate work to anyone else?

Josh: Right. I do it all myself.

Jody: Describe your responsibilities with regard to meetings.

Josh: I prepare memos and reports for distribution at staff meetings and for the executive committee; by that I mean I coordinate the materials and collate everything. Sometimes she asks me to prepare PowerPoint presentations. I enjoy that. But of course she checks each slide and usually ends up changing something.

Jody: What do you enjoy about preparing PowerPoint presentations?

Josh: I like being creative.

Jody: But you mind when your boss changes some of the slides?

Josh: I guess I do—I mean, why ask me to do something if you're going to change it?

This partial interview illustrates the importance of writing down facts as they relate to the duties and requirements of a job. Jody correlated each question to a particular responsibility listed in the job description. As the applicant responded, Jody might have jotted down the following key words and phrases:

Sr. sec'y.—VP PR

Schedules appointments, meetings and trips—prob. w/hotel in Rome: ". . . can't be hld respon. 4 . . . clerk/Rome does."

Screens visitors; offers help; puts through if urgent

Opens, sorts and prioritizes all mail, including confidential

Boss = "control freak" re: mail, calls, greeting peo. O.K. with app.—". . . less 4 me 2 do!"

No super/delegation

Coord./collates memos/reports for meetings (staff & executive)

Occas. preps. PP slides—likes creative; doesn't like when boss changes slides: "why ask me . . . if ur going to change it?"

After the applicant has left, Jody can review these thoughts and elaborate on her notes. By once again referring to the position's requirements, she can determine overall job suitability. The final set of notes, based on this portion of the interview, might read like this:

Applicant has worked as secretary to VP, public relations, for 3 years.

Job requires scheduling appointments and meetings: applicant schedules appointments and meetings.

Job requires making travel arrangements: applicant makes travel arrange. Problem with hotel in Rome—said, ". . . can't be held responsible for what some hotel clerk in Rome does."

Job requires screening calls and visitors: applicant screens visitors; offers help; puts through if urgent.

Job requires opening, rerouting and disposing of correspondence: applicant opens & prioritizes all mail, including "confidential."

Refers to boss as "control freak" re: mail, calls, greeting people; O.K. with applicant—". . . less for me to do."

Job requires supervising and delegating work to clerical staff: applicant has no super/delegation experience.

Job requires preparing reports for meetings—board of directors, shareholders, and executive committee: applicant coordinates and collates memos and reports for staff and executive meetings.

Occasionally prepares PowerPoint slides—likes creative aspect; doesn't like when boss changes slides: "Why ask me to do something if you're going to change it?"

Everything written is a job-related fact, including the three quotes. Since Josh lacks experience with some of the essential tangible and intangible requirements of this job, Jody feels confident about eliminating him from further consideration. Should her decision be challenged, she can confidently turn to her documentation of the interview for validation.

Be Descriptive

A second documentation technique enables interviewers to better recall specific applicants. It entails recording a description of the applicant's behavior, speech, attire, or appearance. Interviewers conducting interviews for entry-level jobs as well as volume interviews in excess of twenty a week may find this technique helpful. After meeting with so many people, interviewers may have difficulty remembering one applicant from another when referring back to each person's application or resume. Even notes that are objective, factual, and job-related may not succeed in jogging their recollection of a specific applicant.

To help you better recall specifics, consider the occasional use of descriptive phrases. Their purpose is limited to identifying the person and aiding you in remembering the particular interview. Take care when using such phrases for two primary reasons: First, descriptive phrases can easily become subjective, and second, even though factual, they're not job-related. To illustrate: "Applicant was dressed entirely in yellow" is an objective descriptive phrase. The addition of just one word, however, makes it subjective: "Applicant was garishly dressed entirely in yellow." Even the objective version, however, is not job-related.

Here are additional examples of objective descriptive phrases:

- Smiled during the entire thirty minutes of the interview
- Hair extended below waist
- Wore black nail polish
- Wore pearl cufflinks
- Twirled hair through entire ninety minutes of the interview
- Played with paper clips
- Tapped fingers
- Taller than 6'6" (doorway to office is 6'6")
- Laughed every time she answered a question
- Chewed gum
- Rocked in chair

Interviewers are cautioned against using any of these descriptive terms as part of the selection process. They are intended only to help you remember the applicant, not to determine job suitability.

Document Applicants with Limited Experience

You may find yourself recruiting for jobs that carry limited experiential or educational requirements. These are usually entry-level positions requiring simple, repetitive tasks. Naturally, when this occurs you can't evaluate someone's demonstrated skill level. In these instances, consider posing hypothetical questions relative to the specific tasks of the job and recording the applicant's reply. For instance, suppose you have an opening for an entry-level administrative assistant. The position calls for the ability to manage a wide variety of assignments simultaneously. During the course of the interview, you might ask an applicant, "What would you do if several managers gave you projects to complete by the same date, but you didn't feel you could get everything done on time?" The applicant might reply, "I would suggest that the managers talk to one another and work it out." Your notes for this interview might then include the following reference to the job-related activity: "When asked how would handle multiple tasks with the same deadline, said, 'Would tell managers to talk and work it out.'"

This way, even interviewers with applicants who lack prior work experience can yield postinterview documentation that is objective, factual, and job-related.

Keep Effective Notes

At this point it's helpful to illustrate both effective and ineffective note taking. To accomplish this, let's revisit the abridged job description for the position of assistant to the director of human resources in Chapters 7 and 8. Now let's expand upon it and add portions from an interview for the position. Note that the interview excerpts include only questions asked by the interviewer and responses by the applicant. They do not include detailed information provided about the job and the company, nor do they include questions asked by the applicant. Following the interview excerpts are examples of effective and ineffective note taking.

Job Description for the Assistant to the Director of Human Resources

1. Recruits applicants for nonexempt-level positions via various recruitment sources.
2. Interviews and screens all applicants for nonexempt positions; refers qualified applicants to appropriate department manager/supervisor.
3. Assists department manager/supervisor with hiring decisions.
4. Performs reference checks on potential employees, by telephone and in writing.
5. Processes new employees in terms of payroll and benefits; informs new employees of all pertinent information.
6. Is responsible for conveying all necessary insurance information to employees and assisting them with questions, processing of claims, etc.
7. Assists in the implementation of policies and procedures; may explain or interpret certain policies as required.
8. Assists in the maintenance and administration of the organization's compensation program; monitors salary increase recommendations as they are received to ensure compliance with merit increase guidelines.
9. Advises managers/supervisors of employee performance review schedule; follows up on delinquent or inconsistent reviews.
10. Is responsible for the orderly and systematic maintenance of all employee records and files.
11. Assists EEO officer with advising managers/supervisors on matters of equal employment opportunity and affirmative action as they pertain to the interviewing and hiring process and employer-employee relations.
12. Assists in the maintenance of up-to-date job descriptions of positions throughout the company.
13. Maintains all necessary HR records and reports; this includes unemployment insurance reports, flow log recording, EEO reports, change notices, and identification card records.
14. Conducts exit interviews for terminating nonexempt employees.
15. Assists HR manager and HR director with the planning and conducting of each month's organizational orientation program.
16. Performs other related duties and assignments as required.

Prior Experience and/or Education

1. Thorough general knowledge and understanding of the HR function.
2. Prior experience as a nonexempt interviewer, preferably in a manufacturing environment.
3. Ability to work effectively with all levels of management and large numbers of employees.
4. Ability to deal effectively with applicants and referral sources.

Partial Interview for Human Resources Assistant

Interviewer: Good morning, Ms. Oliver. Thank you for coming in. Please be seated.

Applicant: Thank you. I'm glad to be here and, by the way, it's Mrs. Oliver, but you can call me Sandra.

Interviewer: Did you have any difficult getting here, Sandra?

Applicant: No, my daughter attends school about two miles from here, so I'm very familiar with the area.

Interviewer: Well, I'm glad that you didn't have any trouble. I'm anxious to begin talking with you about your interest in our opening for the assistant to the director of human resources.

Applicant: Oh, I'm ready! I've been looking forward to this all week. I really want this job!

Interviewer: Fine. Then why don't we begin discussing your qualifications as they relate to the responsibilities of this job.

Applicant: Sure, no problem.

Interviewer: To begin with, this job requires recruiting, interviewing, and screening applicants for all of our nonexempt positions. Please describe your experience in this regard.

Applicant: Well, that's exactly what I've been doing for the past year at Circuits, Inc.

Interviewer: Please explain what you mean.

Applicant: Well, whenever I receive an approved job requisition, it's up to me to start recruiting. The first thing I do is talk with department heads to make sure I understand the requirements and duties of the job. I also try to visit the department to get a feel for the work environment and to see firsthand what the person will be doing. It also helps beef up my rapport with the department head. Let's see, where was I? Oh, yes, then I start to explore different recruitment sources.

Interviewer: Such as?

Applicant: The usual: agencies, want ads, employee referrals, you know.

Interviewer: Any others?

Applicant: That's usually all it takes. We don't have any trouble attracting applicants. We have a fine reputation in the manufacturing industry, as I'm sure you know.

Interviewer: Please continue.

Applicant: Well, I interview and screen all the applicants and then refer those qualified to the department head.

Interviewer: Where did you learn to interview?

Applicant: I have a degree in HR administration, as you can see from my resume, and then I received on-the-job training when I first joined Circuits, Inc.

Interviewer: How much time was devoted to on-the-job training?

Applicant: About three months. Then I was left on my own.

Interviewer: I see. Please go on.

Applicant: Okay. As I said, I refer qualified applicants to the department head. Then we get together and decide on whom to hire.

Interviewer: Who finally makes the actual hiring decision?

Applicant: The department heads and I usually agree, but if we disagree, then they decide. After all, they're the ones who have to work with the person.

Interviewer: What are your responsibilities with regard to reference checks?

Applicant: I run both written and telephone references on only those applicants we're interested in.

Interviewer: Tell me about a reference check that didn't confirm the information you had on an applicant. What happened?

Applicant: That's happened several times, actually. Each time I tried to get at least two additional references to confirm either the employer's information or the applicant's. Then I turned all the information over to the department manager for a final decision.

Interviewer: Tell me about a time when you felt it appropriate to discuss the conflicting information with the applicant. What happened?

Applicant: There was this applicant who warned me in advance that I might get some negative information from his old boss. He was right. I called the applicant and told him what his former employer had said. He called the guy who ended up calling me to explain why he said what he did. It was pretty amazing. We ended up hiring the guy; he worked out fine.

Interviewer: Once an applicant is selected, what do you do?

Applicant: I arrange the starting date and schedule them for orientation. It's also my job to put them on payroll and take care of their benefits.

Interviewer: So then, is it your responsibility to explain all the company benefits?

Applicant: No, not exactly. I just process the paperwork. Someone from the benefits department explains all that during orientation.

Interviewer: I understand. Tell me, Sandra, does Circuits, Inc. have a policies and procedures manual?

Applicant: Yes, it does.

Interviewer: What are your responsibilities with regard to this manual?

Applicant: Sometimes if my boss, the human resources manager, isn't around, I try to answer questions from department heads.

Interviewer: Give me a specific example.

Applicant: Well, last week one of the managers from accounting called for clarification on our vacation policy for part-timers.

Interviewer: Were you able to help?

Applicant: Yes.

Interviewer: Good. Tell me, in addition to recruiting, interviewing, screening, and processing payroll and benefits paperwork, what other areas of human resources are you involved with?

Applicant: Well, let's see. Let me think for a minute. Oh yes, I'm in charge of performance reviews.

Interviewer: In what way are you in charge of performance reviews?

Applicant: I keep a log of when each nonexempt employee's review is due and notify the department head if they don't get them in on time.

Interviewer: Tell me about a time when a department head didn't submit a past-due review despite repeated requests.

Applicant: We have this one department head—I won't name names—who never gets anything in on time. So what I did was start bugging him about two months before the review was really due. By the time he finally got around to sending it in, it was only a little late!

Interviewer: I see. That's certainly an interesting approach. Tell me about your responsibilities with regard to salary administration.

Applicant: I don't have any. We have a compensation manager who takes care of that.

Interviewer: What about equal employment opportunity and affirmative action?

Applicant: Nope. Our EEO officer handles that. I know a lot about those areas though.

Interviewer: You know a lot about EEO and affirmative action?

Applicant: Yes. I studied it in school and attended a three-day seminar on it about six months ago. I'd like to specialize in EEO some day.

Interviewer: That's very interesting. What other human resources responsibilities do you have at Circuits, Inc.?

Applicant: Well, I help with job descriptions.

Interviewer: In what way?

Applicant: Whenever there's a nonexempt job opening, I check with the department head to make sure that the job hasn't changed significantly and that the existing job description is still valid. If it needs revamping, I tell my boss and she takes over from there.

Interviewer: What are your responsibilities with regard to HR record keeping?

Applicant: I keep an applicant flow log and make sure employees update their records online.

Interviewer: Do you personally process any other forms?

Applicant: None that I can think of.

Interviewer: What about your involvement with exit interviews?

Applicant: Oh, yes, I forgot about that! I do all exit interviews for nonexempt employees. I enjoy that!

Interviewer: What is it that you enjoy about it?

Applicant: I like finding out why a person is leaving and what the company might do in the future to prevent good people from leaving.

Interviewer: I see. That's very interesting. Describe for me a specific exit interview and what you learned as a result.

Applicant: We recently lost a great programmer/analyst because we ignored his request for a transfer to a less technical department. He didn't care about making less money; he just wanted to change fields. Even though he was really good at being a techie, he just didn't enjoy it. I felt badly about that; we should pay attention to what people want to do as much as what they can do.

Interviewer: What other aspects of your work do you enjoy?

Applicant: I like the interviewing, you know, talking to so many different people.

Interviewer: Tell me about one of the most interesting people you ever interviewed.

Applicant: There was an applicant who came in with a snake draped around her neck—honest! She said it was her pet and that she took it wherever she went!

Interviewer: That's certainly unusual. What don't you like about your job, Sandra?

Applicant: If I had to pick one thing, I guess it would be making sure employees update their records via the Intranet; you know, like when they've completed a course at school or learned a new skill. All that has to go into their files and they're responsible for doing it, but I'm kind of a watchdog over the entire process.

Interviewer: What aspect of your job do you find to be the most difficult?

Applicant: I guess that would be my part in the monthly orientation program.

Interviewer: You participate in the orientation program?

Applicant: Yes, didn't I mention that? I have to give an opening talk of about twenty minutes about the history of Circuits, Inc., why it's such a great place to work, that sort of thing.

Interviewer: What is it about doing this that you find difficult?

Applicant: I get nervous talking in front of people.

Interviewer: I see. Sandra, I'd like to get back for a moment to your educational training in HR administration. What made you interested in this field?

Applicant: It seemed challenging and varied. It also seemed to offer a lot in the way of growth opportunities.

Interviewer: What level do you ultimately want to achieve?

Applicant: I think I'd like to be an EEO officer.

Interviewer: If we contacted your college, what would they tell us about your grades, both in HR courses and other courses?

Applicant: I graduated with a 3.0 average. I did pretty well in everything except math. I got a "D" in statistics.

Interviewer: What did your HR curriculum consist of?

Applicant: Everything. The degree prepared me to be a generalist.

Interviewer: I know you said that you particularly like EEO. What aspects of human resources do you enjoy the least?

Applicant: That would have to be benefits. I really find it kind of dry and boring.

Interviewer: I understand. Sandra, I have just a few more questions to ask you. Can you tell me about a time when an applicant acted up? By that I mean, became aggressive or otherwise emotional.

Applicant: I did have a guy start screaming at me when I told him the job he was applying for was already filled. I tried to calm him down by telling him we could still talk, then if something suitable opened up in the future I could call him. It worked. I knew I had to remain objective if I was going to evaluate him fairly.

Interviewer: It sounds like you got a good handle on the situation. Sandra, what does the prospect of this job offer you that your present job does not?

Applicant: It's time for a change.

Interviewer: A change?

Applicant: Yes. One year in Circuits, Inc. is long enough. It's not the most exciting place in the world to work.

Interviewer: What's your idea of an ideal work environment?

Applicant: One where employees who prove themselves can grow; also, where managers don't look over your shoulder all the time. Of course, I'd like to be paid more, too!

Interviewer: What type of employee are you?

Applicant: I like to work independently. I don't need close supervision.

Interviewer: What do you feel you could offer our company, Sandra? Please be specific about three of your attributes, and examples of when you've applied them in your current job.

Applicant: Let's see. Well, I'm objective. I gave you an example of that before with the applicant who was screaming at me. I'm also a hard worker. In the last month alone I've worked overtime at least a dozen times without getting paid for it. And I care about keeping good people once we hire them—that's why I get so much out of exit interviews. I also want to say that I love the field of human resources.

Interviewer: Is there anything else I should know about your qualifications that would help me to make a hiring decision in your favor?

Applicant: I can't think of anything else.

Interviewer: Fine, Sandra. I'd like to thank you again for coming in. We'll be interviewing for the next five days or so, and will make our decision at the end of that time. If you have any questions in the interim, please feel free to contact me. I've enjoyed talking with you.

Applicant: Thank you. I've enjoyed talking with you, too. I really want this job!

Interviewer: I understand. Good-bye, Sandra.

Applicant: Bye.

Example of Ineffective Notes

Here are the ineffective notes taken during the course of the interview with Sandra:

Married; young daughter

Too anxious

Tends to ramble

Only nine months' real experience; degree okay

Likes P&P involvement

Had trouble remembering what else she does

Interested in EEO; I smell trouble

No real J.D. experience

Light record keeping

Sounds like a troublemaker; loves to find out why people leave

Dislikes doing orientation

Dislikes benefits

Light experience with problem applicants

Bored with present job; didn't give it much of a chance

Wants more money and to move up in a hurry

Doesn't like supervision

Summarizing Statement

I don't feel Sandra would make a very good HR assistant. She just doesn't seem reliable. Also, she hasn't demonstrated a thorough knowledge of HR.

As you can see, these statements are highly subjective. In addition, several of the comments are not job-related and some violate EEO regulations.

Example of Effective Notes

Now let's review effective notes based on the same interview (to be subsequently elaborated upon in relation to job-specific requirements and responsibilities as identified in the job description):

Circuits, Inc., manufacturing

Nonexempt interviewing experience: 9 mos.; 3 mos. OJT

Degree in HR admin.

Recruiting, interviews (enjoys), screens, and recommends for hire

Telephone and written references

Processes payroll and benefits form

P&P manual; most questions handled by HR mgr. (boss)

No sal. admin. respon.

Expressed interest in pursuing field of EEO

Checks on accuracy of existing JD's

Flow log and employee updates (enjoys least)

Exit interviews for all nonexempt employees (enjoys)

Participates in monthly orientation prog.: "nervous talking in front of people"

Least favorite: benefits

Reason for leaving: "time for a change"

Has dealt with applicants who have acted up; knew it was important to remain objective

"Like to work independently"

"I'm a hard worker; I love the field of human resources."

Summarizing Statement

This job calls for a thorough general knowledge and understanding of human resources as well as prior experience as a nonexempt interviewer. Ms. Oliver has had three months' on-the-job training and nine months' actual experience in the following areas of HR at Circuits, Inc.: nonexempt recruitment, interviewing, screening, references, processing payroll and benefits forms, checking accuracy of job descriptions, flow logs and employee updates, exit interviews, monthly orientation. Also has a degree in HR administration. Recommends hiring; interested in EEO; enjoys exit interviews; least favorite—benefits. "Wants a change"; "Likes to work independently"; "hard worker"; "loves HR."

These statements are all objective, factual, and job-related. Anyone reading them would have an immediate understanding of the applicant's skill level as it relates to the requirements of the job.

Adhere to Documentation Guidelines

Effective documentation requires adhering to a set of simple, yet critically important, guidelines:

1. Take notes using an interview evaluation form; do not write on the application form. The application is a legal document and should bear the handwriting of the applicant only.
2. Write only key words or phrases during the interview; elaborate immediately afterward.
3. Refer to the job description to relate accomplishments with specific requirements.
4. Take notes reflecting positive as well as negative attributes and comments.
5. Use objective language, avoiding subjective terminology.
6. Provide concrete support for all opinions.
7. Record job-related facts.
8. Write down portions of specific questions and directly quote applicants' responses.
9. Record descriptive terms if needed to distinguish applicants from one another.
10. Use terminology likely to be understood by anyone, never codes that may be misconstrued.

Summary

Notes serve as a permanent record of an interview. They also help interviewers assess an applicant's job suitability in relation to the job description and as compared with other applicants, are useful to the original interviewer and others considering rejected applicants for future openings, and can be used as evidence in employment discrimination suits.

Effective documentation relies on objective language. Additionally, any personal opinions should be supported by job-related information.

There are two effective documentation techniques that enable interviewers to assess job suitability. The first requires that only job-related facts be referred to. The second technique relies on a description of the applicant's behavior, speech, attire, or appearance to help interviewers differentiate between applicants.

Directly quoting applicants' responses can prove useful for those jobs that do not carry any experiential or educational requirements. They are also helpful when an applicant meets the concrete aspects of a job, but falls short with regard to one or more intangible requirements.

CHAPTER 12

Preemployment Testing

Following World War II, testing was used extensively as a means for selecting new hires. The popularity of testing as a selection tool continued for several decades, only to decline toward the end of the 1990s. However, due in part to an increasingly competitive global economy, heightened security concerns (especially post 9/11), worries about workplace violence, and shortages of skilled labor, preemployment tests are once again becoming a favored means for selection. For HR practitioners, this may mean re-examining existing or previously used tests to support an increasing array of computer-based test options, while remaining sensitive to certain applicant populations, e.g., older workers, who may be more comfortable with more traditional tests. It may also mean revisiting areas to be tested. Quantifiable skills, such as computer knowledge, and personal qualities, like honesty, are among the most common testing categories, but also popular are interest tests and tests that purport to measure learning and thinking ability. HR test givers must also be ever vigilant about possible adverse impact, job-relatedness, and overreliance on test scores as the basis for selection.

Can tests accurately predict how individuals are likely to perform in any given job? Even the strongest supporters of tests will agree that not all tests are created equal and that care must be exercised in their selection, implementation, and interpretation. Therefore, employers that administer tests are urged to consider test results as only one basis for selection.

How Preemployment Tests Are Used

Employers typically use preemployment tests to accomplish two primary objectives: eliciting an applicant's undesirable traits and identifying characteristics that most closely match the qualities required for the available job. Specifically, tests given to prospective employees may help to:

- Predict acceptable or unacceptable on-the-job behavior
- Minimize or eliminate bias in the interview and selection process
- Allow employers to identify potentially unfit workers
- Identify responsible individuals, capable of working under certain working conditions

- Reduce the cost of recruiting, hiring, and training
- Identify future "superstars"
- Identify additional job factors that should be taken into account
- Safeguard against so-called "professional applicants" who pride themselves on being able to mislead interviewers
- Identify workers who will need extra assistance or training
- Flush out factors that could prove to be detrimental on the job

Advocates of preemployment testing believe that employers can acquire this information through the use of a wide range of tests, including skills and aptitude, integrity, personality, psychological, drug, and physical. The exams may be conducted at any point in the selection process, depending on the extent of an employer's commitment to test scores. Firm believers in testing generally require applicants to complete one or more tests as the first step. If the applicants achieve a predetermined minimum score, they will be interviewed and given further consideration. If not, they are rejected. Employers who place a greater value on the face-to-face meeting usually require tests only after the interview process is completed. These employers place little weight on test performance unless it conflicts with information acquired during the interview or through reference checks. Employers who place an equal emphasis on each of three main tangible aspects of the selection process—interviewing, testing, and references—usually first discuss various aspects of the job with the applicant, then conduct tests, talk further with the applicant, and, finally, conduct reference checks. The results of each phase are then studied and a hiring decision is reached.

HR practitioners are urged to work closely with their hiring managers and come to an agreement as to the role preemployment testing plays in the selection process.

Testing Advantages and Disadvantages

In the simplest terms, preemployment and employment tests are defined as procedures for determining job suitability. This is accomplished by examining the skills, knowledge, or physical capabilities of employees or employment applicants according to a predetermined set of objective guidelines. The results are assessed in relation to the requirements and responsibilities of a given position and conclusions are drawn as to the appropriateness of the individual's qualifications.

Testing Advantages

Proponents of workplace testing maintain that the process enables employers to match an individual's abilities and potential with the requirements of a given job. It also identifies certain desirable and undesirable traits. Among the positive traits are honesty, reliability, competence, emotional stability, integrity, and motivation. Negative characteristics to be screened out include substance dependency and a propensity to steal. In security-sensitive jobs, ferreting out such traits becomes particularly important. Another popular reason for workplace testing is to protect against charges of negligent hiring, the charge employers sometimes face when they fail to exercise reasonable care in hiring or retaining employees. Increasingly, employers are being held responsible for the criminal, violent, or negligent acts of their employees, both in and away from the workplace. Generally, the deciding factor is whether an employer can establish that it exercised reasonable care in ensuring the safety of others. One way of accomplishing this is through preemployment and employment testing.

Some test proponents also support workplace testing as a substitute for reference checks. Fear of being charged with defamation of character has led many employers to refuse to divulge all but the most basic information, such as dates of employment and job titles, about former employees. This is unfortunate; more information than is commonly given could, in fact, be shared since the common law doctrine of qualified privilege states that an exchange of job-related information is in the best interest of both employers and the general public. Still, the sharing of reference-related information is often limited; consequently, employers are turning to other means—like testing—to determine job eligibility.

Another advantage of workplace testing is its overall objective nature. Assuming it's been validated, a test can help employers make unbiased job-related decisions. When tests are fair representations of the skills and knowledge needed to perform a given job, employers are likely to be portrayed as impartial; this in turn may enhance the overall image of an organization.

Finally, tests may help distinguish between otherwise similarly qualified applicants. Although no two applicants may ever be perceived as identical in terms of skills, abilities, and potential, it's sometimes difficult to choose the one person likely to be the best overall fit. Tests may help with the final decision.

Testing Disadvantages

One of the greatest concerns expressed by testing opponents is the tendency to rely too heavily on tests. Certainly this is true when employers conduct tests prior to interviewing applicants, immediately dismissing those who do not score at a minimum level. This frequently occurs with interviewers who aren't confident in their ability to ask questions and interpret answers, usually due to a lack of training or experience. It also occurs in an organization that has been "burned," or involved in some sort of legal action that may have been avoided by a more thorough selection process.

Another common complaint about preemployment testing stems from the tendency to believe that tests can point to people who *will* do well, as opposed to those who are *likely* to do well in a given job or work environment. The predictive abilities of any exam are limited; results can only indicate which individuals are most likely to succeed. This is true even if a test is well-designed and properly used.

Opponents of testing additionally point out that many people react negatively to the mere idea of a test. There are individuals who may be qualified but do not score well on tests, which results in a distorted or incomplete picture of their abilities if tests are overemphasized. Rejecting such an applicant is a disservice to the person and possibly to the organization as well.

Concern that tests may be misused is also on the negative side of the testing ledger. Test misuse can occur when employers are interested in seeing what abilities an applicant possesses beyond those called for in a given job. This is usually done to help evaluate potential and future growth; after all, what employer doesn't want its employees to stay for a long time? This motivation cannot be faulted, but the method is inappropriate. Tests should be given only to evaluate specific skills, abilities, and traits as called for in the available job.

Testing may also be inappropriate when the qualities being sought can be acquired through a minimal amount of on-the-job training or education. In such instances, testing is an unnecessary expenditure of time, money, and energy. Finally, testing is too commonly viewed as the solution to numerous employment problems. Sometimes, improved employer-employee relations best address workplace conflicts.

A summary of testing advantages and disadvantages appears in Exhibit 12-1.

Test Validation

In 1978 the U.S. Equal Employment Opportunity Commission, the U.S. Civil Service Commission (renamed the Office of Personnel Management), the Office of Federal Contract Compliance of the U.S. Department of Labor, the U.S. Department of the Treasury, and the U.S. Department of Justice together adopted the Uniform Guidelines on Employee Selection Procedures (UGESP), under Title VII of the Civil Rights Act of 1964. The primary purpose of the UGESP is to provide a framework for determining the proper use of tests and other selection procedures when they are to be

Exhibit 12-1. Testing Advantages and Disadvantages

Advantages

- Enables employers to match an individual's abilities and potential with the requirements of a given job
- Identifies certain desirable and undesirable traits
- Protects against charges of negligent hiring
- Substitutes for reference checks, which may be difficult to acquire
- Is inherently objective, if validated
- Distinguishes between otherwise similarly qualified applicants

Disadvantages

- Substitutes for effective interviewing skills
- Attempts to predict who will do well
- Screens out qualified individuals who do not test well
- Attempts to evaluate future job suitability
- Substitutes for on-the-job training in jobs requiring minimal learning
- Viewed as solving multiple employment problems

used as the basis for any employment decision. The term "test" covers all formal, scored, quantified, or standardized techniques of assessing job suitability. "Other selection procedures" refers to application forms, interviews covering education and work experience, reference checks, performance evaluations, training programs, and any other means for determining job suitability. The guidelines are also intended to preclude the use of any selection procedure that has an adverse impact on the hiring, promotion, or other employment opportunities of members of either sex or of any race or ethnic group. When two or more substantially equal selection procedures are available, employers are expected to use the procedure that has been shown to have the lesser adverse impact on members of any protected group. These guidelines apply to private employers with fifteen or more employees, state and local governments, and most employment agencies, labor organizations, and contractors and subcontractors of the federal government.

Validation studies are required as a means of "proving" that a certain test or other selection procedure really works and does not discriminate against members of protected groups. The keys to proving validity are job relatedness and evidence that the test is a proven indicator of job success.

In broad terms, validation begins with a thorough job analysis to identify the requirements of a job. The next step entails identifying selection devices and standards that will isolate applicants or employees who meet the job requirements. Employers should then prepare a detailed validation report that outlines and documents the steps taken. The last part of the study is a summary explaining the study's conclusions and stating that the study found the selection procedure used to be valid and nondiscriminatory. Validity studies should be carried out under conditions ensuring the adequacy and accuracy of the research and the report. Here's some information on types of validity studies.

Types of Validity Studies

The UGESP recognize three specific methods of determining validity:

1. *Criterion-related validity* refers to a statistical relationship between scores on a test or some other selection procedure and the actual job performance of a sample of workers. There must be evidence that the selection procedure is predictive of job performance. For example, a study proving that college graduates perform a particular job better than high school graduates would be criterion-related.

2. *Content validity* pertains to selection procedures that test a sample of significant parts of a particular job, that is, a demonstration that the content of a selection procedure is representative of important aspects of job performance. For example, the analysis of computer skills for an administrative assistant's position would constitute a content validity study.

3. *Construct validity* describes a relationship between something believed to be an underlying human trait or characteristic and successful job performance. Honesty,

for example, might be such a characteristic, the presence and measure of which might be measured by a given selection procedure.

For all three methods, the guidelines specify that cutoff scores must be "set so as to be reasonable and consistent with normal expectations of acceptable proficiency within the work force."

Although the uniform guidelines do not state a preference for one validity method over the others, it is generally agreed that the criterion-related process, though effective, can be a long and expensive procedure. Construct validity has been the source of much debate and is considered to be the most difficult of the three to establish. Consequently, most employers rely on content validation, believing that it most accurately predicts job success.

The guidelines do not specify how frequently or under what conditions validity studies should be reviewed for currency. They do, however, urge employers to keep abreast of changes in the labor market, relating such changes to the validation strategy originally used and revising their validation studies accordingly.

Employers may use tests and other selection procedures that have not been validated provided a legitimate validation study is underway. Until it is completed, however, employers are discouraged from making hiring decisions based on invalidated test results.

Testing and Bias

Misuse of preemployment tests can violate federal employment laws if employers use them to intentionally discriminate or if they disproportionately exclude individuals in any protected group, unless employers can justify a test despite its discriminatory impact. Here's what some federal employment laws have to say about testing and bias:

Title VII of the Civil Rights Act of 1964

According to section 703(h) of Title VII, it is not "an unlawful employment practice for an employer to give and to act upon the results of any professionally developed ability test provided that such test, its administration or action upon the results is not designed, intended or used to discriminate because of race, color, religion, sex or national origin." Neutrality is best ensured by tests prepared by industrial psychologists or other testing professionals and validated according to the standards set forth in the UGESP. Employers choosing to bypass professionally developed tests and use instead their own in-house tests may find themselves facing charges of Title VII discrimination, since "homemade" tests are more difficult to validate than professionally researched tests.

There are two important Title VII terms that impact testing. The first is *disparate treatment*. This may occur if, for example, employers test the abilities of nonwhite applicants but not those of white applicants. The second, called *disparate impact* or *adverse impact,* prohibits employers from using non-job-related neutral tests or selection procedures that have been statistically shown to have a greater negative impact on members of a protected group, such as an endurance test that screens out a disproportionate number of women. Employers can negate any suggested or apparent disparate impact if they can show that the selection procedure or test is job-related and consistent with business necessity—in other words, that it is necessary for the safe and efficient performance of the essential functions of the job. Even then, however, the selection procedure may be challenged if a less discriminatory alternative is shown to be available.

Employer liability may occur under Title VII as it relates to numerous forms of testing, among them:

• *Drug or Alcohol Tests.* Employers should make certain that individuals are not singled out for drug or alcohol testing on the basis of race, color, religion, sex, or national origin. Ideally, either all applicants and employees should be tested or none. If a random testing program is in place, employers should avoid testing a disproportionate number of members from any particular group. Employers successfully demonstrating that their drug and alcohol testing program is a result of business necessity are less likely to be held liable, even if an adverse impact is found.

• *Psychological Tests.* All general intelligence and aptitude tests must be validated to avoid the potential for adverse impact. Employers must be prepared to not only produce evidence of validation, but to demonstrate that the test is valid for specific jobs.

• *Personality Tests.* Charges of adverse impact, particularly as they concern women, may result from improperly conducted personality testing. This is because certain personality characteristics may be interpreted differently when it comes to men and women. For example, a male applicant may be viewed as detail-oriented, whereas a similarly qualified female candidate may be labeled as demanding.

• *Physical Ability Tests.* Physical ability tests must be based on a thorough job analysis and show that they are related to the job. Employers who have never used a physical test before and then institute a testing procedure must be prepared to present a business necessity defense. Physical ability tests are most frequently challenged on the basis of sex and age discrimination.

Age Discrimination in Employment Act of 1967

Generally speaking, the Age Discrimination in Employment Act (ADEA) prohibits the disparate treatment of individuals aged 40 and over. With regard to testing, the act identifies specific prohibited behaviors, such as the issuance of physical agility tests only to those over age 50 based on a belief that they are less physically able to perform a particular job than are younger potential employees. The ADEA also blocks employers from using neutral tests or selection procedures that have a discriminatory impact on individuals 40 and older, unless such tests or procedures are based on a reasonable factor other than age.

Rehabilitation Act of 1973

The Rehabilitation Act deals with the issue of preemployment physical exams. Businesses that have not required physicals in the past must prove necessity if they wish to start conducting them. Additional stipulations apply:

- Physical exams must be issued to everyone, not only to those with disabilities.
- They cannot be the first step in the application process.
- They may be required after a conditional job offer has been made.
- Physical fitness for work requires a qualified physician who must phrase any negative findings in specific, objective, job-related terms.
- The results of the exam must be shared with the applicant.

Applicants who are unable to perform the essential functions of a job without harming themselves or others, even with reasonable accommodations on the part of the employer, are effectively denied protection under the Rehabilitation Act.

Americans with Disabilities Act of 1990

Title 1 of the Americans with Disabilities Act (ADA) prohibits private employers and state and local governments from discriminating against qualified individuals with disabilities based on those disabilities, specifically when employers may require examinations that will identify physical or mental impairments. As with the Rehabilitation Act of 1973, employers may not require medical exams until after making a conditional job offer. At that point, they may ask disability-related questions as long as they do it for all individuals being hired for the same job. Employers may also ask questions about a disability or require medical exams if they have a reasonable belief, based on objective information, that a potential employee will be unable to perform the essential functions of a job, or if they receive a request for a reasonable accommodation from the individual.

The ADA requires organizations that conduct tests of any kind to do so in a place and manner accessible to persons with disabilities. Individuals with impaired sensory, manual, or speaking skills must be offered modified tests or appropriate auxiliary aids to accommodate their disabilities.

Preemployment psychological and personality tests are not expressly prohibited by the ADA, but they cannot be used to identify disabilities, including mental or psychological disorders. If their purpose is to assess personality traits, behavior, attitudes, or a propensity to act in a certain way, psychological and personality tests may be conducted at any stage of the employment process.

Tests used to screen out individuals with disabilities must be shown to be job-related and consistent with business necessity.

Genetic Information Notification Act

Under Title II of the Genetic Information Notification Act (GINA), it is illegal for employers to discriminate because of genetic information. This includes requesting, requiring, purchasing, or disclosing information about an individual's genetic tests or the genetic tests of an individual's family members. Family medical history is referenced in GINA because it is often viewed as relevant in determining whether someone is predisposed to getting a disease, disorder, or condition.

Employers are expressly prohibited from using genetic information in making a hiring decision.

Test Administration

Test administration encompasses a number of components, including who should take tests, who should administer tests, test standardization, test security, and language consistency. Exhibit 12-2 highlights each of these components.

Exhibit 12-2. Components of Test Administration

Test Takers	Applicants and employees who need to demonstrate specific skills and knowledge essential for the successful performance of a particular job
Test Administrators	Professionals on staff Someone on staff sent for professional training Outside professionals
Test Standardization	Same environment

	Same conditions: Duration
	                                      Instructions
	                                      Materials
	                                      Physical factors

	Eliminate distorting influences: Tools in poor repair
	                                      Excessive noise
	                                      Interruptions
	                                      Uncomfortable seating
	                                      Poor lighting
	                                      Poor ventilation

Test Security	Keep separate those who have taken tests from those who have not yet been tested Limit access to tests and answer sheets Keep tests locked Assign random seating
Language Consistency	Avoid unfamiliar words or word usage

Test Takers

Many people believe that it's most equitable to require testing across the board, that is, a test for every applicant applying for every job. Each external job applicant should be tested, as should each employee under consideration for transfer or promotion. Across-the-board testing precludes claims that certain individuals have been singled out for testing. This method may seem fair on the surface, but it is actually laden with bias, since not all positions require tests. It's far better to first identify in a written job description the specific skills required to perform a particular job, then ask yourself a simple but crucial question: "What do I hope to accomplish by conducting a test?" The answer—"I hope to identify those individuals who possess specific skills and knowledge deemed essential for the successful performance of a given job"—should help determine who should take tests.

Test Administrators

According to the American Psychological Association (APA) Standard 6.6 of "Responsibility for test use should be assumed by or delegated only to those individuals who have the training and expertise necessary to handle this responsibility in a professional and technically adequate manner."

The level and type of expertise of the tester should be commensurate with the complexity and level of the job in question and with the type of test involved. For example, individuals with a minimal degree of training and test administration knowledge can generally conduct multiple-choice tests. On the other hand, administering tests that assess personality or mental ability usually requires extensive training. Test publishers generally indicate the degree of psychological training required to administer and interpret their tests. A third type of testing, work sample tests, may be conducted and rated by individuals who are knowledgeable about the details of the job. This may include line supervisors as long as they are also familiar with basic testing procedures, including how to set up for the test, give instructions, and score the test.

Depending on the type of test in question, employers may select a professional already on staff to manage their testing programs, send someone on staff for professional training, or hire outside professionals. Employers need to carefully evaluate the credentials of outside vendors and check their reputation in the field. In addition, it is prudent to review the test's underlying research and its relevance for meeting an organization's goals.

Test Standardization

Each time a test is administered it should be given in exactly the same way, in the same environment and under the same conditions, including duration, instructions, materials, physical factors, and any other aspect that might affect testing outcome. It is only when precise standards are adopted and all applicants are allowed to react to the same set of stimuli that legitimate conclusions may be drawn about test scores and job suitability. A possible exception may be made for certain online tests that are computer adaptive, meaning that answers to the current question determine what the next question will be. But this method of testing is more difficult to design in an equitable way and may be challenged for being invalid or having an adverse impact.

Every effort should also be made to eliminate or minimize distorting influences. This includes test administrators who mumble or speak with a pronounced accent, using tools that are in poor repair, excessive noise, interruptions during the test, uncomfortable seating, or poor lighting or ventilation. Of course, if a particular job is routinely performed in a noisy atmosphere, then simulating that environment as part of the test would be appropriate.

Test Security

The APA's Standard 15.3 calls for "reasonable efforts to be made to assure the validity of test scores by eliminating opportunities for test takers to attain scores by fraudulent means." To accomplish this, some employers opt to limit the number of people who have access to copies of the tests and answer sheets, as well as keeping all exams locked away in a safe location. Further, during exams, they may separate individuals who know one another to minimize cheating. Although such measures could result in negative feelings on the part of some test takers, they are often necessary for fair and meaningful test results.

Language Consistency

Linguistic factors may adversely affect the test performance of speakers of dialects or those who are unfamiliar with certain terms or situations. Unfamiliar words or word usage may be a distraction or may create negative attitudes toward the test and testers, which would have a negative impact on test results. Employers must make every effort to ensure that there is no bias in the language of their tests. Maintaining consistency of language helps ensure equitable testing conditions.

Testing Policies

Organizations that conduct tests should have written testing policies. The policy should include the primary objective of testing; the organization's commitment to compliance with relevant employment laws; which applicants will be tested; who will conduct and interpret test results; a description of testing conditions; and a description of all tests currently used. Everyone concerned with conducting or interpreting tests, in addition to all those involved in any stage of the employment process, should become familiar with the policy through training workshops in which all the components of the organization's testing program are fully discussed and explained:

- *The primary objective of testing.* A general statement will usually suffice: "As part of (JavaCorp.'s) commitment to hire qualified individuals to fill positions as they become available, selected preemployment testing may be conducted. Resulting test scores will contribute to making the final selection."

- *The organization's commitment to compliance with employment laws.* A clear and concise statement will express the company's position: "It is (JavaCorp.'s) policy to employ qualified individuals regardless of race, creed, religion, national origin, sex, age, or disability status. When an equally valid means of assessing applicants is known to be available, it will be used if it has less of an adverse impact on groups that are subject to discrimination."

- *Information pertaining to which applicants and employees will be tested.* First, a statement regarding the testing of similarly situated applicants should appear: "All applicants applying for a position identified as suitable for testing will be given the same test. Such tests will be job-related and relevant to the selection process. Reasonable accommodations will be made for individuals with disabilities." This statement should then be followed by a list of those positions that currently require tests.

- *Who will conduct and interpret test results.* A general remark concerning the competency of test administrators should begin this section: "All testing will be carried out by those individuals having the training and expertise necessary to assume this responsibility in a professional and technically competent fashion. The actual degree and type of expertise will be commensurate with the complexity and level of a given job."

- *A description of testing conditions.* Begin by addressing the issue of standardization: "Each time a test is administered it must be given in exactly the same way, in the same environment and under the same conditions. This includes identical duration, instructions, materials, and physical factors." Next, provide a detailed description of where tests are administered. If tests are not always conducted in the same place, describe the ideal testing environment. Include such factors as type of seating, lighting, ventilation, tools, and materials. In addition, this section should address the issue of security to ensure fair test results, as well as the importance of eliminating any linguistic factors that may adversely affect test performance.

- *A description of all tests currently used.* Begin with an introductory comment concerning the validation status of tests in the organization: "All tests used by (JavaCorp.) have been found to be valid and nondiscriminatory, both in content and in practice." Then identify all of the tests currently being used, noting that these tests are reviewed on a regular basis for currency.

Testing Programs

The Society for Industrial and Organizational Psychology, Inc. (industrial-organizational psychology is the scientific study of the workplace) identifies what they consider important elements of a testing program. They suggest that employers consider consulting with professionals with training in test development and evaluation before proceeding:

- Clearly identify what knowledge, skills, and abilities are required of a given job, then ask: can these requirements be measured via testing?
- Select an appropriate test. If you are going to purchase a test, ensure reliability and validity. Reliability refers to the consistency of test results; validity refers to whether the inferences made on the basis of a test score are correct. Determine, too, how the test was developed, evidence of reliability and validity, confirmation that the test lacks bias, and data to help with the interpretation of test scores.
- Consider developing your own test. Often, a "homegrown" test will meet your needs better than a prepublished generic one.
- Work with an industrial-organizational psychologist to isolate the pros and cons of different kinds of tests and what they can be expected to reveal about the test taker.
- Ensure the expertise of those who administer, score, and evaluate test results. These experts' responsibilities include ensuring consistency and keeping accurate records of test scores.

(See http://www.siop.org/workplace/employment%20testing/effectivetesting.aspx.)

Testing Categories

Several tests are classified in more than one way. For example, some achievement tests measure physical abilities and could therefore be categorized with physical testing; other achievement tests measure knowledge, placing them under the heading of psychological testing. Similarly, motor work samples may be considered a form of physical testing, but they are also a type of achievement test and could therefore be classified as psychological. Drug tests are clearly physical tests, but because of their popularity they are frequently given their own category. The same holds true for integrity testing: Although technically a form of personality testing, integrity tests usually stand on their own.

Exhibit 12-3 organizes some of the most common forms of testing into categories, and further by specific types. The list is not meant to be all-inclusive.

Drug Testing

The controversy over whether to test applicants and employees for drug use remains unresolved. Sound arguments can be made both for testing and for not testing. Proponents point to the risks linked to substance abuse and maintain that testing will ferret out offenders and rid the workplace of numerous ills. But those who oppose drug testing are quick to point out that some courts have criticized a "zero tolerance" policy, designed to deter drug use off the job as well as on the job, as an unwarranted invasion of privacy. Popular methods used for detection, such as urine analysis, may also be considered invasive and a violation of an individual's privacy.

Exhibit 12-3. Testing Categories

Drug

- Blood
- Critical tracking (assess on-the-spot employee fitness by measuring fine hand-eye coordination and reaction time)
- Hair analysis
- Saliva
- Sweat
- Urine (screening; confirmatory)

Psychological

- Achievement (measure current skills, knowledge, and accomplishments)
- Aptitude (what a person can accomplish on the basis of what she knows)
- General intelligence
- Interest and vocational inventories
- Job knowledge or trade
- Work sample

Personality

- Ipsative (forced choice scale requiring test takers to compare two or more options and pick the one that is most preferred)
- Personality inventories (seek to uncover personal characteristics, thoughts, feelings, attitudes, and behavior)
- Projective (describe, interpret, or attach meaning to certain unstructured stimuli)
- Self-report inventories (test takers rate the degree to which they agree or disagree with statements)

Integrity

- Polygraphs
- Honesty tests
    - Overt or clear-purpose (measure attitudes relating to dishonest behavior)
    - Veiled-purpose (pose seemingly irrelevant questions)

Physical

- Preemployment physical exams
- Tests of physical ability (psychomotor tests)

Opponents also object to drug testing because they fear it will subject companies to potential legal liability. Applicants or employees who have been accused of drug use may allege that positive test results do not prove any act of wrongdoing. For example, urine can retain traces of drugs for anywhere from a few days, in the case of cocaine and amphetamines, to a month, as with the drugs classified as cannabinoids. Consequently, although a urine test may indicate use of an illegal drug, it cannot establish with certainty that the drug was used during working hours, impaired the employee's ability to perform his work, interfered with the work of colleagues, or endangered the safety of others. Lawsuits may also stem from false positive test results caused by the use of legitimate, over-the-counter drugs. This is most likely to occur when urine-screening tests are used, since they frequently report "drug detected" without distinguishing which drug is involved. To reduce this possibility, it is advisable to ask test takers to identify all drug products used in the weeks prior to the test.

In addition, no matter how sophisticated a test may be, it does not always correctly identify all individuals who use drugs. Temporary abstinence, faked samples, and false negatives are all obstacles to accurately identifying drug abusers. Also, few tests are able to differentiate users from abusers—an important distinction. Hence, the relationship between testing positive for substance abuse and job performance is debatable.

To help you determine whether testing is appropriate for your company, consider these questions:

- Are there safety- or security-sensitive jobs where substance abuse might endanger lives or property?
- Are other companies in my field conducting drug testing?
- How successful have other companies with drug-testing programs been?
- How receptive are members of management and the workforce to drug testing?
- If my organization decides to implement a drug-testing program, will it be part of an overall workplace antidrug program?
- If we make a job offers conditional on passing a drug test, will word spread, affording applicants ample opportunity to "test clean"?

Applicant Drug Test Consent

If your company adopts a drug-testing policy for applicants, it's advisable to test all job applicants as a condition of employment. Acquire the permission of applicants prior to conducting drug tests. Applicant consent forms can be simple and straightforward: "I agree to submit to drug testing as part of (Avedon Industries') employment selection process. I understand that positive test results, refusal to be tested, or any attempt to tamper with test samples or results will result in the withdrawal of my employment application, offer of employment, or termination of employment, depending on when the results are made known."

These forms might also call for applicants to list current medications, including over-the-counter drugs. Additionally, they could be asked include a statement that the applicant agrees not to file any action against the company or its laboratory testing service. Prior to issuance, legal counsel should review consent forms.

Psychological Testing

Psychological tests are viewed by proponents as tools for identifying and predicting behaviors that are relevant to a given position. For example, many industrial psychologists believe that an individual's propensity to leave an organization prematurely can be anticipated through testing. Similarly, in evaluating applicants for sales positions, a psychological test might be used first to identify the characteristics judged most valuable in a sales representative and then to assess the likelihood that a particular applicant will exhibit those traits. Psychological tests are also increasingly being used to evaluate specific traits, such as managerial effectiveness, business ethics, company loyalty, stability, cooperation, and independence.

To determine whether such testing is appropriate, employers need to explore answers to these questions:

- Can psychological tests really identify traits and predict behavior?
- Is it safe to assume that an individual's behavior, and therefore test scores, will remain relatively stable over time?
- Are they effective measures of intelligence or ability?
- Can employers rely on test projections?

Objectors to and Supporters of Psychological Testing

Here are some of the most commonly voiced objections to psychological testing in the workplace:

- The tests are intimidating.
- They invade the privacy of individuals.
- They set a negative tone for the workplace.
- They cannot accurately measure intelligence because intelligence defies definition.
- They promote labeling—for example, referring to someone as "bright" or "slow."
- They may contain questions on topics with which test takers are uncomfortable.
- The results may be misleading or misused.
- They promote reliance on testing to the exclusion of other selection factors.

On the other hand, employers who are fearful of charges of negligent hiring, are unsuccessful at obtaining comprehensive references, or are uncomfortable with their ability to conduct effective employment interviews are turning to psychological tests as a means of "knowing" a person before making a hiring decision. They argue that responsibly administered psychological tests designed to select employees whose abilities match the requirements of a job can be more objective than other selection procedures. In addition, they reason that psychological tests:

- Can be more cost-efficient than other screening devices
- Have a deterrent effect on deviant conduct among those hired
- Produce a more productive workforce

- Provide employers with peace of mind
- Provide employers with a competitive edge

Types of Psychological Tests

Currently, employers may choose from among thousands of commercially available standardized psychological tests, including general intelligence tests that measure a wide range of traits; aptitude tests that predict what a person can accomplish on the basis of what she knows; achievement tests that measure current skills, knowledge, and accomplishments; job knowledge or trade tests that require applicants to demonstrate their degree of existing knowledge on how a given job is performed by answering written or oral questions; interest and vocational inventories that purport to determine what jobs individuals are most suited for; and work sample tests that require test takers to demonstrate their existing level of skills using actual or simulated job-related equipment.

Employers must make certain that the tests selected comply not only with federal and state laws, but with appropriate ethical standards as well. The ethical use of tests can be controlled to some extent by a code of ethics to which professional testers and publishers subscribe. Both the American Psychological Association (APA) and the American Personnel and Guidance Association (APGA) are bound by ethical codes pertaining to test administration and other psychological services. These codes cover such issues as test validity, reliability, standardization, and administration. Test publishers must also control the release of tests to qualified persons only: those trained to use tests for their intended purposes alone. Publishers and distributors of psychological tests must make certain that the tests they market are designed properly and are of potential value to a particular organization and society as a whole.

Employers obtaining psychological test results must understand exactly what is being measured by the tests given to prospective employees, as well as what is not being measured. It is especially important for employers to realize that test scores are not fixed measures of an individual's mental status; rather, tests of general intelligence and special aptitudes reveal only the probability that a test taker will succeed in a particular job or field. In addition, test scores are susceptible to errors of measurement and to changes in abilities and achievements.

Personality Testing

Personality tests are designed to assess the degree to which a person has certain characteristics or predict the likelihood that a person will engage in certain conduct. Should personality be a consideration when making a hiring decision? The answer to this question will vary with each job. Clearly, some tasks will be carried out more effectively if the incumbent possesses certain intangible traits. For example, a friendly receptionist is certainly more desirable than one who is abrasive or abrupt, because a receptionist is generally the first contact a client or visitor has with a company. Similarly, an interviewer who appears disinterested or judgmental could make an applicant feel uneasy and hesitant about revealing important background information. In these instances, certain aspects of an applicant's personality are job-related. On the other hand, personality has less relevance for programmers or those hired to conduct research, since they will have limited interaction with others.

Job-relatedness, then, is the key to whether personality should be a consideration when making a hiring decision. But how can the job-relatedness of an intangible be determined? One way is to ask yourself if an applicant without certain traits can perform a given job as effectively as another who possesses those traits. If the answer is no, and you can document why, then the personality requirements are probably valid. If the answer is yes, but an applicant with certain characteristics could probably do a better job, then the answer is less clear. If the answer is yes, but you would prefer to hire a particular personality, then the requirement is probably invalid and should be stated as more of a preference.

Even when personality traits are job-related, employers are cautioned that judgments about personality are subjective, and as such are susceptible to challenge. Care must be taken to avoid weighing personality too heavily or to use it as the sole basis for selection or rejection. As stated earlier, intangibles are most useful when there are two or more applicants with similar tangible skills or when there are no concrete requirements at all.

Advocates and Opponents of Personality Testing

Advocates of personality testing view it is a valid indicator of job success. They maintain that a workforce made up of individuals who have been selected in part because of their responses to personality test questions will be more compatible and work more efficiently together, thereby improving productivity. Additionally, having been properly "matched" with their jobs, members of such a workforce are more inclined to stay with one employer for a longer period of time. Proponents also argue that personality tests provide employers with a more complete picture of an applicant than do other selection criteria, such as application forms, resumes, face-to-face interviews, or reference checks. In addition, supporters of personality testing maintain that information may be gathered in such a way that applicants are unaware of exactly what is being revealed. Hence, there is little potential for allegations of discrimination and resulting lawsuits. Finally, supporters claim that personality tests reduce recruitment costs, in that tests can accurately identify those workers best suited for specific jobs, virtually eliminating wasted time, effort, or money.

Opponents of personality tests strongly disagree with these claims. They argue that personality is extremely difficult to measure and that labeling personalities is an imprecise process. Even if it is shown that a particular quality prevails over others, there may be unusual circumstances to take into account, perhaps a significant event in the applicant's life that after a certain period ceases to be influential. Opponents express concern over the assumption that personalities do not change over time and reject the idea that matches deemed appropriate or otherwise at one time will necessarily remain so. They also voice concern that employers who conduct personality tests might erroneously assume that a given job can be successfully performed by only one specific personality type. This kind of thinking not only discriminates against qualified applicants, but it also may hurt the company.

Employers who decide to use personality tests to help make better hiring decisions should make certain the tests are developed in full compliance with the UGESP, be validated, and be administered by individuals skilled and knowledgeable in matters of personality testing. Test questions should also be worded to minimize the potential for violating an individual's privacy and an individual's protection against self-incrimination.

Integrity Testing

Integrity tests may reveal significant information relating to a person's honesty, dependability, trustworthiness, and reliability. Stated another way, they are used to identify individuals who are likely to engage in counterproductive behavior at work.

Supporters of integrity tests point to reduced costs through the identification of individuals who are less likely to engage in inappropriate or unacceptable behavior, such as theft. Detractors express concern that applicants may provide inaccurate or dishonest information, thereby resulting in a false foundation upon which to make a decision.

Polygraph Tests

Polygraph tests, or lie detector tests, were once among the most popular forms of tests used by businesses. The Employee Polygraph Protection Act now prohibits most private employers from using lie detector tests. Exceptions may apply when employers hire workers for security-sensitive jobs and pharmaceutical work, or for those employers involved in manufacturing, distributing, or dispensing controlled substances. Individuals suspected of theft, embezzlement, or other behavior that results in economic loss to the employer may also be asked to take a polygraph test. Additional exemptions apply, including for federal, state, and local governments. Employers that are exempt may not use the results of the polygraphs as the sole basis for making an employment-related decision.

Strict standards govern the use of polygraphs, including the issuance of written notice prior to testing. Individuals may also refuse to take, or discontinue taking, a test. They also have the right not to have test results disclosed to unauthorized persons.

Honesty Tests

Not surprisingly, since the Employee Polygraph Protection Act virtually bans the use of the most popular form of integrity testing, there has been an increase in the use of honesty tests. Most of these tests pose a series of direct and indirect questions related to thievery and deceit, while others seek out the potential for unsafe work habits, drug abuse, and counterproductivity. These tests generally take about twenty minutes to complete and are scored by computer in approximately six seconds.

While most would agree that honesty tests are less intimidating than polygraphs, there is a great deal of concern expressed over their validity. Test publishers argue that their honesty exams are highly accurate and based on extensive research. Many experts, however, express concern over the ability of such test results to determine job suitability.

Physical Testing

Physical tests are intended to ensure a workforce that is physically capable of performing the essential functions of each job and not threaten the health or safety of others. Preemployment physical exams and physical ability/psychomotor tests are the two primary forms of physical testing used by employers as preemployment hiring tools.

Preemployment Physical Examinations

Preemployment physical examinations can identify individuals who are not physically able to perform the essential functions of a job in a safe and effective manner. More specifically, such exams may disclose a person's past and present state of health or prior exposure to harmful substances or an injurious environment. Predictive screening, while controversial, can also assess an applicant's susceptibility to future injury.

Employers are subject to the preemployment physical restrictions and guidelines of their respective states. These generally include requiring the employer to pay for the entire cost of the exam, providing the employee with a copy of the results, and maintaining the confidentiality of the results. State regulations may also control the timing of tests and who may not be tested. Some states restrict preemployment physicals to those applicants receiving an offer of employment. In these instances, employment is generally conditioned on the successful completion of the medical exam. Other jurisdictions stipulate that preemployment medical exams must be given to all applicants. Depending on the test results, accommodation for those with physical or other impairments may be required, barring undue hardship to the employer. Note also the provision in the Americans with Disabilities Act that people with disabilities cannot be singled out for physical exams.

Employers are advised to familiarize themselves with relevant state requirements before implementing or continuing with preemployment physicals. Examining state fair employment or civil rights acts and consulting with an attorney can help in this regard.

In these litigious times, ever-increasing numbers of employers are requiring applicants and employees to sign a waiver acknowledging that the company does not guarantee the accuracy of its physician's conclusions. This sort of waiver is an attempt to limit the employer's liability for negligence if the employee later suffers an on-the-job injury because of a condition that was not detected during the preemployment physical. Consult with legal counsel before implementing such a waiver.

Preemployment physical exams can be significant detective and evaluative tools, assuming the administering physician is familiar with those tasks that are essential to the performance of each applicable job and evaluation is limited to the applicant's ability to perform those tasks. Test results are not always accurate, however, and they offer limited predictive qualities. Consequently, physicals are effective, but as with most other tests, only as one of several selection devices.

Physical Ability and Psychomotor Tests

Many on-the-job injuries occur because the tasks require more strength and endurance than employees can exert without excessive stress. These injuries can lead to increased absenteeism and turnover, not to mention claims for workers compensation and health insurance. Since it is extremely difficult, if not impossible, to judge a person's strength and level of endurance on the basis of body size and appearance, physical ability tests—also known as strength and endurance tests—can be helpful preemployment selection devices for positions requiring physical performance. On the other hand, they are typically more likely to differ in results by gender than other types of tests. In addition, opponents point to the time and cost involved, as well as logistical problems associated with administering physical ability tests in standard office environments.

The preferred validation method for physical ability tests is content validity. This means a thorough job analysis has determined that a given test accurately reflects the primary duties and responsibilities of a job. Many employers contact private agencies or clinics for assistance with physical ability testing.

Psychomotor tests measure such abilities as manual dexterity, motor ability, and hand-eye coordination. They are used primarily for semiskilled, repetitive work, such as packing and certain forms of inspection. Most psychomotor tests are simulation tests. The most valid psychomotor test should call for the use of the same muscle groups as required on the job. Custom-made tests that reproduce the combination of motor abilities needed have been shown to have fair validity.

Computer-Based Testing

Computer-based tests (CBTs), also known as e-assessments, are tests in which the answers are electronically recorded and evaluated. CBTs come in many forms, the most popular of which is the computerized adaptive test (CAT), also known as tailored testing. With CATs the computer "adapts" itself according to the test taker's ability by selecting the next question based on the answer to the previous question. If the test taker answers a question correctly, the level of difficulty increases for the next question. On the other hand, if the test taker answers a question incorrectly, the next question is less difficult. The process continues until either the accuracy of the test score reaches a certain level or the test ends after a predetermined number of questions are administered. Questions for CATs are chosen from a pool of possible questions categorized by content and difficulty. Individual test takers are exposed to specific questions that are appropriate to their ability level. Hence, CATs are highly personalized.

Computerized classification tests (CCTs) are a variation of CATs in that they are also adaptive. The goal with CCTs is to classify the test takers into two or more broad categories, such as pass or fail, rather than to determine a specific score. Some CCTs provide an immediate pass or fail score and provide detailed scoring later.

Advantages of CBTs

Proponents of CBTs maintain that these procedures eliminate any possibility of administrative bias, ensuring standardized testing procedures. Other advantages include:

- *Accuracy.* There is a reduced chance for transcription errors that accompany written "bubble" answer sheets.
- *Consistency.* Well-controlled test environments and consistent test administration are by-products of CBTs.
- *Convenience.* CBTs offer test takers a wider choice of testing locations and testing dates.
- *Diversity of questions.* CBTs offer a wide range of question types pulled from numerous types of exams. They can randomize the order of questions or devise exams instantaneously by selecting questions from a variety of subjects.
- *Ease.* The tests are reportedly easier to take than pencil-and-paper tests, in that tutorials demonstrate how to take the test and test takers can simply click on an answer.
- *Efficiency.* CBTs offer shorter test-taking time and faster score reporting. In fact, results are usually available immediately.
- *Security.* CBTs offer increased security due to the relative ease in handling and protecting electronic files.
- *Varied presentation.* Information is presented in a wide range of formats, utilizing graphics, voice-activated responses, and split screens to simultaneously display text and questions.

Disadvantages of CBTs

There are three primary concerns about using CBTs:

1. *Computer literacy.* CBTs are thought to favor test takers who are more computer literate, e.g., Millennials and GenXers, despite tutorials that allow users to become familiar with the computer and learn how to read the questions and indicate their responses prior to taking the actual test.

2. *Lack of flexibility*. Some test takers complain that CBTs prevent them from returning to a previously answered question. In addition, they can't jump around within a section.

3. *Cost.* Costs related to the start-up, software, and maintenance of CBTs are perceived by some as prohibitive.

All variations of CBTs are subject to the standards and requirements for selection procedures as outlined in the UGESP.

Summary

Employers typically use a wide range of preemployment tests to accomplish two primary objectives: eliciting an applicant's undesirable traits and identifying characteristics that most closely match the qualities required for the available job.

There are numerous testing advantages and disadvantages that should be weighed before using any test. Proponents argue that testing is inherently objective and that in addition to matching an individual with a job and identifying specific traits, tests can protect against charges of negligent hiring. Opponents maintain that there is no substitute for effective interviewing and that tests cannot predict who will do well or evaluate future job suitability. Furthermore, tests may screen out qualified individuals who simply do not test well.

Tests and other selection procedures must be validated. The keys to proving validity are job relatedness and evidence that the test is a proven indicator of job success.

Proper test administration includes identifying who should take tests, who should administer and evaluate them, standardization of testing conditions, security, and language consistency. All of this should be covered in an organization's testing policy.

There is a vast array of testing tools from which to choose, including aptitude tests designed to measure a person's potential ability, achievement tests intended to measure current skills, and physical tests that may ensure performance of tasks without threatening the health or safety of others. There are several significant types of exams within each of these broad testing categories including drug, psychological, personality, integrity, and physical. These, in turn, are broken down further into hundreds of specific tests.

Computer-based tests are thought by many to be superior to traditional written tests due to their ease in implementation and efficiency of use. Opponents express concern that they appeal only to Millennials and GenXers.

All tests are subject to the standards and requirements for selection procedures as outlined in the Uniform Guidelines on Employee Selection Procedures.

CHAPTER 13

References and Background Checks

Most interviewers know it's unwise to make a hiring decision without first checking an applicant's references and, in many instances, conducting a thorough background check. Despite well-honed recruiting, screening, and interviewing skills, even the most seasoned interviewers feel uncomfortable extending a job offer without more closely examining information about the person selected.

Reliance on references and background checks has increased, due in part to concerns over charges of negligent hiring and retention. In addition, there is greater anxiety over identify theft. News of executive embezzlement and unscrupulous behavior has also left employers wary of hiring without first conducting reference and background checks on all individuals, regardless of position or level.

Employers conducting reference and background checks need to be able to distinguish between the two forms of information gathering, consider relevant legal guidelines, and become familiar with both reference essentials and the fundamentals of background checks.

Internet-based references will be explored in Chapter 14.

References Versus Background Checks

While "references" and "background checks" are both part of the selection process, each focuses on different aspects of an individual's past.

Distinction Between References and Background Checks

References probe an individual's work- and education-related background. The primary purpose of any reference check is to (1) verify information provided by the applicant throughout the application process and (2) establish job suitability. Most employers have a statement on their application forms informing would-be employees that a job offer is contingent upon satisfactory references and that falsification of any information is grounds for rejection, or termination if such information is acquired after hire. Reference checks also allow potential employers to view would-be hires through the eyes of former employers.

Background checks explore aspects of an individual's background that have nothing to do with previous jobs or education and are more personal in nature. Typical areas of focus include criminal records (generally dating back as many as seven years), credit reports, medical records, and workers compensation records. The extent of preemployment background checks should relate to specific job requirements. For example, conducting a Department of Motor Vehicles investigation would make sense when hiring a crane operator, but it would not be appropriate when hiring a secretary.

Most employers conduct reference and background checks only on those applicants they are interested in hiring. Since background checks are often conducted by outside vendors for a price, many businesses bypass this step and focus on HR-conducted references.

Reference and Background Checklists

Checking the references and backgrounds of new hires can require a good deal of time and energy, especially during periods of high-volume interviewing.

A colleague of mine, Josh, winces when asked to retell a reference and background check horror story that happened because he didn't stay on top of the process. As the HR manager for his company, Josh felt his job ended when the hiring manager made her final selection. At that point, he turned the paperwork over to his assistant, whose job was to contact their vendor for a routine background check while she conducted educational and experiential reference checks. Meanwhile, a letter offering employment was sent to the soon-to-be new hire, contingent upon satisfactory reference and background checks. In this particular instance, the vendor apparently needed additional time for its investigation, but didn't say why. Josh's assistant didn't think anything of it and proceeded with her part of the process, calling the applicant's former employer. She was unable to acquire any information and was told instead that his employment records were sealed. When she asked why, she was told it was "a confidential matter." She later said she'd intended to bring the matter to Josh's attention but became busy and simply forgot. Time passed, and the applicant's starting date rolled around. There were still no references on him and no feedback from the vendor. Again, no one followed up. He started work, and six months later he was caught stealing computers and other office equipment during the night. Another employee, working late, confronted him and was assaulted for his efforts. Later it was revealed that the new employee had been fired from his previous job for his part in a physical altercation with another worker. In addition, the criminal background check that the vendor had failed to conduct unveiled two previous larceny-related convictions. The last time I spoke with my colleague, he was knee-deep in negligent hiring and retention charges brought by the assaulted employee.

In this regard, two simple checklists could have helped prevent a most unfortunate situation. Once an applicant is selected for hire, use one or both checklists, depending on whether you use outside vendors for background checks. Using these in conjunction with the exempt and nonexempt reference forms (Appendixes H and I) will help preclude on-the-job problems once an applicant becomes an employee. The Reference Checklist appears below as Exhibit 13-1; the Background Checklist appears as Exhibit 13-2.

Legal Guidelines

Employers are advised to familiarize themselves with certain legal guidelines, including those on the state level, as they relate to references and background checks. State laws differ as to what a potential employer can consider with regard to criminal records. Some states, such as Colorado and Connecticut, require a connection between a job and crime committed before an employer can refuse to hire an individual; Illinois, Maryland, and others will not consider convictions that have been expunged or sealed; and Hawaii generally requires that a contingent offer be made before ordering a criminal records check. Always consult with legal counsel before proceeding.

Defamation of Character

Former employers frequently hesitate to cooperate when asked to provide information about an individual's employment to would-be employers. This resistance is

Exhibit 13-1. Reference Checklist

Name: *Date:*

Conducted by:

Reference Checklist Instructions:

- Beginning with the most recent work or education experience, list all experiential and educational reference checks to be attempted.
- Identify each attempt by date, and assign each a number according to the following:

   (1) Reference information received and consistent with information the applicant provided; no further action required.
   (2) Reference information received and inconsistent with information the applicant provided; further action required.
   (3) Reference information received and causes concern; further action required.
   (4) Reference information requested and pending; follow-up required.
   (5) Reference request denied. Reason given is _____.

- Document the results of each attempt and place in individual's file.
- Determine job suitability based on the results of the reference checks, and choose one of the following:

   (1) Results of applicant's reference checks are consistent with interview and other selection devices and confirm job suitability.
   (2) Results of applicant's reference checks raise concerns about job suitability.
   (3) Results of applicant's reference checks refute job suitability.

Exhibit 13-2. Background Checklist

Name: *Date:*

Vendor:

Monitored by:

Background Checklist Guidelines:

- Have I clearly communicated to the vendor conducting the background check exactly what it is expected to determine? _____ yes _____ no.
- Have I submitted information required for the vendor to conduct its background check? _____ yes _____ no.
- Date information submitted to the vendor: _____
- Date information received from the vendor: _____
- Results of background check (choose those that are appropriate and follow up accordingly):

  (1) Background check is complete; results are satisfactory.
  (2) Background check is complete; results are questionable.
  (3) Background check is complete; results are unsatisfactory.
  (4) Background check is incomplete.

---

usually founded on the fear of being sued by past employees for giving less-than-flattering references. Accordingly, many employers only verify dates of employment in an effort to mitigate any legal exposure to a defamation of character charge. Indeed, even if an applicant was off by a month when recording his dates of employment, a former employer may simply state that these dates are incorrect without offering the correct dates or an explanation. This might leave you to wonder how far off the applicant was and if he was trying to conceal something.

Although it's understandable that employers want to err on the side of caution in this regard, they may be overly careful and fail to realize that a great deal of information can be legitimately and legally imparted without fear of retaliation from former employees. Since apprehension of being sued for defamation motivates many employers and prevents them from seeking or providing employment-related information, understanding twelve key elements of defamation could help to alleviate this concern:

1. Defamation may occur when one person makes a statement about another that is implied to be factual, but is instead intentionally false or could potentially harm the person's personal or professional reputation.

2. Statements made with reasonable belief that they are true are generally treated the same as true statements.

3. Defamatory statements may be either oral or written: Oral defamatory statements could lead to charges of slander; written defamatory statements could lead to charges of libel.

4. The person to whom you are providing information must have a right or a need to know it, e.g., a potential employer.

5. Disclosed information must be employment-related.

6. The information you provide must be truthful, even if it is negative.

7. Information must not be communicated with malicious intent to do harm. Malice occurs when you deliberately provide information that will harm an individual in some way.

8. You may not volunteer information, even if it is employment-related.

9. The information you provide may not be of a personal nature.

10. If a former employer gives a prospective employer a false and damaging reason for an employee's termination, or gives the discharged person a false basis for the discharge and the applicant repeats this to a prospective employer, then this "self-disclosure" may result in charges of defamation.

11. Disputable opinions or statements are protected by a limited privilege; that is, such communications must be malicious to be actionable.

12. Employers are advised to seek legal advice regarding their state's statute of limitations for filing charges of defamation, that is, how long the plaintiff legally has to sue the person who made the false or damaging statements.

Common Law Doctrine of Qualified Privilege

Employers are further protected by the common law principle of qualified privilege. This doctrine is premised on the public policy that an exchange of information relative to the job suitability of individuals is in the best interest of both employers and the general public. Consequently, if such information is defamatory but without malice, it may be deemed privileged.

This privilege is not without certain limitations, however. The information must be provided in good faith and in accordance with the questions asked. For example, if a prospective employer asks about a former employee's ability to work unsupervised, the voluntary statement that she had a problem getting in on time is not protected, even if true. Also, information about an individual's private life should not be offered unless it is relevant to work performance (this is rarely the case). Moreover, former employers should ensure that the information is being provided to the appropriate party and is relevant to the requirements of the job.

Failure to comply with any of these conditions could eliminate the protection provided by qualified privilege. The doctrine does not protect statements that can be proven to have been made with malicious intent.

Good-Faith References

The number of states with reference-checking laws is increasing. These laws protect employers that provide good-faith job references of former and current employees. This added protection enables employers to give and receive references and go beyond the typical "play it safe" policy of only verifying dates of employment for former employees. Even with such legal protection, however, the trend is to proceed cautiously, providing only documented information that can be easily defended in court.

References and Negligent Hiring

Despite the degree of protection afforded former employers by the common-law doctrine of qualified privilege and individual state laws, many still fear liability and hesitate to provide references. The result has been a proliferation of lawsuits based on negligent hiring and retention. The only effective defense against charges of negligent hiring is a complete investigation of all job-related facets of an applicant's employment and educational background prior to employment. Background checks of previous convictions and driving record violations may also be deemed appropriate, depending on the job.

This presents quite a dilemma for employers: former employers can be sued for defamation when providing improper references, and prospective employers can be sued for negligent hiring and retention if references are not properly checked.

Some employment experts suggest a possible solution: requiring job applicants to sign waivers, thereby relieving former employers of liability if the applicants are not hired due to unflattering references.

Here's a sample statement that might appear on a waiver form:

> I fully authorize (JavaCorp.) to investigate and verify all statements made by me both on my employment application and during the course of all employment interviews in relation to my application for the position of (operations manager). I further authorize (JavaCorp.) to contact all previous employers, educational institutions, or other individuals or organizations listed on my application, resume, or other materials I have submitted relative to my prospective employment. In addition, I authorize all said previous employers, educational institutions, or other individuals or organizations listed on my application, resume, or other materials I have submitted relative to my prospective employment to provide (JavaCorp.) with any information requested that may be relevant and useful in making a hiring decision. In so doing, I release all persons, organizations, and entities from legal liability for making such information available.

Such waivers are of questionable legal enforceability. Do not proceed without advice from legal counsel.

I-9 Compliance

While conducting reference or background checks is at the discretion of an employer, compliance with the Immigration Reform and Control Act of 1986 (IRCA) is required by law. The act prohibits all employers from hiring illegal aliens. More specifically, it requires verification that all individuals hired after November 6, 1986, be legally eligible to work in the United States. Such verification comes in the form of the Employment Eligibility Verification Form, commonly known as the I-9. The I-9 expressly requires new hires to provide employers with documents that confirm their identity and employment eligibility.

The I-9 form has undergone several revisions since the onset of IRCA, with the most recent changes occurring in 2009. These modifications include a requirement that employers accept only unexpired documents.

Employers can access the most recent version of the I-9 at http://www.uscis .gov/files/form/i-9.pdf.

Employers must consider their legal exposure with relation to the I-9 form, including administrative fines. I-9 violations can be avoided by providing new hires with I-9 forms, instructions for completion, and a list of acceptable documents to establish identity and work authorization. The form must be signed no later than the first day of hire and completed within three business days from the employment start date.

I-9s must be kept for three years from date of hire, or one year after termination, whichever is longer.

Reference Essentials

Typically, employers check references to:

- Reduce legal liability, i.e., charges of negligent hiring
- Confirm credentials
- Assess past performance as an indicator of future performance
- Reduce the chances of theft, embezzlement, or other criminal activity
- Ensure a safe work environment for all employees
- Assess the overall fit of an individual within the corporate culture
- Confirm salary history

Exploring a potential employee's previous employment, education, and other categories can yield valuable job-related information, if you can get former employers to talk with you. Despite legal protection for employers who truthfully provide factual, job-related information about former employees, many employers still hesitate to verify much more than dates of employment for fear of being sued for defamation of character. As a result, many employers sigh and say, "Why bother trying?" The answer is that there are a number of very good reasons to bother; there are many problems you could head off if you succeed in acquiring reference information. These include falsified credentials, possible charges of negligent hiring and retention, workplace violence, poor productivity, and employee theft.

Let's consider what happened at a small advertising agency in Chicago, as it illustrates how it can be well worth the effort to conduct reference checks. The ad agency retained the services of an executive search firm to hire a temporary book-keeper. The woman they hired did such an excellent job during the week she was there that the ad agency offered her a permanent bookkeeper position. They assumed that the search firm had checked her references and hence did not run any checks themselves. Besides, they reasoned, she was doing such a good job, what could they possibly learn that would be relevant? That turned out to be a huge mistake. Within months of hire, the woman began taking blank checks from her employer and forging signatures, ultimately stealing more than $70,000 before being caught. It turns out that just two months before taking the initial temporary assignment with the agency, she had pleaded guilty to embezzling nearly $200,000 from another employer and had been sentenced to four years' probation and one hundred hours of community service. That was a lesson learned the hard way.

Applicant Authorization

Your company's application form should include a statement that authorizes prospective employers to conduct reference checks as a condition of employment. Often these statements encompass permission to conduct background checks as well. Sample wording appears in Appendix F as part of "Conditions of Employment," and reads as follows:

> *References and Background Checks:* I understand that my employment may be based on receipt of satisfactory information from former employers, schools, and other references, as well as satisfactory results of a background check, including criminal history, credit history, and social security number verification, if deemed appropriate. I authorize JavaCorp. and its representatives to investigate, without liability, any information supplied by me. In addition, I hereby provide permission to authorized representatives of JavaCorp. to conduct a legal Internet search, including public information appearing on social media sites. I further authorize listed employers, schools, and references, as well as other reference sources, to make full disclosure to any relevant inquiries by JavaCorp. and its representatives without liability. In the event that JavaCorp. is unable to verify any information included on this application, it is my responsibility to furnish the necessary documentation.
>
> ( ) You may contact my current employer at this time.
> ( ) You may not contact my current employer at this time. Should I receive and accept a formal offer of employment, you may contact my current employer at that time.

Variation on the wording is fine, as long as the content clearly states that the applicant is granting permission for you to investigate her background as it relates to the available position. Be sure, too, that the applicant signs and dates the statement.

Telephone References

Telephone references are still considered the most effective means for gathering information about an applicant under consideration for hire. In addition to hearing what the former employer has to say about the applicant's work performance, telephone references enable you to evaluate tone of voice and voice inflection. They also allow for clarification of comments that may have a double meaning, such as "You'll be lucky to get him to work for you." Not only is a telephone reference check likely to produce valuable information, it takes less time to conduct than does a written reference.

Conducting telephone reference checks is similar to conducting an interview. Many of the same skills, like active listening and encouraging the other person to talk, are employed. In fact, just about the only facet of an employment interview that cannot be incorporated into a telephone reference check is nonverbal communication. Because of this similarity to an interview, preparation for a telephone reference check is key.

Begin by deciding whom to call. Ask the applicant for the names of her former manager and anyone else qualified to comment on the quality of her work. Also get the name of someone to contact in the HR department. It may be necessary to speak with more than one person. The manager and others with whom the applicant directly worked will be able to discuss work performance; HR will provide information regarding such matters as job title, dates of employment, absenteeism, tardiness, and salary history.

Bear in mind that even if it turns out that you're unable to speak with an applicant's former employer, the applicant can't be certain of this. Sometimes, just asking an applicant for a reference can inspire her to volunteer valuable information. I recall an instance when I was nearing the end of an interview that had up to that point gone fairly smoothly, although I had some concerns about the applicant's ability to work under pressure. When I asked her for the names of three managers with whom she'd had regular dealings, she immediately became agitated. That was a huge red flag, and so I waited for a moment. Then she began, "I guess I might as well tell you since you're going to find out anyway." She proceeded to describe a recent incident involving a team of managers and an assignment she said she had "botched." Her account revealed a great deal about her ability to meet deadlines while working under pressure and confirmed some of my concerns about her in this regard. As it turned out, I was unable to speak to any of the managers she'd named. Had she not described the incident, I never would have learned about it.

It's helpful to prepare a phone-reference form in advance. As with written reference forms, you may want to have one for exempt positions and another for nonexempt positions. The same form can be modified for written references. In designing the forms, however, keep in mind that phone references will yield more information. It's also likely that you'll ask questions other than those on the form. Therefore, allow ample room between questions to take notes. A sample reference form for exempt positions is provided in Appendix H, and a sample for nonexempt positions is found in Appendix I.

When conducting a telephone reference check, begin by identifying yourself, your organization, and the reason for your call. To illustrate:

> **Good morning, Mr. Salerno. My name is Peter Fisher. I'm the HR manager at JavaCorp., and I'm conducting a reference check on your former employee, Ms. Susan Downey.**

If there is any reluctance on the part of the previous employer, offer your phone number and suggest that he call back to verify your identity.

Always begin by confirming the information provided by the applicant. This will help the former employer recall specific information about the person. For example:

> **Ms. Downey has informed me that she worked for your company as an industrial engineer from June 2009 through December 2011. She indicated that she regularly fulfilled four key responsibilities during that time: analyzing current operating procedures; developing flowcharts and linear responsibility charts to improve operating procedures; implementing systems by programming personal computers and by training staff; and advising management of project feasibility after conducting studies. Would you agree with this summary of her primary responsibilities?**

While listening to your opening statement, the respondent's thought speed will enable him to think about other aspects of the former employee's work. At this point, you'll be able to proceed with the other categories on the reference form. As soon as you anticipate that the former employer is willing to continue, shift from closed-ended questions to competency-based and open-ended questions. Be prepared to ask probing questions when more in-depth information is needed.

If the person is closed-mouthed, refusing to provide any information beyond verification of dates of employment and possibly eligibility for rehire, try saying, "I understand you're hesitant to say anything for fear of being sued for defamation of character, but did you know that defamation may occur only when a former employer makes a statement about a former employee that is intentionally false or could potentially harm that person's reputation? Not only that, but employers are protected by the common law principle of qualified privilege. That means an exchange of information relative to the job suitability of employees is in the best interest of both employers and the general public. So even if such information is defamatory but without malice, it's deemed privileged. You just have to make sure the information is provided in good faith and in response to job-related questions."

That's a mouthful, and referencing specific legislation can be daunting, but it may be just what's needed to get the person talking.

Another tactic you can try is to say something like, "Put yourself in my shoes. Wouldn't you want to verify a person's work experience before extending a job offer?" That might do the trick.

If the person still hesitates to answer your questions, try asking him if there's someone else with whom you can talk—another manager, perhaps—someone familiar with the former employee's work even if that manager is no longer with the company. Sometimes that will work. Even if he still won't communicate, you may get the name of someone who will.

Written References

Written references usually consist of form letters designed to verify facts provided by the applicant. Unless directed to the attention of a specific manager or department head, these forms are usually routed to, and completed by, HR staff relying on the former employee's file for information. Even when addressed to the applicant's former manager, these inquiries may routinely be turned over to the company's HR department for a response that generally consists of verification of dates and little more.

Another drawback to a written reference is that it generally takes one to two weeks to get a reply. This is valuable time lost if you're waiting for the reference to be returned before making a hiring decision. In fact, the person you finally select may have accepted another job offer in the interim.

Make certain that your written request is comprehensive but not time-consuming. Each question should be straightforward, easy to understand, and work-related. It's also advisable to have two separate form letters: one for exempt employees and another for nonexempt employees. Appendixes H and I may be modified for use when conducting written references. You may also want to call this person prior to sending the letter. This way, you can make certain she's still employed with the company; in addition, you can stress the importance of a speedy reply. Follow up with a phone call three to four days after mailing your request to help expedite a reply.

While faxing is certainly faster than snail mail, and e-mail is even faster, these methods are not recommended when conducting written references checks. References contain confidential information and their contents should not be casually disclosed.

Educational References

Applicants must provide written consent before a school can release educational records to a prospective employer. The Family Education Rights and Privacy Act (Buckley Amendment) allows students to inspect their scholastic records and to deny schools permission to release certain information. A space for this permission should appear on the application form or a separate release form. Once the proper release has been obtained, the prospective employer, usually for a small fee, may ascertain academic information.

Be certain to ask about the following when you check educational credentials: dates attended, major and minor courses of study, specific courses relevant to the position applied for, degree and honors received, attendance record, work-study program participation, and grades.

In considering this last point, remember that the value of scholastic achievement varies from school to school. An overall grade-point index of 3.5 in one college might be equivalent to an index of 2.8 in another. Therefore, it's important to know something about the standing and reputation of a particular school before weighing an applicant's grade-point average. Also factor in the degree of difficulty of the courses they studied, their course load, extracurricular activities, and outside employment.

Be careful, too, about drawing conclusions based on grades. Not everyone does well on tests or in a classroom setting. This doesn't mean, however, that the applicant hasn't gained the knowledge needed to perform a particular job. Likewise, outstanding grades do not, in and of themselves, mean that someone will excel in a position.

Educational references are generally most useful in confirming the validity of information provided by an applicant. This can be important, since applicants have been known to claim degrees that they don't have. Educational references may also prove to be valuable when an applicant has had little or no previous work experience. Remember, however, that these references should only be conducted when a job description clearly calls for specific educational achievements.

Personal References

Some application forms ask job seekers to provide names of personal references. Usually three names are called for, along with their respective occupations, number of years having known the applicant, and contact information. Although asking someone to provide the names of references certain to offer only praise seems like a waste of time, many interviewers check personal references and maintain that the information gleaned is valid and useful. Specifically, personal references may reveal significant information relevant to the issue of negligent hiring and retention. Some go so far as to ask the references to refer still others who can discuss certain qualities and behavior characteristics. By talking with people not directly referred by the applicant, employers feel they are more likely to get a complete and accurate picture. Still others believe that the type of person used as a reference is significant, that is, whether the person is a doctor, lawyer, teacher, or religious leader.

As with employment references, personal reference checks may result in charges of discrimination if potential employers do not abide by the legal guidelines described earlier. Some employers incorrectly believe that these guidelines do not apply when talking with a reference not connected with the applicant's former employment, prompting non-job-related and even illegal questions in the belief that an acquaintance is more likely to reveal information relevant to important intangible qualities.

Generally speaking, personal references should be avoided unless interviewers have absolutely no other source of employment or educational information. When personal references are checked, the information acquired should be sifted carefully, and any information that appears biased or not factual should be filtered out.

Evaluating References

While obtaining reference information is important, it has no real value if it's not properly evaluated. By and large, reference checks should be viewed as an interview; that is, the person conducting the check must listen to or read the information carefully in relation to the requirements and responsibilities of the job. In some ways, references are more difficult to assess than are interviews because they tend to be more subjective. Regardless of how well your questions are worded, former employers may provide biased, albeit truthful, positive and negative responses, which may cloud your perception of an applicant and justify additional checking. Poor performance in or loss of one job does not necessarily mean failure in another, nor does it indicate employee deficiencies. It's conceivable that termination could have been avoided if there had been a more appropriate job match or if the employee's work habits had been more compatible with that of her manager.

The safest way to approach and evaluate reference checks is to view them as just one of the factors to consider in making a final selection. This doesn't diminish their value; it merely puts them in proper perspective.

Guidelines for Releasing and Obtaining Information

When it comes to references, most employers have been on both the giving and receiving ends. When contacted about a former employee's work performance, they're probably stingy with information; but when trying to get information, they want to know everything possible about a potential hire and are undoubtedly frustrated when their efforts are inhibited.

It would be ideal if every employer worked from the same set of guidelines governing both the release and ascertainment of reference information. That way, everyone would be abiding by the same rules. While that's not likely to happen, you can set up a set of workable guidelines to eliminate any internal confusion as to what to do when asking for or providing reference-related information.

Guidelines for Releasing Information

When it comes to releasing work-related information about a former employee, consider these guidelines:

• One person, or a limited number of persons, should have the responsibility of releasing information about former employees. These individuals should be trained in legal matters such as defamation of character and qualified privilege. Typically, this task falls to HR practitioners.

• During exit interviews, tell terminating employees what information will be provided during a reference check. If the employee is being asked to leave, make sure she knows the reason and signs a statement to that effect.

- Try to obtain a signed consent form from a terminating employee authorizing you to provide relevant reference information to prospective employers.
- Always tell the truth and make certain you have documentation to back it up. Provide factual, job-related examples to support your statements.
- Make certain that the person to whom you are providing reference information has a legitimate and legal right to it.
- Be certain all information provided is job-related.
- Do not volunteer information, even if it's job-related.

Guidelines for Obtaining Information

To increase your chances of obtaining meaningful information about potential employees, consider these guidelines:

- Conduct all reference checks in a uniform manner. Never single out those applicants who strike you as "suspect." Inconsistency may be viewed as discriminatory.
- If an applicant is ultimately rejected because of a negative reference, be prepared to document the job-related reason.
- If while conducting a reference check you discover that an applicant has filed an EEO charge against her former employer, keep in mind that it is illegal to refuse to employ someone for this reason.
- Obtain permission from applicants—on the application or on a separate form—to contact former employers.
- Carefully question the validity of comments made by former employers. Despite possible legal ramifications, it's not uncommon for employers to express negative feelings toward a good employee who resigned for a better position. Likewise, employees terminated for poor performance sometimes work out a deal with their former employers that ensures them of positive reference checks. Probe for objective statements regarding job performance.
- Exercise caution when interpreting a respondent's tone of voice, use of silence, or implication. Be aware, too, of phrases that may be interpreted in more than one way. For example, if a former employer were to say, "She gave every impression of being a conscientious worker," it would behoove you to ask for clarification.
- Since reference checks are generally reserved for applicants making it to the final stage of consideration, give these individuals the opportunity to refute any information resulting from the reference check that contradicts impressions or information obtained during the interview.
- If possible, check with a minimum of two previous employers to rule out the possibility of either positive or negative bias. This may also disclose patterns in an individual's work habits.

- Ideally, the person who interviewed the applicant should conduct reference checks. If representatives from both HR and the department in which the opening exists conducted the interview, the HR specialist typically does the checking.

- Do not automatically assume that a reported personality clash is the applicant's fault.

- Having been fired does not necessarily mean that an applicant is a bad risk. Employees are terminated for many reasons; get an explanation before jumping to conclusions.

- Tell applicants that any job offer will be contingent upon a satisfactory reference from their current employers. This is a wise step to take since most applicants do not grant permission to contact their present employers.

Fundamentals of Background Checks

Even though employers hire the services of outside vendors to conduct background checks, they are still responsible for making certain all information requested and acquired is in full compliance with the Fair Credit Reporting Act.

Fair Credit Reporting Act (FCRA)

The FCRA, a federal law enforced by the Federal Trade Commission (FTC), pertains to a great deal more than a person's credit history and standing. The FCRA governs the acquisition and use of a wide range of background information on applicants and employees, including Department of Motor Vehicle record checks and criminal background, character, general reputation, personal characteristics, and mode of living checks. Employers should look into whether they have additional state regulations governing background information and/or investigative reports. As of this writing, the states that regulate background checks are Arizona, California, Colorado, Georgia, Kansas, Louisiana, Maine, Maryland, Massachusetts, Minnesota, Montana, New Hampshire, New Jersey, New Mexico, New York, Oklahoma, Rhode Island, Tennessee, Texas, Vermont, Virginia, and Washington. Of these, California has the most stringent requirements, including a set of unique procedural steps for compliance. Organizations with multistate locations are advised to comply with the laws of the states where the individual investigated resides and the employer requesting the information has its principal place of business. The FCRA generally does not preempt state consumer reporting laws; there are, however, a few areas in which it does. Employers are advised to err on the side of caution and abide by both federal and state laws to ensure compliance. As in all areas concerning legal matters, consult with an attorney. The full text of the FCRA can be obtained by visiting http://www.ftc.gov/os/statutes/fcra.htm.

The FCRA was amended by the Fair and Accurate Credit Transactions Act of 2003 (FACT Act). Many of the revisions serve to increase consumer protections against identity theft and improve the accuracy of consumer reports.

Reports

The FCRA applies to two types of reports: consumer and investigative consumer.

Consumer Reports   The FCRA defines *consumer report* as a report prepared by a consumer reporting agency that investigates an applicant's or employee's creditworthiness, credit standing, credit capacity, character, general reputation, personal characteristics, or mode of living. Examples of consumer reports include criminal background investigations, Department of Motor Vehicle inquiries, and credit history checks. The information is gathered and used for employment purposes, defined as hiring, termination, reassignment, or promotion. The report must be prepared by a consumer reporting agency (CRA) to qualify as a genuine consumer report under the FCRA. In some instances, drug test results may also qualify as a consumer report.

Investigative Consumer Reports   An *investigative consumer report* is defined by the FCRA as a subset of consumer reports in which information about an applicant's or employee's character, general reputation, personal characteristics, or mode of living is acquired via interviews with the person's friends, neighbors, or business associates. Examples of investigative consumer reports that are conducted by a CRA include employment verifications and interviews with former employers and coworkers.

Employers can learn more about consumer reports and investigative consumer reports by accessing a document titled "Notice to Users of Consumer Reports: Obligations of Users Under the FCRA," available at www.ftc.gov/os/statutes/2user.htm.

Basic FCRA Compliance

Employers are obliged to comply with three steps whenever they request a background check or investigation under the FCRA:

1. Employers must provide applicants or employees with a special notice in writing that they will request an investigative report, and they must obtain signatures of consent. In addition, employers are required to present a summary of rights under federal law. Individuals wanting a copy of the report must so indicate.

2. Employers must certify to the background check or investigation company that they will comply with applicable federal and state laws by signing a form typically provided by the investigation company.

3. Employers must provide a copy of the report to the individual investigated if an adverse action is to be taken as a result of the report. Employers should include a description of the adverse action, which could be, for example, withdrawing an offer of employment. Employers are further obliged to wait a reasonable period of time (generally three to five days) before taking adverse action to allow the individual investigated time to dispute the accuracy or completeness of any information in the report.

When hiring the services of investigation companies to conduct background checks, employers must ensure that the agencies are aware of prevailing laws. In addition, employers need to ensure that these agencies do not reveal information they are not entitled to disclose. For example, agencies are not permitted to divulge information about bankruptcies that are more than ten years old or tax liens that exceed seven years.

Background Checks Policy

Companies that intend to conduct background checks should have a written policy along with accompanying procedures for HR or others to follow.

Purpose   The policy should begin by stating its overall purpose. For example, you could start out by saying:

> (Avedon Industries) is committed to hiring individuals whose skills and backgrounds are compatible with the position for which they are applying. In addition, we are obliged to provide a safe environment for our employees. Accordingly, background checks will enable (Avedon Industries) to obtain and confirm job-related information that will, in turn, help us determine an applicant's overall employability and ensure the protection of (Avedon's) employees, its property, and its information.

Contents   The policy should include:

- What background checks could cover, e.g., information about an applicant's or employee's character, general reputation, personal characteristics, or mode of living.
- A statement to the effect that you are only collecting information that pertains to the quality and quantity of work performed.
- The name(s) of CRAs retained to gather information about an individual's creditworthiness, criminal record, and the like.
- References to the required steps for compliance with the FCRA, as described earlier.
- Identification of prevailing laws. For instance, if you plan to collect credit information, you might say:

> (Avedon Industries) is permitted to collect credit-related information consistent with the guidelines of the FCRA, provided it (1) certifies to the consumer reporting agency that it is in compliance with the FCRA, (2) obtains written authorization from the applicant, (3) informs the applicant of his right to request additional information as to the nature of the report, (4) informs the applicant as to what the report will encompass, (5) provides the individual with a summary of his rights under the FCRA, and (6)

informs the applicant as to any negative results, intended adverse action, and sufficient time in which to contest the negative results.

Perhaps you plan on conducting a criminal investigation as part of your background check. In that event, your policy should state:

It is the policy of (Avedon Industries) to conduct a criminal investigation as part of its background check on potential employees. As part of this investigation, (Avedon Industries) is permitted to make inquiries concerning criminal records as long is it does not violate Title VII of the Civil Rights Act of 1964 with regard to using information acquired as a basis for denying employment, unless it is determined to be job-related or dictated by business necessity.

Record Keeping

Your policy should clearly stipulate that the information acquired as a result of any background check will only be used as part of the selection process and will be kept strictly confidential. Here's a sample:

(Avedon Industries) recognizes the potentially sensitive nature of information that may result from background checks. (Avedon) assures its applicants that all information acquired as a result of any background check will only be used as part of the selection process and that said information will be kept strictly confidential. Only those with a ''need to know'' will be permitted access to this information.

Selecting a Consumer Reporting Agency or Vendor

Background checks may be conducted by a consumer reporting agency, nationwide specialty consumer reporting agency, or information furnisher.

The top national CRAs are Equifax (www.equifax.com), Experian (www.experian.com), and TransUnion (www.transunion.com). These three are regulated by the FCRA. The CRAs are required by law to provide a central source website for consumers to request their reports.

The FCRA classifies information technology companies as "nationwide specialty consumer reporting agencies" to produce individual consumer reports. A partial list of companies classified as nationwide specialty consumer reporting agencies includes Acxiom, Central Credit, ChoicePoint, Innovis, Integrated Screening Partners, Lexis-Nexis, Medical Information Bureau, and Teletrack. Nationwide specialty consumer reporting agencies must establish a simplified process for consumers to request consumer reports.

There are also companies called "information furnishers." These are companies that provide information to consumer reporting agencies and may include collection agencies, creditors, and banking institutions.

For our purposes, nationwide specialty consumer reporting agencies and information furnishers are referred to as "vendors." The identification of specific vendors is not meant as an endorsement, nor are the vendors identified intended to represent an all-inclusive list.

Here are some helpful guidelines when selecting a CRA or vendor to conduct background checks:

- *Be patient.* Most credible CRAs or vendors will require as many as five days to conduct a thorough background check, although some can effectively be accomplished in as few as three. Rushing through the process could result in overlooking important information, so if a third-party vendor tells you it requires a week to do a thorough job, be patient and think about how you'll feel knowing you didn't cut any corners.

- *You get what you pay for.* The cost of conducting a background check can range from less than ten dollars to upward of several hundred dollars, with a background check on an executive costing even more. If an applicant has moved around from state to state, the cost is likely to be higher.

- *Be vigilant about how the vendor acquires its criminal history information.* There are three main methods for acquiring this data: using in-house researchers, contracting local court retrieval service companies to go to the courts for them, and doing database searches. Most credible firms relay on a combination of the three. If you are considering an agency that relies on third-party databases to conduct criminal history record checks, ask if the court sanctions the database and how often the material is updated.

- *Make certain that the vendor is well-insured.* In the event of a negligent hiring lawsuit, employers usually want to assign liability to the vendor. This makes insurance an important component.

- *Ensure the legal knowledge base of the vendor.* For example, any credible firm that conducts background checks should be knowledgeable about the FCRA, which governs how background information can be used. It should also be willing to consult with HR to ensure that the company knows how to legally use the information it supplies.

- *Conduct a test run.* Some experts recommend testing the abilities of a vendor before signing on with them by providing a name of someone known to have a criminal record to see how thorough and accurate they are.

Summary

Most interviewers know it's unwise to make a hiring decision without first checking an applicant's references and, in many instances, conducting a thorough background check. However, this is not always easy to do.

Employers often hesitate to disclose relevant information about former employees, fearing defamation of character lawsuits. Others are afraid to explore background information because of prevailing legislation, such as the Fair Credit Reporting Act. Concerns prevail despite what employers are entitled to know according to the common law doctrine of qualified privilege and regardless of state laws protecting employers that provide good-faith job references.

References and background checks are both part of the selection process, but each focuses on different aspects of an individual's past. References probe an individual's work- and education-related background, while background checks explore other aspects of an applicant's life, such as criminal matters, character, general reputation, personal characteristics, and mode of living. Legal guidelines, including many on a state level, prevail regarding both references and background checks.

Once application authorization has been acquired, references may be conducted via phone or in writing, with the former being the preferred method. Organizations that intend to conduct background checks should have a written policy along with accompanying procedures for HR and others to follow. The policy should state its purpose, identify what background checks could cover, and stipulate how records of any acquired information will be maintained.

The careful selection of a consumer reporting agency, nationwide specialty consumer reporting agency, or information furnisher to conduct your background checks will help ensure the best possible fit.

CHAPTER 14

Social Networks and Hiring

The 1979 movie *The Jerk* is about a naïve character who invents slip-proof eyeglasses. At one point the character played by Steve Martin is euphoric upon seeing his name in the new phone book. He remarks, "Page 73—Johnson, Navin R. I'm somebody now! Millions of people look at this book every day! This is the kind of spontaneous publicity—your name in print—that makes people. I'm in print! Things are going to start happening to me now!"[1]

Fast forward to the present day and substitute Facebook for the phone book. The rewrite might read something like this: "I'm somebody now! Millions of people log onto Facebook every day! This is the kind of publicity that makes people. Things are going to start happening to me now!"

While few people could ever claim to be as excited about seeing their name in a phone book as Navin Johnson, the underlying similarity between then and now is both apparent and relevant to this chapter. In varying degrees, most people enjoy seeing their names in print and the social interaction that comes with it. That interaction currently comes in the form of social networks, touching our lives on both a personal and professional level.

For some, like most members of the Millennial generation, the sharing of information through social networks is not only acceptable, but a necessary part of their daily routine; they wouldn't have it any other way. Others find the inherently intrusive nature of social media excessive, quickly learning that once connected with friends, family, colleagues, and in many instances total strangers, your life becomes public in a way unlike ever before. For them, sharing is one thing; living in a fishbowl twenty-four hours a day, every day, is another.

Not surprisingly, with hundreds of millions of users sharing information and interacting online, our uses of social networks continue to evolve at a rapid pace. Social networks have expanded into, and become part of, how we make employment decisions. What started out primarily as a means to socialize has turned into a way for individuals to look for jobs and for employers to gather information about whom to hire.

Using social networks as evaluative instruments to help make hiring decisions is not without its challenges. Let's look at some of these sites and see how employers use and misuse them.

Social Networking Primer

Many of you may already consider yourselves social networking pros, while others struggle to wade through the quagmire of terms and options. It doesn't help that some of these sites pop up, are hugely popular for a time, and then fade from sight seemingly overnight or are gobbled up by another social network. An example of this is Myspace, which was once the world's fastest-growing social network. Once Facebook entered the picture, though, Myspace faded into the background to a state of near oblivion.

For those of you who dare to admit you can't keep up with all the social networking sites and offerings out there, here's an overview of some of the networking players, current as of this writing:

Facebook

Whatever you may think of social networks in general, it's hard not to be impressed by what Facebook has achieved to date. It is probably the most popular social networking service of all time. Cocreated by Mark Zuckerberg while he was a student at Harvard and launched in 2004, the site reports that 50 percent of its more than 750 million active users log on to Facebook daily, spending more than 700 billion minutes on Facebook per month. More than 250 million active Facebook users access the site through their mobile devices.

Significantly, Facebook has international appeal, reporting some 70 percent of users outside the United States availing themselves of more than seventy translations. It has also expanded its scope of attraction with social plug-ins launched in 2010, which allowed the integration of more than ten thousand new websites daily.

In addition to exchanging the more than 250 million photos that are uploaded every day, registered users ages 13 and up can create personal profiles, exchange messages with friends, and join common-interest groups. Its focus, then, is more on personal matters such as friends, family, celebrations, interests, hobbies, and events, as opposed to business.

To put it simply, Facebook has changed the way people communicate.

That said, one of the greatest areas of controversy with regard to social networks in general, and with Facebook in particular, is privacy. Facebook's continuous news feed and facial recognition technology that is used to identify people in photographs puts the company in the foreground of issues concerning confidentiality and discretion. Many believe that Facebook's policies will ultimately define standards for privacy in cyberspace.

In an effort to provide users with added control over privacy, Facebook recently announced a series of changes, among them that each time a user adds content to his profile page, the user can determine who has access to it. This control extends to all personal user information and replaces the long-standing separate privacy page. Members can determine how much or how little they allow others to see, including information about their gender, date of birth, family members, relationship status, sexual orientation, and religious views, all topics savvy interviewers know to avoid. Yet if interviewers come upon this information during a legitimate Facebook search, it becomes difficult to ignore or prove that they didn't factor any of it into the decision-making process.

There is controversy among privacy advocates as to whether these changes are sufficient. Supporters maintain that the changes provide users with more control over who sees what—that it's a departure from the network's previous approach in which much of what was posted was widely accessible. Detractors express concern that Facebook users can still publish information about another's whereabouts without that person's consent. So if the publisher of a photograph in which you appear cannot place it on your profile page, but can still keep it on his own page, does that extend the privacy option, now called "public," far enough? If you click public, can anyone who is online—including prospective employers—see what you're posting?

Other Facebook changes, including modifications to its news feed and friend lists, the implementation of a subscribe button, and the addition of a live feed of what's happening at any given moment, are considered by many to go too far into allowing a deeper look into a member's past.

By the time you're reading this, Facebook will undoubtedly have made numerous additional changes, perhaps rendering moot the details described here. But what will not change is this: Employers seeking employment-related information on this giant social media site must exercise extreme caution. Just because it's out there doesn't mean it's there for the taking.

LinkedIn

Considered the world's largest business-related network, LinkedIn has been around since 2003—a long time in the world of social media—and currently has more than 120 million members in 200 countries and territories worldwide. Members create profiles describing their professional background, and LinkedIn allows registered members to network with others, called "connections," in their professional fields or as friends. Users can invite anyone, including those not currently signed on to LinkedIn, to become a connection. Individuals use connections to expand upon existing contacts, find jobs, and review profiles of companies they may be interested in working for. In July 2011, the company added the feature "Apply with LinkedIn" on their job listing pages. This allows applicants to apply for positions using their LinkedIn profiles as resumes. Employers can use LinkedIn to list jobs and search for potential employees. All users can post their own photos and view photos of others. In addition, the network supports the formation of interest groups ranging in size from 1 to more than 300,000.

Employers who want to review what an applicant says about himself on various social networks are advised to search LinkedIn, since it's designed as more of a professional site than is, say, Facebook. While members are permitted to provide personal information, few do; their focus is on professional, job-related information. It's also less likely that members will post pictures other than an identifying photo or that they will post inappropriate comments.

Twitter

Founded in 2006 and launched a year later, Twitter is a social networking and microblogging site on which users can send text-based posts up to 140 characters in length by way of short message service (SMS is a text messaging service component of phone, web, or mobile communication systems), instant messaging (IM), or e-mail to the Twitter website. Tweets answer the question, "What's happening right now?" As of 2011, Twitter claimed more than 200 million users, generating more than 200 million tweets per day.

Users tweet through the Twitter website or by SMS. They can update their profiles through their mobile phones by text messaging, or through apps on smart phones and tablets. The content of most tweets can be categorized as "peripheral awareness," conversation, pass-along value, self-promotion, spam, news, and gossip.

Tweets are publicly viewed unless senders restrict message delivery to specific followers. One individual forgot this golden rule of tweeting when he received a job offer from Cisco. He tweeted, "Cisco just offered me a job! Now I have to weigh the utility of a fatty paycheck against the daily commute to San Jose and hating the work." A Cisco employee read the tweet and passed the information along, and the company withdrew its job offer.[2]

Twitter collects "personally identifiable information" (PII) that may be used to identify or contact someone. PII may include a person's name, date and place of birth, driver's license number, vehicle registration plate number, and credit card numbers. This information can currently be shared with third parties.

Twitter supporters applaud the ease with which busy people can stay in touch; opponents suggest that the sharing of minutiae is trivial.

Delicious (Originally Known as "Del.icio.us")

Delicious is a free social bookmarking service that allows users to tag, save, manage, and share web pages. All bookmarks posted to Delicious are publicly viewable unless users identify them as private. Imported bookmarks are private by default. Delicious allows for a single set of bookmarks on all of a user's computers and access to his bookmarks from someone else's computer via the Delicious website. It also allows users to check out prevalent tags, view the most popular bookmarks for a tag, and thus explore topics of interest.

The site was operated by Yahoo! until July 2011, when it was sold to Avos Systems.

Digg

Digg is a content-sharing site. Users can submit stories, articles, images, and videos to Digg and registered users click "Digg it" if they like it. Once the feature reaches a "tipping point," it's promoted on the site's homepage. Users can select those categories that are of the greatest interest and hide others. They can also add friends to see what they're "Digging."

Users can add photos to their profile, as well as links to Facebook or other favored web pages. Privacy settings allow users to control what's displayed to others.

Google Plus

Considered by some to be a possible rival of Facebook, Google Plus launched in June 2011. Its focus is on sharing within small social group subsets known as "circles." Examples of circles include friends, family, and coworkers. Circles allow users to share different information with different people. Google Plus also offers a feature called "hangouts," whereby someone clicks, starts a hangout, and triggers a message among members of varied social circles so others can join in and "chat." A variation on hangouts is the "huddle," which converges multiple conversations into one group chat. Some view this as a viable alternative to trying to text several people at once about the same topic. The site also provides users with "sparks," that is, articles and videos that are likely to be of interest to individuals based on information they've provided.

Ning

Through built-in integration with online services such as Facebook, Twitter, Google, and Yahoo!, Ning members share photos and voice opinions in comments, blogs, videos, group forums chats, and activity streams. Individuals and organizations alike can use premade templates or create custom social networks built around a particular topic or need, thereby appealing to specific membership bases. Initially, Ning offered both free and paid options; in April 2010, it switched over to three levels of paid service, with each level offering different degrees of features and customer support.

Uses

When asked about what kind of information they're looking for on social networks, most employers respond as follows:

- Bad-mouthing of previous or present employers and colleagues
- Comments that put into question an applicant's maturity or judgment
- Discriminatory remarks pertaining to race, gender, sexual orientation, disabilities, national origin, or religion
- Deviant sexual behavior
- Evidence of providing "do good" services, such as community or other volunteer work
- Excessive use of foul language
- Extreme responses to certain situations
- Lies about qualifications, experience, and other information shared during the interview or appearing on the application or resume

- Links to criminal behavior
- Membership in clubs and organizations
- Photos placing applicants in questionable situations
- Poor communication skills as evidenced in entries and profiles
- Posting questionable or inappropriate content
- Provocative attire and/or poses in photos
- Radical political views
- References to, or images of, drinking and/or drug use (remember, drugs are illegal)
- Revealing confidential information about previous or present employers
- Unrealistic career goals vis-à-vis organizational goals
- Verification of job-related affiliations, associations, and activities
- Violent or antagonistic tendencies and behavior

It seems, then, that employers using social networks as a selection device are largely looking for reasons to reject someone. Of the twenty items listed, only two are positive: evidence of providing "do good" services, such as community or other volunteer work, and verification of job-related affiliations, associations, and activities. One other could go either way: membership in clubs and organizations could be of a personal or professional nature. This contrasts with the long-standing purpose of reference checks, which is to confirm information that supports the selection of one applicant over others.

Interesting, too, is the allegation by some businesses that they're suspicious if an applicant appears on the more personal types of social networks like Facebook projecting a professional and employer-friendly image. They think the look may be staged, especially if it's a twenty-something fresh out of college—and it very well may be. But can you know for certain one way or the other? You're either going to believe what you read and see or you're not; you can't have it both ways.

And that leads us to an interesting observation: Employers admit that they don't necessarily believe what they see or read on Facebook, but they still want to know what's out there so they can decide whether they're willing to take a chance.

This scenario illustrates how one employer uses social media to decide which of two qualified applicants makes the best fit.

A senior HR recruiter, Blake, has been searching for an assistant vice president of marketing for his company for more than a month. After screening and interviewing a dozen promising applicants, he reviews both tangible and intangible requirements and tasks of the job, and together with the vice president of marketing narrows the field to two equally viable possibilities: Sophia and Mackenzie. Now comes the challenging part, how to acquire sufficient reference information on each of them to determine who will make the best fit. Blake dismisses the glowing feedback he receives from each contender's personal references, deciding that they cancel one another out. He focuses, instead, on what their previous employers have to say.

Phone references reveal that Sophia and Mackenzie are both held in high esteem. They are, at this point, running neck and neck. Blake knows there's another source, albeit one that carries some legal risks: social media sites. He's looking for something that will break the tie, and so he decides to take a tour of their respective Facebook and LinkedIn pages, hoping to get a clearer picture of each applicant.

First Mackenzie: Among other things, he learns that in her spare time she is actively involved in Big Brothers Big Sisters, a youth mentoring program. She also delivers meals to the homes of senior citizens once a week (evidence of providing "do good" services). He learns, too, that she is an active member of the Woman's National Democratic Club (membership in clubs and organizations). Regrettably, upon reading about her professional goals on LinkedIn, Blake learns that Mackenzie hopes to become VP of marketing within a year's time—an unrealistic objective in Blake's estimation. He wonders how he could have missed covering her short-term goals during the interview. Sophia, on the other hand, appears to devote the majority of her after-work hours to the martial arts. In fact, she has a second degree black belt in jujitsu. Blake, knowing what kind of dedication it takes to achieve that level of expertise, is impressed, yet he wonders if this means she spends too much time in the dojo and not enough time at work. Still, her references indicate that she works hard and puts in whatever hours are needed to get her work done.

Since they are practically identical in terms of their skills sets and both received outstanding recommendations from prior employers, Blake decides to use the information he acquires from the social networks to make his decision; he's going to recommend hiring Sophia. His concern over Mackenzie's goal of becoming VP of marketing in a year is the deciding factor.

Assuming Blake accessed the information on these social sites legally and that the information both applicants posted is 100 percent true, then using social network sites as a tiebreaker serves as a useful tool in the selection process. He needs to be wary, however, of possible discrimination charges brought by Mackenzie based on non-job-related, highly personal information he had access to, even though he maintains he didn't use it to make a hiring decision.

Blake is one of thousands of employers who use social networking sites daily to learn about future employees. In fact, according to several 2010 studies, including one by Cross-Tab, which was commissioned by Microsoft, between 70 and 79 percent of recruiters and hiring managers use social media sites for screening and rejecting applicants.[3] The primary reason given for using these over other reference sources is ease of use. In truth, nothing could be easier or more cost-effective, that is, unless you get sued for failure to hire or charged with invasion of privacy (more on the legal ramifications shortly). In addition, social networks are frequently used to scope out new college graduates who have limited work experience.

But can employers assume that social media sites yield accurate information? Should you assume that whatever an individual posts on Facebook or LinkedIn is completely true? While considered among the most business-oriented social sites available, LinkedIn does not verify the authenticity of the information its members provide. This leads to a disturbing possibility: that employers could be basing their decision to reject or hire someone based on unreliable, dated, or inaccurate information. The fact of the matter is that information you find on social media sites may be in part or wholly incorrect, or intentionally misleading. In fact, someone pretending to be someone else could even place it there.

When I conduct face-to-face interviews I expect applicants to be prepared with answers to standard questions, have relevant questions of their own, dress to impress, and behave appropriately. Yet some of what I've seen and heard makes me want to ask, "What were they thinking?" This same line of reasoning applies to social media content. One might assume that anyone looking for a job is not going to want to leave a trail of incriminating information, such as pictures of rowdy parties with heavy drinking, drug use, or other unprofessional and in some instances illegal conduct. Yet even when advised in writing that employers may explore social media sites in conjunction with an applicant's interest in a job, some applicants make no attempt to conceal inappropriate behavior. Maybe they don't believe you'll really check. This raises an interesting question to which there is no definitive answer, as of yet: If an employer hires someone based on information that individual posted on his social network and later learns that the information was false, can it hold the applicant accountable for posting inaccurate information even if there was no requirement that the site be truthful? The outcome of this scenario becomes even trickier if the employer did not inform the applicant that it might explore social networks, even though it conducted a public search.

Legal Risks

Employers who are fans of social networking maintain that sites such as Facebook allow for a greater understanding of the likelihood that a potential employee will fit in with their company's culture. They point to tweets, photos, and other bits of information that do not appear on the standard resume, which focuses on education and employment experience. This raises serious concern since an employer's emphasis should be on an applicant's job-related experience, not her personal life.

Due to the immense popularity of these sites, the question must be asked: Is there social media information unrelated to education and experience that can legally be used to make an employment decision? For example, if an employer learns, through something he reads on an applicant's social media site, that an applicant called in sick but in truth was nursing a hangover, can it eliminate that person from consideration? The answer is, "It depends." Read on.

Despite the ease with which social networks can be used and the useful application of the information employers gather about applicants, there are legal risks that are not to be minimized. Using social media sites to help determine job suitability is relatively recent in terms of the law; it takes far less time to figure out new ways to use social networks than it does to pass relevant legislation. But there are concerns. Has social networking given employers another way to potentially discriminate during the hiring process? Erring on the side of caution and consulting with legal counsel when in doubt is the way for savvy employers to go.

Discrimination

One of the greatest legal concerns when it comes to exploring social media has to do with what employers are legally entitled to access and use. According to Jackson-Lewis attorney Chad Richter, Facebook profiles of more than 24 million users are public, 73 percent of social media profiles can be found through public search engines, and 77 percent do not restrict viewing of their photos.[4] That's good news for employers; once an applicant posts something on a public domain, an employer is free to view it. The problem is that you're likely to see more than you should. This could result in intentional or unintentional discrimination based on protected-class status. For example, suppose you legitimately access the Facebook profile of an applicant and discover that she sings in her church choir along with her husband and two kids. In fact, there's a photograph of the entire family wearing choir robes. You've just learned three bits of information you have no business knowing: her religious affiliation, marital status, and that she has children. If you decide to hire someone other than her, the burden is now on you to show you did not use the personal information you learned on Facebook against her.

Failure-to-Hire Claims

In Chapter 6 we explored various federal laws prohibiting discrimination on the basis of categories such as race, color, religion, sex, national origin, age, disability, and genetic information. Additional state statutes prohibit discrimination based on sexual preference and other factors. We also discussed how your liability regarding the use of this information does not change merely because it was the applicant who provided the non-job-related information. That line of thinking applies to visiting social media sites. Just because an individual "invites" you to share in what she posts by virtue of her public status does not mean you can use anything you learn or see as the basis for a hiring decision. It's far more likely that you'll discover something illegal on a social site than you would during the course of a structured employment interview largely consisting of competency-based, job-related questions, or through a traditional reference check. Whether this discovery is the whole reason, partly the reason, or irrelevant to the reason for rejecting an individual is not going to prevent someone from filing a claim of discrimination.

Discrimination charges based on inappropriate use of social media start out no differently than other discrimination claims. All an individual has to do is establish a prima facie case, which consists of these four components:

1. She is a member of a protected class.
2. She is qualified for the job in question.
3. She was rejected despite her qualifications.
4. The position remained open after she was rejected and the employer continued to seek applications from others with similar qualifications.

The burden is now on you to show that the rejection was based on legitimate, nondiscriminatory reasons. Even though this may be 100 percent true, the fact remains that you did explore the person's social media site—albeit legitimately—and you must acknowledge that you saw, as illustrated earlier, that she sings in her church choir and has a family. You must now argue that this information did not contribute to your decision not to hire her.

Failure-to-hire claims resulting from the use of social media in the making of employment decisions are relatively new. It is expected, however, as businesses increasingly rely on social networks to support rejection or hiring decisions, that we will be hearing more about this. One additional word of caution: Even if an individual's social networking site is public, certain forms of speech and individual action are protected under the law, e.g., legitimate complaints about working conditions. As always in matters concerning the law, when in doubt, consult with legal counsel.

Invasion of Privacy

Ryan, a recent college graduate seeking a "serious" job, approached me for advice on whether he should modify his social networking profiles. After reviewing the contents I suggested he strive to make his profiles more employer-friendly. I offered three specific suggestions:

1. Remove pictures that could send the wrong message, including those of him as the "life of the party."
2. Delete the use of what would likely be considered inappropriate language in a work environment.
3. Steer clear of affiliations with groups whose names or activities could turn off potential employers.

Ryan responded by saying, "I didn't ask you to give me a whole new identity!" I asked him how he thought a potential employer might perceive him if he left everything as it was. His reply: "It's none of their business." I explained that if his settings were public, then they could legitimately be explored and relevant information on his profiles might be used. I further suggested that if he wanted to leave them as is he should change his settings to private. Ryan was clearly getting annoyed with me. He waited a moment and then said, "I don't want to do that because then they'll think I have something to hide. But I don't want to change who I am either. I have a right to have a public profile and not have what's on it used by some random company."

Even though they allow their profiles to be viewed by the general public, some individuals, like Ryan, maintain that prospective employers should not be permitted to use any information from social networks when making a hiring decision. They argue that the information is personal and should have nothing to do with work. Legally, a claim of invasion of privacy is largely based on whether an individual has "a reasonable expectation of privacy in the information viewed." Most experts agree that applicants who allow their profiles to be viewed by the public give up their right to privacy. Of course if someone poses as a "friend" to gain access to restricted information or uses other covert methods, then the individual's claim of privacy invasion may be valid.

Sidestep the possibility of invasion of privacy claims by adding a statement similar to the following in the Reference and Background Checks section of your company's application form: "I hereby provide permission to authorized representatives of (JavaCorp.) to conduct a legal Internet search, including public information appearing on social media sites." The applicant's signature should weigh heavily toward negating future invasion of privacy claims.

Disparate Treatment and Disparate Impact

Disparate treatment refers to intentionally treating members of a protected class differently than others. To avoid charges of disparate treatment in conjunction with social networks, apply the golden rule that pertains to testing: If you're going to test one applicant, test them all. Don't decide based on some arbitrary gauge that one person meets the requirements of a job and therefore does not need to be tested, while another does not. Likewise, if you decide to check out the social profiles of only one out of three finalists, you could find yourself facing charges of disparate treatment. For example, if one of the applicants under serious consideration is a woman and the other two are men, and you decide to conduct a search of social media only for the woman, you could be accused of looking for reasons not to hire her, e.g., pictures of her or comments about her children. Also, if you discover similar information about all three applicants but interpret it differently for the woman than for the men, you could be accused of disparate treatment.

Disparate impact can occur when a seemingly neutral employment practice has a great negative impact on one particular group. For example, only considering applicants with certain information on their social networking profiles, or having profiles at all, could have a disparate impact on members of a protected class who are statistically shown to be less likely to have a social media profile, for example, older workers.

What should you do if not everyone has a social networking profile? You're not likely to know that until you conduct a search. Upon discovering that an applicant does not have a presence on a social media site, you may have already explored the profiles of one or more other applicants. Document the fact that you made the effort. The key is consistency.

Social Media Policy

It's evident that gathering information about potential employees through social networking sites can be complicated and laden with risks. You might therefore be tempted to say it's not worth it and not bother. As employers increasingly use various social networks as evaluative instruments to help make hiring decisions, however, some experts project that we will see negligent hiring extend to encompass social media. That is, the pressure on employers to exercise reasonable care in hiring employees could include checking social network sites in addition to conducting traditional reference checks.

Whether this scenario plays out or not remains to be seen. Even if it does not, however, there's no denying that social networking and the workplace are tightly intertwined. Every organization, then, should have a written policy concerning social networks and hiring to maximize benefits and minimize risks. Here are some of the key points to include in a social media policy:

• Ask all applicants in writing—preferably on the employment application form—for permission to conduct a social media search.

• Create a list of all social media sites that will be searched for each applicant under consideration.

• Identify what job-related information will be sought based on a position's accompanying job description.

• Conduct social media checks only on applicants under serious consideration.

• Have neutral parties conduct the search, that is, someone who is not involved in the decision to reject or hire an applicant. That person can brief decision makers as to any job-related information acquired as part of the search and omit any protected information.

• Inform managers that they are not to conduct social networking searches of potential employees on their own.

• Conduct social media checks at the same point in the process for all applicants under serious consideration.

• Document any information discovered on a social networking site that results in a decision not to hire someone. Where possible, include screen captures in your documentation since social network profiles may change.

• Determine whether a disproportionate number of members of a protected class are rejected as a result of social network checks.

• Compare the information you get from social network checks with what you learned from the interview, test scores, and the results of traditional reference checks.

• Maintain records relating to your decision: the information you looked at and your decision based on that information.

• Become familiar with individual state laws concerning the use of social media in hiring decisions. For example, some states ban decisions based on leisure activities.

• Give applicants prior notice when using third-party vendors to conduct background checks that include searching social networks. If applicants are not informed that a third party might explore their social media profiles, you could be in violation of the Fair Credit Reporting Act.

Social Media Versus Traditional Reference Checks

As stated in Chapter 13, reference checks can help deflect charges of negligent hiring. That statement applies to traditional means to help determine job suitability, but it may potentially extend to social media checks.

Proponents of Social Media Reference Checks

Social media supporters offer these arguments in favor of using information found on an applicant's social networking profile to determine job suitability:

- Social media searches yield more information than traditional reference methods, since former employers are often tight-lipped about revealing any information about workers for fear of being sued for defamation of character.
- Social networking sites are more comprehensive, yielding more information than employers can get through traditional checks.
- Employers can gain greater insight into an applicant's expanded professional life, making it easier to determine if the applicant will fit into the organization's culture.
- Examples of inappropriate behavior are more likely to be revealed through social media sites than traditional reference checks.
- It takes less time to explore social networks than it does to conduct traditional reference checks.

With the possible exception of the last point, these statements are not supported by sufficient empirical information to conclude they are facts. Even the last point can be challenged; it's awfully easy to become distracted and lose track of time when on a social media site, which could greatly extend the length of time devoted to reference checks.

Opponents of Social Media Reference Checks

The overriding objection to conducting social media reference checks is the limited evidence supporting their validity. In addition:

- The jury is still out with regard to the definition of privacy when it comes to social media.
- Allowing managers and others who are directly involved with the decision-making process to perform social media reference checks could violate employment laws, putting the company in jeopardy.
- Misuse of social media sites by employers could damage the reputation of those sites, not to mention the reputations of employers themselves.

- In addition to verifying information provided by an applicant through the interview and resume, a traditional reference check provides someone else's perspective of the job suitability and likely overall fit with a particular corporate culture.

Traditional reference checks offer two additional advantages over social media checks: (1) Phone reference checks—the preferred method—allow a prospective employer to hear and carefully interpret tone of voice to support what the former employer is saying, and (2) skilled interviewers conducting phone references may be able to engage a former employer in a conversation, thereby learning more about the applicant's qualifications.

Employers who decide to conduct reference checks through social media are advised to conduct a controlled search about job-related tangible and intangible factors only. While tangible information, such as verification of prior employment, should serve as the foundation of a reference check, social media sites often focus instead on intangibles. That can work as long as the intangibles are job-related. For example, the ability to work well under pressure when considering applicants for a manager's job would be a relevant intangible trait, supportable by specific examples from the applicants' former jobs. Suggesting, however, that an applicant's second job at night tending bar in a less-than-reputable neighborhood is job-related is not likely to hold up. It's also not information you're likely to access during a phone reference check, which makes its applicability questionable.

The veracity of information posted by an applicant on his social media site may also be challenged.

The bottom line is this: Do not use information uncovered during a social media search if it's inconsistent with information that could legally be obtained during a traditional reference check. If you're intent on conducting a social media reference check, run a traditional check as well.

Summary

Use social networks judiciously and look for consistency between what they reveal and what you've learned as a result of interviews, tests, and traditional reference methods. Base your hiring decision on an overall objective assessment of the applicant and not just on information from social media sites.

Social networking sites such as Facebook, LinkedIn, Twitter, and others have changed how employers and applicants communicate. Employers increasingly rely on social media to learn as much as possible about potential employees, including whether they demonstrate inappropriate behavior such as drinking, have made discriminatory or disparaging comments, or are prone to violence.

There are numerous legal risks connected with using social media in hiring decisions, including failure-to-hire claims, invasion of privacy, disparate treatment, and disparate impact. Because of these risks, employers are urged to develop social media policies that begin with asking all applicants, in writing, for permission to conduct a social media search.

When it comes to conducting social media checks, experts agree that it is best to also perform traditional references.

CHAPTER 15

The Selection Process

You've conducted legal, competency-based interviews, effectively documented each one, conducted relevant tests, and run comprehensive reference and background checks on the finalists. You've also considered your company's affirmative action goals and assessed its organization-wide and departmental diversity levels. Hopefully, the hiring manager and HR interviewer agree on whom to hire; if they don't, the manager will probably make the final decision, with the HR representative documenting his reasons for disagreeing. At last, it's time to extend an offer of employment to the one applicant who stands out among the rest.

Final Selection Factors

Before committing to one applicant and extending a job offer, take a moment to review these final selection factors:

• *Review your objective.* Remind yourself of the role this job plays and how it fits in with other positions in the department, division, and organization overall. Consider, too, its projected impact on both departmental and organizational goals.

• *Review the job description to ensure thorough familiarity with the concrete requirements, duties, and responsibilities of the position.* Identify the essential and nonessential functions of the job, as well as the approximate amount of time devoted to each task.

• *Consider the intangible requirements of the job.* Remember that certain intangible qualities, although subjective by definition, can still be job-related. Identify and evaluate only those intangibles that have a bearing on job performance.

• *Evaluate applicants' reactions to various questions and statements.* For example, if the job requires extensive overtime and standing for long periods of time, review the applicant's reaction to this information.

• *Compare an applicant's verbal and nonverbal communication patterns.* Recollect nonverbal patterns during the interview in response to certain questions and carefully interpret what was being expressed by way of certain gestures, movements, and microexpressions. Determine, too, if they were consistent with verbal responses.

- *Take salary requirements into consideration and compare these with the salary range for the available position.* The salary offered should be one that is acceptable to both the prospective employee and the company.

- *Assess reasons for leaving previous employers.* If you see a pattern emerging every two years or so, such as "no room for growth," it's possible that within a short time your company's name will appear on the applicant's resume with the same claim.

- *Consider the applicant's potential, especially if the opening is a stepping-stone to other positions.* It's all right to favor a future employee whose strengths are most likely to further the company's goals; just don't reject someone because they don't demonstrate potential.

- *Consider whether this job and the organization overall appear to be appropriate for the applicant.* Does what your company offers in the way of career growth and other opportunities seem to reflect what the applicant is looking for? You don't want someone to grow restless shortly after coming aboard and decide to move on upon discovering there's a mismatch.

The Final Meeting

Based on your review of these selection factors, you should now be ready to extend a job offer to the final standout applicant. This last step of extending an offer of employment should be fairly effortless, although there are still some critical components remaining to ensure a smooth transition from the status of applicant to employee. Call or e-mail a job-offer letter, asking the recipient to either decline or accept. Assuming the answer is "yes," set up a time to discuss the particulars of the offer. Unless logistics prove prohibitive, this conversation should take place in the form of a face-to-face meeting.

So often, employers assume that new employees know certain basic information about the job, only to learn after starting that they do not. Here's one of my favorite stories to illustrate this point: A young woman named Delia was selected to work as a public relations assistant for a small publishing company. She was thrilled and looked forward to starting her new job. Because she was concerned about the commute, Delia allowed plenty of time to make sure she wouldn't be late on her first day. As it turned out, she'd planned her travel schedule exceedingly well and arrived at her new job by 8:15, forty-five minutes early. The next day she left home at the same time and once again she arrived early, this time at 8:18. She did this for the remainder of the week with the same results, give or take a few minutes on either side of 8:15. She then began to relax. Delia was the only one arriving that early, and she was no longer concerned about being late. She decided to take a later train from that point on. The following Monday, she arrived at 8:45, still fifteen minutes early, allowing her ample time to get settled and ready to begin work. She noticed that others were already at their desks, but she didn't give the matter much thought. She'd arrived in plenty of time to begin her day and that's all that mattered. For the next three mornings she was at her desk no later than 8:50. On Friday, Rupert, her manager, summoned her into his office, clearly agitated. She didn't have much time to try to figure out what was wrong because he started right in by bellowing, "What exactly is it that you think you're doing? You've been here for two weeks and have shown up late five days in a row! I hope you've got a good explanation, because this is not the way to make a good impression on me!" Delia was stunned. "What are you talking about? I've been early every morning since I've started. True, I'm not as early this week as I was last week, but I'm still here ten to fifteen minutes before I'm supposed to be!" Rupert settled down and looked at her. Then he had a disquieting thought: "Delia, what time did they tell you in HR that we start in this department?" Delia replied, "They didn't tell me anything, so I just assumed the job was 9 to 5. Aren't those the hours I'm supposed to work?" Rupert sighed. "No, Delia. Our hours are 8:30 to 5."

Reading this scenario you might think that Delia should have asked HR what her hours were supposed to be. But Delia had only worked at one other job before this one, and in that office the schedule was 9 to 5. Since no one had said otherwise, she assumed the hours were the same at this job. Yes, she should have confirmed the actual hours of work, but the onus was on HR or her manager to communicate all the particulars about the job before she began, including something as basic as her schedule.

Final Meeting Checklist

To avoid creating employer-employee rifts such as the one between Rupert and Delia, develop a checklist that reflects all the particulars of the available position. The checklist should represent a review of topics previously discussed with the applicant, as well as new topics such as the actual starting salary and some specific benefits. Exhibit 15-1 is a comprehensive generic checklist that can be used as a model. Some of the topics may not apply to all jobs, but it's better to start out with more than less.

Once you and the prospective employee sit down and go over the list together, check off each topic discussed. It's a good idea to give the individual a copy of the list so she can also keep track of everything as well. It's most important to indicate whether you and the individual are in agreement about each topic. If there are any discrepancies, clearly indicate the nature of the disagreement, as well as the next step to be taken. For example, the employee may have assumed that she was entitled to the same number of vacation days she receives at her current job. If this becomes a point of contention, make a note before moving on to the next topic. Toward the end of the meeting, return to the matter of vacation days and see if you can come to an agreement. If not, you may need to get back to her. The reason it's a good idea to move on and then return to the subject is that you don't want to get bogged down at any point. Get through all the topics on your checklist and then revisit any that require additional discussion. This approach will also give you an overview of how many areas of controversy there are, as well their levels of severity. In addition, applicants have a chance to reconsider their thinking. You will also have a better

Exhibit 15-1. Final Meeting Checklist

Topic	☑ Discussed	☑ Agreed	☑ Further Discussion Needed
Job title			
Exemption status			
Department			
Report to			
Primary duties and responsibilities (List or attach a job description)			
Start date			
Schedule			
Hours			
Days			
Shifts arrangement			
Location			
Fixed			
Rotate			
Salary			
Base salary (weekly or biweekly)			
Bonus			
Commissions			
Signing bonus			
Overtime			
Comp time			
Travel allowance			
Schedule of salary reviews			
Employment-at-will relationship			
Conditions of employment			
Satisfactory reference check			
Satisfactory background check			
Proof of employment eligibility in the U.S.			
Satisfactory results of company-issued physical exam			
Satisfactory results of company-issued drug test			
Union/Nonunion status and requirements			
Benefits (detailed coverage during orientation)			
Holidays			
Personal days			
Sick days			
Vacation (eligibility; number of days)			

(continues)

Exhibit 15-1. Continued.

Topic	☑ Discussed	☑ Agreed	☑ Further Discussion Needed
General health benefits including:			
Medical			
Dental			
Vision			
Insurance: life, accidental death, disability			
Profit sharing, stock options, ESOPs			
Pension plan, 401(k)			
Tuition reimbursement			
Additional Offerings:			
Electronic devices			
Health club membership			
Laptop computer			
Company car			
Noncompete agreement			
Additional conditions of employment			

sense of where you can afford to yield, thereby gaining leverage to hold out regarding more significant points.

Exhibit 15-2 illustrates how the discussion relating to vacation might be indicated on the final meeting checklist.

Final Meeting Problems and Solutions

The procedure to follow during the final meeting between the HR representative and soon-to-be-employee is simple: use the checklist as a guide, review each topic as it relates to the job he's about to fill, and answer any remaining questions he may have. Then, as indicated earlier, return to any areas of disagreement at the end of the meeting and try to reach a resolution.

This process, while simple, sometimes unveils significant discrepancies to the extent that some of the most seemingly benign areas of dispute can become deal breakers. For instance, a man I know was interviewing for the position of director of HR—the topmost position in the department, reporting directly to the president of the company. Eli was satisfied with the job description, had no argument with the salary or benefits, but wanted a title change: Instead of director of HR, he wanted "vice president of HR." This title would be in line with the heads of other departments company-wide, all of whom were vice presidents. Anything less, he argued, would diminish the credibility of the HR function. The president would not budge. Despite acknowledging that one of her goals was to position HR to take on a more

Exhibit 15-2. Final Meeting Checklist. Disagreement about Vacation

Topic	☑ Discussed	☑ Agreed	☑ Further Discussion Needed
Vacation (eligibility; number of days)	☑		☑ Re: # of days. Applicant currently gets 20 days; level of job warrants 15. Applicant is adamant. Suggest allowing 5 unpaid days, if dept. mgr. agrees, but cannot take 20 consecutive days. App. will consider & call w/in 24 hrs.

strategic role in achieving business missions, she remained steadfast: the HR department had never been headed up by an officer and she felt it would represent too dramatic a departure to do so now. Eli grew concerned that the president's thinking was reflective of how the organization functioned; if she refused to get on board with a title change, how would he convince her to implement the many improvements he knew were needed to increase productivity? He ultimately decided to decline their offer.

With this illustration in mind, let's look at a final meeting from the perspective of the applicant in terms of some of the problem areas that could develop, along with potential solutions. Note that the discussion that follows presumes that the HR representative avoids presenting anything new or different about the job during the meeting.

Topic: Job Title

Possible Problems: The title fails to accurately reflect the full scope of responsibilities, is not comparable to other titles with similar levels of responsibility, or certain words in the title, such as "clerk," or "assistant," are objectionable.

Possible Solutions: Explain how job titles are part of specific job families and that to change a specific title would impact the entire job family, as well as incumbents performing similar functions. Suggest that applicant begin work at the existing job title, with the commitment that HR will review its continued appropriateness after three months. Confirm that the applicant will accept the existing job title, as well as any suggestions, before proceeding.

Topic: Primary Duties and Responsibilities

Possible Problem: The primary duties and responsibilities encompass tasks the applicant didn't realize were part of the job.

Possible Solutions: First, explain that this is the same job description that she reviewed during the interview. Then together focus on unveiling the real problem:

Are these tasks she doesn't feel qualified to perform? Perhaps on-the-job training or an outside workshop is the solution. If, on the other hand, there are responsibilities that she doesn't feel should be part of the job, then make clear that the job description reflects the tasks expected of everyone hired for this position. If she's uncomfortable with any of the duties identified, ask her what she realistically expects to happen. This is a critical point in the meeting. If she expresses a high level of discomfort, then you may have to ask if this means she's no longer interested in the job. If, however, she says she initially misunderstood certain aspects of the job but is now clear about and fine with them, confirm that she is willing to accept the responsibilities as identified in the job description before proceeding.

Topic: Start Date

Possible Problem: Applicant requires more time before beginning work than you consider reasonable.

Possible Solution: Find out why he needs more time. If it's because he feels obliged to his current employer, offer to talk with his manager once he's given notice. If, however, it's because he wants time off between jobs, suggest a compromise, such as an abbreviated break coupled with an initial modified work schedule, such as two to three days per week for the first two weeks.

Topic: Schedule

Possible Problems: Agreed-upon hours, shift arrangement, and/or days are no longer acceptable.

Possible Solution: Be careful that the problem doesn't have to do with a religious conflict; if it does, you're obliged to reasonably accommodate the person's religious conviction. If the problem does not concern religion, explain that the schedule is the same as the one described during the interview. Ask what has happened since that time to make it a problem, making sure not to discuss personal matters. If her explanation strikes you as plausible, see if there are alternative work schedules you can explore. For example, does your company offer flextime, a compressed workweek, or telecommuting? If so, consider the impact this would have on the workload and morale of the rest of the workforce and the workload in the department.

Topic: Salary

Possible Problem: Applicant's salary expectations have increased since the time of the interview.

Possible Solutions: Salary is a thorny topic. The final salary agreed upon has to be acceptable to both parties: If either side feels disgruntled, the employer-employee relationship is doomed to fail before it even begins. Depending on the level of the position, most employers have some latitude in terms of what they can offer. In fact, many applicants believe they're expected to reject your first offer and negotiate. Therefore, before the final meeting you need a clear vision of just how much base salary you're prepared to offer and what additional aspects of salary—such as bonuses, commissions, or travel allowance—invite discussion. Consider this multi-stepped approach:

1. Listen closely to everything the applicant is saying while asking yourself if there's a sound basis for his demands.

2. Ask meaningful questions, including, "Why do you feel you're worth the additional money?" "What's changed since our last interview?" "Why do you think your current employer doesn't pay you this amount?" "Did you consider how I would react to your request for more than I'm prepared to offer?" "What will you do if I tell you right now that we cannot pay you more than the sum I've offered?" "If you were me, what would you do?"

3. Look for areas of compromise. For example, if the applicant is dissatisfied with the base salary being offered, a one-time signing bonus could alleviate the problem. Or perhaps adjusting the method of calculating commissions might prove satisfactory.

4. Keep in mind how much "wiggle room" you have. How much beyond what you were prepared to offer are you willing to pay in order to have this person work for you?

5. Consider the likely impact this person's salary will have on incumbents functioning in a similar capacity at a lesser rate of pay.

6. Consider how badly the organization wants or needs this person. Was the position open a long time before you finally found the one you believe will make the best fit? Is this a hard-to-fill position for which only a handful of individuals possess the skills and knowledge required? What can this person offer that someone requiring less compensation cannot?

Topic: **Conditions of Employment**

Possible Problem: Applicant does not want her current employer contacted for references until she receives a letter extending an offer of employment, at which time she will give notice.

Possible Solution: This shouldn't be a problem. Explain that conditions of employment could extend to beyond her start date; in other words, under certain circumstances, a person could start work without all of the conditions being met, with the understanding that appropriate action would be taken after hire, if need be. For example, all reference checks may not come back prior to the agreed-upon start date.

Topic: **Benefits**

Possible Problems: There could be any one of a number of issues regarding benefits, including number of and eligibility for vacation days, general health benefits, profit sharing, and tuition reimbursement.

Possible Solutions: Most benefits are set by the company, leaving HR little room to negotiate, although some benefits, such as number of vacation days, can sometimes be recalculated. State this clearly, suggesting that the applicant raise specific benefits-related questions during the employee orientation. If, however, the applicant has concerns that preclude his ability to proceed beyond this point, pause and, if plausible, set up a meeting or phone call between the applicant and someone in benefits. Hopefully, you'll be able to proceed shortly thereafter.

Topic: **Additional Perks**

Possible Problem: The applicant wants more "stuff," such as a laptop computer, that wasn't part of the original agreement.

Possible Solution: If you decide to grant additional perks, bear in mind the likely impact such acts of generosity are likely to have on the new hire's colleagues. These extras may make her happy for now, but this could affect the morale and productivity of other employees later.

Topic: **Noncompete Agreement**

Possible Problem: The applicant refuses to sign a noncompete agreement.

Possible Solution: Noncompete agreements are for a specified period, often one to two years, and are intended to take effect upon termination. Employees may be restricted from working for a competitor, working at the same or a comparable job in the same industry, or working in a defined geographical area for a competitor. Because these are often intricately worded agreements, you may need to get your attorneys involved if applicants refuse to sign or require modifications to your organization's standard noncompete agreement.

Note that you are obliged to confirm that the applicant will not be violating a noncompete agreement he may have with his current or previous employer.

As you wade through the details of this list of possible problems, try not to view matters from the prospective of the applicant. Remind him about some of the benefits of working for your company and mention any awards or recognition bestowed upon your organization (e.g., "Malstrom Electronics has been voted one of the top 10 places to work in Vermont for three years in a row"). Also, bear in mind that prospective employees want to hear about staff recognition, advancement possibilities, and any unique aspects of the corporate culture.

To exemplify this last point, the HR manager from a small business in upstate New York once contacted me regarding an interesting choice her company offers new hires. Since they know they can't afford to offer the same salaries as their competitors, they look for other ways of attracting and retaining employees. They came up with an idea whereby applicants are offered an unusual choice: If hired, they can either have fully paid pet insurance and enjoy other pet-related services, such as a free dog-walking service; or they can have on-site child care and at-home babysitting services of comparable value. If they opt for the pet package, employees can bring their pets to work one day a month; likewise, if they prefer the child-care perk, they can have their children at their workstations once a month. According to the HR manager, applicants seem to love having a choice, and so far as I know, no one's been bitten. (NOTE: Look into insurance and liability issues before allowing animals at work.)

Notifying Selected Applicants

Assuming all goes smoothly during the final meeting and you've exchanged a verbal agreement concerning the terms of employment, it's time to extend an official offer in writing.

A job-offer letter could be viewed as a legally binding employment contract; ensure that the contents absolutely and accurately reflect what you and the applicant agreed to during the final meeting.

The HR representative should send two copies of the letter to the prospective employee: one for him to sign and return to the employer, the other for him to keep. Also, send a copy to the hiring manager.

The contents of the letter should be concise and clear, leaving no room for misunderstanding. Much of what was discussed during the final meeting should be included:

- Job title
- Exemption status
- Department
- Primary duties and responsibilities (list or attach a job description)
- Start date
- Schedule
- Location
- Salary in weekly or biweekly terms
- Employment-at-will relationship
- Conditions of employment, including satisfactory reference and background checks, physical and drug tests, and I-9 verification
- Arrangements regarding:
  —Preemployment physical (may warrant a separate letter)
  —Preemployment drug test (may warrant a separate letter)
- Union status, if relevant
- Benefits highlights
- Identification and instructions for the completion of any materials enclosed, such as benefits forms
- Additional offerings
- Noncompete agreement (may warrant a separate letter)
- Other topics relating to the terms and conditions of employment
- Whom to contact with questions

Exhibit 15-3 is a sample letter reflecting this plethora of topics. As you can see, it is a highly formalized, comprehensive letter of considerable length. Depending on the nature of the job, certain aspects may not be necessary, such as referencing the signing bonus. Also, your company may not require preemployment physicals or

Exhibit 15-3. Sample Job Offer Letter

January 23, 2XXX

Mr. Richard M. Reason
20 Foxrun Circle
Secona, Nevada 55555

Dear Mr. Reason:

We are pleased to confirm our offer for the nonunion, exempt-level position of industrial engineer in the operations department of Hardcore Industries. The attached job description reflects the primary duties and responsibilities for this job, as discussed during our meeting on January 21, 2XXX.

As agreed, you will begin work on February 28, 2XXX. At 9:00 A.M. on that date, kindly report to your manager, Claire Hinton, in the operations department at Hardcore's headquarters located at 477 Jackson Boulevard in Secona. For your convenience, you may park in space number 47 in the south employee parking lot. This will be your regular parking space as long as you're employed by Hardcore. When you are required to visit any of Hardcore's other locations, you will be able to park in their rotating employees' parking lots.

Your regularly scheduled core hours will be 10:00 A.M. to 4:00 P.M., Monday through Friday, with an additional two hours of work preceding or following these hours each day. These additional hours will be determined between yourself and your manager. This will total eight hours of work daily, including a one-hour lunch period.

As further agreed, your base starting salary will be $2,846.15 per week. In addition, you will receive a signing bonus of $8,000, payable in a lump sum, effective immediately upon hire. The entire amount will be returned should your relationship with Hardcore be severed either by you or us, according to the terms and conditions of Hardcore's at-will agreement (see below), within six months of the date of hire. The signing bonus has no bearing whatsoever on any salary increases for which you might be deemed eligible during your unspecified term of employment.

Hardcore's at-will agreement reads as follows:

Employees hired by Hardcore Industries may terminate their employment at any time, with or without notice or cause. Likewise, Hardcore may terminate the employment of any of its employees at any time, with or without notice or cause.

I understand that my employment is not for any specified period of time, and if terminated, Hardcore Industries is liable only for wages earned as of the date of termination.

I further understand that no representative of Hardcore Industries, other than the president or a designated official, has any authority to enter into any agreement, oral or written, for employment for any specified period of time or to make any agreement or assurances contrary to this policy.

Nothing in this letter, in the employee handbook, or any other Hardcore document shall be interpreted to be in conflict with or to eliminate or modify in any way the employment-at-will status of Hardcore's employees."

This offer of employment is contingent upon certain conditions:
1. Satisfactory results of a Hardcore-initiated background check.
2. Satisfactory results of a Hardcore-initiated reference check.
3. Submission of acceptable documents that establish your identity and eligibility to work in the United States, in accordance with the Immigration Reform and Control Act (IRCA) of 1986.

4. Satisfactory results of a Hardcore-issued preemployment physical.

5. Satisfactory results of a Hardcore-issued drug test.

With regard to items (4) and (5), our medical office has been advised of your start date and will be expecting you for your preemployment physical exam and drug test anytime within one week of that date; that is, no later than February 21, 2XXX. The medical office is open Monday through Friday, between 8:00 A.M. and 12:00 noon. Please call extension 6488 for an appointment and instructions as to how to prepare for these two exams.

The extension of an offer of employment is also contingent upon your agreement to abide by Hardcore's noncompete clause. You will receive a letter under separate cover from Hardcore's legal department essentially asking that you commit to (1) being free of any agreement limiting your ability to work for Hardcore, and (2) upon termination from Hardcore, agreeing not to work at the same or a comparable job for a competitor for a period of one year. Upon receipt, please call Jocelyn Wright in the legal department at extension 6420 with any questions concerning the noncompete agreement.

The attached schedule of benefits identifies such matters as holidays, personal days, sick days, vacation, general health benefits, insurance, Hardcore's pension plan, and tuition reimbursement. As discussed during our meeting on January 21, 2XXX, all of these and other benefits will be fully explained and your questions answered during employee orientation, beginning on February 28, 2XXX. At that time you will also be asked to complete certain benefits and payroll forms. Should you have any questions that you would like addressed prior to that date, please feel free to contact Hardcore's benefits manager, Lou Briscoe, at extension 6499.

As part of your employment package, you are entitled to free membership in the Live-Long health club, a Smartphone, and a laptop computer. You will also receive reimbursable expenses in conjunction with approved Hardcore-related business, according to the enclosed schedule. These entitlements will continue until either party evokes their employment-at-will status.

As agreed, you will resign from your current position upon receipt of and agreement with the conditions of this job offer. Upon doing so, please notify this office in writing so that we may conduct a reference check with your current employer.

Kindly indicate your understanding and acceptance of the terms and conditions of Hardcore's offer by signing below and returning a signed copy of this letter in the enclosed envelope no later than February 1, 2XXX.

It is my sincere pleasure to extend this offer of employment with Hardcore Industries. If you have any non-benefits, non-health, or non-legal questions, please do not hesitate to contact me at extension 6815.

Sincerely,

Wes Lohan
Manager of Human Resources

I, Richard M. Reason, understand and accept the terms of Hardcore Industries' terms and conditions of employment as identified in this letter.

_____   _____
(Signature)   (Date)

conduct drug tests for all potential employees. It also may not have a noncompete agreement requirement. Even without these references, however, this is a long letter. You may choose, therefore, to remove certain segments and communicate them under separate cover. In addition to the noncompete agreement, sections suitable for isolation and individual reference include any requirements concerning physical exams and drug tests.

Some companies opt not to reference the employment-at-will statement in their offer of employment, reasoning that it renders the letter too formal. After all, the individual signed the application form containing the at-will clause, and the statement probably appears in the employee handbook that the person will receive soon after starting work. Others, myself included, recommend including the employment-at-will statement in the letter offering employment. This is a critical document and the at-will statement is a vital part of the employer-employee relationship. A duplication of effort is preferable over omission.

Notifying Rejected Applicants

Once you've received a signed letter from the applicant accepting your offer of employment, it's time to notify the other applicants. Except for those individuals you absolutely knew would not be considered as soon as their interviews ended, it's best to wait to send out letters of rejection until you have a firm commitment from the person you want to hire.

Rejection letters should refer to the specific position for which an individual applied. In other words, don't reject the person overall; you may want to consider her for another position in the future.

The tone of a rejection letter should be professional and sincere. Avoid including detailed information about the successful candidate—doing so without permission of the new hire could be considered an invasion of privacy. In addition, a rejected applicant could use your disclosures as the basis for a discrimination claim.

Rejection letters should be brief, beginning and ending on a positive note. As with letters offering employment, the HR representative who interviewed the applicant usually sends them.

Following is a sample letter encompassing these points:

February 1, 2XXX

Ms. Amy I. Morris
128 Field Avenue
Union City, Nevada 55535

Dear Ms. Morris:
Thank you for taking the time to meet with us to discuss Hardcore Industries' opening for an industrial engineer. We learned a great deal about your accomplishments and aspirations and appreciate the interest you expressed in our company.

When filling an opening, Hardcore looks at a number of factors, such as experience, demonstrated skills, knowledge, and the ability to handle key job-related situations. This can make the selection process difficult when we are fortunate enough to attract many qualified applicants. With only one opening, however, we are forced to turn away many fine interviewees. Accordingly, we regret that we are unable to extend an offer of employment to you at this time.

Thank you again for your time and interest, Ms. Morris. We hope you consider us again for employment in the future.

Sincerely,

Wes Lohan
Manager of Human Resources

What Could Go Wrong?

Congratulations! You're all done! The letter offering employment has been sent out; all that's left is for the applicant to sign it and return it to you. Then you'll proceed with any remaining steps, such as the physical and drug test, schedule him for orientation, and that will be that. Right?

Well, technically, there is nothing left to do. But that doesn't mean things can't still go wrong. Let's look at three possible last-minute scenarios and what you can do to avert a disaster. In each instance, bear in mind that even if the worst possible scenario—that you're going to lose the applicant—seems imminent, it may be preferable to being held hostage by unreasonable, last-minute demands that could be a sign of trouble later on.

Scenario 1: The applicant calls you upon receipt of the offer letter, claiming you changed the mutually agreed-upon salary.

Response: Ask her what figure she believes should have been recorded and offer to call her back. Immediately check your notes; it's possible, although unlikely, that you made a mistake. Upon confirming that the figure in her letter is the salary you both agreed to, call her and state, "Ms. Chisholm, I've reviewed my notes; the salary I referenced in the letter is correct. In addition, I recall our discussion concerning salary and that you agreed to a starting salary of $85,000 per annum, or $1,634.62 a week." At this point, do not say anything further. Here's a possible response from the applicant: "I remember that $85,000 is what you offered, but I said I was worth more—at least $5,000 more." "Yes, Ms. Chisholm, you did say you believed you were worth more money; but if you'll recall, I clearly stated that I cannot offer you more than $85,000 at this time." Again, don't say anything more; the ball is in her court. She could come back with any one of a number of responses, including rejecting your offer outright. In the time between your last statement and her next one, you need to decide what you're prepared to do. You can either stand your ground, compromise, or acquiesce. It's up to you, of course. How valuable is this person? My inclination would be to stand pat. If she continues to argue, say, "Ms. Chisholm, I wish we could discuss this further, but there's nothing more to be said. I need to know at this time if you are comfortable accepting the agreed-upon salary of $85,000. Our offer is firm."

Scenario 2: The applicant calls to say he's received a better offer. He prefers working for you, however, and wants to know if you can sweeten the pot.

Response: This is a variation of the first scenario in that this applicant wants more than was agreed to. In this case, it could be more money, greater benefits, or additional perks. Whatever the case, unless this person is a one-in-a-million find for a hard-to-fill position, my advice is the same: do not alter your offer. The time for negotiations is past. The applicant agreed, and last-minute grandstanding is only going to make a bad impression. Accordingly, you could respond with, "I'm sorry to hear that you're not interested in keeping your oral commitment to us; I'll send you a letter confirming this conversation and withdrawing our offer." He might come back with, "That's not what I said. I want to work for you; it's just that I have this other offer and they're making it very tempting." Again, remain firm: "I understand, Mr. Stars, but the time for discussing the particulars of your employment is past; we both agreed to the same terms of employment." If the applicant really does have another offer, he may withdraw his verbal commitment. Chances are, though, he doesn't have another offer and is just trying to get more from you. If that's the case, he may then say something like, "I was hoping to get you to match their offer, but I'd rather work for you even though I'll be earning less."

Scenario 3: The applicant calls upon receiving the offer letter and says she needs more time before making a final decision.

Response: Ask her if there are any specific questions you can answer that will help. She might say, "I don't know what it is; I'm just not sure if I really should leave my current job. They really need me here." It's tempting to get annoyed with this response, but you need to remain objective. Consider asking, "Ms. Polymer, are you saying that you're rejecting our offer of employment?" At this point she might ask for more of an incentive to switch jobs, or she might actually say, "Yes, I guess that's what I'm saying. I'm sorry, but I realize I'm better off staying here."

This is probably the worst thing you can imagine happening at this point. You'd closed the book on this job and now you're faced with the prospect of starting all over again. But the picture may not be as grim as you might think. First, have her formally reject your offer of employment, in writing. Then go to your pile of rejected applicants and look at any who came in a close second. If you're lucky you'll find someone who will work out as well or nearly as well as your first choice. This may add some time to the start date, but pat yourself on the back for not sending out rejection letters before you received a firm commitment.

Sometimes unforeseen events happen and there's nothing to be done. Consider the applicant who worked for three and a half days, and on the afternoon of his fourth day he said he had a headache and needed to run to the corner drugstore for some pain reliever. That was the last anyone saw of him. E-mails and phone calls remained unanswered. The following week he sent a curt text to his supervisor: "I guess by now you know I won't be coming back."

Summary

The final step of extending an offer of employment should be fairly effortless, although there are still some critical components remaining to ensure a smooth transition from applicant status to employee.

Before making your final decision, review some critical factors, including your objectives, the job description, the credentials of your finalists, and their respective salary requirements. Also assess reasons for leaving previous employers. Once you offer the job to your top contender and that person accepts, set up a meeting so you can discuss some of the particulars, such as duties and reporting relationship, salary, benefits, and a starting date.

In preparation for this meeting, and to ensure coverage of all the salient points, develop a checklist representing relevant topics. Once you and the prospective employee go over the list together, check off each topic discussed and indicate whether you and the individual are in agreement. If there are any discrepancies, clearly note the nature of the disagreement. Before ending the meeting, return to any areas of dispute and try to come to an agreement.

Sometimes significant discrepancies are unveiled during the final meeting. Typical problem areas that can result in disputes include job titles, primary duties and responsibilities, start dates, schedules, salary, conditions of employment, benefits, additional perks, and noncompete agreements. Some of these disputes can mushroom into deal breakers.

As you wade through the details of your checklist, try not to get bogged down by issues to the extent you lose sight of your main objective: to make this applicant an employee. If you hit a snag, take a step back; remind yourself why you want this person and reiterate some of the benefits of working for your company to help the applicant remember why she wants the job.

Assuming all goes smoothly during the final meeting and you've exchanged a verbal agreement concerning the terms of employment, extend an official offer in writing. The contents of the letter should be concise and clear and should leave no room for misunderstanding. Much of what was discussed during the final meeting should be included.

Once you've received a signed letter from the applicant accepting your offer of employment, it's time to notify the other applicants. Except for those individuals you knew absolutely would not be considered as soon as their interviews ended, it's best to wait to send out letters of rejection until you have a firm commitment from the person you want to hire.

After you've sent out the letter formally offering employment, there's really nothing left to do, but that doesn't mean things can't still go wrong. If this should happen and the worst possible scenario—you're going to lose the applicant—seems imminent, it may still be preferable to being held hostage by unreasonable, last-minute demands that could be a sign of trouble later on.

Orienting New Employees

CHAPTER 16

Organizational Orientation

Everyone knows that starting a new job can be unnerving. Until an employee becomes familiar with his surroundings, feels comfortable with the details and routine of a typical day, and develops an understanding of what's expected of him, it's likely to be difficult to focus on job performance. Most businesses recognize this and provide some form of new hire organizational orientation that covers a range of topics and varies in duration. Do orientation programs succeed at putting new employees at ease and familiarizing them with their work environment? Some do; others do not. Programs that succeed do so because they're well-planned and thoughtfully organized in terms of format and content. But for those employers to whom the term *orientation* means sending new employees to a brief meeting during which someone from HR describes the company's history, rules, and benefits and leaves little if any time for questions or interaction among attendees, there's little hope for success. After all the time, effort, and expense you invested in finding the best possible person for a job, why risk losing him at the outset?

In this chapter, we'll explore the elements of successful "live" organizational orientations. Departmental orientations will be discussed in Chapter 17, and self-directed, or web-based, orientation will be explored in Chapter 18.

Objectives

First and foremost, organizational orientation programs should focus on affirming a person's decision to join your company. There's nothing worse than changing jobs only to have regrets shortly thereafter. The orientation process should therefore expand upon what the employee learned during his interviews, such as the company's values and corporate culture, and how individual goals can align with those of the organization. Orientation should also focus on encouraging each person to feel like a contributing member of your company from the outset. Overall, then, your goal is to have them leave at the end of their first day feeling like valued employees, not like new hires. In other words, you want to make a good first impression.

First Impressions

There's a great deal of talk concerning the merits of first impressions. Usually the discussion has to do with how applicants can impress their prospective employers, and later how they come across as employees once they start work. No doubt this is important, but so too is the first impression employers make on their newest employees. Employers sometimes forget—especially during economic times when jobs are scarce and the applicant pool is brimming with talent—that an effective employer-employee relationship requires effort on both ends; that effort begins on day one.

It can take very little time to form an opinion about someone, yet what happens in the span of a few hours, minutes, and even seconds can leave an indelible mark. Sometimes that impact can spread, albeit unfairly, to others. Consider, for instance, what happens to Caleb during the first hour of orientation. He's on time, but the orientation begins late. The HR officer does not explain the delay, nor does he introduce himself (the only reason Caleb knows he's the HR officer is because there's a printed agenda and his name is first). He starts by asking, "Can anyone tell me the most important reason you're here?" His tone does not invite a response, but Caleb, as well as others, volunteer answers such as "to learn about the company" and "to find out what's expected of me." The HR officer is expressionless, silent, and clearly unimpressed. After hearing a handful of answers, he flatly states, "Wrong. The most important reason is that we're paying all of you a great deal of money and we want to make sure we get our money's worth." Caleb thinks this is supposed to be funny, but the officer's voice is humorless and his body language stiff, and no one is laughing. Caleb endures the remainder of the orientation and later that day starts his job, glad the so-called orientation is over. Later that day he receives an e-mail from HR concerning some outstanding forms that require completion. Caleb's immediate reaction is negative. The mere thought of dealing with HR makes him uneasy. He goes, meets with someone other that the officer from orientation, and immediately dislikes her even though she is quite pleasant and helpful. Still, because of that negative first impression, he has trouble being objective when dealing with anyone from HR.

Now let's join Ian for his first orientation experience. He's accepted a job paying less than he made in the past, but he's been out of work for nearly a year and grateful to be working. He knows he has a bit of a chip on his shoulder, however, starting out with the attitude that he deserves more than he's getting. He sits with his arms folded, not talking with any of the others in attendance or eating from the breakfast buffet in the back of the room. At exactly 9:00, the designated start time, one of the people he assumed was an attendee approaches the front of the room and introduces herself: "Hi, everyone. My name is Olivia and I'm going to try really hard to make the next two hours both informative and enjoyable for you." And that's exactly what she does. Ian unfolds his arms and starts to listen. Within minutes, Olivia's relaxed style wins Ian over. His focus is no longer on how he's worth more money than he's getting; instead, he starts to think about how this may work out after all.

Simply stated, a positive first impression is golden.

With the prevailing objective of making a positive first impression in mind, some employers take proactive measures to convert a person's new hire status to that of employee well before orientation begins. Some e-mail a welcome packet to the individual, including a checklist of topics that will be covered during orientation. Others send home the individual's new business cards in advance as a means of beginning the psychological conversion process. One company sends a box titled "logo lottery." Inside, new hires find T-shirts, hats, mugs, and other items inscribed with the company logo. The reasoning behind these offerings is simple: The company wants soon-to-be employees to feel like they already work for the company before walking through the door on their first official day of work.

In addition to affirming a person's decision to accept your job offer, here are other reasons for conducting organizational orientation:

• *Decrease anxiety.* Everyone feels anxious when starting a new job. Orientation can go a long way toward making new employees feel at ease and comfortable.

• *Answer questions.* You probably know from your own work experiences that it becomes increasingly difficult to ask questions the longer you're on the job. Orientation is an opportunity for new hires to ask what certain acronyms stand for, how varying departments interrelate, and a host of logistic questions such as where to park, without worrying about sounding foolish.

• *Negate future disciplinary action.* Clearly communicating organizational expectations and policies can go a long way toward preventing future misunderstandings.

• *Increase employee retention.* With employee turnover costing as much as two and a half times an employee's annual salary, it behooves any organization to do what it can to keep employees motivated and interested in staying put from the outset.

• *Promote good public relations.* Your goal is to have new employees talk positively about your orientation program to family members and friends, describing it as a worthwhile experience. The people they tell could well become future employees.

Benefits

Done right, organizational orientation programs benefit employers and employees alike.

Benefits to Employers

Many employers don't realize the many ways they themselves can benefit from well-prepared and well-implemented orientation programs. To begin with, recognize that orientation sets the tone for overall effective employer-employee relations. Savvy employers view this forum as an opportunity to convey their strong commitment to the well-being and development of the company's workforce. In return, new employees are usually motivated to reciprocate by doing their best. Demonstrate your dedication to the development of the workforce by describing some of your most well-received employee-friendly programs. Select examples that go beyond what employees are likely to expect, like basic medical coverage, to demonstrate how great it is to work for your organization. Instead of beginning an organizational orientation session by describing the rules of the company (necessary, but let's face it, not a crowd pleaser), start out with something like this:

> We care about what our employees want! How do we know what you want? We ask you! Just last year as a result of multiple surveys, our employee suggestion program, and one-on-one conversations with members of our management team, we revamped our cafeteria menu and set up an employee lounge. In fact, we're in the process of expanding that lounge to include a nap room! The year before that we implemented our "walk-in-our-shoes" program, whereby managers volunteer to perform an employee's least desirable task for a day. As you might imagine, that's been a huge hit! So welcome to Hardcore Industries, everyone—we know we can count on you to work hard for us. In return, we want to make your experience at Hardcore the best it possibly can be! In fact, before leaving today, we want each of you to tell us about one perk that would make working at Hardcore ideal. You never know, that may be what I talk about during our next orientation program!

Once you have their attention, move on to some details. While it's not advisable to start off by describing company rules, new employees certainly need to know what's expected of them, as well as what happens if they fail to comply with these expectations. But there are ways of discussing these matters that are more palatable than others. For instance, instead of saying "we're going to talk about Hardcore's rules and regulations," say, "Let's look at some of Hardcore's policies and procedures." The first sounds punitive, the latter informative. Consider introducing this subject by saying something like the following:

> You've all been given a copy of Hardcore's employee handbook. In it you'll find many company policies concerning such matters as schedules, vacations, and holidays. You'll become familiar with all that Hardcore offers its workforce, as well as what we expect in return, regarding such matters as attendance and punctuality. In just a few moments, we'll begin to review its contents. But first I want to stress that all of Hardcore's policies reflect our strong commitment to a reciprocal relationship between employer and employee.

Introducing company expectations in this manner benefits employers by establishing an atmosphere of mutual respect—a cornerstone for productivity.

Organizational orientation programs can also help shorten a new employee's learning curve, which is a huge benefit for employers. Learning entails a great deal more than how to do one's job; that's part of the departmental orientation. There's also the important matter of becoming familiar with the prevailing corporate culture. Talking with other new employees and listening to representatives of HR, senior management, and various departments will help accomplish this. If employees feel part of the corporate culture from the start, they're more likely to focus on their work.

Benefits to Employees

Employees tend to look at the benefits of orientation programs differently than employers do. Whereas employers take a long-term holistic view of the process, employees want, first and foremost, to feel welcome. Making employees feel at ease can be accomplished with little effort. As mentioned, some employers start this process prior to orientation with packets of information, business cards, and baskets of goodies. Others share announcements of their start date with current staff. These traditional approaches set a welcoming tone well before the new hire's first day. You might also want to consider a more creative approach, such as the one adopted by a manager who stated that he could never understand why people throw parties when employees leave. He thought it made more sense to have a "welcome aboard" party. HR supported his idea and now orientation starts out with a celebration, complete with balloons, noisemakers, and cake. The entire event lasts only about fifteen minutes, but it makes a huge impact on new hires.

New employees are also less interested in the history of the company or what it earned last year than they are on those topics that affect them personally and immediately. That said, they will likely gain from information about:

- *Food:* Is there a company cafeteria? What about restaurants in the area? Are there coffee stations on every floor?
- *Clothing:* What attire is appropriate? Do we have casual Friday? What's considered appropriate on that day? What if there's an important meeting on a Friday—is attire still casual?
- *Parking:* Where am I supposed to park? Do I have an assigned space? Are there certain spaces where I shouldn't park? Which lots fill up first? How long does it generally take to get out of the parking lot at the end of the day?
- *Supplies and equipment:* Where do I go for supplies? Are there forms to fill out for special supplies? Where's the copy machine? Do I do my own copying?
- *Phones:* How does the phone system work? What should I say when answering the phone? Where can I find phone numbers for key staff members? What's my phone number?
- *Computers:* How do specific programs work? How do I access the intranet? Whom should I contact if I have questions about using my computer? Is e-mail the preferred method of communication? What's my e-mail address? Where can I find a list of e-mail addresses for my department? What about the rest of the company?
- *Personal hygiene:* Where are the restrooms? What about an employee lounge? What are the "rules" concerning use of the lounge?

• *Salutations:* How am I expected to address coworkers? Managers? Members of senior management?

If you're not sure which topics are important to new employees, just think about your workplace and consider all that you now know innately but didn't know when you first started; there's your list of topics.

In addition to being interested in those things that enable them to function effectively on a daily basis, new employees want to know about benefits, including what they're entitled to, when they start to earn them, and to whom they go with questions.

If all of this sounds self-serving, it is. Only after employees feel secure about their place in the organization are they likely to turn their attention to more global concerns, such as: What are the company's goals? What's my role in helping to achieve these goals? Who are our competitors? How are we positioned in relation to our competitors? And what are the major external issues that affect us?

Recognizing that new employees have different priorities puts you ahead of the employer-employee relations game and more likely to nurture a healthy, long-term relationship.

Characteristics of a Successful Program

Before discussing specific components, let's consider those characteristics that are likely to contribute to a successful organizational orientation:

• *Develop targeted goals.* Design orientation so that employees are likely to leave feeling valued and wanted. If they leave feeling good about the overall experience and believe that the company had their best interests in mind when they developed the program, that's going to go a lot further than whether they remember what you said about the location of each department. Once you identify your objectives in terms of employee satisfaction, you can focus on the more tangible goals of the components, participants, timing, duration, and location.

• *Involve members of senior management.* A few remarks made in person or via DVD by someone in senior management can send a strong message of commitment to new employees.

• *Bring in other speakers.* In addition to having someone from senior management present, other organizational representatives can keep the session interesting and varied. Select individuals based on their presentation skills, not job titles.

• *View the orientation from the perspective of new employees.* If you were attending, what would you want to hear? Of equal importance, what would you not want to hear? Survey current employees and ask them two questions: (1) what did you get out of your organizational orientation, and (2) what would you have liked for it to cover if you had had a choice? You might be surprised at the answers.

• *Make presentations interesting.* In general, presentations that are interactive are more interesting. This is true even when discussing topics that are probably not likely to be noteworthy. Is there a way to cover these subjects in a way that's appealing? Of course. Think creatively: Instead of reading from the employee handbook, or showing wordy PowerPoint slides, come up with a variety of scenarios, games, and other activities that will make each topic not only palatable, but memorable.

• *Cover only what's likely to be retained in one sitting.* Pace yourself. One of the biggest complaints new employees express is that too much is thrown at them all at once. A good way to avoid information overload is to separate every one to two topics with a break or activity.

• *Keep it simple.* Follow the basic rules of reporting: With each topic, think in terms of who, what, where, when, why, and how. If you can't apply each of these terms to a topic, then rethink the relevance of integrating it into the program. Remember to make your presentation of each topic interesting—that's the all important "how."

• *Serve food.* Just like in the movie *Field of Dreams*, feed them and they will come. Okay, I know, they're coming whether there's food or not, but I've conducted enough orientation sessions where employees are told they have to attend to know that hands down, programs serving food make for happier participants.

• *Be the topic of conversation at the dinner table.* When a new employee completes orientation, you want him to go home and talk to family members about how interesting and informative it was. If he can talk about feeling valued and wanted, you've gotten him off to a good start, and chances are he'll be with you for awhile.

Components

It's advisable to create and distribute a written agenda when determining the components of your company's orientation program. This removes the element of surprise for new employees and helps ease any anxieties. An agenda also projects a professional and polished image, conveys the message that the company takes orientation seriously, and enables you to adhere to a structured presentation without inadvertently overlooking anything.

In addition to a written agenda, prepare a checklist of information pertaining to all the forms employees need to complete and sign. These may include W-4 and I-9 forms, as well as paperwork concerning emergency notification, employee handbooks, and the company's harassment policy. Be sure to include directions for completions, instructions for submission, and due dates.

Content

Basically, all topics covered during an organizational orientation fall into one of two categories: (1) what employees can expect from the organization, and (2) what the organization expects to receive from employees. Within these two broad areas are a wide selection of additional topics from which employers can choose, suitable to their work environment and relevant to a particular group of participants.

When identifying the specific content of an orientation program, keep in mind that information retention can be as low as 15 percent on the first day of work, so be judicious in what you choose to cover and when.

As mentioned, it's generally not advisable to start off by describing the organization's history, products, services, or organizational structure; likewise, avoid lengthy explanations of how the organization sets itself apart from its chief competitors, or its philosophy, mission, or goals. The employer who starts off by describing some of its benefits and employee-friendly programs has the right idea. It's an attention grabber and establishes the organization's commitment to its workforce. When it's time to discuss policies and procedures, focus first on those that benefit employees, and then ease into a discussion of company expectations.

The exact content of an organizational orientation program will vary depending in part on the size of your company and the average number of new employees. Generally, topics fit within five broad categories:

1. *Employer Commitment to Employees.* Possible topics include a harassment-free workplace, growth opportunities, a safe and secure work environment, a drug-free workplace.

2. *Employer Expectations.* This may include conflicts of interest, standards of performance, following company rules of conduct, confidential and proprietary information, ethical and legal business practices.

3. *Benefits.* This may cover federally mandated benefits, dental insurance, educational assistance, employee assistance programs, financial counseling, flexible benefits, holidays, life insurance, medical insurance, membership in clubs and organizations, personal days, pretax programs, short- and long-term disability insurance, sick days, pension plan, profit sharing plan, retirement saving plan, vacation time, wellness plan.

4. *Policies and Procedures and the Employee Handbook.* Possible topics include introductory employment period, employee rights and responsibilities, employment classifications, attendance and punctuality, work schedules, employee records, paydays, breaks, work/life balance, career planning, performance reviews, compensation, employee recognition, job posting, employee referrals, employment of relatives, suggestion program, training, disciplinary matters, grievance procedures, illness, leaves of absence, use of company communication systems, dress and grooming, outside employment, use and maintenance of company equipment and property, drug and alcohol use, smoking, solicitation, safety, workplace violence, inclement weather.

5. *The Organization.* Areas of coverage could include history, products or services, comparison with competitors, mission statement, philosophy, goals and strategic objectives, corporate culture, size and composition, organizational structure.

Tours

Assuming it's logistically feasible, a tour of key departments and other locations will help acclimate new employees. Telling someone the cafeteria is on the third floor, but can only be accessed by the elevator on the first floor, is not as helpful as actually showing them.

Typically, tours take place toward the end of the first day or at the conclusion of the entire orientation, if it's less than a day long. Some companies like to insert the tour in between content, perhaps immediately following or preceding an especially detailed portion of the orientation, such as benefits. Others schedule the tour for a day when no other components of orientation are being presented or discussed.

What do new employees want to see? Be practical and include the basics, such as locations serving food, coffee stations, restrooms, and the like. Then consider key departments of interest or importance, such as HR, where most employees will likely need to go at some point.

Depending on how extensive your tour is you may want to prepare and distribute maps highlighting the locations visited. Adding a word or two about who the people are in each location and what they do will enhance the experience.

Most orientation tours last from twenty to sixty minutes. It's generally not important that you let departments you'll be visiting know in advance of your plans to swing by with a group of new employees, since you're only passing through. Occasionally, a manager may see the group approaching and decide to say a few words about her department. That kind of impromptu interaction can go a long way toward solidifying the message of employer commitment to its employees. Just make sure the comments are brief, taking no more than two or three minutes, so you can stay on schedule.

Participants

When planning the composition of your company's organizational orientation program, think in terms of two groups: company representatives and attendees.

Company Representatives

Whom do you immediately think of when it comes to organizational orientation? My guess is you said HR. If you did, you'd be right. HR should play the primary role in planning, preparing, and conducting orientation. Because of this wide range of responsibilities, the HR representative selected should have in-depth knowledge of the organization and possess effective interpersonal skills. If you have more than one HR person who possesses this dual set of qualifications, set up a rotational schedule to keep their respective presentations fresh.

Others should also participate. First and foremost, new employees need to see and hear from a member of senior management to convey a message of commitment to new employees. Also, representatives from different departments might briefly describe the primary functions of their respective departments and discuss how each unit relates to the organization as a whole. This will add to the employee's holistic view of the company. Ideally, select individuals who are representative of your diversity-driven work environment.

New employees may also benefit from hearing existing staff members talk about some of the best aspects of working for the company. Even well-intentioned employers can miss some of the details that their workers value most, such as that the best bakery within thirty miles is located less than a block away!

Sometimes, too, it's helpful to invite subject experts to participate. Representatives from the benefits department usually top the list, which also includes salary administrators and members of the training and development department to discuss growth opportunities. These topical experts should be well-versed in the workings of the company and possess effective verbal communication skills. This is especially important with experts who are discussing topics that many may consider important but "dry," such as insurance. Regardless of the subject, if it's important enough to be included in the orientation, those selected to speak about it should be able to generate interest and facilitate retention.

Attendees

There are mixed views as to who should attend an orientation program. There are those who favor the one-size-fits-all approach. After all, everyone is working for the same company and should therefore be exposed to the same information about its history, goals, and the like. Others—often large corporations—prefer to have one program for exempt employees and another for nonexempt employees, or one for technical employees, one for sales and marketing staff, and so on. This is typically done when there is a substantial difference in the specific information offered, such as managerial benefits and policies pertaining to executives. Some employees have reported discomfort with this approach, saying that they felt isolated and left to wonder what the others were learning in their sessions. Still other companies separate employees new to the workforce from those with prior experience. The former group may consist of new graduates needing help in making the transition from the academic to the business world. Some businesses also consider employees' schedules and offer shift workers orientation in line with their respective hours or work.

While organizational orientation programs are designed with new employees in mind, consider inviting existing staff to attend select segments as well. A refresher on such matters as corporate goals and standards of performance can prove to be useful to all employees. It can also motivate existing employees to feel they are of continuing importance to the company. Having existing staff attend the same session as new employees also allows for an informative exchange between the two groups.

Because discussion is an important element of an effective orientation program, the number of participants should be limited to a maximum of twenty. The ideal group size is from twelve to fifteen. This encourages an exchange between the new employees, while allowing for questions. Having fewer than four employees is generally not recommended, as this can make the participants feel conspicuous and self-conscious.

Format

Orientation information can be imparted in a variety of ways. In fact, variety is considered essential to the success of a program, especially when a great deal of information is being presented.

It's especially important to appeal to different learning styles: visual, auditory, and kinesthetic, i.e., learning through physical movement. Presentation techniques for visual learners include flip charts, PowerPoint presentations, written materials, DVDs, samples or models, and other visual representations of what they're learning. For those who are primarily auditory in how they learn, provide brief lectures, soft instrumental music during any group discussions, and sound effects to highlight certain points. Also, be certain to speak clearly and vary vocal speed and volume. Orientation participants who learn best through physical involvement will prefer small-group or paired discussions, demonstrations, role playing, and tours.

Timing and Duration

Most companies schedule new employees to begin orientation as soon as possible, usually the first day of work. Employees are not yet caught up in the details of their jobs, and there's little chance of receiving inaccurate information from other sources.

Coverage of the key topics can take anywhere from a few hours to several days. If the latter is likely, consider breaking discussion up over a series of half days; better yet, conduct several two-to-three-hour modularized sessions. The employee's retention rate is bound to be higher and fatigue is less likely to set in. Also, their managers are probably more receptive to releasing them for a few hours at a time than for several full days. Take a progressive approach, going from general to detailed information to ensure greater retention.

Location and Setting

The site selected for your organizational orientation program should be centrally located and convenient for most employees. It should easily accommodate the number of people scheduled to attend, but should not be too large. Tables should be provided, since literature is likely to be distributed and employees will probably want to jot down notes during the session. Tables and chairs should be arranged in a casual manner; round tables are preferable over a classroom-style arrangement. For these reasons, auditoriums should be avoided.

Employee Feedback

You may think your company's organizational orientation program is great, but if employees don't find it worthwhile or if they fail to come away with an understanding of the salient features, then your efforts will have been wasted.

Your program should be continually evaluated in terms of its components, organizational representatives, format, timing and duration, location and setting, and overall impact. The latter can be determined by obtaining feedback through employee surveys at the end of the sessions. Then review and compare the survey results over a period of time. Sample questions and statements appear in Exhibit 16-1, Organizational Orientation Feedback.

Ask presenters for their feedback as well. In particular, ask about the overall structure of the program; the balance, completeness, clarity and relevance of information; and the overall tone of the program. Ask, too, how they think attendees responded, and compare these impressions with employee feedback.

Some organizations also approach employees several months after they've attended orientation to conduct "follow-up" surveys. The contents of follow-up surveys appears in Exhibit 16-2, Organizational Orientation Follow-Up Feedback.

Summary

Everyone knows that starting a new job can be unnerving. Until an employee becomes familiar with her surroundings, feels comfortable with the details and routine of a typical day, and develops an understanding of company and departmental expectations, it's likely to be difficult for her to focus on job performance. Most businesses recognize this and provide some form of organizational orientation covering a range of topics and varying in duration.

Well-developed organizational orientation programs should affirm a person's decision to join your company. They can also help with employee retention, negate future disciplinary action, and promote good public relations.

Done right, organizational orientation programs benefit employers and employees alike. Employers are able to establish an atmosphere of mutual respect—a cornerstone for productivity—and employees can learn about that which will enable them to function effectively on a daily basis.

Characteristics of a successful orientation program include targeted goals, viewing the program from the perspective of new employees, making presentations interesting, and avoiding information overload. Your goal is to have employees leave the orientation feeling good about themselves and their new employer.

While the specific content of an organization's orientation program will vary according to that company's size and the average number of new hires, all topics will fall into one of two categories: what employees can expect from the organization and what the organization expects to receive from employees. This usually translates into five broad categories: employer commitment to employees, employer expectations, benefits, policies and procedures, and the organization overall. A tour of key locations within the organization is another important component.

Businesses that evaluate their orientation programs in terms of the components, participants, content, format, timing and duration, location and setting, and overall impact will ensure more productive and longer-lasting employer-employee relations.

Exhibit 16-1. Organizational Orientation Feedback

1. Which segment of the orientation did you find most informative? Least informative? Why?
2. Which segment of the orientation did you find most interesting? Least interesting? Why?
3. Was the order in which topics were presented effective?   Yes No
4. What order of topics would you have preferred?
5. Was the appropriate amount of time devoted to each category of information? Specifically:
   - Employer Commitment to Employees   Yes No
   - Employer Expectations   Yes No
   - Benefits   Yes No
   - Policies and Procedures   Yes No
   - The Organization   Yes No
6. Indicate whether the following categories of information should have receive more or less time:
   - Employer Commitment to Employees   More Less
   - Employer Expectations   More Less
   - Benefits   More Less
   - Policies and Procedures   More Less
   - The Organization   More Less
7. Identify what you learned about each of the following categories of information as a result of the orientation:
   - Employer Commitment to Employees
   - Employer Expectations
     Benefits
   - Policies and Procedures
   - The Organization
8. On a scale of 1 to 5, with 1 representing excellent and 5 signifying poor, rate the following:
   - Duration   1 2 3 4 5
   - Format   1 2 3 4 5
   - Location   1 2 3 4 5
   - Number of participants   1 2 3 4 5
   - Quality of printed materials   1 2 3 4 5
   - Quality of visuals   1 2 3 4 5
   - Range of topics   1 2 3 4 5
   - Relevance of topics   1 2 3 4 5
   - Room setup   1 2 3 4 5
   - Selection of speakers   1 2 3 4 5
9. As a result of the orientation, do you fully understand your benefits?   Yes No
10. As a result of the orientation, do you fully understand the company's policies and procedures and content of the employee handbook?   Yes No

(continues)

Exhibit 16-1. Continued.

11. On a scale of 1 to 5, with 1 representing the most effective and 5 signifying the least effective, rate each presenter in terms of his ability to convey the subject matter, sustain your interest, and respond to questions. (List presenters by title, and topics each presenter addressed.)

12. On a scale of 1 to 5, with 1 representing the most helpful and 5 signifying the least helpful, rate the usefulness of the tour.   1   2   3   4   5

13. On a scale of 1 to 5, with 1 representing the highest and 5 signifying the lowest, describe your level of interest in the orientation overall.   1   2   3   4   5

14. What suggestions do you have for improving the organizational orientation program? Please be specific.

15. Please provide a summarizing statement reflecting your overall evaluation of the orientation program.

16. Would you recommend this orientation program to other new employees?   Yes   No

---

Exhibit 16-2. Organizational Orientation Follow-Up Feedback

Dear Valued Hardcore Employee,

Our records show that you attended our Organizational Orientation on (date). Now that you've been on the job for (number of months), we'd like your input concerning the degree of usefulness of some of the topics that were covered.

Please react to the following categories by circling a number from 1 to 3: 1 signifies "extremely helpful," 2 signifies "helpful," and 3 signifies "not at all helpful."

- Made me feel welcome   1   2   3
- Enabled me to get to know other employees   1   2   3
- Learned about Hardcore's commitment to its employees   1   2   3
- Learned about Hardcore's expectations of its employees   1   2   3
- Learned about Hardcore's employee benefits   1   2   3
- Learned about Hardcore's policies and procedures   1   2   3
- Learned about Hardcore overall   1   2   3
- Do you have any suggestions as to how orientation can be improved? Yes   No
  Please be specific.

Thank you for your feedback. Your signature on this questionnaire is optional.

_____

(optional signature)

CHAPTER 17

■ Departmental Orientation

Consider and contrast these scenarios:

Scenario #1: Amelia is a manager, awaiting the arrival of her new administrative assistant, Emma. It's 8:41 on Monday morning, and Amelia already feels as if she's put in a full day since arriving less than an hour ago. These past five weeks have been rough. Her assistant quit with less than a week's notice, and Amelia has had to ask her colleagues' assistants to do her work while HR found and hired a replacement. Amelia thinks Emma will work out well, but unfortunately she felt compelled to give two weeks' notice to her current employer, pushing back her start date until today. It's now 8:46. Amelia is growing impatient. She knows Emma isn't supposed to start until 9:00, but shouldn't she want to arrive early the first day to make a good impression? Now it's 8:47. Amelia sits at her computer and continues to amend the list of all the work that needs to be done when she hears a polite "ahem." She turns and sees Emma standing in the doorway, smiling. "Finally!" Amelia cries out. "Let's get started."

Scenario #2: Ava arrives for her first day at her new job and is greeted cheerfully by the receptionist, who clearly knew she was coming. She is escorted to her office where Ava finds a nameplate on the door, a vase of fresh flowers on the desk, her drawers filled with supplies, and an agenda of that day's activities, including organizational orientation in the morning, lunch with her manager, and a departmental orientation in the afternoon. As she takes all this in, she hears a light rap on the door. She turns to see her manager, Adam, smiling. "Welcome, Ava!" exclaims Adam. "Why don't you settle in and grab some coffee, and I'll walk you over to our training room for organizational orientation. It's recently been revised and I hear really good things about it. I'm looking forward to your feedback when we meet for lunch. You're going to have an exciting first day!"

Scenario #3: Told to report to his manager's office on Monday morning at 9:00, Eric arrives promptly and is asked by the receptionist to please have a seat. He sits and waits. After ten minutes pass, he again approaches the receptionist, who says, "She knows you're here; it'll just be another minute." Ten minutes stretch into fifteen. Eric feels uneasy and left to wonder if he's made a mistake accepting this job. Finally his manager emerges from her office, carrying a folder and a key. Eric stands up, ready to follow her, when she says, "Sorry—I'm already running behind this morning. Here's a folder with some departmental procedures. You can go through them and if you have any questions ask Cora." Eric asks, "Who's Cora?" The manager says, "She's the other analyst in our department. I'll try to catch up with you later. Oh, I almost forgot. Here's the key to the men's room. Welcome aboard!"

Scenario #4: Cody reports to his new job only to discover that HR has forgotten to notify the department that he was starting that morning. His office is still being used for storage, so there's no place for him to sit. His manager is out of town and no one knows quite what to do with him. He's sent to HR for orientation, which, it turns out, consists of filling out forms. He returns to his so-called office, which, thankfully, has been cleared of boxes and now has a desk, a chair, and a computer. As he takes all this in, the receptionist says she has a message for him from his manager. It reads, "Sorry I'm not there. Introduce yourself to the rest of the department and see if there's anyone who can bring you up to speed as to what we're working on. And have IT give you a password so you can access the Jamison file and start going through it. Hang in there—I'll be in tomorrow and we'll talk then."

Which of these scenarios can you relate to? All of them are true, and unfortunately scenario #2 is the exception; for every good first day a new employee has, there are several that are similar to the ones experienced by Emma, Eric, and Cody. What an employee experiences during his first day of work can set the tone for the duration of his employment. This critical first impression can result in either a motivated, productive employee, or one who begins to update his resume that evening.

A crucial part of this initial impression is departmental orientation. Regardless of how effective the organizational orientation may be, an employee needs to develop a strong connection to her department beginning on day one. Departmental orientations need not be as formalized as organizational orientations. Sometimes, there's only one new hire in a department at any given time, so the process is informal, but it is no less important.

Preparation

Effective departmental orientation is built on a foundation of preparation that's established well before a new employee's first day of work. Consider what simple steps Adam took to ensure a warm welcome for Ava: notifying the receptionist of Ava's arrival; arranging for a nameplate on the door to her office; ordering flowers; filling her desk with supplies; and providing an agenda outlining her first day, including lunch and departmental orientation with her boss. In addition, Adam personally greeted her and escorted her to the morning's organizational orientation session. Who wouldn't appreciate all that? Overall, Adam's investment of time was minimal, but the payoff was potentially huge.

Here are ten preparatory steps any manager can take to ensure a positive response on the part of a new employee on her first day of work:

1. *Spread the word.* Once there is an official exchange of signed correspondence between an employer and an applicant confirming the offering and acceptance of a

job, the new employee's manager can plan to distribute an internal memo or e-mail to members of the department. Typically, this is done about two weeks before the employee's start date. The purpose of this message is to inform existing staff as to when the new employee will be joining the department, his title and responsibilities, and a brief statement about his background. The tone should be friendly, the content informative. To illustrate:

> *From:* **Claire Hinton**
> *To:* **Operations staff**
> *Subject:* **Richard Reason**
>
> **We are pleased to announce the hiring of Richard Reason to the position of industrial engineer in our operations department. Richard has six years' prior experience as an industrial engineer, working first at Zanza Corp., and most recently at Boma Products. Richard will come aboard beginning on February 27. Please try to be available on that date to give Richard a warm welcome to our staff.**

2. *Think like a new employee.* Ask yourself: What would I want my first day on the job to consist of? Compare your thoughts with these first-day-on-the-job comments: "An opportunity to get the lay of the land," "A chance to meet my colleagues," "Access to one person I can turn to with questions," "Alone time with my boss," and "A little time to myself so I can sort through everything I'm being exposed to." Sounds good to me.

3. *Prepare an agenda.* Providing new employees with an agenda of their first day or even the first week provides structure and gives them a sense of direction. Here's a sample agenda for day one:

9:00 a.m.	Good morning, Richard. Welcome to the Operations Department of Hardcore Industries! Enjoy the muffins and juice; coffee is right down the hall to your left.
9:15 a.m.	Meeting with Claire Hinton—review the day's agenda
9:30 a.m.	Organizational orientation
12:00 noon	Departmental introductions and tour
1:00 p.m.	Lunch with Claire Hinton and Bella Ingermann—your personal operations partner
2:30 p.m.	Familiarization with the department and various functions
4:30 p.m.	Meeting with Claire Hinton: go over the events of the day, answer questions, discuss tomorrow's agenda

This agenda gives the new hire an overview of how his time is going to be spent during his first day. The agenda could be more detailed and extend beyond the first day, depending on what the manager has planned; what matters is that the employee has a clear sense of what to expect and when to expect it.

4. *Provide necessary supplies and other provisions.* Managers need to make the employee's workstation or office ready for his arrival. At a minimum, this should consist of:

- *Essential supplies.* We may rely on computers to perform much of our work, but everyone still uses basic supplies. Have someone stock the new hire's work area with supplies and information relating to his computer, including a list of e-mail addresses (including the employee's own e-mail address) and instructions for accessing the intranet. Provide writing materials and instruments, as well as basic office supplies, such as paper clips. In addition, provide a telephone directory, a list identifying the employee's phone number, key personnel with their extensions, and instructions on how to use the phone system, including how to access voice mail. If relevant, provide a calculator and any other equipment that may be needed. Also provide the name and extension of whom to call if any supplies are missing.

- *Map/floor plan.* Provide a map and/or floor plan to help the employee navigate during the first few days. Be sure to highlight certain locations, including emergency exits, restrooms, the employee lounge, medical office, child care and elder care facilities, vending machines, and the cafeteria.

- *Organizational and departmental charts.* While organizational charts will probably be reviewed during company-wide orientation, it's a good idea to go over the names and functions of key players, especially if it's likely that the new employee will interact with any of them. It would be helpful, too, if he could see photos to go along with names. You never know when he might be in the elevator, standing alongside the company's president. Then do the same with reporting relationships within the department.

- *Reading materials.* Supply the new hire with company literature and any required departmental documents, such as a procedures manual, as well as recommended readings that may enhance his ability to do his job. In addition, prepare a glossary of industry- or company-specific terminology and acronyms. Be sure to remove any files belonging to the new employee's predecessor if they are not relevant to the new employee's work.

- *Answers to questions.* Some companies provide a stack of "No Such Thing as a Dumb Question" cards. These can be used any time the new employee has a question but feels uncomfortable about asking it. Be generous in the number of cards you provide and exclude an expiration date.

- *Access to materials.* Provide any access passes or keys, passwords, and security codes necessary to enter the building.

- *Food/beverage locations.* If you have a company cafeteria, provide its hours of operation and a menu or list of typical offerings along with prices. Indicate, too, where the employee can grab a cup of coffee in the morning, along with a list of favorite restaurants in the area.

5. *Be available.* There's a wonderfully memorable exchange between characters Major Major Major Major (that's his rank, first, middle, and last names) and his First

Sgt. Towser in the 1970 movie *Catch-22,* during which the Major tells his Sergeant to allow people into his office only when he's not there. The dialogue is witty and makes me laugh every time I read or hear it, but it becomes less amusing when I recall managers who consciously or inadvertently duplicate Major Major Major Major's style of leadership; that is, to make themselves scarce when employees need advice, guidance, or assistance. The most effective managers are available to their employees, especially at the beginning of an employer–employee relationship.

6. *Anticipate questions.* As with step #2, "Think like a new employee," managers would do well to consider what they would want to know if it were their first day on the job. In addition to the topics already identified, likely categories include department structure, departmental and individual responsibilities, and department culture.

7. *Have reasonable expectations.* Even the most eager employees who are capable of absorbing a great deal of information at once need time to process what they see, hear, and learn. Setting reasonable expectations as to when new employees can actually start work may be frustrating at the outset, especially when departments are backlogged with work, but this approach will ultimately pay off. Increased exposure to departmental routines and methodologies will serve to indoctrinate new members in the culture of the department, thereby making the transition from applicant to employee that much smoother.

8. *Make the first day as typical as possible.* Many years ago, I worked in the HR department of a bank. We had an opening for a junior compensation analyst, reporting to JP, vice president of HR. JP knew his unit was underrepresented in terms of ethnic and racial categories, and so felt compelled to seek out and hire a minority for the position. He hired Paul, a recent college graduate and a member of a protected group with absolutely no work experience or knowledge of compensation. That didn't matter to JP. He was focused on addressing his affirmative action goal. When Paul reported to work on his first day, JP made a huge fuss, devoting the morning to introducing Paul to one executive after another, people Paul was unlikely to meet, much less interact with given his job level. As lunchtime rolled around, JP rounded up select members of the HR department and heralded us along with Paul to the executive dining room. We knew it would be the one and only time Paul would ever ride that private elevator reserved for officers. Throughout this shameless display, Paul sat quietly, although noticeably both flattered and overwhelmed. Lunch ended and we all went back to work, and that's when reality set in for Paul: JP was done. He led Paul to a barren desk situated outside his office, gave him a manual, and left without a word. Paul had no idea what to do. A couple of the other analysts tried to describe what they were currently working on, but Paul wasn't clear as to what his job was. For the remainder of the afternoon, Paul sat at his desk trying to focus on the manual before him, but he was clearly confused. The next day was a repeat of the former afternoon, although JP left a curt note on his desk with instructions. This continued throughout the entire week. JP had no time for Paul, except for a note on his desk now and then. Paul grew increasingly distraught and disenchanted. Not surprisingly, he resigned after a few weeks. As I recall, JP described him as "ungrateful."

I relate this incident as an example of just about the worst thing a manager can do to a new employee. Interacting and dining with levels of management an employee will probably never see again, and then providing absolutely no support or resources, is a far cry from making the first day as typical as possible. What JP could easily have done was take a few minutes in the morning to describe what constitutes a typical day in the compensation department and highlight a junior compensation analyst's responsibilities within that day. Then he could have assigned someone to work with Paul and duplicate that typical day as closely as possible.

9. *Don't take anything for granted.* Even if a new employee has attended organizational orientation, review some details that are department-specific. For example, hours of work can vary from unit to unit; likewise, lunch hour rotation schedules may be dictated by departmental work flow. Clarify such matters at the outset to avoid misunderstandings down the road.

10. *Arrange for a "partner."* A partner program involves a one-to-one relationship between a new employee and another employee from the same department, whereby the latter is assigned to answer questions, offer encouragement, and provide whatever assistance may be needed. Assigning a partner to a new employee will extend the welcoming and instructional quality of the first day.

Content

The sample agenda described earlier in this chapter reflects a first day devoted to introductions and settling in. Day two in the department is generally more content-driven. There are numerous topics considered relevant for inclusion in this stage of a departmental orientation. Some managers take a "she'll learn as she goes along" approach. Others believe in a checklist method, sitting down with the new employee and going over each topic in detail. The latter is preferable to the "sink or swim" approach, but it doesn't require an approach that is formalized or strictly structured to the point of exhaustion. Casual discussions over lunch or coffee can lend balance to in-office meetings. Managers can also gather members of the department for informal, round-table discussions about matters germane to the new employee's areas of responsibility.

Managers are cautioned against trying to cram everything into a day or two. Departmental orientation is not meant to be a crash course. Small doses of information will likely result in greater retention. Some of the information can be written, be made available online, or conveyed verbally, supported by some written form for confirmation. Some of what managers review may have been covered during the organizational orientation, such as policies concerning personal computer use during working hours. A duplication of effort is preferable to omission.

Here are some topics for inclusion in departmental orientation, not in any particular order of importance:

• *Confidentiality.* Identify areas of work considered confidential and the ramifications of violating confidentiality.

- *Department structure.* Identify specific functions by task and incumbent.
- *Departmental culture.* Describe any unique features of the department, including "rituals" such as birthday celebrations and the annual Thanksgiving feast.
- *Departmental responsibilities.* Discuss the department's overall function and long- and short-term goals.
- *Equipment.* Explain how to use required equipment and materials safely and efficiently, and review safety rules.
- *Hours of work.* Remind the employee of starting and quitting times and any alternative schedule options.
- *How to access information.* Explain how to contact employees within and outside the department and throughout the organization.
- *Information about the company.* Include information about the organization's mission, goals, products or services, and customers or clients.
- *Interrelationship between the department and other departments.* Talk about the flow of work between departments and key individuals to contact in other departments.
- *Job duties and responsibilities.* Together, review the new employee's job description, discussing specific areas of responsibility and how these tasks dovetail with those of other employees.
- *Meal and break periods.* Describe how meal times are scheduled as well as the frequency and duration of breaks.
- *Payroll.* Inform the employee as to the frequency of being paid and any information relevant to direct payroll deposit. Also, if the employee will spend a significant amount of time in the field, explain the company's travel and entertainment policy, as well as its expense reporting procedures.
- *Performance expectations.* Discuss performance goals and appropriate benchmarks and the concepts of ongoing coaching and counseling and when they might be appropriate; define regularly scheduled performance evaluations and salary reviews.
- *Use of phones and computers for personal use.* Identify circumstances under which personal telephone calls are permitted and stipulations concerning the use of company computers for personal use. The latter refers to sending and receiving e-mails as well as surfing the Internet, playing computer games, or entering chat rooms. Discuss, too, rules about texting during working hours.
- *Reporting relationships.* Define direct and indirect reporting relationships throughout the department and organization-wide, as well as who's typically in charge when key personnel are out of the office.
- *Vacation scheduling.* Explain how vacations are scheduled, who approves vacation requests, and how far in advance requests should be made.

Participants

Managers are not the only ones involved in a new employee's departmental orientation.

Other Members of the Department

Introducing a new hire to others with whom she'll be working should be one of the first objectives of any departmental orientation. These introductions should include individuals from the same department as well as employees in other units. If there are more than half a dozen introductions, prepare a sheet in advance with everyone's name, title, office location, and contact information. This way, the new hire won't feel pressured to memorize everyone's name upon introduction.

As you take the new employee around, be careful not to express your opinions about others. For example, "Janet, the next person you're going to meet is Bob Johnson. Watch out for him during staff meetings; he's notorious for stealing ideas and submitting them as his own." Or "When I introduce you to Fred Waters, don't take it personally if he acts as if he doesn't like you. He applied for your position but was rejected. He thinks you cheated him out of a promotion."

Seemingly positive statements should be avoided as well. For example, "Janet, I'd like you to meet Rod Perret. Rod can always be counted on to help you meet impossible deadlines."

New employees should be permitted to form their own opinions about coworkers, so avoid statements that are subjective or judgmental. Instead, focus on being descriptive. As you approach the office or workstation of each employee, briefly describe her overall function. Think in terms of action words, like the ones used in job descriptions. For instance, you might want to say, "The next person you'll be meeting is Terry Carson. Terry is our office manager. She receives all the work prepared by the department's assistant vice presidents, distributes it among the secretaries, reviews the final product, and then returns it to the appropriate AVP." If the new hire is taking notes, she could quickly write, "Terry Carson: office manager: receives, distributes, and returns work to AVPs." You could also have this information written out for her in advance.

Partner Program

The partner program, also referred to a sponsor system, is a one-to-one relationship between a new employee and another worker from the same department who answers questions, offers encouragement, and provides whatever personal assistance may be needed as the new employee becomes acclimated to his work environment. The partner programs serves to help ease the new employee's transition into the new work environment, lessening the stress of "fitting in" by providing access to someone who is both familiar and comfortable with the department's culture and expectations.

While some employees are lucky enough to immediately link up with someone who's willing to help them out during their first few days on the job, most are not. Outside of organizational and departmental orientation programs that may or may not be beneficial, new workers are usually left to fend for themselves. A formalized partner program guarantees that every individual has one person to guide her through the inevitable confusion that accompanies a new work environment. Here are just a few of the benefits of a partner program:

- The initial anxiety and uncertainty experienced to a lesser or greater extent by all new employees is greatly reduced.
- New hires can be assured of comprehensive, straightforward answers to important questions about day-to-day matters.
- Managers have more time to deal with employees on work-related issues.
- New employees are likely to develop increased confidence and self-esteem, leading to greater productivity.

Whereas managers provide valuable information about the organizational structure and departmental guidelines, partners take new hires "behind the scenes," offering a peek at some of the company's unwritten rules. In no way is the partner's role to substitute for that of the manager.

Partner programs are similar to mentoring in that the process is a developmental, helping relationship: one person invests time, ability, and effort in enhancing another person's knowledge and skills in preparation for greater productivity or future achievement. As with mentoring, everyone wins in the end. The new hire gains insights into the inner workings of his department and the company; the partner gains additional recognition by the organization and adds another dimension to her leadership skills; and the organization benefits by building a stronger team.

Partner programs can range from a casual transfer of information or ideas from one person to another, to a structured system with a specific agenda. Regardless of how informal or ordered the program is, the new employee's partner should take a proactive stance. She should regularly approach the employee with information rather than waiting for the employee to come to her asking for help.

Ideally, partner programs should begin before the new employee's first day of work. A letter of welcome could read something like this:

February 22, 2XXX

Mr. Richard Reason
20 Foxrun Circle
Secona, Nevada 55555

Hi Richard,

My name is Allie Rowens. I'm an industrial engineer in Hardcore's operations department, and I've been with the company for three years. As part of Hardcore's Partner Program, I'm going to be available to you during your initial weeks on the job to answer any questions you may have. View me as a friendly source of advice, information, and introductions. If you want to call me before starting next week, my extension is 6339.

Hardcore is a great place to work and I'm looking forward to making your introduction to the company as smooth and pleasant as possible. I look forward to meeting and working with you.

Sincerely,

Allie Rowens

This same message can be conveyed in a phone call or e-mail; what matters is that contact is made before the person's first day on the job.

Depending on the level and complexity of the job and nature of the work environment, the partner relationship typically lasts from a minimum of a week to as long as three or more months. By then the employee should have developed solid relationships with his colleagues and learned about the prevailing departmental and organizational cultures.

Selecting a Partner

Some employees make better partners than others. Their length of service and knowledge of the department and the company are important, but those should not be the sole basis for selection. Managers should select someone who will make a lasting impression, someone who is personable, patient, and can explain things clearly and concisely. Also, select an employee with high personal standards of performance and a positive attitude. Ideally, a partner should be someone whose style of communication and approach to work is flexible enough to suit that of the new employee. In this regard, partners are encouraged to familiarize themselves with the approach to learning preferred by the new employee. Some need examples, some need to talk, and others need to experiment with different methods of learning and accomplishing tasks. Regardless of the preferred methodology, partners need to practice active listening, offer information and suggestions, avoid making assumptions, remain objective, and provide frequent feedback.

Make certain, too, that the employee selected is able to budget her time and not fall behind in her work as she takes time away from her job to assist the new employee with his. Managers are responsible for ensuring that this doesn't happen. They are also responsible for overseeing the partner relationship to ensure that the two are properly matched. If for any reason it appears that the partner's style or personality is ill-suited for the new employee, managers shouldn't hesitate to assign a new partner midstream.

It's best if HR conducts a brief training session for employees interested in joining the partner program. The purpose of the training is to teach coaching skills and reinforce the most salient points of partnering. The agenda for this session should include explaining or defining:

- The purpose and anticipated results of the program
- The role of the partner and the nature of the relationship
- Mandatory aspects and topics of the program
- A partner's availability requirements
- Partners' reporting responsibilities to management
- Confidentiality
- Duration of the program

Employees who volunteer their time to be partners should be appropriately acknowledged and rewarded.

While personalized one-to-one partnering has the greatest potential for trust and learning, sometimes it's not as practical as group or team partnering. During times of mass hiring, for example, having one partner available to a group of up to six new employees is by far more cost- and time-effective. In these instances, participants can learn from one another as well as from their designated partner.

Onboarding

Scene:	Breakfast at a local diner on a Saturday morning.
Cast:	Two friends—Ethan and Rob—both of whom have recently started new jobs.
Dialogue:	*Rob:* This has been the most boring first week on a new job that I've ever had.
	Ethan: What made it so boring?
	Rob: Orientation! Every morning I had to sit with other newbies and listen to HR go on and on about how lucky we were to have jobs in this economy and even luckier to be working for what they keep calling the "greatest company on this planet." As if repeating it makes it true. Then I had to spend each afternoon with my manager.
	Ethan: What did your manager talk about?
	Rob: Honestly, I tuned out after the second day. He kept reading stuff from a manual. It was obvious that someone told him he had to do this, know what I mean?
	Ethan: Can't say that I do; orientation at my job's been great. In fact, it's still going on.
	Rob: What are you talking about? You started your job over three months ago!
	Ethan: Yup, that's true. Actually, it's not really orientation anymore. It's called "onboarding." It's super intense, but very effective. It really enhances employer-employee relations. I'm learning a lot, and I really feel as if the company cares about me as an individual.

Wouldn't you like to hear your employees talk about your company the way Ethan talks about his?

Some employers use the term *onboarding* interchangeably with orientation, along with *alignment, assimilation, integration, transition,* and even *organizational socialization.* But onboarding differs from these processes in several ways. As David Somers, director of consulting services for Cornerstone OnDemand, observed, "Onboarding begins with the first contact you have with a prospective new hire and actually ends with the conclusion of their employment at the company."[1]

Whereas orientation is an introduction to and overview of a company, onboarding is a loosely structured, ongoing process of learning and applying what is learned. Specifically, onboarding:

- Aligns what is learned at organizational and departmental orientation with practical, day-to-day goings-on
- Builds relationships
- Continues far beyond the point at which orientation programs typically end: formal onboarding programs can last as long as a year, and successful executive transitions can take more than two years. In fact, to paraphrase David Somers, they're never-ending.
- Improves employee engagement
- Is customized to focus on the areas of greatest need to support each individual's role in the company
- Lessens the learning curve
- Links new employees with more colleagues and introduces them to other aspects of the company
- Makes clear performance objectives from the outset
- Provides specialized resources and intensive support
- Reduces misunderstandings
- Supports a closer connection between an employee and his manager

You might say, then, that orientation leads to, and lays the foundation for, onboarding, or that onboarding picks up where orientation leaves off. Done well, onboarding leads to greater motivation and increased productivity, improves talent retention, and reduces turnover costs.

Onboarding Programs for Executives

Successful executives are often thought of as quick thinkers, effective decision makers, and backed by a knowledgeable, supportive team. But it's unreasonable to expect that even the best among them will start with a new company functioning at maximum capacity. Even if an executive brings in some of her own staff, it takes time to establish new working relationships and learn the intricate details of how a company functions. Experts report that newly promoted or hired executives face many major challenges during their first four months. Some executives often get off to a slow start or fail in the execution of their new responsibilities due to a lack of clear direction. Others take on too many tasks and try to meet unreasonable deadlines. Executives can avoid making these mistakes if they receive the proper guidance.

In some organizations, onboarding targets employees hired for or promoted into leadership roles. In this regard, onboarding is intended to:

- Ensure that new leaders are thoroughly indoctrinated in the workings, priorities, objectives, brand identity, strategic direction, decision-making processes, initiatives, results achieved, and culture of the company

- Offer in-depth information relevant to how the company measures success
- Provide a systematic approach to ensure that new executives succeed in their jobs and remain with the company
- Ensure alignment between organizational and individual goals
- Foster increased exchange of information between members of the leadership team
- Focus on creating and nurturing solid employer-employee relationships
- Increase job satisfaction
- Decrease job turnover

Some onboarding programs for new leaders combine personal coaching with the use of a web-based application that allows the executive to access onboarding resources and advice online. Others bring in professional onboarding consultants to work one-to-one with new executives over a period of months, providing feedback along the way.

Duration

Think back to your childhood and recall your favorite songs: I'll bet many of them had verses that reoccurred over, and over, and over, and . . . well, you get the point. These "loop" songs were sung in rounds or relied on the repetition of certain words, making them virtually impossible to forget, even well into adulthood. Managers can apply a take-off on this loop concept (without singing a single note!) by viewing departmental orientation as an ongoing, never-ending process, rather than as a single event. This form of thinking is especially relevant during an employee's first several weeks on board. By reiterating the same theme—that is, a commitment to ensuring that the assimilation process is as seamless and useful as possible—managers can establish a foundation of effective employer-employee relations that is likely to prevail for a long time. For instance, each day during a new employee's introductory period—usually ninety days—managers can introduce or share something additional about the composition of the department, its contribution to meeting organizational goals, fun facts, and the like. This is more casual than onboarding in that it is completely informal and often unplanned.

Here are some examples that are sure to trigger more of your own:

- Best "Casual Friday" outfit ever worn.
- Best suggestion ever made by an employee, how much money it saved the company, and what the employee received in return.
- Examples of how members of the department have pulled together as a team.
- Food in the cafeteria that draws the biggest crowd (and food to avoid).
- How the efforts of the department have contributed to making the company number one in its field for the past three years.

- The day last August when the company bought ice cream for all the employees and the air conditioning broke down.

- The record for greatest number of hot dogs eaten at the company's annual Fourth of July picnic.

- The role of fun in the department.

- Tips as to the best spots in the parking lot if you need to make a quick getaway at the end of the day.

- What to expect at the next holiday party based on last year's event.

- Why this department is the best in the company.

It may only take a matter of minutes for managers to share these tidbits, but they serve to keep new employees connected with their managers during the critical introductory stage of their employment. The result of very little effort could translate into a hugely productive and mutually satisfying long-term relationship.

Summary

Departmental orientation focuses on the relationship between new employees and their managers. The process is built on a foundation of preparation prior to the new employee's first day of work. These preparatory steps will go a long way toward ensuring a positive response on the part of the new employee on his first day of work.

The first day of departmental orientation usually focuses on introductions and settling in, while day two is generally more content-driven. Managers are cautioned against trying to cram everything into a day or two, however. Departmental orientation is not meant to be a crash course. Small doses of information will likely result in greater retention.

Managers are not the only ones involved in departmental orientation. Individually assigned partners answer questions, offer encouragement, and provide whatever personal assistance may be needed as the new employee becomes acclimated to his new work environment. Managers provide valuable information about the organizational structure and departmental guidelines, and partners take new hires "behind the scenes" to offer a peek at some of the company's unwritten rules.

Whereas orientation is an introduction to and overview of a company, onboarding is an ongoing process of learning and applying what has been learned. Effectively, orientation leads to, and lays the foundation for, onboarding.

Managers are advised to view departmental orientation as an ongoing process rather than as a single event. For each day during the new employee's introductory period, managers can introduce or share something additional about the composition of the department, its contribution to meeting organizational goals, fun facts, and the like.

CHAPTER 18

Web-Based Orientation

"Orientation at my last company was online; it was cool. I learned at my own pace and no one made me participate in dumb, getting-to-know-you types of activities. Sorry, I guess that's the techie in me talking. I just prefer learning on my own."

Does that sound like something the majority of your employees would say? If so, then perhaps you'll want to consider implementing a web-based organizational orientation program.

Overview

Web-based orientation programs are designed to allow new employees to experience many or all of the same components of conventional programs, either by joining others in virtual classrooms, webinar-style, or on their own time. This second method is commonly referred to as "self-directed." In both instances, individuals generally receive e-mails with login instructions, a user name and password, and navigation tools and tips. A schedule is enclosed with dates and times for those opting to participate in the live chat, classroom format; self-directed participants are notified as to when recorded and archived live sessions will be available for viewing. Employees can then upload files of these sessions and undergo orientation later on at the time and location of their choosing.

Not unlike conventional organizational orientation programs, web-based programs can range anywhere from the equivalent of a few hours to several days or more, although they are generally shorter than conventional programs due to their overall format. Electronic versions also differ in that the information is imparted in a series of modularized presentations usually lasting about an hour to an hour and a half each. The length of time between virtual classroom sessions is generally three or four days.

Content is largely presented in the form of live lectures, streaming videos, and PowerPoint slides. Participants in virtual classrooms are able to ask questions of the orientation leader by typing them on their computer monitor, usually receiving an oral response before the session ends. Employees who view archived files must submit questions via e-mail to orientation presenters and wait for a reply.

Some web-based organizational orientation programs are greatly condensed, offering only a minimal amount of information. They present topics with just a few accompanying bullet points via PowerPoint slides, relying on employees to access designated contacts for details. Information about whom to contact about specific topics is provided, but not much else. While time-efficient, this condensed version is considered among the least effective of all approaches. It removes responsibility from the employer to provide important organization-related information and places it instead in the hands of new employees, who must obtain it on their own while learning their jobs.

At the end of each module, employees may be asked to answer some questions to show they understand the unit's contents. They may also be required to complete an assignment for review at the beginning of the next module. Upon concluding the program, employees are usually asked to sign and submit a statement declaring understanding and completion of the orientation contents. Electronic signatures may result in legal complications; this will be addressed later in the chapter.

Sample Program

A modularized approach effectively defines web-based organizational orientations. Depending on their length, one or more modules may be scheduled for each virtual classroom session. For instance, a module lasting thirty minutes could be combined with the next one that is sixty minutes long, requiring participants to be at their computers for a total of ninety minutes.

Here's an example of a program consisting of forty topics, delivered in eight modules, lasting a total of eight hours:

Module One: Introduction (forty-five minutes)

- Welcome to the company
- Orientation overview and objectives
- Instructions
- Topics to be covered in subsequent modules
- Format
- Timeline
- Employee requirements at the conclusion of each module
- Contact information for questions or problems

Module Two: Virtual Tour (forty-five minutes)

- Food services
- Security
- Supplies
- Key locations, e.g., HR, accounting, executive offices

Module Three: Employer Commitment to and Expectations of Employees (sixty minutes)

PART I: EMPLOYER COMMITMENT TO EMPLOYEES (THIRTY MINUTES)

- Harassment-free workplace
- Growth opportunities
- Safe and secure work environment
- Drug-free workplace

PART II: EMPLOYER EXPECTATIONS OF EMPLOYEES (THIRTY MINUTES)

- Conflicts of interest
- Standards of performance
- Company rules of conduct
- Confidential and proprietary information
- Ethical and legal business practices

Module Four: Benefits (ninety minutes)

- Insurance: medical, dental, life, disability
- Programs and plans, including educational assistance, employee assistance, financial counseling, retirement savings, pension, profit sharing, wellness, employee services, and amenities such as health club memberships and store discounts
- Paid time off, including holidays, vacation, sick days
- Other benefits

Module Five: Employee Rights and Responsibilities: The Employee Handbook (ninety minutes)

- Introductory employment period
- Rights. Topics may include work/life balance, career planning, performance reviews, salary increases, training and development
- Responsibilities. Topics may include attendance and punctuality, disciplinary matters, use of company communication systems, outside employment, use and maintenance of company equipment and property, drug and alcohol use

Module Six: The Organization (sixty minutes)

- History
- Products/services; comparison with competitors
- Who's who in the company: photos, names, and titles
- Mission statement and philosophy
- Goals and strategic objectives
- Corporate culture
- Size, composition, and organizational structure

Module Seven: Confirmation of Completion (sixty minutes)
- Final steps, including responding to questions about each topic to signify understanding
- Procedure to follow for the completion of certain forms in HR

Module Eight: Orientation Evaluation (thirty minutes)
- Purpose
- Instructions for completion
- Overall usefulness of contents
- What could have been added or eliminated
- Amount of time devoted to each module
- Most/least interesting topics
- Most/least informative topics
- Quality/usefulness of visuals
- Quality/usefulness of virtual tour
- Recommended to other new employees

Many of the topics in these modules can be expanded, can stand alone, or can be combined with topics from other modules. For instance, the eight modules could be presented as follows:

- *Modules One and Two:* Introduction and Virtual Tour—could constitute one session, totaling ninety minutes.
- *Module Three:* Employer Commitment to and Expectations of Employees—sixty minutes in duration, could stand alone.
- *Module Four:* Benefits—ninety minutes in duration, could stand alone.
- *Module Five:* Employee Rights and Responsibilities: The Employee Handbook—ninety minutes in duration, could stand alone.
- *Module Six:* The Organization—sixty minutes in duration, could stand alone.
- *Modules Seven and Eight:* Confirmation of Completion and Orientation Evaluation—could constitute one session, totaling ninety minutes.

How you group together modules all depends on how much effort you're willing to invest in the process and how much detail you want to impart.

Much of what's recommended for inclusion in these modules will sound familiar if you read Chapter 16, although some of the topics are grouped differently than they were for a conventional orientation program. The length of time recommended for each grouping of topics is likely to be considerably less for a web-based approach due to the lack of interaction between company representatives and new employees, and other differences in format.

Advantages

Those in favor of a web-based approach to organizational orientation offer numerous advantages.

- *Consistent delivery of uniform content.* Closely adhering to a strictly structured agenda and time frame for each module ensures consistent delivery of each segment of the orientation's content. Upon completion, every employee—regardless of function or department—will have been exposed to the same materials. This is less likely to occur with a conventional approach since topics can be added or condensed depending on the group attending.

- *Convenience.* The convenience of web-based orientation fits right in with the lives and work styles of many of today's workers. Rather than being told they have to report for orientation at a designated time and place for a predetermined number of hours or days, employees can choose for themselves—within a certain framework—when and where they will participate. If they opt for a virtual classroom setting, all they need to do is make certain they're in front of their computers at the designated time. Or if they prefer, they can upload archived files of live sessions and "participate" later, perhaps before work, during lunch, or late in the afternoon when they've reached a certain point in their work for that day. Since the material is modularized, scheduling becomes more manageable.

Web-based orientation is especially convenient for those working at or living near satellite locations. It also proves advantageous for shift workers. If you had to travel several hours or worked a 4:00 p.m. to midnight shift, would you want to attend orientation from 9:00 a.m. to 4:00 p.m.? Even if the session were half a day, it would be far less time-consuming or taxing to be able to sit in front of your computer at a time of your choosing.

- *Cost-effective.* There are numerous costs associated with conventional orientations, including updating and duplicating materials, refreshments, and reimbursement of employees' travel expenses, especially those commuting from satellite locations. Web-based orientations are comparatively inexpensive, even when updates are required.

- *Easy updates.* Since web-based orientations are modularized, segments can be quickly and easily updated without disrupting the content of the other segments.

- *Greater detail.* Although web-based orientation generally takes less time to deliver, its strictly structured format and lack of interruptions from participants, other than questions presenters opt to answer, actually allows for greater in-depth coverage of topics. For those employees who choose to take the self-directed approach, they can stop, start, and repeat segments as often as they want, thereby increasing the likelihood of retention.

- *Millennials expect it.* Those born between 1981 and 1999, and even younger GenXers, are intrinsically linked with electronic forms of communication and interaction. It's therefore likely that they'll expect orientation to be at least partially web-based. Does this mean they won't do well in a conventional setting? Certainly not. But it all comes back to first impressions, that is, feeling they're part of an organization that's committed to being current and technologically savvy.

- *Likely to ask questions.* At the end of a three-day workshop I recently conducted, one of my students approached me and apologized for not participating more. She explained that she was shy and didn't like speaking up in class. I acknowledged what she said and asked if that posed a problem for her at work. She said it was something she was working on. Then she volunteered an interesting bit of information: New to her current job, she had recently completed a web-based orientation program. She had the choice of a self-directed or virtual live classroom format and selected the latter. She told me that she felt entirely at ease asking questions of her orientation presenters in a virtual format. In fact, as more and more of her questions were answered and she received affirmation and encouraging feedback like, "Jenny's just asked another really good question!" she was inclined to continue. As long as no one saw her and she was unable to witness reactions to her questions, she was completely at ease.

Jenny's not the first person to confide that asking questions in a classroom is unnerving, whereas they're completely at ease communicating through some electronic means. Since you don't want new employees to leave orientation with their questions unanswered, web-based sessions are worthy of consideration.

•   *Able to revisit topics.* Web-based orientation allows employees to go back and reread or listen to certain topics. Perhaps they're exploring the module on benefits and having trouble understanding some of the offerings. Repetition can help clarify matters. Even if employees choose to participate in virtual classrooms, they can later upload an archived session and revisit it.

•   *Self-paced.* The self-paced nature of self-directed web-based orientation is ideal for employees who want to take their time with some topics and move more quickly with others. For example, an employee may have conducted extensive research on the company before interviewing for her job and learned a great deal about its history, philosophy, goals, corporate culture, and organizational structure. She would not need to spend as much time on that section. On the other hand, she may have a particular interest in the contents of the employee handbook and might choose to spend more time reviewing the details of that module.

•   *Time-efficient.* Although web-based orientation sessions cover many of the same topics as conventional programs, they usually take less time to complete. In fact, they are typically designed to be efficient, packing a maximum amount of information in the shortest possible period of time.

Drawbacks

Not surprisingly, those who favor a more conventional approach to organizational orientation cite several drawbacks to a web-based method. The greatest of these is the lack of face-to-face interaction with other new employees, the orientation leader, and other speakers. Participants cannot feed off one another's questions, comments, and observations, nor can they react to body language. This can be significant, for as we learned earlier, as much as 55 percent of communication is nonverbal. Typing questions on one's computer screen also negates the instructor's ability to hear the employee's tone of voice. This is also important since 38 percent of communication is attributable to tone of voice. In fact, only 7 percent is verbal.

Exchanges during conventional orientation sessions can be lively and highly interactive, such as during games and activities that provide variety and serve to enhance the learning process. Electronic orientation, by its very nature, precludes the possibility of incorporating these and other aids. While there are likely to be enticing PowerPoint slides, DVDs, and other visuals, the fact remains that an employee is left to experience them alone. Web-based orientation also prevents employees from gravitating toward or connecting with others in the same virtual classroom who will be working in different departments. Future opportunities to meet these individuals may be limited or may not occur at all due to logistics.

In addition to citing a lack of two-way communication, limited variety of presentation tools, and the lack of opportunity to meet and talk with new employees from other departments, critics of web-based orientation point to the fact that there are those who simply are uncomfortable with a web-based approach. Employees who are not technologically savvy—and do not need to be, based on the jobs they've been hired to perform—start out feeling uneasy and are therefore less likely to get as much out of the experience as they might during a conventional orientation presentation. This discomfort may also extend to those for whom English is not a first language. If they've been hired for a job where they are not required to excel in the use of the English language, then web-based orientation puts them at a disadvantage.

Virtual classrooms and self-directed web-based orientation also require greater employee initiative than conventional programs. Presenters are unable to monitor the extent of individual employees' attention or involvement since they cannot observe when participants daydream, cut corners, or slack off. It's harder to hide in a class of twenty people than behind a computer screen.

Additionally, managers who know that their new employees have a choice of participating in live chats scheduled during working hours, or self-directed sessions that may be viewed at any time, may not be willing to allow employees time during the day to participate, requiring instead that they "attend" on their own time.

Legal Concerns

As with turning to electronic recruiting sources and social networks as reference tools, conducting web-based orientation sessions can carry certain legal risks. The primary potential problem has to do with an employee's electronic signature, which is easier to forge and harder to authenticate than a handwritten signature.

Electronic Signatures

The Uniform Electronic Transactions Act (UETA) was developed in 1999 by the National Conference of Commissioners on Uniform State Laws to make electronic signatures as legal as handwritten signatures. It has been adopted by forty-seven states and the District of Columbia (New York, Illinois, and Washington have their own statutes). Section 2 of the act states that an electronic signature is "an electronic sound, symbol, or process attached to or logically associated with a record and executed or adopted by a person with the intent to sign the record." It effectively validates the use of electronic signatures and creates a presumption in favor of the validity of electronic signatures if each party has agreed to conduct transactions by electronic means. In matters of employment, this means that employers need to educate employees about electronic signatures and what they mean, and obtain their consent in writing—that is, obtain their handwritten signature—for the use of electronic signatures on HR documents. The UETA provides that a contract may not be denied legal effect solely because it is in electronic form. This last statement is significant in that certain employment-related documents, such as the employee handbook, may be legally binding and viewed as a contract, depending on the wording.

The overall intent of UETA notwithstanding, issues may arise challenging the validity of electronic signatures. Case in point is *Neuson v. Macy's Department Stores, Inc.* (Case No. 28968-1-III) (Wash. Ct. App., 2011). Neuson, hired as a sales associate in the shoe department for Macy's Department Store, worked in two separate locations in Washington beginning in 1994. In 2008, she injured herself on the job, filed a workers compensation claim, and took medical leave. She returned to work approximately two months later with lifting and carrying restrictions. Neuson claimed that Macy's responded with hostility and discharged her unfairly, and she claimed disability discrimination and wrongful termination. Macy's invoked their in-house arbitration through "Solutions InSTORE," a program they'd implemented in 2004. They offered Neuson's electronic signature as proof that she had notice of Macy's arbitration program. The employee responded that the electronic signature could have been completed and backdated by someone else.

The Washington court of appeals refused to enforce Macy's procedure, ruling that Macy's did not show how or why the electronic signature would be unavailable to anyone other than the employee or how the electronic signature is the same as a handwritten signature.

While this case specifically questioned whether an employee's electronic signature meant she knew about and understood the company's arbitration policy, this same challenge could apply to any other HR document employees read and sign electronically. Employers are cautioned in this regard and urged to take one of two measures:

1. Require that employees provide a handwritten signature on all agreements that signify their receipt and understanding of policies and documents, e.g., employee handbooks and harassment policies.

2. In those instances where you wish to require electronic signatures, consult with an attorney in establishing an electronic signature policy that is read and signed by all employees (handwritten signatures, that is).

From a legal perspective, this is still relatively new territory. Because of this, most attorneys agree that employers should rely on handwritten signatures in matters of arbitration, noncompetition, executive, and employment agreements. Included in the latter would be verification of an employee's understanding of his job duties and employer expectations. Edel Cuadra, an attorney with Constangy, Brooks & Smith in Dallas, put it best: "We can all relate to being bewildered by technology. Ultimately, an individual's signature is still among the most persuasive pieces of evidence on which we rely. While an individual can claim a computer glitch resulted in her affirmation of a policy, the individual cannot as easily say that she mistakenly provided her handwritten signature."[1]

That said, attorneys also suggest that at some point in the not too distant future, as electronic signatures become increasingly commonplace, they are likely to be considered legally acceptable on all sorts of documents. In the meantime, take heed and proceed with caution.

Conventional Versus Web-Based Orientation

Let's clarify some of the primary distinctions between electronic and conventional programs so that you can make a more informed decision as to which approach is best for your workplace. These distinctions in Exhibit 18-1, while accurate, depend on the degree of commitment your organization is willing to make to orientation, as well as the thoroughness with which you wish to treat each aspect.

Blended Learning

Blended learning refers to the formal combination of two or more delivery modes to meet a specific set of learning objectives. Typically, the delivery modes are technology-based lessons and traditional classroom instruction. The goal of blended learning is to simultaneously support organizational objectives and meet the unique development needs of each individual, while optimizing the cost of program delivery. This hybrid approach has broad appeal across generational lines, offering both the preferred conventional approach for Matures and Baby Boomers and the electronic method favored by Generation Xers and Millennials.

Applying a blended learning approach to organizational orientation is growing in popularity. The process allows companies to impart critical information about an organization in an efficient yet still personalized way. It integrates different learning styles (visual, auditory, and kinesthetic) and recognizes the continued limited computer comfort level of some individuals. It acknowledges that time and money restraints prohibit many organizations from devoting the requisite number of hours to classroom orientation, but it respects the indisputable benefits of face-to-face communication and interaction.

Here's a step-by-step example of how the concept of blended learning might integrate elements of conventional and web-based organizational orientation programs:

Exhibit 18-1. Conventional Versus Web-Based Orientation

	Conventional	**Web-Based**
Adhering to a strictly structured agenda	Less likely to occur	More likely to occur
Adhering to a strictly-structured time frame	Less likely to occur	More likely to occur
Two-way communication	Extensive	Nonexistent
Convenience	Less convenient	More convenient
Body language	Extensive	Nonexistent
Cost-effective	Less cost-effective	More cost-effective
Tone of voice	Presenters: yes Employees: no	Presenters: yes Employees: no
Updates	Less ease	Greater ease
Variety	Extensive	Limited
Content detail	In-depth coverage requires more time	Allows for greater in-depth coverage of topics in less time
Direct interaction with other employees	Extensive	Nonexistent
Appeal to Millennials	Less likely	More likely
Discomfort with technology	Irrelevant	Relevant
Likely to ask questions	Possibly unnerving	Less unnerving
Employee initiative	Easier to monitor	Cannot monitor
Able to revisit topics	More difficult	Less difficult
Managerial interference	Less likely to occur	More likely to occur
Self-paced	Nonexistent	Extensive
Legal concerns	Less likely to occur	More likely to occur
Time-efficient	Not necessarily designed to be efficient	Designed to be efficient

Step 1: New employees meet for an introductory session. After introductions are completed, an HR representative presents an overview of the orientation process, including its format, content, and duration. She describes the blended learning approach and explains how the process will impact each stage.

Step 2: Employees complete a series of self-paced, web-based tutorials covering five key categories: (1) the employer's commitment to employees, (2) employer expectations, (3) benefits, (4) policies and procedures and employee handbooks, and

(5) the organization. While Step 2 is self-paced, there's still an outside date for the completion of all tutorials.

Step 3: As employees complete each category in Step 2 they fill out a questionnaire reflecting their understanding of the contents of each tutorial.

Step 4: As the outside date for the completion of all the tutorials approaches, the HR representative contacts the original group of attendees and arranges a meeting. The purpose of this meeting is to discuss any questions employees may have as a result of the web-based tutorials. Employees bring the web-based questionnaires they completed as the basis for this discussion.

Step 5: Employees return to the web-based portion of orientation and complete an additional questionnaire that solidifies their understanding of all they've learned.

Step 6: Employees complete a web-based orientation evaluation, providing feedback about the blended learning process and making suggestions for future improvements.

The particulars of each step will vary depending on a number of factors, one of which is the preferred learning style of attendees. For instance, if your organization separates its orientation programs according to special interest groups, you might skew your blended learning approach to favor one over the other. You might lean toward a more conventional approach if the group consists of sales professionals, who tend to respond best to collaborative, visual, and verbal methods of learning. On the other hand, a group of IT professionals would likely be more responsive to a linear, factual, and self-directed web-based approach to orientation.

Since most organizations do not have sufficient numbers of new hires in one particular job classification to warrant a specialized organizational orientation session, blended learning becomes more challenging. Determining how much emphasis to place on a conventional approach versus web-based learning can be made easier if you isolate and evaluate certain variables about your organization. Exhibit 18-2 provides a preliminary blended learning guide to help you with this process.

Experts project that organizations will become increasingly comfortable with blended learning as it pertains to organizational orientation. As the process becomes more refined, companies will learn to better combine the best features of conventional instruction with the most desirable aspects of web-based learning.

Summary

Web-based organizational orientation programs allow new employees the choice of joining others in a virtual classroom at scheduled times or taking a self-directed approach and participating on their own time. Not unlike conventional programs, web-based sessions can range anywhere from the equivalent of a few hours to several days or longer. Electronic versions, however, differ in that the information is imparted in a series of presentations, usually lasting forty-five to ninety minutes

Exhibit 18-2. Preliminary Blended Learning Guide for Organizational Orientation

Instructions: Read each statement and identify its degree of applicability to your organization. Circle the most appropriate number from 1 through 5, in keeping with this scale:

    1 = completely applicable
    2 = applicable in most instances
    3 = applicable in many instances
    4 = applicable in some instances
    5 = rarely applicable

After responding to each statement, add up your scores and divide that total by 20. Locate where your answer fits according to the following key:
- A score of 1.0 to 2.0 suggests that your organization would probably benefit from a greater emphasis on web-based learning blended with a small amount of conventional instruction.
- A score of 2.1 to 3.5 suggests that your organization would probably benefit from a balanced blend of web-based learning and conventional instruction.
- A score of 3.6 to 5.0 suggests that your organization would probably benefit from a greater emphasis on conventional learning blended with a small amount of web-based learning.

- -

1. Our employees have demonstrated a keen interest in, and high comfort level with, web-based learning.   1   2   3   4   5

2. Collectively, our employees have demonstrated a high level of resiliency and receptiveness to change.   1   2   3   4   5

3. Members of the management team have demonstrated a keen interest in, and high comfort level with, web-based learning.   1   2   3   4   5

4. Collectively, members of the management team have demonstrated a high level of resiliency and receptiveness to change.   1   2   3   4   5

5. Members of the HR department have demonstrated a keen interest in, and high comfort level with, web-based learning.   1   2   3   4   5

6. Collectively, members of the HR department have demonstrated a high level of resiliency and receptiveness to change.   1   2   3   4   5

7. Observations of employee learning styles suggest that blended learning would be well-received.   1   2   3   4   5

8. Overall, evaluations of our current organizational orientation program suggest that blended learning would be well-received.   1   2   3   4   5

9. Evaluations of our current organizational orientation programs suggest a low level of responsiveness to its interactive components.   1   2   3   4   5

10. Evaluations of our current organizational orientation programs suggest a low level of responsiveness to presentations by management.   1   2   3   4   5

11. Evaluations of our current organizational orientation programs suggest a low level of responsiveness to completing forms.   1   2   3   4   5

12. Current orientation content is conducive to blended learning.   1   2   3   4   5

13. Our current orientation content is due for a major overhaul.   1   2   3   4   5

14. The web-based aspect of blended learning would not be problematic because of employee access to or ability to use computers.   1 2 3 4 5
15. The conventional aspect of blended learning poses logistical problems since not all employees are in a central location.   1 2 3 4 5
16. Current organizational orientation sessions must adapt to varying employees' schedules.   1 2 3 4 5
17. Managerial preference is of utmost importance.   1 2 3 4 5
18. Employee preference is of utmost importance.   1 2 3 4 5
19. Keeping up with our competitors by integrating technology into our orientation program is of utmost importance.   1 2 3 4 5
20. Keeping orientation costs low is of utmost importance.   1 2 3 4 5

each. This condensed, modularized approach effectively defines web-based orientation.

Some web-based programs are streamlined, offering only a minimal amount of information. They present topics with just a few accompanying bullet points, relying on employees to access contact points for additional information.

Those in favor of a web-based approach to organizational orientation offer numerous benefits including convenience, cost-effectiveness, easy updates, and appeal to Millennials. Those who favor a more conventional approach express particular concern over the lack of two-way communication. They cite the inability to see and react to body language, limited variety of how materials are presented, and the lack of opportunity to meet and talk with new employees from other departments as additional drawbacks. The greatest concern has to do with potential problems connected with the legality of electronic signatures.

After identifying primary distinctions and levels of effectiveness between electronic and conventional orientation programs, some employers opt for the increasingly popular blended approach, a combination of technology-based lessons with traditional classroom instruction. The goal of blended learning is to simultaneously support organizational objectives and meet the unique development needs of each individual while optimizing the cost of program delivery.

Appendixes

Appendix A:
Job Posting Form

Job Title:
Department/Manager: Location:
Primary Duties and Responsibilities:

Exemption Status: Grade/Salary Range:
Work Schedule:
Working Conditions:
Minimum Qualifications and Requirements:

Closing Date:

Job Posting Eligibility Requirements

1. Employee of JavaCorp. for at least twelve consecutive months.
2. In your current position for at least six consecutive months.
3. Meet the minimum qualifications and requirements listed above.
4. Most recent evaluation must reflect a minimum overall rating of satisfactory.
5. Notify your manager of your intent to submit a job posting application.

Job Posting Application Procedure

1. Complete and submit a job posting application form to HR, with a copy to your manager, by the closing date.
2. Someone from HR will contact you within forty-eight hours of receipt.

Appendix B:
Job Posting Application Form

Position Applied For:
Date of Application: Closing Date for Available Position:
Name: Tel. Ext./E-Mail Address:
Current Job Title: Manager's Name:
Dept.:   Location:
Summary of Duties and Responsibilities:

Grade/Salary: Work Schedule:

Job Posting Eligibility Requirements

1. Employee of JavaCorp. for at least twelve consecutive months.
2. In your current position for at least six consecutive months.
3. Meet the minimum qualifications and requirements listed on the job posting notice for this position.
4. Most recent evaluation must reflect a minimum overall rating of satisfactory.
5. Submit a copy of this job posting application to your manager.

Job Posting Application Procedure

1. Complete and submit this form to HR, with a copy to your manager, by the closing date.
2. Someone in HR will contact you within forty-eight hours of receipt.

Appendix C:
Sample E-Mail Cover Letter

From: John J. Wilderson (JJWilderson@gmail.com)
Subject: Off. Mgr. w/3 yrs. law office exper. (Job #HR-7/2462—Office Manager)
Date: December 10, 2012 9:28:14 AM EDT
To: Hillary Yardley (HYardley@BickerBecker.com)

Dear Ms. Yardley:
I have worked as an office manager for the past three years at the prestigious law firm of Sooter, Tucks, Ulrich and Weeds. Having regularly supervised from eight to twelve office workers and reported concurrently to four attorneys, I am capable of meeting the high-pressure demands of an Office Manager (job #HR-7/2462) at Bicker and Becker.

I am accustomed to putting in whatever time and effort is required to complete any given task. My accomplishments have been acknowledged in consistently outstanding performance appraisals in every category as well as recognition by the firm's senior partners in the form of a plaque for superior work.

I am confident that my skills as an office manager and knowledge of the legal profession will be an asset to Bicker and Becker, especially now that you have expanded your services into the areas of immigration and e-commerce law, two specialties with which I have experience.

I look forward to hearing from you.

Sincerely yours,

John J. Wilderson (JJWilderson@gmail.com)

Appendix D:
Work Environment Checklist

Physical Working Conditions
  Exposure to chemicals or fumes
  Extensive standing or sitting
  Extensive computer use
  Noise level
  Types of machinery or equipment
  Ventilation
  Workspace

Geographic Location of the Job
  Central office
  Satellite branch
  Permanent
  Temporary
  Rotational

Travel
  Purpose
  Degree of advance notice
  Locations
  Frequency
  Duration
  Means of transportation
  Reimbursement of expenses

Work Schedule
  Full-time
  Part-time
  Contingency
  Job sharing
  Flextime
  Compressed workweek
  Telecommuting
  Days of the week
  Hours/Shifts
  Meals and other scheduled breaks

Appendix E:
Job Description Form

Job Title: Location:
Work Schedule: Department:
Reporting Relationship:
Salary Range: Grade: Exemption Status:

Summary of Duties and Responsibilities:

Primary Duties and Responsibilities:
(E) = Essential Functions; (N) = Nonessential Functions

Approx. % of time for each task	Essential (E) or Nonessential (N)		Duties and Responsibilities
_____%	E/N	1.	
_____%	E/N	2.	
_____%	E/N	3.	
_____%	E/N	4.	
_____%	E/N	5.	
_____%	E/N	6.	
_____%	E/N	7.	
_____%	E/N	8.	
_____%	E/N	9.	
_____%	E/N	10.	

Performs other related duties and assignments as required.

Education, prior work experience, and specialized skills and knowledge:

Physical environment and working conditions:

Business machines and computer software:

Other factors, such as access to confidential information or contact with the public:

Job Analyst:

Date:

Appendix F: Employment Application Form

Note to readers: The following information is suitable for paper or electronic employment application forms. To adapt to a paper format, use color, borders, columns, boxes, varying type sizes, boldface type, heads and subheads, upper and lowercase lettering, and the like. To adapt to electronic use, modify the design to reflect selected fields and offer job seekers the option of submitting a text-based application that they can copy and paste into an e-mail.

JavaCorp.
Application for Employment

JavaCorp. is an equal opportunity/affirmative action employer and abides by all federal, state, and local laws prohibiting discrimination in employment based on race, color, religion, sex, national origin, age, disability, veteran status, citizenship status, sexual orientation, and all other protected groups.

Please answer all of the following questions, even if you have attached your resume.

Name _____ Date _____
Position applying for _____
Address _____
        No.   Street   City   State   Zip Code
Home Phone _____ Cell Phone _____ E-Mail Address _____
Availability ( ) Full-Time ( ) Part-Time ( ) Days ( ) Evenings ( ) Seasonal
Referral Source _____
Have you ever worked for JavaCorp. before?   ( ) No ( ) Yes Dates _____
Have you ever applied at JavaCorp. before?   ( ) No ( ) Yes Dates _____
Have you ever been convicted of a crime?   ( ) No ( ) Yes
If yes, please explain _____

(A positive response will not necessarily affect your eligibility for employment. Applicants are not obliged to disclose sealed or expunged records of conviction.)

Are you able to perform the tasks required to carry out the job for which you have applied with or without accommodation?   ( ) No ( ) Yes

Language(s) you speak, read, and/or write, relative to the position applied for:

_____ Degree of fluency? _____

Record of Employment
List current or most recent employment first. Include military service, if any.

Company Name, Address, Tel. No.	Manager	Title/ Function	Dates of Employ.	Salary History	Reason for Leaving

Professional licenses, awards, publications: _____
_____

Relevant professional associations _____
Computer software/business machines _____

Education and Training
List all schools attended, including high school, college, graduate school, business school, trade and technical institutions.

Type	Name/ Location	Number of Yrs. Completed	Degree/ Diploma

Academic achievements or extracurricular activities relative to the position applied for:
_____

Additional knowledge, skills, or qualifications relative to the position applied for:
_____
_____

Business and/or academic references, excluding employers or relatives:

Name	Occupation	Years Known	Contact Information
1.			
2.			
3.			

Conditions of Employment:

References and Background Checks. I understand that my employment may be based on receipt of satisfactory information from former employers, schools, and other references, as well as satisfactory results of a background check, including criminal history, credit history, and social security number verification, if deemed appropriate. I authorize Java-Corp. and its representatives to investigate, without liability, any information supplied by me. In addition, I hereby provide permission to authorized representatives of Java-Corp. to conduct a legal Internet search, including public information appearing on social media sites. I further authorize listed employers, schools, and references, as well as other reference sources, to make full disclosure to any relevant inquiries by JavaCorp. and its representatives without liability. In the event that JavaCorp. is unable to verify any information included on this application, it is my responsibility to furnish the necessary documentation.

( ) You may contact my current employer at this time.
( ) You may not contact my current employer at this time. Should I receive and accept a formal offer of employment, you may contact my current employer at that time.

Any information received is to be used exclusively for the purpose of determining my acceptability for employment with JavaCorp.

Drug Testing. Except as limited by law, I accept that JavaCorp. may test applicants and employees for the use of illegal drugs and controlled substances prior to or during employment.

Employment-at-Will. I understand that employees hired by JavaCorp. may terminate their employment at any time, with or without notice or cause. Likewise, JavaCorp. may terminate the employment of any of its employees at any time, with or without notice or cause. I further understand that if hired, my employment is for no definite period of time, and if terminated, JavaCorp. is liable only for wages earned as of the date of termination. In addition, no representative of JavaCorp., other than the CEO, president, or a designated official, has any authority to enter into any agreement, oral or written, for employment for any specified period of time or to make any agreement or assurances contrary to this policy. Nothing in this application shall be interpreted to be in conflict with or to eliminate or modify in any way the employment-at-will status of JavaCorp. employees.

Minimum Age Compliance. If I am under the minimum working age I agree to furnish a work permit prior to hire.

Immigration Reform and Control Act of 1986 Compliance. I understand that in compliance with the Immigration Reform and Control Act of 1986, I will be expected to produce the required documentation to establish my identity and eligibility to work. Employment by JavaCorp. is contingent upon my producing the required documentation or evidence of having applied for it within three calendar days of hire.

JavaCorp. Policies. If hired, I agree to abide by the policies, procedures, and regulations of JavaCorp.

Confidentiality. If hired, I agree to be discreet when discussing any financial, proprietary, trade, or other confidential information related to JavaCorp. business activities. I understand that revealing such information is grounds for immediate termination.

Noncompete Agreement. If hired, I commit to being free of any agreement limiting my ability to work for JavaCorp., and upon termination from JavaCorp., agree not to work at the same or a comparable job for a competitor for a period of one year.

Application Content Certification. I certify that all the information contained in this application is true and complete to the best of my knowledge. Falsification of any information is grounds for rejection or termination.

Signed _____ Date _____

© Copyright 2012 by Arthur Associates Management Consultants, Ltd., Northport, NY.

Appendix G:
Interview Evaluation Form

Applicant: Interviewer:

                                                                   Date:

Position: Department:

Summary of relevant experience _____

_____

Summary of relevant educational accomplishments _____

_____

Relationship between job requirements and applicant's qualifications:

       Essential Tangible Job Requirements   Applicant's Qualifications
1. _____   _____
2. _____   _____
3. _____   _____
4. _____   _____
5. _____   _____
6. _____   _____
       Job-Related Intangible Requirements   Applicant's Qualifications
7. _____   _____
8. _____   _____
9. _____   _____
10. _____   _____
       Additional Desirable Qualities   Applicant's Qualifications
11. _____   _____
12. _____   _____
13. _____   _____
14. _____   _____
Other relevant factors (e.g., test scores) _____

_____

Overall Evaluation: ( )   Strong Candidate
                       ( )   Average Candidate
                       ( )   Weak Candidate
Support for Overall Evaluation _____

_____

■ Appendix H:
Exempt Reference Form

This is a detailed employment reference form for exempt applicants. While intended for use when conducting a telephone reference, it may be modified and submitted as a written request. Although it is unlikely that all questions will result in answers, the form targets a sufficient number of categories relevant to exempt-level positions so that even if only some are answered, a prospective employer is likely to gain valuable insight into an applicant's qualifications.

Applicant   Position
Person Contacted/Title
Company/Address/Contact Information

Reference conducted by   Date

The above-named person has applied to us for employment. He/She has listed you as a former employer and has authorized us to conduct a reference check. We need your assistance in verifying and providing certain information regarding his/her work performance.

1. _____ worked in the _____ department as a(n) _____ from _____ to _____.

   ( ) Correct   ( ) Incorrect

   If incorrect, please explain.

2. His/her primary responsibilities were:

3. He/she stated that his/her reason for terminating employment with your company was _____.

   ( ) Correct   ( ) Incorrect

   If incorrect, please explain.

4. How would you evaluate his/her overall work performance?

5. What were his/her greatest strengths?

6. What areas required improvement and/or additional training?

7. What made him/her an effective manager?

8. Describe a job-related situation involving pressure.

9. Describe how he/she handled a difficult job-related task.

10. Describe his/her management style.

11. Describe his/her decision-making style.

12. Describe his/her approach to time management.

13. Describe a situation involving delegation.

14. Describe a deadline he/she had to meet.

15. How did he/she handle repetitious tasks?

16. Describe how he/she responded to a new assignment.

17. Describe any work-related travel required, in terms of location, duration, and frequency.

18. This job calls for the ability to _____.
    What experience did he/she have in doing this? (This question can be expanded to encompass several different factors. Use your job description as a guide.)

19. How effectively did he/she interact with peers? Senior management? Employees? Customers/clients? Please be specific.

20. Would you rehire him/her? ( ) yes ( ) no. If no, why not?

Appendix I:
Nonexempt Reference Form

This is a detailed employment reference form for nonexempt applicants. While intended for use when conducting a telephone reference, it may be modified and submitted as a written request. Although it is unlikely that all questions will result in answers, the form targets a sufficient number of categories relevant to nonexempt-level positions so that even if only some are answered, the prospective employer is likely to gain valuable insight into the applicant's qualifications.

Applicant   Position

Person Contacted/Title
Company/Address/Contact Information

Reference conducted by   Date

The above-named person has applied to us for employment. He/she has listed you as a former employer and has authorized us to conduct a reference check. We need your assistance in verifying and providing certain information regarding his/her work performance.

1. _____worked in the _____ department as a(n) _____ from _____ to _____.

   ( ) Correct   ( ) Incorrect

   If incorrect, please explain.

2. His/her primary responsibilities were:

3. He/she stated that his/her reason for terminating employment with your company was _____.

   ( ) Correct   ( ) Incorrect

   If incorrect, please explain.

4. How would you evaluate his/her overall work performance?

5. What were his/her greatest strengths?

6. Describe some tasks that he/she performed particularly well.

7. What areas required improvement and/or additional training?

8. How closely did you need to supervise his/her work?

9. Describe his/her ability to successfully perform multiple tasks. Please be specific.

10. How did he/she handle repetitious tasks?

11. Describe how he/she reacted to being given a new assignment.

12. Tell me about some of the questions he/she has asked when confronted with a new assignment.

13. Was there ever a time when he/she performed an assignment unsatisfactorily? Tell me about it.

14. How did he/she react to criticism? Give me a specific example.

15. How effectively did he/she interact with coworkers? With management?

16. How would you compare his/her work upon termination with his/her performance at the time of hire?

17. This job calls for the ability to _____.
    What experience did he/she have in doing this task? (This question can be expanded to encompass several different factors. Use your job description as a guide.)

18. Would you rehire him/her?   ( ) yes   ( ) no. If no, why not?

Notes

Chapter 1: Recruitment Challenges

1. These guidelines are based on material from Diane Arthur, *The Employee Recruitment and Retention Handbook* (New York: AMACOM, 2001), 117–122.
2. www.twainquotes.com/Laughter.html.
3. http://www.helpguide.org/life/humor_laughter_health.htm.
4. Herb Kelleher, CNBC video interview, "iam.cnbc.com," May 8, 2007, http://www.cnbc.com/id/25330616/.
5. S. P. Robbins and T. A. Judge, *Organizational Behavior*, 13th ed. (Upper Saddle River, N.J.: Pearson Prentice Hall, 2009), 572.
6. http://www.hyland.com/careers.
7. http://www.baltimoremagazine.net/features/2010/best-places-to-work.
8. http://money.cnn.com/magazines/fortune/bestcompanies/2011/snapshots/4.html.
9. Ibid.
10. Rita Zeidner, "Questing for Quality," *HR Magazine*, July 2010, 24.
11. http://www.montekids.org/whoweare/standards/.

Chapter 2: Applicant and Employer Perspectives

1. Kathy Gurchiek, "Survey: Work/Life Balance Off-Kilter in U.S.," September 15, 2010, http://www.shrm.org/Publications/HRNews/Pages/WorkLifeOffKilter.aspx.
2. SHRM online staff, "Employee's Choice: Top Companies for Work/Life Balance," May 12, 2011, http://www.shrm.org/hrdisciplines/benefits/Articles/Pages/Employees Choice.aspx.
3. Ibid.
4. Ethisphere, "2010 World's Most Ethical Companies," http://ethisphere.com/wme 2010/.
5. "Sn's top 75 retailers for 2011," March 3, 2011, http://www.srginsight.com/index .php?option = com_articles&task = detail&id = 16.

Chapter 4: Electronic Recruiting

1. http://www.dol.gov/ofccp/regs/compliance/faqua/lappfazs.htm#Q2GI.
2. Joe Light, "For Job Seekers, Company Sites Beat Online Job Boards, Social Media," 2010, Jobs2web Inc.

3. Ibid.

4. Andrea Siedsma, "Marriott Hopes to Win With Facebook Game," July 2011, http://www.workforce.com/archive/feature/software-technology/marriott-hopes-win-facebook-game/index.php.

5. Ibid.

6. Gillian Flynn, "E-Recruiting Ushers in Legal Dangers," Workforce Management Research Center, http://www.workforce.com/archive/article/23/10/03.php.

Chapter 14: Social Networks and Hiring

1. http://www.imdb.com/title/tt0079367/quotes.

2. Joseph Paranac Jr., Esq., "To Tweet or Not to Tweet," Summer 2010, http://www.nysshrm.org/site/files/HRNow_Summer2010.pdf.

3. Forchelli, Curto, Deegan, Schwartz, Mineo, Cohn & Terrana, LLP, The Counselor, Vol. IV, Winter 2011, http://www.forchellilaw.com/newsletters/counselor_winter2011.pdf.

4. Steve Bruce, "Can You Base Hiring Decisions on Information from Social Media Sites?" August 23, 2011, http://hrdailyadvisor.blr.com/archive/2011/08/23/Hiring_Recruiting_Job_Descriptions_Blogging.aspx.

Chapter 17: Departmental Orientation

1. http://www.cpa2biz.com/Content/media/PRODUCER_CONTENT/Newsletters/Articles_2008/Careers/Employee_onboard.jsp.

Chapter 18: Web-Based Orientation

1. Allen Smith, "Obtain Handwritten Signatures on Agreements Employers Intend to Enforce," May 2, 2011, http://www.shrm.org/LegalIssues/FederalResources/Pages/Handwritten Signatures.aspx.

Index